THE OLDER POPULATION
OF THE UNITED STATES

A VOLUME IN THE CENSUS MONOGRAPH SERIES

THE OLDER POPULATION
OF THE UNITED STATES

by

HENRY D. SHELDON

Bureau of the Census

with introductory and summary chapters by

CLARK TIBBITTS

U. S. Department of Health, Education, and Welfare

for the

SOCIAL SCIENCE RESEARCH COUNCIL

in cooperation with the

U. S. DEPARTMENT OF COMMERCE

BUREAU OF THE CENSUS

JOHN WILEY & SONS, INC., NEW YORK

CHAPMAN & HALL, LIMITED, LONDON

FOREWORD

The statistical results compiled by the Bureau of the Census constitute a tremendous mass of detailed information about the population of the United States and its characteristics and economic activities. To meet the requirements of government agencies, business concerns, and investigators of social problems and to satisfy the needs of individual citizens, facts must be gathered and published, showing the distribution of the population in each large and small political unit with respect to age, sex, color, marital status, occupation, income, education, national origin, and other characteristics. This information provides the basis for apportionment of representatives in Congress, for answering many questions by direct reference, and for formulating many plans, at least in preliminary form.

It is the first business of the Bureau of the Census to put into print the census results that directly answer as many such questions as possible. Along with these results, similar data from one or two previous censuses are usually included. Limitations of time, space, and money prevent any extensive statement of the relations between particular results, the long-term trends of significant totals and subtotals, the shifting proportions of the people belonging to different categories, various interesting and important relations such as those between income, occupation, and age. It is not that the Bureau of the Census fails in any sense to appreciate the value and need for such analyses, but rather that it must concentrate on its basic concern with the summary statistics that constitute its unique contribution to knowledge.

When plans for the 1950 Census were made, the need for more extensive analysis was recognized and a series of census monographs similar to those issued after the 1920 Census was proposed. Because of the pressures caused by the depression in the early 1930's and by defense and war in the early 1940's, plans for monographs based on those censuses could not be carried out. Late in the 1940's interested persons from business, research, and government agencies expressed the need for a series that would provide analyses of the most significant results of the 1950 Census. The Social Science Research Council, with the assistance of Russell Sage Foundation, took the lead in stimulating the formulation of suitable plans and in June 1950 appointed a Committee on Census Monographs to cooperate with the Bureau in organizing this project. The members of the Committee are:

Ralph G. Hurlin, Russell Sage Foundation (Chairman)
Robert W. Burgess, formerly Western Electric Company, since February
   1953 Director of the Bureau of the Census
John D. Durand, United Nations
Ernest M. Fisher, Columbia University
F. F. Hill, Cornell University
Frederick F. Stephan, Princeton University
Conrad Taeuber, Bureau of the Census
Ralph J. Watkins, Dun & Bradstreet, Inc.
Paul Webbink, Social Science Research Council

J. Frederic Dewhurst, Twentieth Century Fund, and William F. Ogburn, University of Chicago, were members of the Committee during the first year and a half.

It is essential in any sound census monograph program to obtain the co-operation of authors with a broad understanding not only of the statistical information provided by the regular tabulations of the current census but also of the results of earlier censuses and other relevant knowledge and points of view from other sources and even from other countries. The preparation of a monograph should include broad exploration of new questions suggested by the new information, as well as narrowing the elements of doubt and controversy on old questions. The Social Science Research Council Committee early undertook, in consultation with leading figures in various professional fields, to develop a suggested list of monograph titles and authors and persuaded experts in the subject areas selected to undertake the preparation of memoranda outlining and discussing the topics proposed. Then, in 1951, arrangements were made for continuing cooperation between the Committee and the Bureau concerning the selection of topics, proposals of authors and consultants, and editorial supervision.

Throughout the conduct of the project there has been close collaboration with a number of interested Federal agencies and with universities and research organizations, which provided staff and facilities to help bring the project to completion. They and the Council, which also obtained necessary funds from the Rockefeller and Russell Sage Foundations, provided assistance without which the monographs could not have been prepared.

The task of preparing monographs is an essential part of the broad function of making the information secured by censuses fully available to satisfy the needs and interests of the community and to constitute a broad base for further studies in the social sciences. As Director of the Census and President of the Social Science Research Council, respectively, we wish to record our full approval of the monograph project. It is not implied, of course, that the views expressed in these reports are necessarily those of the Bureau of the Census, the Department of Commerce, or the

Social Science Research Council. The views are those of the individual authors, each of whom has been given the freedom to interpret available materials in the light of his technical knowledge and competence. This freedom of the individual authors is an essential element in making the most useful analyses and interpretations generally available to the community.

ROBERT W. BURGESS, DIRECTOR
BUREAU OF THE CENSUS

PENDLETON HERRING, PRESIDENT
SOCIAL SCIENCE RESEARCH COUNCIL

PREFACE

In this monograph, census data on age, as they relate to other characteristics of the population, are examined in the context of the many issues which have been raised by the current interest in our older population and its place in our society. This examination is focused not only on the position of older people as reflected in such characteristics as employment, living arrangements, and income but also on the development of this position as indicated by changes in these characteristics with age.

Chapters 1 and 9 were written by Clark Tibbitts of the Department of Health, Education, and Welfare. I am indebted to him for this contribution, which serves to indicate the context in which the study was undertaken and to bring together and interpret its findings, as well as for guidance in solving the many problems encountered in the course of the study.

I should also like to express my appreciation for the many helpful criticisms, both as to substance and organization, of the persons who reviewed the final manuscript—Dr. Conrad Taeuber of the Bureau of the Census; Dr. Ralph Hurlin of the Russell Sage Foundation; Dr. Paul Webbink of the Social Science Research Council; and Dr. Ernest W. Burgess, Professor Emeritus of the University of Chicago.

Finally, I wish to acknowledge the assistance of David Kaplan and Gertrude Bancroft of the Bureau staff in advising me with respect to the use of statistics in their respective subject matter fields, and of Merrill Rogers, Josephine Hemphill, and Mildred Russell in editorial review.

HENRY D. SHELDON
Bureau of the Census

Washington, D.C.
April 1958

CONTENTS

xi

CHAPTER 1

THE PHENOMENON OF AGING

The second half of this century has been marked by a rapidly growing interest throughout the country in what may be termed the phenomenon of our aging population and in the many problems that have followed in its wake. Seldom has a fundamental challenge to the economic and social well-being of the Nation gained so great a recognition in such a comparatively brief period.

The growth of interest in aging

Attention was first drawn to older people on a recognizable scale during the 1920's and early 1930's when, in several States, it was found that private charity was no longer able to provide sufficient support for the growing number of dependent aged, and that relatives were unable to provide the necessary care and shelter. Some of the more progressive business firms and industries began to set up pension plans for their retired employees, though they were too few in number to have any broad effect. The problem of old age security was dealt with more effectively in 1935 when Congress established a national system of old-age insurance for workers 65 years of age and over retiring from active employment, and also a Federal-State program of old-age assistance for those needy aged who did not qualify under the insurance program.

Concern over the health of older people gained momentum during this period. The number of people reaching the age with which long-term illness is commonly associated provided a new focus for the thinking of medical and public health workers. Pioneering studies culminated in the National Health Survey of 1935–1936. This survey revealed, among other things, that 1 out of 6 people in the United States had some form of long-term illness or disability, that one-half of these were over 45 years of age, and that at least one-half of all persons 65 years of age and over suffered from one or more of these conditions. One result of these studies was the establishment of the National Cancer Institute in 1937 which was followed by other institutes for research doing work in the areas described above.

In the meantime, the problem of the older worker was claiming public attention. Management, organized labor, and public employment officers were feeling the pressure of elderly workers reluctant to leave the work force, when there was little guarantee of income security in retirement.

1

Hiring policies in much of business and industry tended to give preference to younger men with dependent families, and large numbers of older workers who had lost their jobs in the upheaval of the depression failed to regain their footing in the labor market. A 1938 study of employer attitudes toward the older worker—the first of its kind made by the Bureau of Labor Statistics—helped to bring the essential problem into clear focus.

The impact of the depression on the country had other consequences. Social and welfare workers throughout the country were swamped with requests for help in meeting the problems of living arrangements for older people without families, or whose families could no longer take care of them. Hospitals, homes for the aged, nursing homes, and institutions for care of the mentally ill were becoming overcrowded with elderly people whose needs for medical and domiciliary care could be met in no other way. And the mounting cost of old-age public assistance was beginning to alarm the legislatures of many of the more heavily populated States.

Thus, by the early 1940's, the United States was well aware of the increasing number of older people within its borders and of the growing impact on its economy and community facilities. But only slowly did it begin to appear, from the research activities of more or less isolated groups and individuals, that the needs of older people cover much broader areas than money and health, and that the difficulties of effective social and psychological adjustment to the later years pose problems of equal significance.

By the mid-1940's, however, action on a national scale began to develop. The Social Science Research Council set up a committee to examine the social aspects of aging and to prepare a research memorandum on *Social Adjustment in Old Age.* Subsequently, several foundations made relatively large grants for inquiries into personal and social adjustment to old age. Washington University in St. Louis stepped up its research in the biological aspects of aging, the University of Chicago began a series of notable studies of the socio-psychological aspects of inactivity, and the University of Michigan initiated a series of annual conferences and pioneered various educational programs for older adults.

Also during this decade the Public Health Service Gerontology Unit was established, the Gerontological Society was born out of the Macy Foundation's Research Club on Aging, and the American Geriatrics Society was founded. The American Psychological Association, the Adult Education Association, and the General Federation of Women's Clubs established permanent sections on aging. And the National Social Welfare Assembly created a special committee on the aging.

By the end of the decade it was evident that a comprehensive review of the entire field was needed. Accordingly, in 1950, President Truman issued a call for a National Conference on Aging. The conference, sponsored by the Federal Security Agency with the help of several other departments and agencies of the Government, met in Washington, D.C., in

August of that year. It provided a forum at which some 800 individuals, representing virtually every field of interest, were able to pool their ideas effectively and to outline a broad program of action.

Action in this field continued with steadily increasing momentum. In 1950 only two or three States, at most, had established official bodies concerned with the broad aspects of aging. But within the next 5 years State commissions or committees on aging had been authorized in a score or so of States, representing well over half the population of the entire country. Some States had enacted broad legislative programs in behalf of their older citizens, had developed a close coordination among the various State Departments, and were giving effective encouragement and support to local community activities in the field. Others, still essentially in the "study and planning" stage were developing intelligently conceived programs for State action and building up public support.

Of particular significance was the extensive study made by the Council of State Governments, *The States and Their Older Citizens.* Among other recommendations, the report proposed the appointment by each Governor of a special assistant in aging, equipped with an adequate staff, to plan and carry out a comprehensive State aging program. It also provided for the establishment of an interdepartmental committee of State government and a citizens' advisory committee.

In the early 1950's there were also parallel developments at the Federal level. Research in the social and economic factors relating to the welfare of our older population continued as an integral part of the old-age and survivor's insurance and the Federal-State old-age assistance program. Likewise, other agencies of the Department of Health, Education, and Welfare—such as the Public Health Service, the Office of Vocational Rehabilitation, the Food and Drug Administration, and the Saint Elizabeth's Hospital—placed increasing emphasis on, and devoted special attention to, those phases of their program which impinged on the problems of aging.

In addition, within the Office of the Secretary, a Committee on Aging was established to serve as a nationwide clearing house of information on all phases of aging and to provide consultation service on organization and programming for a large number of State and local groups active in the aging field.

Similarly, the Department of Labor found several of its Bureaus involved in the field. The Bureau of Employment Security, in conjunction with State Employment Services, initiated several studies on obstacles to older worker employment and undertook to develop special counseling and placement services in local employment offices. The Bureau of Labor Statistics made special studies of living costs of older persons and of participation of older workers in the labor force. The Women's Bureau undertook vigorous measures to promote training and employment of middle-aged women.

The Housing and Home Finance Agency sponsored important legislation

designed to make easier the financing of many types of housing for older
people and to give priority to older applicants for local public housing.
The Department of Agriculture was brought into the picture through its
interest in nutrition, family life, and rural housing. The Veterans' Administration developed important medical, rehabilitation, and domiciliary
services for older veterans. The Department of Commerce, through the
Bureau of the Census, furnished much of the basic data in the aging field.
And scattered through the Federal Government were a number of other
programs which in one way or another relate to aging.

In 1956, President Eisenhower established a Federal Council on Aging
with membership drawn from a dozen or so of those agencies and departments of the Government which administer such programs. Its purpose
was to explore the scope of Federal activities and responsibilities in the
aging field, to coordinate current programs, and to develop a broader
range of Federal activities.

The increasing tempo of activity in the field of aging after 1950 was by
no means confined to the State and Federal Governments. In hundreds
of towns and cities, community programs were organized to deal with one
or more aspects of the problem. The growth of senior citizen organizations and "Golden Age Clubs" (largely of a recreational and social nature)
was nothing short of phenomenal. Activity centers, sponsored by the
municipality or by voluntary organizations, increased in number. Community groups organized programs to provide older citizens with better
health facilities, job counseling, and opportunities for employment. Housing
geared to their special needs and pocketbooks, homemaker services, recreation facilities, and opportunities for adult education were offered.

Engaged in the effort were physicians, medical and social research
people, social workers, recreation workers, educators, clergymen, Federal,
State and local government officials, civic leaders, representatives of
women's organizations, business executives, labor union officials, as well
as a large variety of ordinary citizens.

The need for more detailed data

Despite the very considerable amount of research and activity that has
already taken place in the field of aging, it is evident that there is a great
need for more comprehensive and detailed data. Groups at all levels have
encountered persistent obstacles in their studies and programming efforts
because concrete information and knowledge which they can apply to the
situation within their own State or community are lacking.

In these terms, this monograph represents an effort to describe, at the
national level, the situation of our older population in 1950 insofar as it
is revealed by census data. If, by so doing, it provides a sounder basis
for further studies, both local and national in scope, which are so badly
needed, it will have served its purpose well.

The evolution of the phenomenon of aging

The phenomenon of aging represents a fundamental and permanent development in American society. The primary factors lie in changes in the birth rate, improved health environment, and revolutionary changes in the economy and in family life. Parallel and interrelated developments in urbanization, mobility, and institutionalization have been contributing factors.

Increasing numbers of older people. With good reason aging is often described as the extension of the length of life and the increase in the number and proportion of persons in the older age groups. Regarded in either of these terms the increases have been enormous, particularly since the turn of the century. The magnitude of these changes and the factors underlying them are discussed in Chapter 2.

The industrial revolution and aging. The problems associated with aging are even more profoundly a consequence of the shift from an agrarian, craft, household, and self-employment economy to a mechanized society based upon natural energy resources and of great concentrations of wage and salary workers living in cities. Mechanization of processes and widespread application of new forms of power in manufacturing, agriculture, transportation, communication, and even in office and professional work, have fantastically increased worker productivity and, with it, the total national product. The consequences and long-range implications for workers, families, and society have been varied and far-reaching.

One obvious result of rising productivity has been the reduction of hours of work, with a corresponding increase in leisure. The average work week declined from about 68 hours in 1890 to 40 hours in 1950, and is still declining. A parallel result of industrialization is the practice of total retirement from work. Over the past 55 years, participation of older men in the work force has declined by 35 percent and is expected to drop still further. Earlier retirement, plus rising longevity, results in more years of retirement.

Further results of industrialization include a shift from self-employment or employment on a family farm or in a neighborhood business to wage and salary employment in the highly specialized occupations of large enterprises, as well as the rapid appearance of new jobs which make others obsolete. Both these factors militate against employment of older workers.

Industrialization and the extension of the length of life have increased the amount of leisure for the older worker, but, at the same time, industrialization has reduced the probability of continued participation in the work force.

Changes in household and family organization. Scientific development and industrialization have also induced basic changes in the pattern of household living and in family life. Most activities, such as growing and preparing food, making clothing, educating children, caring for the sick, and providing religious instruction, formerly carried on by household members, have moved out of the home into factories and community institutions. Machines have lightened most of the household tasks that remain. As a consequence, the multigeneration, largely self-sufficient household of the agrarian-craft economy has been replaced by the single-generation family of man and wife and the 2-generation unit of parents and children whose needs are satisfied with the aid of community institutions and agencies.

The result of these changes is that the generation of young adults with their children and the older generation of parents have become increasingly independent of one another. This fact, coupled with the extension of life, means that most men and women are completing their parental roles during the 45-year to 55-year decade of life. They become free to develop new interests of their own, but they also lose most of their claim on the extended kinship group for support and social participation and are forced to look elsewhere to find new ways of satisfying their needs for usefulness, status, and companionship. One measure of the change is supplied by the following comparison. The average couple marrying in 1890 could look forward to 31 years together although one spouse would die 2 years before the last child was married. By contrast, the average couple married in 1950 can anticipate 41 years of married life, one-fourth of it coming after the last child has left home.

Ancillary contributing factors. Beyond the changes just described, there are a number of others, including urbanization, rapid social change, mobility, and institutionalization, which have had an important bearing on the circumstances of older people.

The marked shift of the population to cities has had important implications for living arrangements, family life, and social participation of older people. Urban living offers little opportunity for household occupation in retirement, in contrast to the many responsibilities and chores open to the older person in preindustrial rural society. Small homes designed for families of urban workers afford little room for aged parents. Former work associates, friends, and relatives tend to be scattered in cities rather than close at hand as in small towns and rural neighborhoods. City life is characterized by competition and expectations of self-sufficiency and self-preservation as opposed to the helpful neighborliness of highly integrated rural society. Upon completion of his parental and work roles, the older individual in the urban setting may easily become withdrawn, socially isolated, and a community responsibility.

One of the outstanding characteristics of American life is the frequency and ease with which large numbers of people move about the country in response to the rise and decline of work opportunities or in search of presumably more attractive climates, cultural or recreational opportunities, etc. High mobility, however, makes for further separation of family generations and contemporaries, hence aggravating the older person's problem of maintaining close personal and social contacts with children and friends.

The very rapidity of social change in a fast-moving technological and industrial society militates against the older person. He is continually threatened with obsolescence of his occupational skills, outmoded goals, values, mode of behavior, and dress. He is deprived of traditional roles of counselor, guide, and example to the oncoming generations.

The decline of family and household functions was noted earlier. Modern, industrial society has become possible only by the assumption of community responsibility for many functions formerly carried out in the home. Health and protective services, transportation and communication, and preparation and distribution of food and clothing are largely in the hands of formal organizations and agencies. The great growth of knowledge and the need for trained specialists have brought about the rapid extension of formal educational institutions and medical care facilities. Formal religion with programs addressed to particular age groups seems to have supplanted home worship and religious instruction. This great shift of family functions to the community has affected the roles of all family members, but more particularly those in the older ages.

In summary. The phenomenon of aging is seen, then, as a new development in the economy and in the social structure. It is an outgrowth of a remarkable increase in the number and proportion of people living into the older ages and a parallel increase in freedom from work and family responsibilities. Combining these two factors, aging may be defined as the extension of that period of life which follows the completion of parental roles with the consequent appearance of a vast amount of leisure time for which there are few well-defined expectations. Other changes arising out of technological and industrial changes aggravate the problems of older people.

What is the older population?

Any consideration of the older population raises, of course, the question of what age group constitutes this population. Gerontologists agree that any definition in purely chronological terms is, necessarily, an arbitrary one. It is now generally recognized that the onset of aging or of old age must be defined with reference to physiological changes, the nature of the requirements placed on the organism, and to the stage one has reached in the life cycle. Moreover, it is recognized that there are great variations among people in their changing capacities and circumstances, and in the requirements of the tasks they are called upon to perform.

Physiologists point out that aging begins even prior to birth and that some psychophysical capacities reach their peak during adolescence. Occupationally, aging may set in during early adulthood. Professional athletes, for example, are "old" at a very early age. On the other hand, it has been said that statesmen, legislators, judges, and teachers often render their most significant service only after years of experience.

Parental roles are completed for most people during the ages 45 to 55, and age may become a liability in seeking employment even prior to this period. Geriatricians report that marked changes in health may be anticipated during the years 70 to 75 and, of course, frequently appear a decade or more earlier.

Aging and old age must, then, be defined in terms of a composite of many contributory factors which affect individuals at different times, in different degrees, and, sometimes, in different ways. It is also well recognized that the later years are not a unitary period of life.

For practical purposes, maturity may be said to begin in the 40's. Old age is commonly assumed to begin with the termination of career employment and increase in the prevalence of long-term disability, usually between 65 and 75 years of age. Obviously, even these 10-year age ranges are not applicable to all, for most individuals age in some respects long before they do in others.

Although in these terms the use of any chronological definition of age is unrealistic, there are many situations in which we are compelled to define the group under consideration in terms of chronological age. The preparation of this monograph is one of these situations. In this study, recognition is given to the inherent variation by examining the trend of various phenomena in relation to age, and by using as many age periods as seemed feasible from the point of view of the analysis and of the user.

C H A P T E R   2

OUR CHANGING AGE STRUCTURE

The increasing proportion of older persons in the population has been one of the principal factors underlying the widespread and growing interest in their status within our society. It is not only the significant increases already recorded that are drawing attention but also the contemplation of future gains. When it could be said that the proportion of the population 60 years and over (about 4 percent of the total in 1850) might increase to 25 percent by the year 2000,[1] then, clearly, the increasing age of the population demanded attention. Although this figure for the year 2000 seems somewhat improbable in the light of demographic trends since 1940, it was projections of this sort, by no means unreasonable at the time they were made, that helped to bring the changing age structure of the American population into sharper focus.

The increasing accumulation of people in the upper ages which has gone on during the past century is not unique to the United States. It is also characteristic of other industrialized countries, notably those of Western Europe. In most general terms, it is a result of the unprecedented declines in birth and death rates which were associated with industrial development. The most common pattern of change in vital rates was an early decline in death rates with a later decline in birth rates. The rapid population growth that began with the decline in death rates was followed, in course of time, by sharp drops in fertility rates and a subsequent decline in the rate of total population growth. It is this latter phenomenon, particularly, that led to the increase in the proportion of older persons. The declining birth rate provided fewer replacements at the younger ages, and, hence, served to increase the proportion at the older ages.

In this context, the United States has had an aging population since early in the 19th century. In 1800 the median age of the white population was 16 years; that is, one-half of the white population was older than 16 and one-half was younger. By 1850 the median age of this group had increased to 19 years, by 1900 to 23 years, and by 1950 to just under 31 years. Total population figures for 1800 are not available, but from 1850 on the trend has been similar at a slightly lower level.[2]

---

[1] Warren S. Thompson and P. K. Whelpton, *Estimates of the Future Population of the United States, 1940 to 2000*, National Resources Planning Board, Government Printing Office, Washington, D. C., 1943, table 13.

[2] Appendix table A–1.

In 1850, persons 60 years and over constituted 4 percent of the total population; by 1950 they had become 12 percent of the total. The number of persons 65 years and over in 1850 (who, in all probability, comprised 2.5 percent of the population) had by a century later increased to 12 million —or slightly over 8 percent of the total population.[3] It is clear, then, that the trend toward an older population in this country is of long standing.

In this chapter materials are presented for the two age groups, 60 and over and 65 and over, and particular attention is focused on persons aged 60 and over—partly because age groups in even 10-year intervals are more readily related to births and to immigration in even decades between census dates, and partly because the use of age 60 compensates to some extent for the bias in the 65- to 69-year age group.[4]

Changes in age structure, 1900 to 1950

Between 1900 and 1950 the total population of the United States almost doubled, increasing from about 76.0 million to 150.7 million. In this same period, however, the population aged 65 and over nearly quadrupled, increasing from about 3.1 million to 12.3 million. As a proportion of the total population, the group 65 and over increased from 4.1 percent in 1900 to 8.1 percent in 1950. For the population 60 and over, corresponding percentages were 6.4 and 12.2.

Data on the over-all change in the age structure are presented in figure 1. The age "pyramid" for 1900 justifies the term, for, beginning with the age group under 5, as age increases, there are successive and relatively regular decreases in the proportion of the population in each 5-year interval. The 1900 pyramid reflects not only the cumulative effects of mortality on successive cohorts of births but also the increases in the number of births over the lifetime of the population of 1900; that is, the proportion of persons aged 60 to 64 in 1900 was smaller than the proportion of persons under 5 years—not only because some children failed to survive to the age group 60 to 64 but also because the number of births in the period 1835 to 1840 (which in large part accounted for the number of persons 60 to 64 in 1900) was considerably smaller than the number of births in the period 1895 to 1900. The age structure of 1900 also reflects, of course, past trends in immigration.

The pyramid for 1950 has a somewhat narrower base than that for 1900; it shows a sharp decline in the proportion in the age groups 5 to 9, 10 to 14, and 15 to 19, and then shows successive increases in the groups 20 to 24 and 25 to 29. Then comes the expected regular decline by age, but to levels somewhat higher than those of 1900. The irregularities at the younger ages reflect, in large part, the relatively large number of births

---

[3] Appendix table A–1.
[4] See Appendix A, section 1.

in the decade 1940 to 1950, and the relatively small number in the late 1920's and during the 1930's.

Changes in age structure between 1900 and 1950 involved declines in the proportion of persons under 30—particularly in the group from 10 to 19—and progressive increases in the ages above 30. The increase in the proportions in these age groups ranged from 4 percent for the group aged 30 to 34 to 133 percent for the group aged 80 to 84. The 1950 population, in contrast to that of 1900, contained relatively more persons in the ages above 30, and this excess, generally speaking, increased with age.

Nativity. Although between 1900 and 1950 all segments of the population showed an increase in the proportion of older persons, this increase was by no means uniform. In general, the increase was greater for the foreign born than for the native population, greater for females than for males, and greater for the white than for the nonwhite population.

Data in table 1 on the percentage of persons 60 and over for the various segments of the population just considered indicate that in 1950 the proportion of older persons among the foreign born was more than two and a half times the proportion in 1900, whereas the corresponding 1950 figure for the native population was twice the comparable 1900 figure. In general terms, this difference reflects differences in the trends in volume of immigration prior to the two years.

Color. In both 1900 and 1950, the proportions of older persons were lower in the nonwhite than in the white population. However, the trends in these proportions for nonwhites were essentially the same as the corresponding trends for the white population. For nonwhites, the proportions 65 and over and 60 and over increased from 3.0 to 5.7 percent and 4.9 to 8.3 percent respectively. Although the rate of increase was slightly less for the nonwhite than for the white population, it is clear that the nonwhite, like the white, is an aging population. The lower proportion of older persons among nonwhites simply reflects higher levels of fertility and mortality.

Sex. For the total population, in both 1900 and 1950, the proportion of older persons defined in terms of either age group—60 and over or 65 and over—was greater for females than for males (table 1). Likewise, the increase in this proportion between 1900 and 1950 was greater among females. This general pattern of difference was characteristic of the native white population but of neither the nonwhite nor the foreign born.

In the foreign-born population, variations from the standard pattern represent the residual effect of the high sex ratio among immigrants to this country in the appropriate periods before 1950 and before 1900. In the native nonwhite population, variations in the pattern probably reflect the vagaries of age reporting among the elderly nonwhite. Among the relatively small foreign-born nonwhite population, variations are attributable to the same factors as those for the total foreign-born population.

FIGURE 1.—POPULATION OF THE UNITED STATES BY AGE AND SEX: 1950 AND 1900

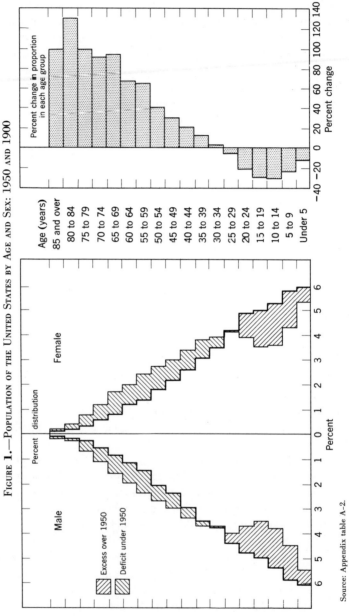

Source: Appendix table A-2.

TABLE 1.—PERCENT OF THE TOTAL POPULATION 60 AND 65 YEARS OLD AND OVER,
BY NATIVITY, COLOR, AND SEX: 1950 AND 1900

Age, nativity, and color	Both sexes		Male		Female	
	1950	1900	1950	1900	1950	1900
60 YEARS OLD AND OVER						
Total..................	12.2	6.4	11.8	6.4	12.5	6.5
Native......................	10.2	5.1	9.6	5.1	10.7	5.2
Foreign born...............	39.1	14.6	39.9	14.0	38.2	15.2
White....................	12.6	6.6	12.2	6.6	13.0	6.7
Native......................	10.4	5.2	9.8	5.1	11.0	5.3
Foreign born...............	39.6	14.7	40.6	14.2	38.6	15.3
Nonwhite...............	8.3	4.9	8.4	5.0	8.2	4.7
Native......................	8.1	4.9	8.1	5.0	8.1	4.7
Foreign born...............	18.8	5.3	19.4	5.1	17.8	6.5
65 YEARS OLD AND OVER						
Total..................	8.1	4.1	7.7	4.0	8.5	4.1
Native......................	6.8	3.2	6.3	3.2	7.3	3.3
Foreign born...............	26.2	9.2	26.0	8.8	26.3	9.7
White....................	8.4	4.2	8.0	4.2	8.9	4.3
Native......................	7.0	3.3	6.4	3.2	7.5	3.4
Foreign born...............	26.6	9.3	26.5	9.0	26.6	9.7
Nonwhite...............	5.7	3.0	5.7	3.0	5.7	3.0
Native......................	5.6	3.0	5.5	3.1	5.6	3.0
Foreign born...............	11.2	2.1	11.5	1.9	10.8	4.2

Source: Appendix tables A-2, A-3, and A-4.

The general pattern of sex differences in the proportion of older persons in the native white population reflects similar differences between the sexes in mortality. In 1900, in terms of either life expectancy or mortality rates, the mortality of males was slightly higher than that of females. Mortality for both sexes declined, of course, between 1900 and 1950, but the decrease for women was appreciably greater than that for men, with the result that the difference increased progressively between 1900 and 1950.

The same general mortality trend is apparent for the native nonwhite population and is reflected in the proportions of older persons. In 1900, however, even though mortality for native nonwhite males was higher than for females, the proportions aged 60 and 65 and over were slightly higher for males than for females. In 1950, although the proportion 65 and over appeared to be higher for females, the proportion 60 and over was identical for each sex. These differences are small and, as previously suggested, they may stem from inaccuracies in age reporting among older persons in the nonwhite population.[5] The sex distribution of the foreign-born population, both white and nonwhite, has of course been affected by the differences between male and female mortality, but the results of these differences are obscured by sharp variations in the sex ratio among immigrants at the time of migration.

[5] See Appendix A, section 1.

Ratio of males to females.   The net effect of these various factors is apparent in the change in the distribution of the population by sex (table 2).   In 1900, in the native population 65 and over, there were 99 males per 100 females; by 1950 this ratio had dropped to about 86.   Corresponding figures for the total population of this age were 102 for 1900 and 90 for 1950.   In absolute numbers, the number of males 65 and over in the total population of 1900 exceeded the corresponding number of females by about 30,000; by 1950 the number of older females exceeded the number of older males by nearly 680,000.   In 1900, for the population 60 and over, the number of males exceeded the corresponding number of females by about 77,000; by 1950, however, there were about 660,000 more females than males.   The excess of females in the population 65 and over in 1950 was greater than the corresponding excess in the population 60 and over, primarily because in 1950 the age interval 60 to 64 was the modal 5-year age group for foreign-born males.

TABLE 2.—MALES PER 100 FEMALES, BY AGE, NATIVITY, AND COLOR: 1950 AND 1900

Nativity and color	All ages		60 years old and over		65 years old and over	
	1950	1900	1950	1900	1950	1900
Total..................	98.6	104.4	93.1	103.2	89.6	102.1
Native.....................	98.2	102.2	88.7	100.4	85.8	99.3
Foreign born................	105.2	119.5	109.9	109.7	104.1	108.6
White....................	99.0	104.9	92.7	102.6	89.1	101.9
Native....................	98.6	102.8	88.1	99.5	85.1	98.9
Foreign born................	103.8	117.4	109.2	109.0	103.5	108.3
Nonwhite.................	95.7	101.0	98.1	108.7	95.1	103.9
Native....................	94.8	98.7	95.6	106.4	93.0	102.7
Foreign born................	175.8	915.3	191.6	717.5	188.1	412.2

Source: Appendix tables A-2, A-3, and A-4.

In summary, then, it is apparent that, with the differential decline in male and female mortality rates, and with the large decline in immigration, the older population has become predominantly a population of women.   Recent statistics on immigration show that the high sex ratios observed in the past are no longer characteristic of immigrant populations; in recent years, in fact, women have outnumbered men in this group.[6]   It seems, therefore, that future immigration will increase the excess of women at the upper age levels—provided, of course, that the recent reversal of the sex ratio among immigrants represents a permanent change.

Natural increase, migration, and age structure

In the foregoing discussion, the general relationships between age structure and fertility, migration, and mortality have been suggested.   These relationships are examined here in more detail.

---

[6] See, for example, U. S. Department of Justice, *Annual Report of the Immigration and Naturalization Service,* 1950–1954, table 9.

The distribution of a native population by any set of age intervals reflects the variations in the number of births in appropriate time periods in the past. Thus, for example, children under 5 in the native population of the United States represented in 1950 the survivors of births in the period 1945 to 1950; those 5 to 9, survivors of births in the period 1940 to 1945; those 60 to 64, survivors of births in the period 1885 to 1890, and so on. Similarly the age structure of a foreign-born population at a given time reflects past trends in the volume of immigration. Although this relationship is somewhat more complicated than the relationship between age structure and past trends in births, it is nevertheless real. Thus, the number of births in appropriate past time periods and the number of immigrants of appropriate ages in such time periods set the upper limits of the size of a specified age group in the current population, and attrition from mortality operating within these limits determines the current size of the age group.

Births. From this perspective it is clear that the native population of 1950 was larger than that of 1900 because, in large part, there were more births in the 90-year period prior to 1950 than in the corresponding period before 1900.[7] There were more native persons 60 and over in 1950 than in 1900 because there were more births in the first three decades of the 90-year period prior to 1950 than in the comparable decades for 1900 (table 3); that is, there were nearly three times as many births between 1860 and 1890 as there were between 1810 and 1840, and, with the differential operation of mortality, slightly more than four times as many persons 60 years and over in 1950 as in 1900.

TABLE 3.—BIRTHS BY PERIOD OF OCCURRENCE AND SURVIVORS AT CENSUS DATE: 1950 AND 1900

Period of birth	Estimated births		Survivors (native population at census date)			Survival rate
	Number (thousands)	Percent	Age at census date	Number (thousands)	Percent	
			1950			
Total, 1860 to 1950.......	218,350	100	Total.......	140,161	100	.642
1890 to 1950.................	163,467	75	Under 60 years..	126,021	90	.771
1860 to 1890.................	54,884	25	60 to 89 years..	14,140	10	.258
			1900			
Total, 1810 to 1900.......	120,213	100	Total.......	65,627	100	.546
1840 to 1900.................	101,750	85	Under 60 years..	62,275	95	.612
1810 to 1840.................	18,463	15	60 to 89 years..	3,352	5	.182

Source: Appendix tables A-3 and A-7.

---

[7] See Appendix A, section 2, for a discussion of estimates of the number of births in the period 1810 to 1910.

Migration.   Just as past trends in the number of births set the general pattern of current age structure in the native population, so do past trends in immigration set the general outlines of age structure in the foreign-born population.   Since age at birth is fixed, but age at immigration is variable, the relationship between migration and age structure is not as simple and direct as the relationship between births and age structure.   In the period under consideration, however, immigration tended to be concentrated in the younger adult years, and the temporal pattern of immigration prior to 1900 was quite different from that prior to 1950.   It is therefore possible to make some rough inferences as to the role of migration in explaining differences in the size of the older foreign-born population between 1900 and 1950.

In the 30-year period (1830 to 1860), 40 years prior to 1900, some 5 million immigrants entered the country, whereas in the corresponding period prior to 1950 (1880 to 1910), the corresponding figure was about 18 million—more than 3.5 times as large.   From these approximate, potential numbers of foreign born 60 and over in 1900 and 1950, the differential attrition from mortality and emigration left approximately 1.5 million foreign born 60 and over in 1900 and about 4 million in 1950 (table 4).   The highly approximate nature of the implied relationship needs emphasis.   Mortality and emigration create a wide gap between the number of immigrants and the net change in the number of foreign born even in a single decade.   Moreover, the assumption that the number of foreign born 60 years and over in either 1900 or 1950 is traceable to immigration in periods 40 to 70 years prior to these dates is extremely rough.   These limitations are not sufficiently great, however, to invalidate the conclusion that a considerable part of the difference in the size of the older foreign-born population between 1900 and 1950 reflects differences in the volume of immigration in appropriate periods prior to these dates.

TABLE 4.—IMMIGRATION IN 70-YEAR PERIOD PRIOR TO CENSUS DATE AND AGE OF THE FOREIGN-BORN POPULATION AT CENSUS: 1950 AND 1900

Immigration prior to census date and age of foreign born at census	1950		1900	
	Number (thousands)	Percent	Number (thousands)	Percent
IMMIGRATION IN 70-YEAR PERIOD PRIOR TO CENSUS DATE				
Total, 70 years..............	29,136	100	18,972	100
0 to 40 years....................	11,406	39	14,061	74
40 to 70 years...................	17,730	61	4,911	26
FOREIGN-BORN POPULATION BY AGE				
Total, all ages.............	10,422	100	10,341	100
Under 60 years...................	6,348	61	8,836	85
60 years and over...............	4,074	39	1,506	15

Source: Appendix tables A-4 and A-5.

Declining mortality. The most popular explanation of the increase
in the number of older persons is in terms of declining mortality. Death
rates have fallen, people are living longer, and thus the number of older
persons is increasing. It is perfectly clear that the expectation of life has
been increasing. Various life tables, based on fragmentary data, indicate
a life expectation of about 40 years during the middle of the 19th century.
The life table of 1900, based on data from the 12 registration States, indicates a life expectation of 49.2 years (table 5). In 1950 the life expectation of the total population, based on complete data for the entire country,
was 68.1 years. These figures indicate a clear downward movement in
mortality—a movement which permitted increasing numbers of persons to
survive to older ages, but had little effect in increasing life expectation at
the older ages. In 1900, life expectation at age 60 was 14.8 years; in 1950,
17.0 years.

TABLE 5.—EXPECTATION OF LIFE AT SELECTED AGES, BY COLOR AND SEX: 1949–1951 AND
1900–1902

Year, color, and sex	At birth	20 years	40 years	60 years	65 years	70 years	75 years
TOTAL							
1949–1951................	68.1	51.2	32.8	17.0	13.8	10.9	8.4
1900–1902[1]...............	49.2	42.8	28.3	14.8	11.9	9.3	7.1
WHITE							
Male:							
1949–1951................	66.3	49.5	31.2	15.8	12.8	10.1	7.8
1900–1902[1]...............	48.2	42.2	27.7	14.4	11.5	9.0	6.8
Female:							
1949–1951................	72.0	54.6	35.6	18.6	15.0	11.7	8.9
1900–1902[1]...............	51.1	43.8	29.2	15.2	12.2	9.6	7.3
NONWHITE							
Male:							
1949–1951................	58.9	43.7	27.3	14.9	12.8	10.7	8.8
1900–1902[1]...............	32.5	35.1	23.1	12.6	10.4	8.3	6.6
Female:							
1949–1951................	62.7	46.8	29.8	17.0	14.5	12.3	10.2
1900–1902[1]...............	35.0	36.9	24.4	13.6	11.4	9.6	7.9

[1] Based on data from original Death Registration States. Figures for nonwhites cover only Negroes who in 1900 comprised more than 95 percent of the total nonwhite population in the registration area.

Source: U. S. Bureau of the Census, *United States Life Tables: 1890, 1901, and 1900-1910*, by J. W. Glover, 1921; and
National Office of Vital Statistics, "United States Life Tables, 1949-1951," *Vital Statistics—Special Reports*, Vol. 41,
No. 1, November 23, 1954.

Although life-table data clearly establish the fact that mortality has declined, they suffer from certain limitations when used as a basis for eval-
uating the contribution of this decline to the increase in the older population of the United States. Life tables for the United States are not available
for periods prior to 1900. Furthermore, the population was exposed not
to the set mortality conditions of life tables for a given date but rather to
shifting mortality conditions between birth and the older ages. By relating an estimate of the number of births in the appropriate periods to the
actual population 60 and over in 1900 and 1950, we can obtain a crude

approximation of the aggregate effect of improved mortality. Figures of this type indicate that, for the native population, about 18 percent of the estimated number of births from 1810 to 1840 were represented in the population aged 60 to 89 in 1900. The corresponding "survival" rate for the population 60 to 89 in 1950 was 26 (table 3).

It is clear then that the decline in mortality contributed appreciably to the increase in the number of older persons between 1900 and 1950—about 4.2 million—on the basis of census survival rates for 1900 applied to the births which accounted for persons 60 to 89 in 1950. The size of this number is, of course, in part the result of the fact that the number of births which account for the native population 60 and over in 1950 was something like three times as large as the corresponding number for 1900. If the number for 1950 had been equal to that for 1900, the contribution of declining mortality would have been 1.4 million. The remaining 2.8 million, therefore, represent the effect of declining mortality on the excess in the number of births contributing to the older population of 1950.

Relative effects of births, mortality, and migration.   Some interest attaches to an estimate of the relative contribution of changes in the number of births, and changes in mortality and immigration, to the increase in the number of persons 60 to 89 years old, or, for all practical purposes, the population 60 and over.

The application of the 1900 survival rate for persons 60 to 89 to the births, which accounted for this age group in 1950, provides a rough notion of how much the increase in births and the decline in mortality have contributed to the increase in the older native population. The remaining portion of the over-all difference—that between the number of foreign born at the two dates—reflects the effects of immigration, combined of course with whatever improvement in mortality occurred in the immigrant group. Thus, of the increase in the total population 60 to 89 between 1900 and 1950 (13.3 million), about 6.6 million, or 50 percent, can be attributed to the difference in the number of births; about 1.4 million, or about 11 percent, to the decline in mortality *per se;* about 2.8 million, or 21 percent, to declining mortality among excess births; and about 2.5 million, or nearly 20 percent, to immigration.[8]

Changes in the proportion of older persons.   So far, consideration has been given primarily to the relative contributions of past trends in the number of births, past trends in the volume of immigration, and the decline in mortality to the increase in the *number* of older persons between 1900 and 1950. The larger issue and the one which may well be the subject of greater concern is the increase in the *proportion* of older persons in this period. The data presented in tables 3 and 4 suggest that both births

---

[8] Appendix A, section 2, and appendix tables A–8 and A–9.

and immigration were more heavily concentrated in the earlier part of the 90-year period prior to 1950 than they were in the corresponding part of the 90-year period prior to 1900; therefore, the higher percentage of the population 60 and over in 1950 is to be expected.

Although the decline in mortality has made an appreciable contribution to the increase in the *number* of older persons between 1900 and 1950, the data suggest that this decline has made but a small contribution to the increase in the *proportion* of older persons. Thus, if the survival rates derived from the period prior to 1900 are applied to the births contributing to the 1950 population, a hypothetical native population is derived in which persons 60 and over constitute about 9 percent—about 1 percentage point less than the percentage actually observed in the native population of 1950. This conclusion rests, however, on the assumption that the trend in births prior to 1950 was fixed, and was independent of the trend in mortality. Actually, if the mortality levels prior to 1950 had been the same as those prior to 1900, fewer females would have survived to the child-bearing ages, there would have been fewer births, and these births would have been more heavily concentrated in the period 1860 to 1890. In short, there are grounds for believing that, had it not been for the lower mortality in the years prior to 1950, the proportion of older persons in the native population might have been higher than the observed proportion.[9]

The same line of reasoning also applies to immigration. To be sure, immigration was concentrated in the latter part of the appropriate period prior to 1900 and in the early part of the period prior to 1950, and these differences are reflected in the sharp increase in the percentage of older persons among the foreign born between 1900 and 1950. In both periods, however, young adult immigrants with their high fertility made substantial contributions to the population under 60 in the years under consideration. Thus, if it were possible to obtain data on the age structure of populations composed of immigrants prior to 1900 and to 1950 and their respective descendants, it might be found that the contribution of immigration to the increase in the proportion of older persons in the total population between 1900 and 1950 would have been considerably less than that implied by the data on the foreign born alone.

It seems reasonably clear, then, that the increase in the proportion of older persons between 1900 and 1950 was for the most part a matter of declining fertility. Estimates, although extremely rough, suggest a crude

[9] Studies of generalized population models, implicit in the fertility and mortality levels of roughly the period 1900 to 1950 in Western European countries and the United States and of characteristic changes within these levels, indicate that within this frame of reference the net effect of declining mortality has been to stabilize and, in some cases, to reduce the proportion of older persons. See, for example, Ansley J. Coale, "The Effects of Changes in Mortality and Fertility on Age Composition," *The Milbank Memorial Quarterly*, Vol. XXXIV, No. 1, January 1956, and George J. Stolnitz, "Mortality Declines and Age Distributions," *The Milbank Memorial Quarterly*, Vol. XXXIV, No. 2, April 1956.

birth rate of about 55 in 1820, 44 in 1860, and about 32 in 1900.[10]   Between 1920 and 1930 the birth rate dropped from 28 to 21, reaching a
low of 18 in 1933.   Between 1940 and 1950 the rate increased from 19
to 24.[11]   Thus, succeeding generations made progressively smaller relative
contributions of births to the population and, as they aged, became in turn
progressively a larger proportion of that population.

Future prospects

A great deal has been written about the future increase in our older population.   Very often the magnitude of the increase, if not exaggerated, has at
least not been underplayed.   This emphasis results partly from earlier population projections in which the "low" fertility—defined in terms of the
birth rate of the 1930's and carried forward for half a century—resulted
in phenomenally high proportions of older persons in the projected populations.   The relatively high fertility of the 1940's and early 1950's has
cast some doubt on the validity of these predictions; although there is
every reason to believe that the *number* of older persons will increase for
some time, it is an open question whether or not the *proportion* of older
persons will increase substantially.

Since the native population that will reach the ages 60 to 69 at each
decennial census from 1960 to 2010 is now living, it is possible to indicate
the number of persons who will enter the population aged 60 and over at
each decade in this period.   The number of persons in this age group probably will increase substantially until 1980 or 1990, although at rates somewhat lower than in the decades before 1950.   In the year 2000, when survivors of the relatively small number of births in the 1930's become 60 to
69, the number in this age group may decline.   In the year 2010, however,
the bumper baby crop of the 1940's will swell the ranks of the older
population.

The future trend in the total population 60 and over probably will
follow, in general, the same trend as that for the age group 60 to 69.   The
fact that more than one decade of births is involved, combined with the
sharp increase in mortality at ages above 60, leads to an averaging effect
which blurs the relationship to births in a single decade.

In the foreign-born population, the number aged 60 and over probably
will be smaller in 1960 than it was in 1950, and this decline may continue
for a number of decades—or until survivors of the heavy immigration of
1900 to 1925 have died.   Thereafter the number will remain relatively
constant, provided that immigration continues at about current levels.   If

---

[10] Appendix table A–8.

[11] National Office of Vital Statistics, *Special Reports*, Vol. 33, No. 8, September 28, 1950; *Vital Statistics of the United States, 1953*, Vol. I, table K.

the volume of immigration were to increase, the effects of such increase would not appear until the immigrants involved had reached the upper age levels. In short, within the next several decades, the number of foreign born in the older population may decrease.

Although the age structure of the 1950 population provides a clue to the general pattern of increase among older people, the actual numbers will also be affected by trends in mortality. Some reduction in adult mortality is generally expected; many people feel that medical science is about to pay handsome dividends by reducing mortality from cancer, heart disease, and other diseases characteristic of middle and later life. At present, however, such predictions are necessarily vague as to amounts of reduction, and as to precisely when the results will become effective.

It seems probable that changes in mortality resulting from medical discoveries will not cause any sharp dramatic drop in mortality (such as that suggested by a life table constructed on the assumption that there will be no deaths from heart disease), but will be spread over a number of decades.

Although a specific estimate of future trends in the older population may be questioned on a number of grounds, predictions as to the future trend in the proportion of older persons in the population are still more problematic, since they involve not only the future course of mortality but also the future course of fertility. If fertility continues at roughly the 1950 level, the rate of increase in the total population will almost keep up with the rate of increase in the population 60 and over, and thus the proportion of older persons will increase but slightly. If, on the other hand, the birth rate should fall to the depression low, the proportion of older persons would increase rapidly; and if this low level continued long enough, persons 60 and over might come to constitute from one-fifth to one-fourth of the total population.

TABLE **6.**—PROJECTIONS OF THE TOTAL POPULATION AND THE POPULATION 60 YEARS OLD AND OVER: 1955 TO 1975

[In thousands. Series AA, A, B, and C imply the following assumptions as to fertility: AA—1954-55 level continues to 1975; A—1950-53 level continues to 1975; B—1950-53 level continues to 1965, then declines to about the "prewar" level by 1975; C—1950-53 level declines from 1953 to about the "prewar" level by 1975]

Projections and age	1955	1960	1965	1970	1975
Total population:					
Series AA...................	165,248	179,358	193,346	209,380	228,463
Series A....................	165,248	177,840	190,296	204,620	221,522
Series B....................	165,248	177,840	190,296	202,984	214,580
Series C....................	165,248	176,452	186,291	196,370	206,907
Population 60 years and over....	20,817	23,048	25,106	27,470	30,053
Percent of total population 60 years and over:					
Series AA...................	12.6	12.9	13.0	13.1	13.2
Series A....................	12.6	13.0	13.2	13.4	13.6
Series B....................	12.6	13.0	13.2	13.5	14.0
Series C....................	12.6	13.1	13.5	14.0	14.5

Source: U. S. Bureau of the Census, *Current Population Reports*, Series P-25, No. 123.

The general role of fertility in relation to the proportion of older persons is illustrated in the revised projections of the population issued by the Bureau of the Census in 1955 (table 6).[12]   These projections made only one set of assumptions with respect to mortality and migration; thus the variation among the four series represents variations with respect to future fertility.   Series AA is based on the assumption that the fertility level observed in 1954 to 1955 continues unabated until 1975, whereas Series C assumes that the fertility level of 1950 to 1953 declines from 1953 to about the "prewar" level by 1975.   Series A assumes that the 1950 to 1953 fertility level continues unchanged to 1975, and Series B assumes that this level continues to 1965 and then declines to about the "prewar" level of 1940.   The 1975 "high" fertility series (Series AA) shows a percentage 60 and over of about 13.2 percent—an increase of about 1 percentage point over the 12.1 percent in 1950.   For the "low" series the percent is 14.5—about 2.3 points over the 1950 level.

Although these assumptions as to fertility are reasonable, they are also conservative.   They do not cover the possibility that fertility might drop back to (or below) the level of the middle 1930's, nor the possibility that there could ever again be birth rates higher than those observed between 1954 and 1955.   Moreover, the assumption as to mortality provides for a continuation of the decline observed in the 1940's, but allows for no improvement thereafter.[13]   In short, it may be that the assumptions understate the probable range of variability in the future trend in the proportion of older persons.

In summary, then, it seems likely that the number of persons 60 and over (which nearly doubled between 1900 and 1925, and more than doubled between 1925 and 1950) will increase substantially in the next quarter of a century, but—even allowing for appreciable reductions in mortality—at a rate somewhat less than in the two previous quarters of this century (table 7).   Moreover, there are indications that in the last quarter the rates of increase will be small.   The trend in the proportion of older persons would appear to follow somewhat the same course, but difficulties in projecting fertility tend to place this conclusion in the realm of speculation.

---

[12] U. S. Bureau of the Census, *Current Population Reports*, Series P–25, No. 123.

[13] If a continuation of the decline in mortality at the upper age levels observed between 1947 and 1954 is assumed, and this trend is used to carry forward the estimate of the 1960 population to 1975, a gain of from 2 to 3 million over the published figure is indicated.   It is perhaps noteworthy at this point that, although in the period from 1900 to 1950 studies of the effects of declining mortality on age structure indicate that mortality has had little effect in increasing the proportion of older persons, a concentration of improvement at the upper ages, which seems not unlikely in the future, may have the effect of actually increasing the proportion of older persons.

TABLE **7.**—POPULATION 60 YEARS OLD AND OVER: 1900 TO 2000

[In millions]

Year	Population 60 years old and over	Increase from preceding date	
		Number	Percent
1900	4.9	...	...
1925	9.0	4.1	83.7
1950	18.3	9.3	103.3
1975[1]	30.1	11.8	64.5
2000[1]	35.9	5.8	19.3

[1] Projections.

Source: Appendix table A-2; *Hearings Before the Subcommittee on Social Security*, 83d Congress, 1st Session, Part I, table 11, p. 18; and U. S. Bureau of the Census, *Current Population Reports*, Series P-25, No. 114.

CHAPTER 3

GEOGRAPHIC DISTRIBUTION OF THE
OLDER POPULATION

Although the migration of older persons to such States as Florida and California has attracted much attention, such migration plays only a small part in the total variation in the proportion of older persons among the geographic areas of the United States.

Large movements of population, both from abroad and within the country, have occurred within the lifetime of our present aging population and have left an indelible imprint on the age structure of the present population of our States. Local variations in these movements have likewise affected the age structure of areas within States—standard metropolitan areas, counties, and cities. Suburbanization has also influenced not only the internal structure of the metropolitan community but also the age distribution within this structure. The effects of these population movements have, of course, occurred within the context of local variations in fertility and mortality.

In this chapter, which brings together data on geography and age, the aging population is sometimes defined as the population 60 and over, and sometimes as the population 65 and over, depending on the nature of the materials.[1] Although the result is a reduction in comparability, only rarely is a generalization based on one level which is not equally supported by data based on the other level. In short, as far as geographic distribution is concerned, the number and proportion of persons 60 and over are highly correlated with the number and proportion 65 and over.

State differences

In 1950, the proportion of persons 60 and over in New Hampshire, 15.4 percent, was about twice that in New Mexico, 7.5 percent. These variations reflect, of course, past trends in births, deaths, and migration. However, an explanation of current age structure in terms of past demographic trends becomes an infinite series of explanations going backward in time. For example, the current size of the population aged 60 and over is determined largely by the number of births 60 years ago and earlier. This

---

[1] The data from the 1950 Census on which the analysis in the chapter is based are described in Appendix B, section 1.

24

leads to a consideration of the number of women of child-bearing age at that time. This number, in turn, is related to the number of births at an appropriate earlier period, and so backward in time, *ad infinitum.* This challenge, however, is rejected here and the analysis is limited to demographic trends in the period 1890 to 1950. In this context, the population under 30 years of age in 1890 may be taken to represent births in the period 1860 to 1890, as well as the generation which became 60 and over between 1890 and 1950.

Within the lifetime of the population of 1950, the continuing redistribution of population by migration—both internal and from abroad—has had a considerable impact on the age structure of the various States. In most general terms, the settlement of the West was completed between 1860 and 1950. In 1860, if we are to take the census of that year literally, there was no population in what are now the States of Oklahoma, Montana, Idaho, Wyoming, and Arizona. Between 1860 and 1950 the population of the Dakotas and the State of Washington increased by something over 20,000 percent. Likewise, this period was one of heavy immigration from abroad, and this trend, in turn, influenced the age structure of certain States.

The effects of migration are perhaps most clearly indicated in a context which takes into account the variations in fertility and mortality levels among the States. To this end, appropriate data for States classified by indexes of fertility and mortality are presented in table 8. In this table the States are classified into four levels of fertility on the basis of the mean fertility ratio, 1900 to 1950, and into four levels of mortality on the basis of a summary State figure for life expectancy as of 1930. Of the 16 categories implicit in the cross classification of these two elements, there were 3 into which not any of the States fell. Specifically, only States at the highest fertility level fell into the highest mortality class.

Within each fertility-mortality category, the States are ranked by the observed percentage of the population 60 and over. In addition, the percentage 60 and over expected had there been no migration between 1890 and 1950 as well as the migration rates for the periods from 1890 to 1920 and 1920 to 1950 are presented for each State.[2]

Role of migration. The examination of migration in relation to the proportion of older persons among the States is made here in terms of a comparison of the actual or observed percentage 60 and over in 1950 and the percentage expected had there been no migration in the period 1890 to 1950. The differences between the observed and expected percentages reflect therefore the net gains or losses in migrants and their descendants, that is, the full impact of migration.

---

[2] The indexes of fertility and mortality on which the classification of States in table 8 is based, as well as the indexes of net migration and the methods used in developing the expected percentage 60 and over are described in Appendix B, section 2.

TABLE 8.—PERCENT 60 YEARS OLD AND OVER, OBSERVED AND EXPECTED, 1950, AND MIGRATION RATES, BY LIFE EXPECTATION AND FERTILITY RATIO, FOR STATES

Fertility ratio: Under 36[2]

Expectation of life, 1930[1]	State	Percent 60 and over — Observed	Percent 60 and over — Expected[4]	Migration rate[3] 1890 to 1920	Migration rate[3] 1920 to 1950
62 years and over	Oregon	13.2	14.9	62	40
	....	...	...	...	...
	....	...	...	...	...
58 to 61 yrs	New Hampshire	15.4	13.5	5	-2
	Massachusetts	14.7	15.0	28	-2
	Connecticut	13.4	13.9	31	11
	Rhode Island	13.3	14.4	26	2
	Illinois	13.3	13.9	15	5
	Pennsylvania	13.1	15.7	26	12
	New York	12.7	17.0	102	96
	New Jersey	12.6	13.9	38	15
54 to 57 yrs	District of Columbia	10.8	21.9	65	49
Under 54 yrs	....	...	...	...	...

Fertility ratio: 36 to 41[2]

Expectation of life, 1930[1]	State	Percent 60 and over — Observed	Percent 60 and over — Expected[4]	Migration rate[3] 1890 to 1920	Migration rate[3] 1920 to 1950
62 years and over	Iowa	15.0	12.9	-8	-14
	Kansas	14.7	12.7	-10	-15
	Wisconsin	13.5	11.5	5	-3
	Washington	13.3	14.5	98	30
58 to 61 yrs	Missouri	14.9	12.9	-9	-7
	Vermont	14.7	11.8	-6	-14
	Maine	14.4	12.0	1	-8
	Indiana	13.4	12.7	...	2
	Ohio	13.3	13.6	16	4
	Pennsylvania	12.8	11.9	9	-9
	Delaware	12.3	12.6	3	-9
	Michigan	11.2	11.9	21	15
54 to 57 yrs	Colorado	12.8	12.5	38	1
	Nevada	10.7	13.8	43	45
	Maryland	10.5	11.9	3	15
Under 54 yrs	....	...	...	...	...

Fertility ratio: 42 to 47[2]

Expectation of life, 1930[1]	State	Percent 60 and over — Observed	Percent 60 and over — Expected[4]	Migration rate[3] 1890 to 1920	Migration rate[3] 1920 to 1950
62 years and over	Nebraska	14.5	12.2	-14	-21
	Minnesota	13.5	11.5	13	-7
58 to 61 yrs	Montana	13.3	10.8	88	-19
	Kentucky	11.5	8.5	-15	-17
	Tennessee	10.4	8.6	-14	-7
	Wyoming	9.9	10.2	60	-2
54 to 57 yrs	Florida	12.5	9.2	33	65
	Texas	9.9	8.5	9	4
	Louisiana	9.6	7.7	-3	-5
	Virginia	9.6	8.0	-8	-2
Under 54 yrs	....	...	...	...	...

Fertility ratio: 48 and over[2]

Expectation of life, 1930[1]	State	Percent 60 and over — Observed	Percent 60 and over — Expected[4]	Migration rate[3] 1890 to 1920	Migration rate[3] 1920 to 1950
62 years and over	South Dakota	12.8	9.9	10	-26
	Oklahoma	12.5	8.9	116	-24
	North Dakota	11.6	8.4	32	-32
	Idaho	11.2	8.9	77	-9
58 to 61 yrs	Arkansas	11.3	7.2	-10	-25
	West Virginia	10.2	7.7	4	-14
	Utah	9.3	7.5	9	-7
54 to 57 yrs	Mississippi	10.0	6.5	-14	-20
	Alabama	9.4	6.9	-8	-16
	Georgia	9.3	7.2	-7	-18
	North Carolina	8.3	6.5	-9	-7
Under 54 yrs	Arizona	9.1	9.1	127	35
	South Carolina	8.0	5.6	-13	-20
	New Mexico	7.5	7.0	16	1

[1] Weighted mean of sex-color groups. State values for the nonwhite population estimated by applying the ratio of nonwhite to white values at the national level to the observed State values for the white population.

[2] Mean ratio, children under 5 years per 100 women 15 to 49 years old, 1900 to 1950.

[3] Aggregate net migration of population 10 years old and over for indicated 3-decade periods expressed as a percentage of expected population at end of period, that is, the difference between the observed (or actual) population and the aggregate net migration.

[4] Percent 60 and over expected on the assumption of no migration between 1890 and 1950.

Source: Appendix tables B-1 to B-5.

The results of this analysis suggest that consistent patterns of out-migration in the period under consideration have increased the proportion of older persons among the States. In such States as Iowa, Kansas, Missouri, and Nebraska—States with appreciable out-migration in the periods 1890 to 1920 and 1920 to 1950, and with intermediate fertility and relatively low mortality—the observed percentage 60 and over was uniformly higher than that expected in the absence of migration. Likewise, among those southern States with appreciable out-migration in the two periods but with relatively high fertility and mortality—such as Mississippi, Alabama, Georgia, North Carolina, and South Carolina—the observed percentages for the same age group were higher than the expected ones. These findings suggest that, in the States under consideration, the loss through out-migration from successive cohorts as they reach the young adult ages meant a loss of potential parents and births, and thus a reduction in the rate of population growth below, and an increase in the proportion of older persons above, the levels expected in the absence of out-migration.

Among such States as North Dakota, South Dakota, Oklahoma, Idaho, and Montana—States which were only recently settled in 1890 and which were characterized by a considerable in-migration between 1890 and 1920, and a substantial out-migration between 1920 and 1950—the observed proportion 60 and over was appreciably higher than expected. In these States it seems not unreasonable to assume that the survivors of the initial in-migration contributed heavily to the older population and that their children constituted a major element in the subsequent out-migration.

In examining the relation of in-migration to age structure, a consideration of those States in which immigration from abroad has been an important element in the total migration into the State is instructive. Among such States are Massachusetts, Rhode Island, Connecticut, New York, and New Jersey. In each of these States there was a high concentration of foreign born in the older population[3] and, with the exception of Massachusetts in the period 1920 to 1950, each was characterized by a consistent pattern of in-migration between 1890 and 1950.

In these States, the observed percentage 60 and over was less than the expected percentage in 1950. Thus, although immigration from abroad made a substantial contribution to the older population, the immigrants with their high fertility made a more than compensating contribution to the population under 60. It was, of course, not entirely a matter of immigration from abroad; in Connecticut, New York, and New Jersey particularly, there was also a substantial in-migration of native population. Nevertheless, these are States in which the aging of the foreign-born pop-

---

[3] The percentage of foreign born in these States ranged from 40.7 in New Jersey to 46.8 in Rhode Island; see appendix table B–6. North Dakota might also have been included in this group but, in that State, the marked shift from in-migration to out-migration seemed to have greater significance with respect to age structure.

ulation might have been expected to raise the proportion of older persons in the total population above expectation.

Finally, there are States in which the rate of in-migration was high throughout the entire 60-year period—Washington, Oregon, California, Arizona, Florida, and the District of Columbia. In four of these States— the Pacific Coast States and the District of Columbia—the proportion of older persons expected in the absence of migration exceeded the observed proportion; that is, the heavy in-migration appeared to have lowered the percentage of older persons. In Arizona, however, the expected and observed percentages appeared to be identical; and in Florida in-migration appeared to have raised, rather than lowered, the percentage of the total population 60 and over.

It is commonly assumed that the ultimate destination of elderly migrants is either California or Florida and the potential impact of such an influx on the economy of these States has been a subject of local concern. Actually, the figures for California suggest that if the growth of the States population had been the sole responsibility of the "native sons" of 1890, the total population would have been slightly less than 1.5 million instead of 10.5 million, and the percentage 60 and over would have been 17 rather than 12. Moreover, of the million or so in-migrants 60 and over living in California in 1950, only some 280,000, or about 25 percent, had entered the State in the decade 1940 to 1950 at ages which made them 60 and over in 1950. The remaining 75 percent were survivors of the in-migrants of earlier decades who had entered the State at ages more acceptable to those concerned with future planning.[4]

In Florida, although without in-migration the 1950 population would have been only about one-third as large as it actually was, the proportion of persons aged 60 and over would have been lower—possibly 9 percent as compared with the observed 12 percent. In contrast to California, more than 100,000, or about 45 percent of the in-migrants 60 and over, migrated in the decade 1940 to 1950. Florida, then, represents a case in which the influx of large numbers of elderly persons did in fact increase the proportion of the total population 60 and over.

In the foregoing discussion specific consideration has been given only to those States in which the volume of immigration was relatively large and the pattern reasonably clear cut. Both the migration rates and the expected percentages 60 and over are at best rough approximations, and, therefore, small migration rates and small percentage differences are open to question.[5] In general, however, in the period under consideration, it appears

---

[4] Thompson is in essential agreement with the position taken here that the older population of California in 1950 was composed in large part of the younger migrants of earlier decades who had aged, rather than recently arrived older migrants. Warren S. Thompson, *Growth and Changes in California's Population*, The Haynes Foundation, Los Angeles, 1955, pp. 56–57.

[5] See Appendix B, section 2, for a discussion of the accuracy of the estimates of net migration and expected percentages 60 and over.

that out-migration increased, and in-migration decreased, the proportion of older persons. This relationship appears to have resulted from the successive gains or loss over a number of decades of migrants concentrated in the young adult years and their eventual descendants.

There is, however, nothing inevitable in this set of circumstances. If, as appears to have been the case in Florida, the migrants are somewhat concentrated at ages above the reproductive period, or if an in-migrant population of relatively low fertility is superimposed on a population of relatively high fertility, the net effect of in-migration may be to increase the proportions at the upper age levels. If, for example, in the future, migration on retirement from the heavily industrialized States of the Atlantic Seaboard to the Gulf Coast States becomes the order of the day, the proportion of older persons in the former States will be reduced by out-migration, and, in the latter States, increased by in-migration.

Fertility and age structure. If attention is focused on the percentages 60 and over expected in the absence of migration, then it appears clear that the level of fertility was, in the period under consideration, related to the proportion of older persons in the expected direction. These percentages, generally speaking, declined as the ratio of children to women increased. The expected age distributions are of course not "pure" in the sense of a stable population. The observed fertility ratios were used which, in precise terms, means that the expected population for each State is based on a unique fertility series. Likewise, since the calculation began with the observed population of 1890, any "abnormalities" in sex and age distribution (such as those which existed in the States but recently settled in 1890) are to some degree reflected in the expected 1950 population. Finally, the 1950 expected populations also reflect differences in mortality levels. Exact uniformity in the percentage 60 and over is therefore not to be expected within fertility classes.

Mortality and age structure. An examination of the expected percentages 60 and over by mortality classes suggests a lower order of relationship than that between fertility and the proportion of older persons. Among the States with relatively low fertility, there appears to be little evidence of a decline in the percentage 60 and over as the expectation of life declines. Among the States with relatively high fertility, there is a suggestion of such a relationship. This lack of a clear-cut relationship is perhaps to be expected. The proportion of women surviving from birth through the childbearing period was greater in the "low" than in the "high" mortality States. Thus, at comparable fertility levels, there were relatively more births in the former than in the latter States. These additional births tended to compensate for the additional persons surviving to the older ages in the "low" mortality States, and thus the percentage of older persons tends to be not materially greater than in the "high" mortality States. In short, the effect is analogous to that described in connection with in-migration.

Some indication of the impact of differences in mortality on the percentage 60 and over is indicated in table 9, in which data are presented for North Dakota and New Mexico.   Both States had about the same mean fertility ratio but, in estimating the 1950 expected population, the lowest survival rates were used for New Mexico and the highest survival rates for North Dakota.   If the application of these two sets of rates is reversed, the expected percentage for North Dakota is lowered by about 0.8 percentage points and that for New Mexico, raised by 0.8 percentage points.   These percentage point differences give some indication as to the magnitude of the difference in the percentage of older persons attributable to differences in mortality level.[6]

TABLE **9.**—Percent 60 Years and Over Expected in 1950 in Absence of Migration, 1890 to 1950, Under Various Mortality Assumptions, for North Dakota and New Mexico

State and percent 60 years old and over	Observed	Expected in absence of migration, 1890 to 1950		
		Observed survival rates	"High" survival rates[1]	"Low" survival rates[2]
Total population:				
North Dakota......................	619,636	659,472	659,472	523,192
New Mexico........................	681,187	454,786	572,476	454,786
Population 60 and over:				
North Dakota......................	72,050	55,347	55,347	39,594
New Mexico........................	51,231	31,688	44,411	31,688
Percent 60 and over:				
North Dakota......................	11.6	8.4	8.4	7.6
New Mexico........................	7.5	7.0	7.8	7.0
Mean fertility ratio:[3]				
North Dakota......................	55.0	55.0	55.0	55.0
New Mexico........................	55.0	55.0	55.0	55.0

[1] Ten-year survival rates developed for Kansas for each decade in the period 1890 to 1950; see Appendix B, section 2.
[2] Similar rates developed for Arizona. The Kansas rates were used as the observed rates for North Dakota and the Arizona rates as the observed rates for New Mexico.
[3] Mean of number of children under 5 per 100 women 15 to 49 years old at each census, 1900 to 1950; see Appendix B, section 2, and table B-1.
Source: Appendix table B-5 and related materials; see Appendix B, section 2.

Urban-rural differences

Since the historical trend in the United States has been toward urbanization, and since the position of older persons in urban areas is somewhat different from that of older persons in rural areas, urban-rural differences

[6] This percentage point difference does not take into account differences in mortality prior to 1890. In the initial estimates, this deficiency is not serious since it can be assumed that the 1890 population had been subjected to mortality schedules roughly homogeneous with those used to bring forward this population. However, in applying the survival rates of a "high" mortality to the 1890 population of a "low" mortality State, it is clear that an adjustment of the 1890 population is called for. It is equally clear that a thoroughgoing adjustment involves a web of "reasonable" assumptions approaching sheer fantasy. In principle, this situation is a sample of a special case of the effect of lower mortality on age distribution. The adjustment in question would decrease the number of survivors 60 and over in 1950, but would also decrease the number of child-bearing age and thus the number of survivors under 60 in 1950. What the net effect on the expected percentage 60 and over in 1950 would be remains an open question. It seems highly unlikely, however, that it would produce a sharp and dramatic decrease in the proportion 60 and over.

in the concentration of the elderly are of some interest. As the figures in table 10 indicate, these differences have been small since 1920, the year in which a classification encompassing the urban, rural-nonfarm, and rural-farm segments of the population was first established.

TABLE 10.—PERCENT OF TOTAL POPULATION 65 YEARS OLD AND OVER, BY URBAN AND RURAL RESIDENCE: 1920 TO 1950

Year	Total	Urban	Rural nonfarm	Rural farm
New urban definition, 1950.........	8.1	8.1	8.6	7.6
Old urban definition:				
1950............................	8.1	8.3	8.0	7.6
1940............................	6.8	6.8	7.3	6.6
1930............................	5.4	5.1	6.6	5.1
1920............................	4.7	4.3	6.0	4.4

Source: *1950 Census of Population*, Vol. II, *Characteristics of the Population*, Part 1, U. S. Summary, table 38; and *1940 Census of Population*, Vol. II, *Characteristics of the Population*, Part 1, U. S. Summary, tables 7 and 9.

In the United States. It is evident, however, that within the limited range indicated there is a consistent pattern of difference. From 1920 to 1940 the percentage of persons 65 and over was highest in the rural-non-farm population, and for the urban population this percentage was either equal to or more than that for the rural-farm population. In 1950, how-ever, the figures based on the old urban definition (identical with that used in the earlier census) show a higher percentage 65 and over for urban than for rural-nonfarm areas. According to the new definition, however, the pattern of the previous years is maintained.

In general, the change in the definition of urban and rural territory, made in 1950, shifted the population of certain suburban territory on the out-skirts of cities of 50,000 or more from the rural to the urban category. Since the population shifted by this change in definition was relatively young—only about 5 percent were aged 65 and over—the net effect was to decrease the percentage of older persons in urban areas and to increase the percentage in the rural-nonfarm population. Thus, if the rural-non-farm population is conceived to be the population of villages and open country (but not farms), the effect of the change in definition was to in-crease the homogeneity of the population in question, and, in one sense, to make the figure somewhat more comparable with those of earlier years. Suburbanization has of course been going on for some time, and strict comparability would involve a similar revision of the figures for earlier years. Since, however, changes in this direction in the decade 1940 to 1950 were considerably greater than in previous decades, the figures com-piled on the basis of the new definition may be the more useful.

Variations among States. Although according to the new definition the figures on urban and rural residence for 1950 present a pattern con-sistent with the past, the pattern among the States is by no means consist-ent. Of the 48 States (the District of Columbia is entirely urban), there were 11 States in which the percentage 65 and over was highest in urban areas, 19 in which it was highest in rural-farm areas, and 18 in which it was highest in rural-nonfarm areas.[7]   There was some indication of characteristic regional patterns.   Of the 11 States with the highest percentage of older persons in the urban population, 9 were in the Pacific and Mountain Divisions.   Although the States with the highest percentage in rural-farm areas were somewhat more heterogeneous in geographic distribution, they included all the South Atlantic States except Florida.   Those States which exhibited the pattern characteristics of the country as a whole were concentrated in the central agricultural area of the country.   They included not only Iowa, Missouri, Kansas, Nebraska, and the Dakotas; but on the northeastern periphery, Minnesota, Wisconsin, and Illinois; and on the southwestern boundary, Louisiana, Arkansas, and Oklahoma.

The differences in the proportions of older persons among urban, rural-nonfarm, and rural-farm populations suggest that the two components of the rural-nonfarm population—unincorporated suburban areas, and places with a population of less than 2,500—have characteristic and contrasting age distributions.

Urban-suburban differences

The population which was shifted by the change in the 1950 definition from the rural-nonfarm to the urban population contained a relatively low proportion of older persons.   This fact suggests a smaller concentration of elderly people in suburban areas than in central cities surrounded by suburbs—a generalization born out by the statistics on the proportion of persons 65 and over in urbanized areas.   In 1950, about 7.8 percent of the total population of urbanized areas were 65 and over.   For the central cities of these areas, however, the percentage was 8.2, and for the urban fringe (that is, the suburban areas), 7.1.   This difference, although small, occurs in each size class of urbanized area (see appendix table B–10).

One explanation of the difference lies in the substantial migration of young adults to cities.   Once settled in the city, they eventually marry and, with the advent of children, they tend to move into single-family dwelling units on the outskirts of the city—usually in new real estate developments. Thus the population of the suburbs is heavily weighted with young adults and their children and, consequently, the proportion of older persons is low.

Regardless of the adequacy of this somewhat oversimplified explanation, if attention is focused on a limited time period, for example, on suburbs which developed between 1940 and 1950, it is clear that suburban areas contain a high proportion of young adults and their children.   This generalization becomes less applicable as the time perspective is broadened, for parents who were in their 20's when they settled in a new development in 1910 are now in their 60's.   In short, the population of a suburb tends to age

---

[7] Appendix table B–7.

with the suburb. Thus, for example, in Oak Park, Illinois, which is an "old" suburb of Chicago, the percentage of people aged 65 and over was 11.7, compared with 7.6 for the central city.

The fact that people grow old in the suburbs as well as in the central cities accounts for the relatively small difference in the proportion of older persons between central city and urban fringe in urbanized areas. The urban fringe frequently contains "old" suburbs with relatively mature populations as well as suburbs settled by young married people. As a consequence, the proportion of older persons in the urban fringe tends to average out at a level which is not materially different from that of the central city.

Suburban contrasts. In terms of actual incorporated places, a striking example of a "new" suburb is such a place as Park Forest, Illinois, a suburb of Chicago. Park Forest, with a population of some 8,000 in 1950, was built up entirely in the late 1940's. In contrast to the city of Chicago, Park Forest is characterized by an age structure in which there were heavy concentrations of the population in the age groups under 10 and between 25 and 34, and relatively few in the age groups 10 to 24 and 45 and over (table 11).

TABLE 11.—POPULATION BY AGE, FOR CHICAGO, FOREST PARK, AND PARK FOREST: 1950

Year and age	Chicago	Forest Park	Park Forest	Percent distribution		
				Chicago	Forest Park	Park Forest
1950						
All ages..................	3,620,962	14,969	8,138	100.0	100.0	100.0
Under 10 years..............	583,326	2,378	2,928	16.1	15.9	36.0
10 to 24 years..............	683,877	2,626	917	18.9	17.5	11.3
25 to 34 years..............	632,776	2,337	2,827	17.5	15.6	34.7
35 to 44 years..............	577,388	2,271	1,070	15.9	15.2	13.1
45 to 64 years..............	869,871	3,768	328	24.0	25.2	4.0
65 years and over............	273,724	1,589	68	7.6	10.6	0.8
1940						
65 years and over............	197,079	1,194	...	5.8	8.0	...
1930						
65 years and over............	134,451	912	...	4.0	6.3	...

Source. *1950 Census of Population*, Vol. II, *Characteristics of the Population*, Part 13, tables 33 and 38; and *1940 Census of Population*, Vol. II, *Characteristics of the Population*, Part 2, Illinois, tables 32 and A-35.

At the other extreme of the age distribution lies Forest Park, Illinois, which first appeared in the decennial census of 1880, with a population of 923. By 1930 the population was approximately the same as in 1950— about 15,000. In contrast to Park Forest, Forest Park's heavy concentrations of population in 1950 were in the age groups 45 to 64 and 65 and over, with relatively low proportions in the groups under 10 and 24 to 34. These differences suggest the hypothesis that the age of suburban populations varies directly with the age of the suburbs themselves.

Proportion of older persons and age of suburb. An examination of this relationship among the several hundred suburbs in the three largest urbanized areas of the United States—the New York-Northeastern New Jersey Urbanized Area, the Chicago Urbanized Area, and the Los Angeles Urbanized Area—suggests that the evidence in support of the hypothesis is more than anecdotal.[8] In this examination a suburb was defined as an incorporated place of 2,500 or more in the urban fringe of the urbanized areas. The census statistics on the year in which dwelling units were built ("year built") provided the basis for classifying the suburbs by age into four groups: those relatively "new" suburbs in which 50 percent or more of the dwelling units had been built between 1940 and 1950; those suburbs in which it was necessary to go back to 1930 to account for 50 percent or more of the dwelling units; those in which 50 percent or more of the dwellings had been built between 1920 and 1950; and, finally, the oldest suburbs, in which 50 percent or more of the dwellings had been built before 1920. The percentage of the population 65 and over was taken as an index of the age of the population of the suburbs under consideration.

As might be expected, the results of this examination, presented in table 12, tend to confirm the hypothesis stated. In terms of the aggregate percentages 65 and over (percentages based on the pooled population for each class of suburb), in each of the three urbanized areas, the proportion of older persons declined as the age of the suburbs declined, and in each case the percentage was greater for the oldest suburbs than for the central city or cities, and smaller for the newest suburbs.

TABLE 12.—PERCENT 65 YEARS OLD AND OVER IN SUBURBS, CLASSIFIED BY PERIOD IN WHICH 50 PERCENT OR MORE OF TOTAL DWELLING UNITS WERE BUILT, FOR SELECTED URBANIZED AREAS: 1950

Component of urbanized area and age of suburb	New York-Northeastern New Jersey	Chicago	Los Angeles
Total urbanized area.....................	7.6	7.3	9.1
Central cities................................	7.6	7.6	9.6
Suburbs[1]..	8.0	6.6	9.8
50 percent or more of dwelling units built--			
1940 to 1950.............................	5.1	3.8	5.9
1930 to 1950.............................	6.1	5.5	10.3
1920 to 1950.............................	8.0	6.6	13.5
Before 1920.............................	8.5	8.5	...
Remainder of area............................	6.2	5.2	6.7

[1] Places of 2,500 or more in urban fringe.

Source: Appendix table B-8.

Although in general the relationship between the age of the suburbs and the age of the population seems to hold, there was obviously a great deal of variability in the percentage 65 and over wthin age-of-suburb classes, and a considerable overlap of these percentages between classes. This sit-

---

[8] See Appendix B, section 3.

uation arises in part from the rather approximate index of the age of suburb used and the great variability in growth patterns. The analysis of this relationship might prove more incisive if it were made in terms of smaller, more homogeneous units such as census tracts. Data for the Los Angeles tracted area indicate a clear-cut positive relationship between median year in which houses were built and the percentage of the population 65 and over; not only for the city of Los Angeles proper but also for such larger suburbs as Long Beach and Pasadena. It seems to follow, then, that in large metropolitan areas an analysis in which the suburb is a unit tends to obscure by an averaging effect the relationship which actually exists.[9]

As in the case of States, the question arises as to the role of migration in accounting for this variability. Is the increasing age of the population of a suburb through time merely a function of the aging of the initial in-migrants? Or may in-migration actually increase the proportion of older persons in given instances? In an effort to find the answers, an analysis was made among Los Angeles suburbs in the period 1930 to 1950. This area was selected because it was hoped that the volume of in-migration was large enough to transcend the fairly wide margin of error implicit in the available data and techniques for measuring net migration, and because in-migration was commonly supposed to have actually increased the proportion of older persons.

With estimates of the complete age distribution of that part of the 1950 population attributable to the 1930 population, and the part attributable to net in-migration between 1930 and 1950—estimates developed by methods similar to those used for States—it was possible to compare the percentage 65 and over in these two segments with the corresponding percentages for the total population in 1950 and in 1930 (table 13).[10] Thus the difference between the percent 65 and over in the surviving population of 1950 and the corresponding percent for 1930 indicates the percentage point increase to be expected in terms of the age structure of 1930, and subsequent fertility and mortality in the absence of migration. A comparison of this percentage point increase with the increase in observed percentage in the total population between 1930 and 1950 indicates the net percentage point gain or loss attributable to net in-migration. For example, the percentage 65 and over in Beverly Hills in 1930 was 4.4. The percentage expected in 1950, on the basis of age distribution in 1930 and the fertility implied in the 1950 figures, was 12.0. Therefore, the expected gain in percentage points was 7.6. The actual percentage point increase between 1930 and 1950 was 6.0. The difference between the two percents, 1.6, indicates the degree to which the percent 65 and over was reduced by in-migration.

---

[9] See Appendix B, section 3.
[10] See Appendix B, section 3.

TABLE **13.**—EXPECTED AND OBSERVED INCREASE IN THE PERCENT 65 YEARS AND OVER, FOR
LOS ANGELES SUBURBS: 1930 TO 1950

[Minus sign (−) denotes decrease]

Suburb	Increase in percent 65 years and over, 1930 to 1950			Percent 65 years and over			
	Expected if no in-migration	Actual	Differ-ence	1950			1930
				Total	Expected if no in-migration	Net in-migrants	
Beverly Hills............	7.6	6.0	-1.6	10.4	12.0	8.5	4.4
South Pasadena..........	6.0	5.6	-0.4	14.5	14.9	13.1	8.9
Arcadia.................	6.5	0.7	-5.8	9.4	15.2	7.7	8.7
Huntington Park.........	5.1	5.4	0.3	10.9	10.6	12.4	5.5
San Marino..............	5.8	2.9	-2.9	8.8	11.7	7.2	5.9
Santa Monica............	4.7	2.5	-2.2	11.3	13.5	9.2	8.8
Culver City.............	4.3	1.3	-3.0	5.6	8.6	4.2	4.3
Torrance................	4.9	1.4	-3.5	4.5	8.0	2.2	3.1
Pasadena................	3.6	4.6	1.0	16.8	15.8	18.5	12.2
Glendale................	3.8	4.3	0.5	11.8	11.3	12.7	7.5
Alhambra................	3.1	3.5	0.4	11.5	11.1	12.0	8.0
Maywood.................	3.4	3.3	-0.1	7.3	7.4	7.2	4.0
San Gabriel.............	3.3	2.9	-0.4	7.6	8.0	7.4	4.7
Signal Hill.............	3.6	3.0	-0.6	8.7	9.3	6.7	5.7
Inglewood...............	3.6	2.8	-0.8	8.5	9.3	7.8	5.7
Sierra Madre............	3.7	2.6	-1.1	13.8	14.9	12.9	11.2
Long Beach..............	3.2	2.0	-1.2	11.2	12.4	9.7	9.2
Montebello..............	3.1	0.9	-2.2	5.9	8.1	5.0	5.0
Burbank.................	3.0	0.0	-3.0	5.8	8.8	4.9	5.8
Monterey Park...........	3.8	0.4	-3.4	7.5	10.9	5.9	7.1
El Monte................	2.0	3.6	1.6	8.5	6.9	10.3	4.9
Whittier................	2.4	3.9	1.5	12.2	10.7	14.9	8.3
San Fernando............	2.3	2.8	0.5	7.7	7.2	9.2	4.9
El Segundo..............	2.2	1.5	-0.7	5.0	5.7	4.1	3.5
Bell....................	2.8	2.0	-0.8	7.6	8.4	6.7	5.6
South Gate..............	2.9	1.8	-1.1	5.8	6.9	4.9	4.0
Azusa...................	2.3	0.6	-1.7	5.8	7.5	3.6	5.2
Redondo Beach...........	2.1	0.0	-2.1	8.6	10.7	7.1	8.6
Compton.................	2.6	0.4	-2.2	5.1	7.3	4.0	4.7
Hawthorne...............	2.5	0.0	-2.5	6.7	9.2	4.4	6.7
Hermosa Beach...........	2.0	-0.8	-2.8	9.3	12.1	7.4	10.1
Covina..................	0.8	2.8	2.0	13.9	11.9	18.4	11.1
Monrovia................	1.7	2.8	1.1	13.9	12.8	15.1	11.1
Lynwood.................	1.4	-0.5	-1.9	5.5	7.4	4.5	6.0

Source: Appendix table B-9.

The figures as a whole, which cover the suburbs in the Los Angeles urban
fringe for which 1930 figures were available, confirmed the commonly accepted hypothesis that in-migration reduces the percentage of older persons
in the population over what might be expected in the absence of in-migration. This hypothesis assumes that, since migration rates for the population 45 and over are considerably smaller than for the age group 20
to 44, in-migration continued over a 20-year period will have made a
greater contribution to the cohorts under 65 than to those 65 and over. In
line with this hypothesis, 25 of the 34 suburbs considered showed an estimated decrease from the expected percentage.

These figures, however, also confirm the supposition that the Los
Angeles area includes suburbs in which in-migration has increased the percentage 65 and over in the period under consideration, and suggest some
sort of selectivity with respect to in-migration. This finding, although it
may be unique to the Los Angeles area, points to the possibility of frequent
exceptions to general assumptions concerning the effects of migration on

age structure. Six of the nine oldest suburbs (those in which 50 percent or more of the dwelling units were built in the period 1920 to 1950) showed estimated increases in the percentage 65 and over as the result of in-migration. For the remaining three suburbs the percentage point losses attributable to in-migration were 1.1 or less. At the other end of the scale—in cities for which figures are available in 1930, but where 50 percent or more of the dwelling units were built between 1940 and 1950— the estimated percentage point loss from in-migration ranged from 1.1 to 5.8 percent, and, generally speaking, the proportion of the population attributable to in-migration was larger in the latter than in the former group.

Conclusion. In general, the suburban population is initially a young population, and its age increases as the age of suburbs increases. Although in-migration tends to retard this aging process, there are suburbs, at least in the Los Angeles area—and these were by and large the "older" suburbs —where in-migration has actually increased the proportion of older persons. This finding suggests that in this area migration is selective with respect to age, and that we are witnessing the development of specialized communities of older persons. Data for selected areas in Florida would in all probability suggest the same phenomena.

Differences by size of place

The rural-nonfarm population, as previously noted, may be classified roughly into two components: the population of unincorporated suburban areas, and of villages and open country. The suburban component, insofar as it is identified by the population shifted from the rural-nonfarm to the urban category by the change in the urban-rural definition, contained a relatively small proportion of older persons, whereas the remaining population (rural-nonfarm, according to the new definition) had a high concentration of older persons. This raises the question of the proportions of older persons in the villages and in nonfarm open country in relation to larger places; in short, the whole question of variations in the proportion of older persons by size of place.

In the United States. The question is answered by the statistics in table 14. The country as a whole, excluding the three urbanized areas with populations of 3,000,000 or more—New York, Chicago, and Los Angeles—showed a steady increase in the proportion of older persons as size of place declined through incorporated places of under 1,000, where the percentage 65 and over was 13.5. The proportion for the open country, however—7.4 percent—was only slightly more than one-half the proportion for the smallest incorporated places and the lowest figure for any size group. This difference appears to be more closely related to size of place than to farm-nonfarm residence. Most of the rural-farm population was in this last size class, but it was matched by a nonfarm population of about equal size. The percentages 65 and over for these two populations were 7.5 and 7.2 respectively (see appendix table B–10).

TABLE **14.**—PERCENT OF THE TOTAL POPULATION 65 YEARS OLD AND OVER, BY SIZE OF PLACE, BY REGIONS: 1950

Size of place	United States	Northeast	North Central	South	West
Total...	8.1	8.8	8.9	6.9	8.2
IN URBANIZED AREAS					
Areas of 3,000,000 or more..............	7.9	7.7	7.3	...	9.1
Areas of 1,000,000 to 3,000,000.........	7.6	8.6	6.7	6.4	8.2
Areas of 250,000 to 1,000,000..........	7.8	8.7	8.3	6.5	9.2
Areas of less than 250,000.............	8.0	9.2	8.5	6.5	8.4
OUTSIDE URBANIZED AREAS					
Places of 25,000 or more................	8.5	10.3	9.2	6.7	8.5
Places of 10,000 to 25,000..............	8.8	9.9	10.2	7.1	8.3
Places of 2,500 to 10,000...............	9.2	10.3	11.4	7.5	8.0
Places of 1,000 to 2,500................	10.3	10.5	12.9	8.3	8.5
Incorporated places of less than 1,000..	13.5	12.0	15.7	11.3	9.6
Other rural territory...................	7.4	9.0	8.1	6.6	6.6

Source: Appendix table B–10.

Regional comparisons. The national pattern in the variation of the proportions of older persons by size of place was also characteristic of the North Central Region, the South, and (with minor variations) the Northeast. Although figures for the West show some divergence from the national pattern, here, again, the highest values were found in incorporated places of less than 1,000 and the lowest values in other rural territory.

As with variations in the proportions of older persons between old and new suburbs, the relationships observed are not inevitable, and the values for any given size class represent an average of the values for the individual places that fall into the class. In the West, for example, the difference between urbanized areas of 3,000,000 or more and those of 1,000,000 to 3,000,000 is the difference between the Los Angeles and the San Francisco-Oakland Urbanized Areas. The percentage 65 and over for urbanized areas of 250,000 to 1,000,000 is higher than that for the immediately higher class because this percentage is lower for the San Francisco-Oakland Areas than for the Seattle, Portland, and Denver Areas. Similarly, the other points at which the West departs from the standard pattern represent, in all likelihood, State differences in the proportion 65 and over, combined with differences in the degree to which States are represented in the various size classes. However, since there are enough smaller places to insure that the percentage for the class is not determined by the unique characteristics of a single place, it is apparent that appreciable numbers of the smaller places have relatively low proportions of older persons in their populations.

Other geographic differences

Variation exists of course in the proportion of older persons among geographic areas of all types—standard metropolitan areas, State economic areas, counties, and cities. Among standard metropolitan areas of 100,000 or more the percentage 65 and over ranged from 12.2 in the Tampa-St. Petersburg Standard Metropolitan Area to 4.1 in the Lubbock, Texas, and Albuquerque, N. Mex., Standard Metropolitan Areas.[11] Among cities of 100,000 or more the percentage ranged from 16.8 in Pasadena to 3.7 in Corpus Christi.[12] The same variability is exhibited among counties. In Florida the percentage 65 and over ranged from 21.6 for Osceola County to 4.1 in Okaloosa County. In California these percentages ranged from 14.8 to 4.1; in Iowa, from 16.0 to 7.8; and in New Mexico, from 11.9 to 0.9.[13] This variability suggests the limitations of inferences regarding the age structure of a particular area from a knowledge of the general class of areas into which it falls.

An explanation of this variability resembles that used in considering the variability in the proportion of older persons among States. In some instances, of course, the explanation is obvious. Osceola County, Florida, had, in 1950, recently established a large-scale community project for elderly retired persons. Since the population of Osceola County was small, participants in the project loomed large in the total population. The population of Los Alamos County, New Mexico—the county created in 1949 as the result of the atomic energy installation in a nearly uninhabited area—consisted almost entirely of the young adult staff of this installation; hence less than 1 percent of the population was 65 and over. In California, Napa County was among the several counties with a high percentage 65 and over. This county had a relatively small population but contained a large mental hospital; the elderly patients in this institution contributed appreciably to the percentage of older persons. Generally speaking, however, the relative size of the older population of any of these areas is the result of past trends in migration and natural increase, and the explanation for any particular area is to be found in the trends unique to that area.

---

[11] *1950 Census of Population*, Vol. II, *Characteristics of the Population*, Part 1, U. S. Summary, table 86.

[12] *Ibid.*

[13] *Op. cit.*, Parts 5, 10, 15, and 31, table 12.

CHAPTER 4

AGE AND EMPLOYMENT

The decline in employment with advancing years is one of the central issues in any consideration of the status of older persons in our society. For men, the extension of life has increased the period in the work force from 39 years to 43 years. Reduction of household responsibility has made possible the marked rise in the participation of women in gainful employment. Simultaneously, the remarkable increase in productivity has enabled young people to delay their entry into the labor force and older workers to retire.

As a consequence, a period of retirement from one's career occupation has been given respectability as a reward for years of productive contribution, and is used as a means of providing employment for young, vigorous newcomers to the labor force. Retirement systems have been set up on a fixed age basis. Public and private pension systems have been created in an effort to provide support for those who have completed their work lives or wish to taper off.

The situation is, however, by no means as clear cut as the foregoing picture may indicate. Despite continuing efforts to improve the circumstances of retirement, most people living on retirement incomes do not have enough to meet their needs. By and large, those who do have enough derive it from continued employment. Moreover, there is a general feeling that a larger population of retired persons would seriously threaten the economy.

This is not all. For men in our society, employment is not only a matter of maintaining an adequate income; it is also a matter of maintaining self-respect. Although a John Steinbeck may contrast the inherent nobility of the down-and-outer and the bum with the petty meanness of the solid citizen, this point of view must be regarded as a minority report; ours is a "job-oriented" society and the lack of a job tends to carry with it some implication of uselessness, irresponsibility, and inadequacy.

Beyond this, as indicated in the opening chapter, gainful work has additional meanings for the individual. It gives order to his life by providing a day-to-day routine, affords opportunity for social participation with fellow workers, and in many cases provides intrinsic satisfaction as an enjoyable pursuit. Thus, although retirement from one's career is coming to be looked upon as a normal phase of the work cycle, there still remain overtones of the negative attitude toward joblessness, along with other problems not solved by the rocking chair or the fishing pole. The retired older man is often at odds with himself and with society.

For women, the situation is somewhat different. Although the unattached woman faces the problem of making a living, she need not be gainfully employed to be respectable; in fact, remnants of the contrary attitude characteristic of the 19th century are still encountered, and homemaking and child rearing still offer serious competition to employment as a career. In view of these circumstances, employment problems of older women will be considered separately.

Since age 65 has been widely accepted as the normal retirement age, primary focus is on workers above that age, although it is recognized that many workers have difficulty finding employment at younger ages.

This chapter examines trends in labor force participation in relation to age and disability, the circumstances under which retirement occurs, the historic decline in the labor force participation of older people, and the availability of retired older persons for employment.

Employment status and age, 1950

Typically, labor force participation rates for men rise from a relatively low level in the early teens to a peak in the late 30's (when nearly all men are in the labor force), and thereafter decline. This decline is relatively slight in the middle years but, beginning with the late 50's, it accelerates to the extent that, for men 75 and over, the rate has fallen to about the same level as that of the early teens. Thus in 1950, for age 15, the labor force participation rate was 18;[1] for the age group 35 to 39, 94.7; for men 50 to 54, 90.5; and for men 75 and over, 18.7 (table 15).

TABLE 15.—PERCENT DISTRIBUTION BY EMPLOYMENT STATUS OF MALES 30 YEARS OLD AND OVER, BY AGE: 1950

Age	Total	Labor force	Not in labor force				
			Total	In insti- tutions	Unable to work	Other (incl. keeping house)	Not re- ported
30 to 34 years..................	100.0	94.0	6.0	1.3	1.0	2.8	0.9
35 to 39 years..................	100.0	94.7	5.3	1.3	1.1	2.1	0.8
40 to 44 years..................	100.0	94.5	5.5	1.3	1.4	2.1	0.7
45 to 49 years..................	100.0	93.3	6.7	1.4	2.0	2.5	0.8
50 to 54 years..................	100.0	90.5	9.5	1.7	3.5	3.6	0.7
55 to 59 years..................	100.0	86.7	13.3	1.8	5.4	5.3	0.7
60 to 64 years..................	100.0	79.4	20.6	2.0	8.9	8.8	0.8
65 to 69 years..................	100.0	59.7	40.3	2.1	18.4	18.8	1.0
70 to 74 years..................	100.0	38.7	61.3	2.4	30.3	27.4	1.3
75 years and over..............	100.0	18.7	81.3	4.8	47.2	28.1	1.2

Source: Appendix table C-1.

[1] *1950 Census of Population*, Vol. IV, *Special Reports*, Part 1, Chapter A, Employment and Personal Characteristics, table 1.

The subcategories of the class "Not in the labor force" provide, of course, a basis for inferences as to the sources of attrition from the working population.[2] One major source of attrition which seems reasonably clear cut is the increase of disability with age. This factor is reflected in data on persons in institutions and persons not in the labor force.

Generally speaking, presence in an institution is evidence of physical or mental disabilities which preclude labor force participation. There are exceptions, of course, such as prisons, but these exceptions account for only a minor fraction of the total institutional population. In 1950, about 1 percent of men aged 35 to 39 were under care in institutions; for men 75 and over, this percentage was about 5.

The second category in labor force statistics which reflects disability is "Unable to work." This category, in theory, comprises cases of chronic mental or physical disability of sufficient duration to preclude labor force activity. In 1950 about 1 percent of all males 35 to 39 were reported as unable to work, and among males 75 and over about 47 percent fell in this group. Thus, if we accept at face value the statistics on persons in institutions and persons unable to work, the proportion of disabled persons increases from about 2 percent at ages 35 to 39 to about 52 percent among men 75 and over.

The residual "other" group among persons not in the labor force reflects retirement for reasons other than disability as defined in the labor force inquiry. In 1950, about 2 percent of the males 35 to 39 fell in this classification, whereas at 75 and over the percentage was about 30. It is among members of this group that answers are to be sought to questions relating to the operation of age discrimination, the proportion of persons retiring voluntarily, and the volume of retirement attributable to compulsory age retirement systems. Before seeking these answers, however, it seems advisable to consider the degree to which persons able to work and persons not able to work can be reliably distinguished.

Disability and employment

The problem of defining disability. It is quite easy to establish that disability increases with age. It is quite another matter to specify exactly the extent of disability at a given age, and to state the exact relationship between disability and employability. In fact, any attempt to answer the question as to whether an individual is able to work is an extremely ambitious undertaking. In the first place, "disability"—even in such apparently obvious defects as impaired sight or hearing—is a highly technical matter, and slight variations in definition lead to wide differences in reported prevalence, particularly in more subtle and complicated disabilities.

In the second place, even a well-defined disability may have quite different implications in different types of work; thus, a knowledge of the

---

[2] The sources of materials relating to labor force concepts are indicated in Appendix C, section 1.

kind and extent of disability by no means insures an accurate prediction as to employability. Perhaps a team of technicians with a formidable battery of tests and questions could obtain a precise answer as to whether an individual is able to work; for the present, however, we must use the available data, which are based on a variety of answers (to a variety of questions) given by respondents to interviewers relatively untrained in the field of health as related to employability.

Variations in reported level of disability. The highest figures on the prevalence of disability among older men not in the labor force are apparently obtained in response to questions on health and disability as related to ability to work, rather than on health and disability in the abstract.

Thus, in the survey of persons 65 and over who were queried in the Current Population Survey of April 1952 (conducted by the Bureau of the Census for the Institute of Industrial Relations of the University of California), the problem of disability was approached directly from the respondent's point of view with the question, "Are you well enough to work now?"[3] From three-fourths to four-fifths of the retired respondents answered "No." Figures from the National Survey of Old-Age and Survivors Insurance Beneficiaries, conducted in 1951, indicate about the same proportion unable to work among retired beneficiaries.[4] Similarly, the survey conducted in early 1953 for the Governor's Commission To Study Problems of the Aged in Rhode Island indicated that approximately 77 percent of the men aged 65 and over reported as not working classified themselves as not able to work—a figure impressively close to the corresponding national level.[5]

If, however, we turn to a serious attempt to relate health or disability to employability, there is a wide range of figures from which to choose. In 1950, as part of a study of older persons in Meriden, Connecticut, sponsored by the Connecticut Commission on the Potentials of the Aging, respondents answered questions relating to health largely in terms of a list of symptoms, and the answers were rated on a sort of employability scale by a physician in the Connecticut State Department of Health. The results of this study for men 65 to 74 not in the labor force, along with descriptive phrases suggesting the level of health at each step in the employability scale, are presented in table 16.

Taking these figures at face value, it appears that, if our concern is with total disability, then only about one-fifth of the men 65 to 74 fell in this category. If, however, attention is focused on all persons suffering to a greater or lesser degree from some disability, then the figure becomes about 67 percent—certainly within striking distance of the figures derived

---

[3] See Appendix C, section 2, for a description of this survey and appendix table C–3.

[4] See Appendix C, section 2, for a discussion of this survey. The proportion of retired male beneficiaries unable to work comes from unpublished data from this survey.

[5] Governor's Commission To Study Problems of the Aged—State of Rhode Island and Providence Plantations, *Old Age in Rhode Island*, table VIII.

from direct questions relating to health and work. It is not assumed, of course, that Meriden represents the United States in microcosm, but the study does serve to illustrate the problem involved.

TABLE **16.**—POTENTIAL EMPLOYMENT STATUS AND DISABILITY FOR MALES 65 TO 74 YEARS OLD NOT IN THE LABOR FORCE, FOR MERIDEN, CONNECTICUT: 1954

Potential employment status	Number	Percent	Cumulative percent
Total...	182	100.0	100.0
Employable without restriction........................ (Persons who are apparently physically fit for any employment)	59	32.4	100.0
Employable with selective placement................... (Persons with minor physical or disease limitation, e.g., persons who should not do heavy physical labor)	47	25.8	67.5
Employable with individual placement.................. (Persons with major physical limitations, and persons with some physical and minor disease conditions, e.g., persons limited to sedentary work)	9	4.9	41.7
Sheltered work only................................... (Persons with a major disease or with a physical and major disease condition, e.g., persons with uncomplicated blindness)	32	17.6	36.8
Unemployable... (Persons who have active tuberculosis, terminal cancer, or are bedridden, senile, mentally affected or in cardiac failure or suffer blackouts).	35	19.2	19.2

Source: *Report of the Connecticut Commission on the Potentials of the Aging*, December 1954, p. 46, and table 91, p. 78.

The same kind of variability in response is also apparent in the respondents' own judgments as to their health condition and ability to work. As noted earlier, about three-fourths of the retired males 65 and over in the Rhode Island Survey reported themselves not able to work. On the other hand, only about 54 percent of the retired group reported themselves in poor health or handicapped, and of the group reporting themselves not well enough to work, 64 percent, in their judgment, were in poor health or handicapped. In short, although three-fourths of the respondents felt that they were not well enough to work, only one-half felt that they were in poor health or handicapped.[6]

Even when the questions and instructions to interviewers are identical, as in the census data on "Unable to work," variation in response may arise among different groups of interviewers (table 17). The figures purport to cover "Persons who cannot work because of a long-term physical or mental illness or disability."[7] Although "long term" is not formally and explicitly defined, questions arising in the interview are settled in terms of a 6-month period; that is, a person is not "unable to work" if he expects to be able to return to work within 6 months. For April 1950, with one exception, there was reasonably close agreement between the Current Population Sur-

[6] *Ibid.*, table VIII.
[7] See Appendix C, section 1.

vey and the decennial census in the percentage of males unable to work at all age levels. The exception was the age group 65 and over, in which the percentage for those unable to work was appreciably higher in the census count.

Enumerators used in the Current Population Survey are a relatively permanent staff, subject to constant training focused particularly on the labor force questions. It seems reasonable, therefore, that they might confine entries of "unable" to cases meeting the definition, whereas census enumerators—trained only once, and with the labor force questions only one item in a wide variety of questions—might take a somewhat more permissive attitude and accept responses of "unable" at face value. This supposition is supported by the slightly higher percentages in the age groups under 65 in the census figures. At 65 and over, this lack of discrimination betweeen presumed "genuine" disability and the respondent's feeling of disability appeared to make a real difference. In both series of figures, in order to obtain a figure covering all types of disability in the civilian population, an estimate of the number of disabled persons in institutions in 1950 has been added to the "unable" category. The percentages are, therefore, somewhat higher than those based on the raw figures from the initial sources.

TABLE 17.—MALES UNABLE TO WORK AS PERCENT OF ALL CIVILIAN MALES AND CIVILIAN MALES NOT IN THE LABOR FORCE, BY AGE: 1950 CENSUS AND APRIL 1950 CURRENT POPULATION SURVEY

[Figures for "unable to work" include estimate of disabled institutional population]

Age	Percent of all males		Percent of males not in labor force	
	1950 Census	Current Population Survey	1950 Census	Current Population Survey
Total, 14 years old and over.....	6.2	3.9	28.9	21.8
14 to 24 years........................	1.2	0.9	2.7	2.6
25 to 34 years........................	1.6	1.2	20.2	20.8
35 to 44 years........................	2.0	1.6	37.9	47.3
45 to 54 years........................	3.8	2.4	47.6	44.6
55 to 64 years........................	8.7	6.3	52.2	41.7
65 years and over....................	33.2	19.5	56.6	35.2

Source: U. S. Bureau of the Census, *Current Population Reports*, Series P-57, No. 94, table 6; *1950 Census of Population*, Vol. IV, *Special Reports*, Part 1, Chapter A, Employment and Personal Characteristics, table 1, and Part 2, Chapter C, Institutional Population, tables 1 to 11.

Role of disability. It is clear, from the foregoing discussion, that there can be no easy statement as to the exact degree by which disability contributes to retirement. Among older men, in their own terms, it looms relatively large; if, on the other hand, the questions are focused on specific disabilities to which names can be given, or the existence of which stands up under cross examination, the proportion retired by disability is considerably lower.

The issue turns, of course, on the definition of "disability," which in the minds of the respondents covers not only specific ailments and handicaps but also the general loss of strength, endurance, and vigor which comes with age. It is also probable that the respondent defines disability in terms of his own work experience, and that he is affected by his conception of available employment in his previous occupation or occupations in which he believes he could still work.[8] Within this broad definition it is difficult to state precisely at what point disability, as an objective measurable condition, stops. The question might well be raised, for example, as to how many of the 74-year-olds classified in the Meriden study as "apparently physically fit for any employment" would be able to operate a pneumatic drill day in and day out, or withstand the rigors of an assembly line in heavy industry. Although it would be extremely difficult to define exactly the lower limit of disability as it relates to employability, investigations in this field would gain a great deal from a standard working definition.

In spite of the difficulties in determining the precise level of disability, it is clear that the ills to which human flesh is heir increase progressively with age; as a generation grows older, an increasing proportion of its members become incapable of working for reasons of health and disability.

Thus, it appears that a decline in the labor force participation rate with age is implicit in the nature of things, and that, although changes or reforms in the social arrangements relating to work—such as age discrimination or formal retirement systems—may serve to postpone retirement, they will not alter the general character of the relationship. For this reason, the relationship between disability and employment, as it varies with age, provides the perspective necessary to an adequate evaluation of the effects of institutional arrangements, and of the probable results of programs designed to alter these arrangements. All this, of course, presupposes that the discovery of a miracle drug which will obviate the physiological concomitants of aging is not imminent.

Circumstances associated with retirement

The over-all relationship between age and physical condition and age and retirement, as indicated by data on the health of retired persons, provides the context in which to examine the problem of employment among older persons at a general level. However, more immediate information on the issue of disability is provided by data obtained from direct questions as to reasons for retirement; such data, in a sense, permit inferences on the basis of the incidence rather than the prevalence of disability. In addition, data on reasons for retirement provide a basis for inferences as to the role of social and economic factors in the increase in volume of retirement with age.

---

[8] Edna C. Wentworth, "Why Beneficiaries Returned to Work," *Social Security Bulletin*, 8, 4, April 1945, pp. 13 and 14.

The circumstances under which an event such as retirement occurs—or, for that matter, an event such as buying a house, getting married, or going to a movie—are varied and interrelated; an explanation in terms of a single category of reasons is usually oversimplified and may well be misleading. From one point of view, the circumstances under which retirement occurs fall into two categories: those relating primarily to the individual—his health, personality, and the like; and those relating to the external situation in which he finds himself—the presence or absence of formal retirement rules, the degree of age discrimination, and the demand for his particular skills. Retirement is then the outcome of the interaction of both sets of factors, and any explanation in terms of only one set is of necessity incomplete.

As an extreme example, of the 40 men classified in the Meriden study as unemployable, 5 were actually employed.[9] Unemployability, as defined in this study, would appear to be a good and sufficient reason for retirement, but in a small number of cases, owing to special circumstances, it was not. Even in terms of the respondent's own definition, surveys conducted by the Bureau of Old-Age and Survivors Insurance in selected areas in the early 1940's suggest that from 10 to 20 percent of the beneficiaries who were employed when the surveys were made considered themselves unable to work.[10] In general, this situation creates the possibility of the selection of single reasons from one or the other of the two sets of circumstances, and the results of the investigation tend to vary according to the degree of emphasis placed in one field or the other.

This discussion does not deny the usefulness of data on reasons for retirement; it merely indicates the need for considering the problem of causality in interpreting data on reasons for retirement, and the need for more intensive research in this field. Significant here are the results of two nation-wide surveys directed in large part to the collection of information on the circumstances surrounding retirement. The first of these is the survey conducted for the Institute of Industrial Relations of the University of California in connection with the April 1952 Current Population Survey; the second is the National Survey of Old-Age and Survivors Insurance Beneficiaries (OASI) conducted in the latter part of 1951.[11]

In comparing these two surveys, several differences in coverage might on *a priori* grounds be expected to produce variations in the results. The University of California survey covered persons 65 and over from the Current Population Survey sample. The OASI sample covered only beneficiaries, thus excluding persons who had been employed in agriculture and self-employed persons in nonagricultural employment. In addition— although in broad terms only retired persons were covered in the OASI sample, and thus data were obtained for a group roughly comparable to

[9] *Report of the Connecticut Commission on the Potentials of the Aging,* December 1954, table 91.
[10] Edna C. Wentworth, *op. cit.,* table 2.
[11] These surveys are described in Appendix C, section 2.

those not in the labor force in the University of California survey—retirement in the OASI survey was defined as the "termination of last covered employment before payment of first old-age insurance benefit." Thus some of the persons interviewed (about 10 percent)[12] were employed at the time of the interview; that is, they had found other employment after their initial "retirement." In table 18 a second column of percentages has been added for beneficiaries who had had no employment for 6 months prior to the interview—a group more nearly comparable to the group not in the labor force in the California survey.

There is no way, however, of correcting for the fact that in the California survey the reasons for retirement refer to retirement from the last job held by the respondent prior to the interview, whereas in the OASI survey the reasons may or may not refer to the last job before the interview, and the difference is greater than that implied by the percentage employed at the time of the interview; something like 20 percent[13] of the beneficiaries had been re-employed at full-time jobs at some time between their initial retirement and the survey date, and something like 35 percent[14] had had employment, full or part time, during the survey year. Finally, in the University of California survey, the group not in the labor force was older than the OASI beneficiaries.[15] Although in comparing the results of the two studies it is necessary to consider these differences in coverage and definition, as well as differences in question wording, they by no means invalidate such comparison. In fact, at some points, they provide additional insight into the problem.

The results of these surveys as they relate to the reasons for retirement are summarized in table 18, which compares those items or reasons that are roughly comparable—the major break between voluntary and involuntary retirement, reasons relating to health and disability, and reasons relating to formal retirement systems. The residual "Other" categories are, as indicated in the footnotes to table 18, quite different from one survey to the other and illustrate the general problem of disparate categories of reasons.

Health. About 60 percent of the respondents in the University of California survey reported that they retired for reasons of health—a figure somewhat lower than the proportion who reported themselves not well enough to work. This difference is to be expected, however, since the first question refers to the time of retirement, whereas the second question has a current reference and thus includes the accretion of disability between the retirement date and the date of the survey.

---

[12] Margaret L. Stecker, "Why Do Beneficiaries Retire? Who Among Them Return to Work?" *Social Security Bulletin*, 18, 4, May 1955, table 4.

[13] *Ibid.*

[14] *Ibid.*, table 6 and unpublished data from OASI survey.

[15] U. S. Bureau of the Census, *Current Population Reports*, Series P–50, No. 44, table 2, and unpublished data from OASI survey.

TABLE **18.**—RETIRED MALES 65 YEARS OLD AND OVER, BY REASON FOR RETIREMENT: 1951–1952

Reason for retirement	All bene- fici- aries	Unem- ployed bene- fici- aries[1]	Reason for retirement	Per- cent
NATIONAL SURVEY OF OLD-AGE AND SURVIVORS INSURANCE BENEFICIARIES: 1951			UNIVERSITY OF CALIFORNIA SURVEY: APRIL 1952	
Total[2]...............................	100.0	100.0	Total[5].......................	100.0
Quit job..............................	55.2	56.0	Voluntary retirement...............	75.9
Unable to work........................	41.5	44.2	Health...........................	59.3
Other................................	13.8	11.8	Other[6]...........................	16.6
Retired voluntarily in good health.....	3.9	...		
All other[3]...........................	9.9	...		
Lost job..............................	44.8	44.0	Involuntary retirement..............	24.1
Reached company retirement age..........	10.9	...	Age compulsory retirement system..	13.7
Other[4]...............................	33.9	...	Other[7]............................	10.4

[1] Unemployed for at least 6 consecutive months prior to end of survey year.

[2] Retired OASI beneficiaries 65 years old and over.

[3] Includes beneficiaries who quit full-time covered job hoping to find a different kind of work or to take a part-time covered job or a noncovered job; who quit after a quarrel with the boss or fellow employees, during a strike, or because of unwillingness to adjust to another kind of assigned work; who were needed at home, etc.

[4] Includes beneficiaries who lost their job because it was discontinued, the employer thought the worker was unable to do the work, and for reasons they did not know or remember except that they were fired.

[5] Males 65 years old and over with work experience and not in the labor force.

[6] Includes persons who retired by reason of age, family decision, and for other reasons.

[7] Includes persons who were discharged by their employer for reasons of age, who were laid off and found other work unavailable, and who lost their jobs for other reasons.

Source: Margaret L. Stecker, "Why Do Beneficiaries Retire? Who Among Them Return to Work?" *Social Security Bulletin*, May 1955, table 2; unpublished data from the National Survey of Old-Age and Survivors Insurance Beneficiaries; appendix table C-3.

The California survey figure on "Unable to work" is considerably higher than the OASI figure—slightly more than 40 percent. This OASI figure appears to be reasonably stable through time. Classified by year of first benefit, the data from the National OASI Survey of 1951 show, by biennium, fluctuations around this figure ranging from 37.7 to 48.1 percent,[16] and data from the earlier studies in selected areas during the decade 1940 to 1950 show somewhat greater variations.[17] Since, roughly speaking, the base for these percentages is persons not in the labor force, some variation in time is to be expected; that is, granting a hard core of disabled persons, such a group will constitute a larger proportion of the total not in the labor force in periods of high employment than in periods of low employment. The figures from the individual studies are, in addition, subject to local variations in employment level.

A part of the observed difference between the two surveys in the proportion retired for reasons of health seems to be related to the fact that the OASI sample contained some employed persons. Thus, the data presented in the second column of table 18 for beneficiaries unemployed for 6 consecutive months prior to the survey date indicate a somewhat higher percentage unable to work than the percentage for all beneficiaries.

[16] Margaret L. Stecker, *op. cit.*, table 3.

[17] Margaret L. Stecker, "Beneficiaries Prefer to Work," *Social Security Bulletin*, 14, 1, January 1951, p. 16.

The difference which remains, however, is substantial. It may be related to the fact that, for beneficiaries, the "retirement" to which the stated reasons apply is on the average more remote in time from the OASI survey date than it is for those respondents not in the labor force in the California survey, and to the fact that the latter group is somewhat older. This hypothesis rests on the assumption that, in a considerable proportion of cases, retirement is not a single definitive event; it is rather a series of forays in and out of the labor market before becoming permanent. In the University of California survey, then, the higher proportion retiring because of inability to work might be expected—given an increase in disability with age, the greater age of respondents, and the fact that the reasons apply to their "last" rather than to their "initial" retirement and thus on the average to a higher age at retirement.

Certainly the OASI data indicate that inability to work, as a reason for retirement, increases with age at "initial" retirement.[18] It might be argued, however, that the labor force attachment of persons employed after "initial" retirement is more tenuous than that of persons employed prior to initial retirement and, therefore, the percentage of persons in the former group who lost jobs might show a greater tendency to keep pace with the percentage who quit for reasons of health. Whether or not this assumption is correct remains an open question.

Another reason for the difference between the proportions of people retiring for reasons of health may be the absence of the self-employed among the OASI beneficiaries. The reasoning here is similar to that outlined in considering the different reference points for retirement. Disability increases with age, and, since employers cannot initiate retirement among the self-employed, they continue to work until disabled. As indicated elsewhere,[19] however, the assumption of greater occupational longevity among the self-employed is somewhat more attractive in the abstract than in the context of available data. To be sure, the self-employed cannot be laid off, but other external factors over which they have no control may terminate self-employment.

Other voluntary retirement. In both surveys the proportion of men retiring voluntarily for reasons other than health was roughly the same, and it is perhaps worth noting that in the OASI sample the proportion retiring voluntarily while in good health was relatively small. Such figures indicate that persons who have spent their lives working prefer to continue to do so rather than to retire. Whether this preference reflects a high value placed on work *per se*, or a choice between the income implicit in continued employment and that implicit in OASI benefits, is an open question. In any event, the figure does suggest that few workers were accepting retirement as a matter of course after their 65th birthdays.

---

[18] Margaret L. Stecker, "Why Do Beneficiaries Retire? Who Among Them Return to Work?" *Social Security Bulletin*, 18, 5, May 1955, table 2.

[19] See following discussion of trends in labor force participation of older men in this chapter and also Chapter 5.

Formal retirement systems. Both surveys indicate that the proportion of persons who retired as the result of age-compulsory retirement plans was relatively low—about 14 percent in the University of California survey and 11 percent in the OASI survey. It is somewhat surprising, therefore, to find so much prominence given to this issue in the literature on the employment problems of older persons and in public discussions. However, with the large-scale development of industrywide pension plans, it is clear that formal retirement systems may considerably increase their contribution to the volume of retirement.

Other involuntary retirement. If persons who retired as the result of formal retirement systems are excluded, the residual group of involuntary retirees constituted about 34 percent of the OASI sample. In the University of California survey, however, the comparable group constituted only about 10 percent of the total. This difference is, of course, the complement of the differences observed in the proportion of people retiring for reasons of health, and as such has essentially the same explanation.

Age discrimination. If compulsory age retirement systems are regarded as a separate problem, the effects of informal age discrimination must be sought among persons who retire involuntarily for other reasons. In terms of the results of the two surveys, age discrimination seems to be operative among less than one-fourth of the retired men represented in the two samples. This conclusion is based on the assumption that since the OASI data, generally speaking, did not cover self-employment, they overstated the proportion of involuntary retirement.

Age discrimination in hiring has been well documented and extensively deplored.[20] According to the conventional description of such discrimination, based in large part on the experiences of State employment agencies, workers encounter progressively greater difficulty in finding work beginning with the early 40's.

It is instructive to visualize this process in more detail. The existence of labor force turnover means that, although some people spend most of their working lives on a single job or sequence of jobs, many others hold a succession of jobs; that is, they lose or give up current work and find other work. In this process age discrimination implies that jobs are more easily lost, and new jobs progressively more difficult to obtain, as age increases. Although age discrimination may begin to operate in the early 40's, the process is long and drawn out. New jobs may be more difficult to find in the early 40's, but in the long run they are found, and it is only in the late 50's or early 60's that attrition from the labor force becomes appreciable.

As indicated earlier, the OASI survey offers some evidence as to the extended character of the retirement process. Of the men 65 and over who

[20] See, for example, Albert J. Abrams, "Barriers to the Employment of Older Workers," *Annals of the American Academy of Political and Social Science*, Vol. 279, pp. 69–77, and U. S. Department of Labor, Bureau of Employment Security, *Older Workers Seek Jobs*, August 1951.

had "retired" initially because of losing their jobs, about one-fourth had been re-employed and about 12 percent were currently working.[21] Thus, even at the upper ages retirement is not necessarily definitive, and some persons who are today retired may tomorrow be employed. It may be argued that the OASI definition of retirement in terms of the termination of last covered employment prior to qualification for benefits is somewhat artificial; on the other hand, reinterviews with the respondents in the University of California survey might well reveal that some persons not in the labor force at the time of the initial interview are now employed.

From the point of view of the individual seeking employment, the process is a matter of progressively increasing odds; at some point the situation seems hopeless and retirement follows. This interpretation is consistent with census data for 1940—a year which, in contrast to 1950, was characterized by a higher level of unemployment and by more intense age discrimination. These statistics indicate that for men the rate of unemployment and its duration were somewhat higher in the age range 45 to 64 than in the range 25 to 44, and thus suggest a tangible manifestation of discrimination and the context in which retirement occurs.[22]

In this context, the fact that the proportion of unemployment and its duration were somewhat lower for males 65 and over may be evidence that many persons faced with this situation had given up and had, in fact, retired. Data from the OASI survey give some quantitative indication of this process. About 15 percent of all beneficiaries reported themselves as unemployed and wanting work, but only 8 percent said they were seeking work. Within the group 65 and over these percentages declined with age, and the percentage seeking work tended to decline more rapidly than the percentage wanting work.[23]

Here, then, is another case in which retirement is the outcome of the interaction of such factors as age discrimination—which make employment difficult to find—and such factors as individual resources—occupational skills, energy, determination, and the like—which are assets in obtaining employment. If a relatively constant pressure on the individual side of the equation and the complete absence of age discrimination are assumed, then some increase in the average age of retirement might be expected; or, in the frame of reference of the surveys examined, some decline in the percentage of involuntary retirement outside of formal retirement rules might result. However, apart from such a hypothetical situation, it would be extremely difficult to specify the exact contribution of age discrimination, as distinct from other factors, to the percentage of persons whose retirement was initiated by the loss of their jobs for reasons other than the provisions of a formal retirement system.

---

[21] Margaret L. Stecker, *op. cit.*, table 4.
[22] *1940 Census of Population, Employment and Personal Characteristics*, tables 12 and 36.
[23] OASI survey, unpublished data.

Conclusions. A review of the two surveys on retirement in 1952 among men 65 and over suggests that answers to the pressing questions in this field must still remain, in part, equivocal. In addition to the substantive questions which this review has raised, it should be emphasized that the data from both surveys are based on small samples (the OASI survey on a somewhat larger sample than the University of California survey); thus, the results are subject to relatively large sampling variability, which means that small percentage differences should be interpreted with caution. It should also be noted that the results are not timeless; they would not necessarily agree with the results of identical surveys taken in 1942 or 1962—although here again, as noted earlier, there appears to be considerable consistency among the various OASI surveys. These cautionary sentiments in no way belittle the substantial and valuable contributions of the studies, but rather emphasize that questions relating to the causes of retirement have not been answered for all time.

On the positive side, the results of these studies might be summarized as follows: In terms of the respondents' judgments, voluntary retirement for reasons of health accounts for the largest proportion of retirement. The size of this proportion is not the same in both surveys, and if it is necessary to assign a specific average value, the average is about 50 percent. Both surveys agree essentially on the contribution of age-compulsory retirement systems, which account for possibly 10 to 15 percent of the retirees. Other involuntary retirement contributes another 35 percent in the OASI survey but only 10 percent in the University of California survey. A part of this difference—and possibly a large part—may be attributed to the differences in coverage and in the reference point for determining reasons for retirement; although certainly, according to common belief regarding the incidence of involuntary retirement, the California survey figure is surprisingly low.

The historic decline in labor force participation among older persons

Although in the course of this century the expectation of working life has increased, this increase reflects the general increase in life expectation rather than the extension of labor force participation at the upper ages. Actually, during this period, labor force participation rates among older men have declined. In 1890, it is estimated, 68 percent of the men 65 and over were in the labor force, and this figure dropped steadily to 42 percent in 1940. The manpower crisis during the war years was reflected in an increase to 49 percent in 1945 but, by 1950, the figure had dropped back to about the 1940 level (table 19).

In terms of health, an interpretation of this historic decline in labor force participation is tenable only on the assumption that the progress in medical science and the reduction in mortality during the past half-century have permitted larger and larger numbers of the physically inadequate to survive to a ripe old age.

TABLE **19.**—LABOR FORCE PARTICIPATION RATES OF MALES 45 YEARS OLD AND OVER, BY AGE: 1890 TO 1950

[Rates for 1890 to 1930 estimated from statistics on "gainfully employed"; estimates for 1890 to 1945 "comparable to 1940 Census data"; rates for 1950 based on 20-percent sample data from 1950 Census]

Year	45 to 54 years old	55 to 64 years old	65 years and over
1950 (April)...................	92.0	83.4	41.5
1945 (April)...................	95.4	89.9	48.8
1940 (April)...................	92.8	84.5	42.2
1930 (April)...................	93.8	86.5	54.0
1920 (January).................	93.5	86.3	55.6
1900 (June)...................	92.8	86.1	63.2
1890 (June)...................	93.9	89.0	68.2

Source: *1950 Census of Population*, Vol. II, *Characteristics of the Population*, Part 1, U. S. Summary, table 118; John D. Durand, *The Labor Force in the United States, 1890–1945*, tables A–6 and A–8.

This view has of course been seriously held in some quarters, but the preponderance of evidence tends to support the contrary hypothesis. The complexity of the issues involved and the nature of the evidence do not, however, permit an unequivocal answer in either direction.

In seeking an explanation of the declining labor force participation among older men in the past 50 years, some examination of the possible effects of the shift in occupational structure during this period is in order. The argument that changes in the occupational structure have resulted in a greater attrition from the labor force at the upper ages proceeds along two general lines:

First, it can be argued that changing technology brings a sharp contraction in the demand for certain skills; thus older persons with special skills are forced out of jobs, they cannot find other jobs utilizing these skills, and at the same time they are in a poor competitive position with respect to other types of work. Second, it can be argued that one aspect of the change in occupational structure has been the shrinkage in the relative number of self-employed persons, and a compensatory increase in the number of salary and wage earners. The self-employed—small business men, professional men, farmers—do not lose employment because of arbitrary decisions by employers or by the provisions of retirement systems. Moreover, since many can carry on their business or profession at a level of activity adjusted to their physical capacities, the self-employed person may be expected to keep on working to a relatively advanced age. Thus the reduction in the proportion of such persons in the labor force over the years, it is concluded, has made an appreciable reduction in over-all labor force participation at the upper ages.

Changing occupational structure. The first of these hypotheses regarding the effects of changing occupational structure on the employment of older persons seems eminently reasonable. Occupational skills, by and large, are acquired early in one's working life; given an accelerated rate of social and technological change, such skills may well be outmoded by the time an individual is approaching the end of his working life. Since the rate of change has been increasing progressively, more workers have been affected by this handicap. Specifically, it has been argued that the competitive position of older workers has been weakened by technological changes in the direction of mechanization and assembly-line production which place more of a premium on speed and physical stamina than on "know-how" gained from long experience.

The evidence, however, raises some question as to the adequacy of this theoretical proposition. Although it is difficult to set up an occupational distribution for the early years of this century which is precisely comparable to a similar distribution for 1950, it is clear that the structure has changed; and that, generally speaking, the changes have involved decreases in the proportion of farmers (but not in the proportions of other proprietors, managers, and officials) and in the proportion of unskilled workers. On the other hand, there were increases in the proportions of professional persons, clerical workers, and semiskilled workers or operatives. It seems reasonable to suppose that the occupational distribution of men 65 and over in 1950 would show traces of the distribution of earlier years, and that this resemblance would be more marked if they were classified not by current occupation but by longest occupation.

Information of this latter type was collected in the University of California survey. A comparison of the distribution by longest occupation of the males 65 and over with the current occupational distribution of all males 14 and over indicated that, as might be expected, the older males were overrepresented among farmers and farm managers and underrepresented among operatives. Likewise, as compared to the total employed, the older males appeared somewhat less frequently among nonfarm managers and officials and among the clerical occupations.[24]

If the current occupational distribution represents current demand for the various occupational skills, then it is obvious that, in terms of their work experience, substantial proportions of older men possess obsolete skills. It is, however, a bold assumption to attribute the decline in labor force participation among older persons to changes in the occupational distribution. In the first place, quite apart from the growth or decline of particular major occupation groups, certain changes in occupational distribution with age would be expected; that is, there are typical career lines which involve shifts from one major group to another. Managers and officials, for example, are recruited in part from clerical and sales personnel, and craftsmen and foremen from operatives; thus it might be expected that the clerical, sales, and operative groups would be more heavily represented in the total than among older persons.

In the second place, it is by no means clear that the contraction of a given occupation displaces more older persons than persons of all ages. Generally speaking, those occupation groups which have been contracting

---

[24] Robert Dorfman, "The Labor Force Status of Persons Aged Sixty-Five and Over," *American Economic Review*, Vol. XLIV, 2, May 1954, table 1.

show unusually high concentrations of older persons.   This situation suggests that the contraction of opportunity in a given occupation is felt first
among younger workers who find it difficult to enter the occupation, whereas
older workers, well established, are in a much more strategic position to hang
on.   Concrete evidence of this mechanism is seen in the regulation of ap-
prenticeship in those craft unions in which the demand for the particular
skills involved has contracted or failed to expand.   This process would not,
of course, preclude the simultaneous displacement of older workers, but it
does leave the general thesis open to some question.   Moreover, among
the few occupation groups in which it is possible to trace a given cohort
from decade to decade, there appears to be little consistent difference in attrition rates between contracting and expanding occupations.   (See
Chapter 5.)

The assumed relationship between obsolescence of occupational skills
and the decline in the labor force participation of older men does not stand
out clearly in the fragmentary statistics in which its appearance might be
expected.   However, the evidence does not completely disprove the
hypothesis in question.   It seems highly probable that the older men who
have been migrating from farms over the past several decades have been
handicapped in finding nonfarm employment; that the physical demands in
terms of speed and stamina of assembly line production place older
workers in an inferior competitive position; and that once an older man
has lost his job, the obsolescence of his occupational skills may contribute
to his difficulty in finding another job.   The occupational structure is, however, vast and complex.   Short of a painstaking analysis of trends among
all the detailed occupation groups, it is unlikely that a definitive answer
can be made as to how, and to what extent, the obsolescence of occupational skills has contributed to the decline in labor force participation of
older men.

Decline in self-employed.   In considering the decline in the proportion of the self-employed as a factor in the decline in the labor force participation among older males, the thesis seems to stand or fall on the basis
of an analysis of what has happened in agricultural employment.   In current census statistics, farmers and farm managers account for nearly one-
half of the self-employed, and certainly in the past they have loomed large
in this category.   For example, special tabulations from the 1910 Census
indicate that about 67 percent of all self-employed gainful male workers
were employed in agriculture.[25]   Although the population of farmers and
farm managers is certainly not identical with the labor force of the rural-
farm population, there is sufficient overlap to justify the consideration of
evidence from this source.

Farming is a contracting occupation.   Although there are problems of
comparability, the figures indicate that the number of farmers in 1950 was

---

[25] Appendix table C–5.

about the same as in 1880, although in this 70-year period the total population increased by a factor of three. The number of farmers reached a peak of about 6.2 million in 1920 and declined to a low of 4.3 million in 1950.[26] In terms of rural-farm population, the decline between 1930 and 1950 was about 7 million—from 30 to 23 million.[27] If it is assumed that the attrition from the labor force among farmers is intrinsically lower than among other members of the labor force, then the decline in the number of persons engaged in agricultural pursuits has been large enough to affect appreciably the labor force participation rates of older men.

The assumption that the occupational longevity is greater for farming than for many other occupations rests, in large part, on the more rapid decline with age of labor force participation rates in the nonfarm than in the farm population, which is indicated by the figures from both the 1940 and the 1950 Census. The figures show that, in the age group 35 to 44, the labor force participation rates are nearly equal for the rural-farm population and the remainder of the population—which, for all practical purposes, can be regarded as the nonfarm population. From this age group, however, the decline in the percentage of males in the labor force is progressively greater in the nonfarm than in the farm population, so that in the age group 75 and over the rate for the farm population is about twice that for the nonfarm population (table 20).

TABLE 20.—LABOR FORCE PARTICIPATION RATES, 1950, AND LABOR FORCE SURVIVAL RATIOS, 1940 TO 1950, FOR FARM AND NONFARM MALES, BY AGE

[Figures for nonfarm population include urban-farm population—283,388 in 1950 and 330,723 in 1940. Farm figures for 1950 adjusted to include institutional population; 1950 figures based on 20-percent sample and 1940 figures, used as base for survival ratio, on complete count]

Age in 1950	Labor force participation rates		Labor force survival rate[1]	
	Farm	Nonfarm	Farm	Nonfarm
45 to 54 years	94.7	91.5	.736	.938
55 to 64 years	88.9	82.3	.605	.783
65 to 74 years	69.8	47.5	.409	.470
75 to 84 years	38.2	16.9	.165	.204
85 years and over	12.7	5.7	.053	.089

[1] Ratio of age group in 1950 to age group 10 years younger in 1940.

Source: Appendix tables C-4 and C-4a.

The conclusion implied by these data is perhaps not as unequivocal as the figures suggest. One inference that might be drawn from the figures is that, since the labor force rates decline more rapidly in the nonfarm than in the farm population, the attrition from a given cohort of males in the

[26] *1940 Census of Population, Comparative Occupation Statistics for the United States, 1870 to 1930,* table 9; *1950 Census of Population,* Vol. II, *Characteristics of the Population,* Part 1, U. S. Summary, table 53. These figures overstate to some extent the decline. Although the number of persons classified as farmers declined by about 2 million between 1920 and 1950, the number of farms declined by only about 1 million.

[27] *1950 Census of Population,* Vol. II, *Characteristics of the Population,* Part 1, U. S. Summary, table 34.

labor force should be greater for the nonfarm population.   Actually the reverse is true.   The figures in table 20 represent the number of persons in the designated age groups in 1950, expressed as a percentage of the number in the same cohorts in 1940, when the same persons were 10 years younger.   These percentages, in short, are a sort of crude survival rate which shows the proportion of persons in a given age group in the labor force in 1940 who, 10 years later, had survived the risks of death and retirement—except, of course, as migration had increased or decreased their number.

Survival rates for each age group considered were higher for the nonfarm than the farm population.   This finding does not necessarily contradict the previous finding that the labor force rate declines less rapidly with age in farm areas, since in the decade 1940 to 1950 there was a substantial net out-migration from the farm to the nonfarm population.[28]   Thus the greater reduction of the rural-farm labor force may reflect the over-all reduction in the farm population.   There is, however, some question whether the higher labor force participation rate in the farm population represents an intrinsic characteristic of that population, or whether it represents a by-product of the net shift of population from farm to nonfarm areas.

If the out-migrants are heavily drawn from the retired farm population, or if retirement and out-migration are highly correlated, then the higher labor force participation rates may simply reflect the fact that the loss from the numerator in the fraction from which labor force rates are computed (which in the absence of migration reverts to the denominator) has also been lost from the denominator.   That is, the retirement rates of both the farm and nonfarm population may be about the same, and the observed difference simply reflects the greater attrition from the retired segment of the farm population.   The assumption that retirement from active farming means retirement to neighboring villages is consistent with the data on size of place, which show high percentages of persons 65 and over in the population of places of 1,000 to 2,500 and in incorporated places of less than 1,000.   In the rural area outside of these places, however, the proportion of older persons is relatively low.[29]

The data for testing this hypothesis are not available.   In one sense, they could never be available, since the question really implied is, "What would the labor force participation rate of the migrants have been had they remained on the farm?"

Analysis of the figures for 1940 and 1950 indicate that this hypothetical rate for migrants at the upper age levels—if it is to equalize farm and nonfarm rates—would have to be considerably below the observed rates in 1950 for either the farm or the nonfarm population.[30]   It is possible, then, that farm workers who remain on the farm have an inherent tendency to

[28] See appendix table C–4a.

[29] See appendix table B–10.

[30] See Appendix C, section 3.

continue working well past the age at which other workers retire, but this tendency is obscured by out-migration. To the extent that this tendency has existed over the past 50 years, out-migration from the farm population has reduced over-all labor force participation rates at the upper ages. In all probability, however, the amount of this reduction is somewhat less than the amount implied by the observed differences between farm and nonfarm participation rates.

In 1950, the nonagricultural self-employed constituted slightly more than one-half of the total self-employed. The data presented in table 21, for a group which approximates the nonagricultural self-employed, suggest that, although this group has shown some decline as a proportion of the total employed since 1910, the decline has not been impressive.[31] More-over, the survival ratios for the cohorts reaching age 65 and over in the decade 1940 to 1950 are slightly lower among the nonagricultural self-employed than among the nonagricultural wage or salary workers. Census statistics provide little support for the hypothesis that a decline in the non-agricultural self-employed has reduced the labor force participation rate of older men.[32] This issue is considered in relation to specific occupation groups in Chapter 5.

TABLE 21.—EMPLOYED NONAGRICULTURAL WORKERS, BY CLASS OF WORKER: 1950, 1940, AND 1910

[Data for 1950 and 1940 adjusted; see Appendix C, section 4]

Year and survival rate	Total		Self-employed			Other
	Number	Percent increase from 1910	Number	Percent increase from 1910	Percent of total	
1910............................	19,146,896	...	2,941,468	...	15.4	16,205,428
1940............................	26,372,100	37.7	3,913,960	33.1	14.8	22,458,140
1950............................	33,900,150	77.1	4,325,010	47.0	12.8	29,575,140
Survival rate, 1950:						
55 years and over, 1940.....	3,759,800	...	986,500	...	...	2,773,300
65 years and over, 1950.....	1,623,810	...	379,860	...	...	1,243,950
Rate.........................	.432	...	.385	...	...	.449

Source: Appendix table C-5.

Other factors. In addition to technological change and declining self-employment, it seems reasonable to assume that changes in age structure since the beginning of the century may also have accelerated the decline in labor force participation among older men. Since 1890, within the population 65 and over, the proportion at ages 75 and over has increased, and because labor force rates decrease with age, this change in age composition may have depressed the over-all rate for men 65 and over. Although something of this sort has happened, the effects appear to be negligible. If the observed age-specific participation rates of 1950 are applied

---

[31] See Appendix C, section 4.
[32] *Ibid.*

to a 1950 population 65 and over having a percentage age distribution identical with that of 1890, the estimated percentage of men in the labor force appears to be about one percentage point higher than the observed percentage.[33]

Generally speaking, within the total population in the same period, the population of working age—persons 20 to 64—has increased. The stated age limits are of course arbitrary and it is possible that a more realistic definition might be obtained by lowering the lower limit a few years and raising the upper limit. Such refinement, however, would not appreciably alter the general upward trend observed in the cruder index. This trend suggests that the number of "producers" in the population has been increasing in relation to the number of "consumers," with the result that the need for manpower was less pressing at the end of the period than at the beginning.[34] In this situation, variations in the employment level of older persons with variations in the demand for labor observed in short-run trends—such as those between the depth of the depression and the years of peak wartime industrial activity—might be assumed to apply, with a resulting downward trend in the employment of older persons.

Finally, the advent of social insurance systems in recent decades provided an alternative to continued employment, an alternative considerably more acceptable than any previously available. Social insurance and its expanding coverage seem likely to become increasingly important in setting the employment level for older persons.

Potential workers among the retired

One obvious answer to the problem of the high proportion of elderly retired men is re-employment, which, it is argued, would not only solve the problem of income maintenance but would also have a salutary effect on morale generally. The logic of this position is so unassailable that much of the literature on age discrimination seems to suggest that, were it not for such discrimination, there would be no problem. In view of this situation, an examination of the evidence relating to potential re-employment is in order.

The materials relating to disability considered earlier in this chapter, which indicate that only something like one-third or one-fourth of the elderly retired men consider themselves "well enough to work," imply certainly that elimination of age discrimination does not eliminate the problem. Questions directed specifically to this issue indicate that the proportion interested in returning to work is considerably smaller. In the University of California survey, only about 200,000 retired men 65 and over (about 8 percent of the total) indicated that they were able to work and interested in working.[35] In the Rhode Island survey, the corresponding proportion

---

[33] See Appendix C, section 5.

[34] *Ibid.*

[35] Robert Dorfman, *op. cit.*, table 7.

was about 16 percent.[36] In terms of actual performance, the OASI figures indicated that about 20 percent of the men who had retired from covered employment had subsequently been employed on a full-time basis for at least 6 months.[37] This figure is not precisely comparable to the previous figures. It is based on a population including some employed persons, and, in a number of cases, "retirement" meant shifting from covered to uncovered employment without any appreciable break; that is, again the reference point is "initial" retirement. In terms of intention, the OASI survey indicates that about 20 percent of the beneficiaries who were not employed at the end of the survey year wanted work, but roughly one-half were reported as seeking work. If these persons are eliminated (in order to approximate the group not in the labor force of the California survey), the proportion becomes approximately 10 percent.[38]

Goldfield and Miller have estimated that in 1952 there were 500,000 potential workers 65 and over of both sexes in the retired population, or slightly more than 5 percent of the total not in the labor force.[39] On this basis, annual average figures for 1952 suggest that the corresponding percentage for males would have been somewhat more than 10 percent. These estimates are based on the assumption that the peak employment rates of older persons during the war years represented the maximum employment potential among older persons, and thus the effective labor reserve in 1952 represented the difference between the actual number of older persons in the labor force and the number expected on the basis of 1945 participation rates.

Although estimates of the proportion under consideration may be expected to vary appreciably from source to source and from time to time, it seems reasonable to assume that only a small number of the retired males 65 and over are employable in terms of current practices. This finding casts not the least doubt on the usefulness of efforts to overcome prejudice in the employment of older persons; it does indicate that creating opportunities for their full employment does not completely solve the problem.

These conclusions, of course, are based on the assumption that the institutional arrangements of the 1950's with respect to hiring practices and conditions of employment are maintained. If these arrangements should be altered to adjust working conditions to the tastes and physical capacities of older persons—if, for example, formal and regular provisions were made for part-time work—an appreciable reduction might be effected in the number of retired older persons, and this reduction might even cut into the group who now consider themselves not well enough to work.

---

[36] Governor's Commission To Study Problems of the Aged *op. cit.*, table VIII.

[37] Margaret L. Stecker, *op. cit.*, table 4.

[38] Unpublished data from the OASI survey.

[39] Edwin D. Goldfield and Herman P. Miller, "How Many Older Workers," *American Economic Security*, October-November 1952, pp. 22–27.

Employment status of older women

Labor force participation among women, as indicated earlier, is quite different from that among men.   There is no "cultural compulsive" which demands that women work; the labor force participation rate of women is substantially lower than that for men, and the pattern of participation by age differs from the pattern for men.   In 1950, for example, the peak of labor force participation among women occurred in the age group 20 to 24. After some decline, a secondary but lower peak occurred in the group 40 to 44, before the beginning of the expected continuous decline with age (table 22).   Among men, the peak occurred in the age group 35 to 39, the rate thereafter showing a continuous decline.

TABLE 22.—PERCENT DISTRIBUTION BY EMPLOYMENT STATUS OF FEMALES 20 YEARS OLD AND OVER, BY AGE: 1950

Age	Total	Labor force	Not in labor force				
			Total	Keeping house	In insti- tutions	Unable to work	Other and not reported
20 to 24 years................	100.0	42.9	57.1	48.2	0.4	0.5	7.9
25 to 29 years................	100.0	32.6	67.4	63.3	0.5	0.6	3.1
30 to 34 years................	100.0	31.0	69.0	65.4	0.6	0.5	2.5
35 to 39 years................	100.0	33.8	66.2	62.6	0.6	0.7	2.3
40 to 44 years................	100.0	36.4	63.6	59.8	0.8	0.8	2.3
45 to 49 years................	100.0	34.8	65.2	60.8	0.8	1.1	2.4
50 to 54 years................	100.0	30.8	69.2	63.8	0.9	1.7	2.7
55 to 59 years................	100.0	25.9	74.1	67.2	1.0	2.5	3.4
60 to 64 years................	100.0	20.6	79.4	68.8	1.3	4.9	4.5
65 to 69 years................	100.0	13.0	87.0	69.0	1.5	10.0	6.4
70 to 74 years................	100.0	6.4	93.6	65.1	2.5	17.6	8.4
75 years and over............	100.0	2.6	97.4	46.6	5.8	34.1	10.9

Source: Appendix table C-8.

This pattern of labor force participation among women reflects the fact that, in spite of increased employment, women still become wives and mothers, and, in spite of increased employment of married women and women with young children, operating a household and caring for children tend to discourage labor force participation.   The peaks of employment for women occur in the years before marriage, in the early years of marriage, and in the middle years when women are freed to some extent from house- hold duties.   From one point of view, "keeping house" might well be re- garded as an occupation in competition with others—a position that might be enthusiastically endorsed by many housewives who learn from the census enumerator that they are "not working."

Marital status, employment, and age.   The labor force participa- tion rates of single women are higher than those of women of other marital status categories and show the least decrease with age (table 23).   In 1950 the rates for single women dropped from about 76 percent at ages 35 to 44 to 27 percent at ages 65 to 74—a decline of about 65 percent.   This was not materially different from the corresponding rate of decrease for all men—about 55 percent.   For all women the rate of decrease between these two groups was 93 percent. The relatively high and persistent participation rates of single women seem to reflect their initial high participation rates, the fact that their working careers are not interrupted by marriage and child rearing, and, in contrast to married women, their greater need for income.

With respect to labor force participation, married women stand at the opposite pole and, to the greatest degree, exemplify the stereotype of the proper "womanly" role. In conformity with this conception, data are presented in table 23 for the wives of household heads; that is, women living with their husbands in households in which the husband is presumptively the head and "breadwinner." As might be expected, labor force participation rates for this group are low and the percentage decrease between the middle and older years is high—about 94 percent. Many of these women are without work experience, or, if they have had such experience, it has been interrupted by marriage. Generally speaking, the pressure of economic necessity is less for this group than for single women.

TABLE **23.**—PERCENT OF FEMALES 35 YEARS OLD AND OVER IN THE LABOR FORCE, BY MARITAL STATUS AND AGE: 1950

Age	All classes	Single	Wife of household head	Widowed or divorced	Other[1]
35 to 44 years	35.0	75.7	26.0	70.4	49.9
45 to 54 years	32.9	70.7	22.6	57.8	45.6
55 to 64 years	23.5	57.2	12.9	35.9	28.7
65 to 74 years	10.3	26.9	5.0	11.7	10.3
75 years and over	2.6	7.0	1.6	2.2	2.6

[1] Married, husband absent, and married, husband present but not head of household.

Source: Appendix table C-9.

Although labor force participation rates for wives of household heads are lower than for any other marital status group, in the middle years these rates are not negligible (about 25 percent at ages 35 to 44), and it is in this group that labor force participation has increased most rapidly in the past half-century.[40] The appreciably lower participation rates of married women who were in their middle years some 20 to 30 years prior to 1950 explain in part the low participation rates at the older ages in 1950. In other words, for women 65 and over in 1950, labor force participation rates represented a "normal" decline from the low rates in the middle years.

Although labor force participation rates for women who in 1950 were widowed or divorced were only slightly lower than those for single women, the rates declined more rapidly with age; by ages 65 to 74, and 75 and over, rates for the widowed or divorced were closer to those for wives than to those for single women. In terms of economic necessity, the widowed or divorced women fare only slightly better than single women. Since, however, they are drawn from a population of married women, they may

[40] See, for example, John D. Durand, *The Labor Force in the United States, 1890–1960*, pp. 24–26.

have been without work experience prior to becoming widowed or divorced; and if they have had such experience, their working careers in many instances have been interrupted by marriage. Thus, at the upper ages, their participation rates stem from the lower rates of married women in earlier years.

In short, widowed and divorced women at the upper ages fall into two groups: those who have been widowed or divorced early in their lives and might thereafter be expected to have the labor force characteristics of single women; and those who have been recently widowed or divorced, and thus might be expected to be essentially similar to wives in level of labor force participation. Since the number of women recently widowed is concentrated at the upper ages and accounts for the major part of the widowed and divorced group, the participation rate for this entire group approaches that for wives.

For the small "other" marital status group—women whose husbands are not household heads or are absent from the household—labor force rates stood intermediately between the wives on one hand and the single and widowed or divorced on the other. The rates in question probably reflected the intermediate position of this "other" group with respect to economic necessity and work experience.

Among single and widowed or divorced women, labor force rates tend to increase as dependence on relatives (as implied in a classification by household relationship) decreases. Thus, the lowest rates are for single women and widows or divorcees who were living as relatives of household heads—the traditional role of the unmarried woman (table 24). Those living as heads of their own households had somewhat higher rates. Some were living on their own in the absence of relatives, but in many of these households there were relatives who conceivably might have contributed to family income. The highest rates, however, appeared among both the single and widowed or divorced women who lived by themselves—as lodgers in private households, or in such quasi households as hotels, residence clubs, and large lodginghouses. The small select group of single women in this category who were 75 and over had a higher participation rate than all men of this age.

TABLE 24.—PERCENT IN THE LABOR FORCE FOR SINGLE AND WIDOWED OR DIVORCED FEMALES 35 YEARS OLD AND OVER, BY HOUSEHOLD RELATIONSHIP AND AGE: 1950

Age	Single				Widowed or divorced			
	All classes	Head of household	Relative of head	Other[1]	All classes	Head of household	Relative of head	Other[1]
35 to 44 years............	78.7	89.3	71.8	88.2	71.1	70.7	67.6	79.9
45 to 54 years............	73.8	84.1	61.0	86.7	58.4	59.8	46.2	73.5
55 to 64 years............	60.0	67.9	42.7	77.7	36.3	38.3	22.9	61.9
65 to 74 years............	28.8	29.1	17.4	50.3	11.9	12.9	5.6	33.4
75 years and over........	8.0	7.3	3.5	19.6	2.3	3.1	0.9	7.5

[1] Unrelated persons in households and persons in quasi households other than institutions.

Source: Appendix table C-10.

The sharp decline in labor force participation with age. The most significant aspect of the employment problems of older women is the sharp decline in participation rates from the middle to the older years. At ages 40 to 44, the rate was 36, but by the time the age group 65 to 69 is reached, the rate had dropped to 13—a decrease of about 64 percent in contrast to 37 percent for men (tables 22 and 15). The explanation of this sharp drop has already been suggested in the preceding discussion of marital status. In most general terms, the cohorts of women reaching the older ages in 1950 were young at a time when the proportions of women entering the labor force were much lower than in 1950, and therefore the "normal" decline was from a much lower level of initial participation. In contrast, the rates for women who were in their middle years in 1950 reflected to a much greater degree the increasing labor force participation of women generally. The difference is amplified by the fact that a majority of women reach the upper ages as either married or recently widowed— that is, from the married state in which the initial rates of participation were low.

Among women, as among men, the decline in labor force participation rates with age also reflects the increased prevalence of disability and the results of age discrimination. The effects of these factors are not so clearly apparent in labor force statistics for women as for men. For women, the category "Not in the labor force" is dominated by the subclass "Keeping house." By virtue of the order in which the labor force questions are asked, women have first the opportunity of classifying themselves as housekeepers and, having done so, they need not consider other reasons that might account for the fact that they are not employed. It is probable, therefore, that the figures on inability to work may be somewhat understated, and that among the women reported as keeping house there are some who, with more searching questioning, might be regarded as in involuntary retirement.

Reasons for retirement. Data on reasons for retirement from the OASI and University of California surveys provide perhaps the best answers as to the role of disability and other factors in the decline in the employment of women as age increases. Since these data apply only to women with work experience, they are comparable in general to the corresponding data for men, and thus for the most part eliminate the complications inherent in the census data on women not in the labor force.

Both surveys agree substantially in showing that, among women, health or disability accounts for one-half of the total (table 25). This means that in the OASI survey the percentage for women is possibly higher than that for men, and in the University of California survey, the percentage is higher for men. Although the University of California study shows a higher percentage of other voluntary retirement than does the OASI survey, both suggest that this category comprises a larger percentage of the total among women than among men. This difference—in so far as it exists to any appreciable degree—may indicate that, even among employed women, the demands of their traditional role lead them to retire in the face of domestic crises.

The two surveys agree substantially on the proportion of women retiring because of compulsory age-retirement systems—about 5 percent. The OASI survey shows a greater amount of other involuntary retirement among men than does the University of California survey, and this applies also to women. Within each survey, however, there is little difference between men and women; the data do not suggest a sex differential in the operation of age discrimination.

TABLE **25.**—RETIRED FEMALES 65 YEARS OLD AND OVER, BY REASON FOR RETIREMENT: 1951–1952

Reason for retirement	All beneficiaries	Unemployed beneficiaries[1]	Reason for retirement	Percent
NATIONAL SURVEY OF OLD-AGE AND SURVIVORS INSURANCE BENEFICIARIES: 1951			UNIVERSITY OF CALIFORNIA SURVEY: APRIL 1952	
Total[2]	100.0	100.0	Total[5]	100.0
Quit job	65.2	66.2	Voluntary retirement	82.2
Unable to work	46.9	48.3	Health	49.8
Other	18.4	17.9	Other[6]	32.4
Retired voluntarily in good health	4.0	...		
All other[3]	14.4	...		
Lost job	34.8	33.8	Involuntary retirement	17.8
Reached company retirement age	5.6	...	Age compulsory retirement system	4.8
Other[4]	29.2	...	Other[7]	13.0

[1] Unemployed for at least 6 consecutive months prior to end of survey year.
[2] Retired OASI beneficiaries 65 years old and over.
[3] Includes beneficiaries who quit full-time covered job hoping to find a different kind of work or to take a part-time covered job or a noncovered job; who quit after a quarrel with the boss or fellow employees, during a strike, or because of unwillingness to adjust to another kind of assigned work; who were needed at home, etc.
[4] Includes beneficiaries who lost their job because it was discontinued, the employer thought the worker was unable to do the work, and for reasons they did not know or remember except that they were fired.
[5] Females 65 years old and over with work experience and not in the labor force.
[6] Includes persons who retired by reason of age, family decision, and for other reasons.
[7] Includes persons who were discharged by their employer for reasons of age, who were laid off and found other work unavailable, and who lost their jobs for other reasons.
Source: Margaret L. Stecker, "Why Do Beneficiaries Retire? Who Among Them Return to Work?" *Social Security Bulletin*, May 1955, table 2; unpublished data from the National Survey of Old-Age and Survivors Insurance Beneficiaries; appendix table C–3.

Conclusions. Among women, the general pattern of employment with age reflects, on one hand, the substantial increase in their labor force participation since the beginning of the century, and, on the other hand, the interaction of the demands of the traditional role of homemaker and mother with those inherent in full-time employment. This situation accounts for the two peaks of labor force participation, the relatively low participation rates among married women, and the precipitous decline in these rates between the middle and later years. The result is that many women arrive at the older ages in need of income (as will be shown in Chapter 8), but ill-equipped by either experience or inclination to obtain income from employment.

The survey data for women with work experience indicate that their reasons for retirement are about the same as those for men. Disability accounts for about the same proportion of retirements among women as among men; other voluntary retirement for possibly a larger proportion of women than men; age retirement systems, in all probability, account for a larger proportion of men than women; and other involuntary retirement for roughly equal proportions of each sex. This last finding does not support the well-documented contention that elderly women, by virtue of both sex and age, are most likely to be objects of age discrimination. It is clear, however, that the survey data do not provide definitive evidence on this issue, and it is likely that age discrimination may have had its major impact on the employment of women well before age 65 is reached.

C H A P T E R 5

AGE AND OCCUPATION

The various types of occupation indicate to some extent the probability of employment at the older ages. For professional athletes, for example, the expectation of occupational life is relatively low, as it is for men in other occupations that require full physical vigor, quick reaction, and other physical and psychological qualities normally blunted by increasing age. On the other hand, such occupations as the professions in which success is based on a long period of training, and on the knowledge and skill which come from long experience, may permit the continuation of working life to advanced ages. Thus, in theory at least, the farmer who operates his own farm, or the independent professional man who is unhampered by the demands of a retirement system, may expect to continue well into the later years—with, if necessary, a declining level of activity. At the outset then, a man's occupation tends to set the pattern for his working career in later years.

Likewise, the current age structure of occupation groups indicates something as to the employment opportunities for older persons who may have lost current employment. Here, again in theory, such opportunities exist in those expanding occupations in which the disabilities incident to aging do not impair performance. Census statistics presented in this chapter throw some light on the extent to which the foregoing generalizations are operative.

The occupational structure is extremely varied and complex, and this situation is reflected in occupational statistics. The detailed classification for 1950 contains 469 separate categories, and these in turn are made up from several thousand occupational titles which include not only the "doctor, lawyer, Indian chief" of the old skipping rhyme but also such specialized titles as "Scleroscope Tester," "Viscosity Man," "Heliotherapist," "Rat Culturalist," "Wharfinger," "Celery Wrapper," and "Hypo Splasher." The problem of classification is complicated by the tremendous variety of occupations as well as by the fact that the occupational structure is in a constant state of flux.[1]

Shifts in occupational structure create a special problem in that they affect not only the numbers in a given occupational category but also the age structure. A comparison of the age composition of occupation groups at a

---

[1] See Appendix D, section 1, for discussion of the census occupation classification.

given time may lead to conclusions that are not valid for an earlier period, nor will they necessarily hold in some future period. Generalizations with respect to the relation between age and various occupations are best derived from an historical series of figures on the subject. This procedure, however, is necessarily limited to comparable categories, and the complexity and change in the whole structure tend to reduce such comparability.

Because of the differences between men and women in the pattern of labor force participation by age, and because these differences are amplified in the occupational distribution, the relation between occupation and age is examined separately for men and for women. For men, the attempt is to examine the entire occupational distribution, whereas for women, the examination is focused primarily on the several occupations that account for an appreciable segment of employed women in the labor force.

Occupation by age, 1950

For purposes of summary, the great variety of occupations has been reduced in the census classification to 12 major groups (table 26).[2] These groups are the lineal descendants of Edward's classification of occupations by social and economic status. The first group—professional, technical, and kindred workers—accounted for approximately 7 percent of the employed males 14 years old and over in 1950. In addition to the commonly recognized professional groups—doctors, lawyers, teachers, clergymen, and engineers—this category includes many related groups which involve the possession of various kinds of technical knowledge usually acquired through specialized education. The second group—farmers and farm managers—accounted for roughly 10 percent of the total employed males. The third group—managers, officials, and proprietors (except farm)—brings together those persons whose activities are primarily managerial, and accounts for about 11 percent of the total.

The fourth and fifth groups—clerical and kindred workers, and sales workers—individually accounted for something more than 6 percent each of the total employed. Craftsmen, foremen, and kindred workers accounted for about 19 percent of the total employed males. These groups include, in addition to such familiar occupations as those of carpenters, plumbers, electricians, blacksmiths, plasterers, and tailors, a wide variety of other skilled occupations. Operatives and kindred workers accounted for about 20 percent of the total employed males, and represent, generally speaking, a wide variety of semiskilled occupations—including the great majority of mass-production occupations.

Private household workers accounted for less than 1 percent of the total in 1950 and represent the survivors of the group formerly classified as servants or domestic workers. Service workers, who constituted about 6 percent of the total in 1950, include protective service workers such as

---

[2] See Appendix D, section 1.

policemen, marshals, watchmen, and constables; barbers, beauticians, and related workers; hotel and restaurant employees; and other allied groups. Farm laborers and farm foremen (including unpaid family workers) accounted for about 5 percent of the total employed males; and laborers (except farm and mine) for about 8 percent. This latter group is extremely diverse and generally may be equated to unskilled labor.

TABLE 26.—PERCENT DISTRIBUTION BY AGE OF MALES 14 YEARS OLD AND OVER, BY MAJOR OCCUPATION GROUP: 1950

Occupation	Total, 14 years old and over	14 to 24 years	25 to 34 years	35 to 44 years	45 to 54 years	55 to 64 years	65 years and over
Total...............................	100.0	21.7	21.0	19.1	15.6	12.1	10.5
Employed...................................	100.0	14.6	24.4	23.5	18.8	13.0	5.6
Professional, techn'l, & kindred wkrs...	100.0	8.1	31.0	26.8	18.4	10.8	4.9
Farmers and farm managers...............	100.0	6.7	18.7	22.7	21.0	18.4	12.5
Managers, off'ls, & propr's, exc. farm..	100.0	3.5	18.9	28.4	26.0	16.7	6.5
Clerical and kindred workers............	100.0	19.4	27.6	21.1	16.5	11.3	4.0
Sales workers...........................	100.0	18.5	26.9	21.9	16.8	10.9	5.0
Craftsmen, foremen, and kindred wkrs....	100.0	9.2	25.8	25.9	20.9	13.9	4.4
Operatives and kindred workers..........	100.0	18.5	28.9	24.3	16.0	9.7	2.7
Private household workers...............	100.0	13.6	14.2	20.2	22.7	17.5	11.7
Service workers, exc. private hshld.....	100.0	13.7	18.3	20.1	20.4	18.0	9.6
Farm laborers, exc. unpaid, & foremen...	100.0	33.8	21.0	16.8	12.8	9.6	6.0
Farm laborers, unpaid family workers....	100.0	76.0	10.0	4.3	2.7	2.8	4.2
Laborers, except farm and mine..........	100.0	21.5	23.6	20.8	16.7	12.4	5.0
Occupation not reported.................	100.0	22.8	22.2	18.7	15.7	12.2	8.5
Other[1]...................................	100.0	41.2	11.5	7.1	7.1	9.4	23.7

[1] Includes Armed Forces, unemployed, and not in labor force.

Source: *1950 Census of Population*, Vol. II, *Characteristics of the Population*, Part 1, U. S. Summary, tables 38 and 127.

A further condensation of the classification is, of course, possible. The professional, managerial, clerical, and sales groups may be generally designated as "white collar" workers, and as such they accounted in 1950 for about 30 percent of the total employed. Craftsmen, operatives, and laborers may be designated as manual or "blue collar" workers; in 1950 this group constituted about 47 percent of the total employed. Farm workers, including farmers, farm managers, and farm laborers, constituted about 15 percent of the total, and the balance (about 8 percent) was represented largely by service workers.

Since, in a pragmatic sense, the proportion in any given occupation may be regarded as an index of opportunities in a particular group, the distribution of the employed population by major occupation group provides the background necessary for considering the variations in participation among various occupations by age and for locating opportunities for older workers. For example, if there is a high attrition rate by age for operatives—the largest single male occupation group—then operatives represent one of the major problems of placement, and, conversely, no program for placing older workers can be focused toward placement in relatively small occupation groups. An analysis, however, based on the general figures of the major occupation groups by age, represents only a very rough approximation to a definition of the problem; also to be considered are past trends and future prospects in the number of opportunities in a given group and the qualifications necessary for holding a position in this group.

Age structure within occupation groups. The age structure among the major occupation groups varied considerably in 1950. Measured in terms of the median age and the percentage of the group aged 65 and over, farmers and farm managers, private household workers, service workers (except private household workers), and the managerial group were relatively old.[3] On the other hand, sales workers, clerical workers, operatives, and farm laborers contained high proportions of younger persons. Figure 2 presents variations in the age structure of each major group relative to the age distribution of all males, and indicates, for each major group, the percentage by which the proportion of persons in a given age group exceeds or is less than the proportion in the total male population. Among farmers and farm managers, for example, the proportion aged 65 and over is greater than in the total population, whereas among operatives and kindred workers this proportion is appreciably smaller.

The general pattern of relationship is indicated, of course, by the profile for the total employed. There was underrepresentation in the age group 14 to 24, overrepresentation in the next four successive 10-year intervals—25 to 34, 35 to 44, 45 to 54, and 55 to 64—and underrepresentation in the group 65 and over. In most general terms, the young age groups in which there is underrepresentation simply reflect the period when individuals are entering the labor force, and variations in this underrepresentation suggest the varying degrees of preparation necessary for entering the occupations in question. Generally speaking, it requires time and preparation to become a farmer or farm manager, a member of the managerial class, or a professional person, whereas one can enter sales or clerical occupations or become a farm laborer at a much earlier age. Overrepresentation or underrepresentation in the upper age groups—55 to 64, or 65 and over—generally reflect variations in attrition from the labor force, but may also reflect occupational mobility and the past trends in the size of the occupation group. Farmers and farm managers, for example, are overrepresented in the age group 65 and over, in part, because these persons represent survivors from a period in which this group was much larger than it was in 1950.

Subgroup variations. In a number of instances, the major occupation groups are extremely heterogeneous with respect to the average age of the component groups. This is particularly true of the professional and craftsmen categories, but instances of wide variations can also be found within each major category. It is of some interest, therefore, to examine the age structure at the intermediate occupation group level, with a view to picking out those occupations which have unusually high percentages of

---

[3] See appendix table D–1.

FIGURE 2.—RATIO OF PROPORTION OF MALES AT EACH AGE LEVEL IN EACH MAJOR OCCUPATION
GROUP TO CORRESPONDING PROPORTION FOR ALL MALES: UNITED STATES, 1950

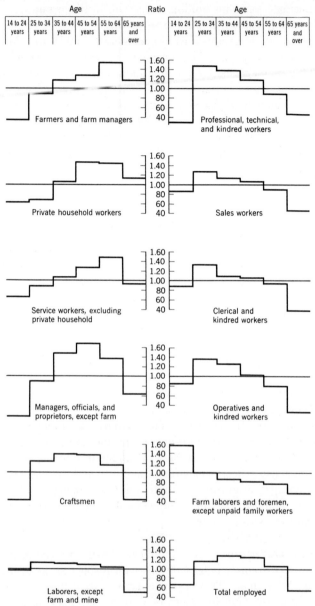

Source: table 26.

older persons. Information on median age and percentage 65 and over for the intermediate groups is presented in appendix table D–1.

Among professional and technical and kindred workers, three groups traditionally viewed as representative of the "professions"—physicians, lawyers, and clergymen—were characterized by having greater proportions of persons aged 65 and over than the comparable proportion for the total male population 14 and over (10.5 percent). At the other extreme, less than 2 percent of the electrical and aeronautical engineers, medical and dental technicians, and chemists were 65 and over.

Among farmers and farm managers, a group commonly thought to contain a high concentration of older persons, the percentage 65 and over was 12.5. Among other managers, officials, and proprietors, only State and local government officials and inspectors had a greater proportion 65 and over than that for the total male population of working age. Although in 1950 most of these managerial groups had relatively high median ages, there tended to be a relatively sharp drop in the percentage between ages 55 to 64 and 65 and over.

The proportion of older persons among occupation groups in the clerical and sales category was in general uniformly low, with the exception of real estate agents with a median age of 50.9 years and a percentage 65 and over of 15.8. The percentage 65 and over for insurance agents was 6.1 and for bookkeepers, 5.3. This proportion for the remaining groups ranged between 3.2 and 4.9 percent.

The craftsmen, foremen, and kindred worker groups were characterized by a variability similar to that of the professional group. The upper extreme of the distribution was represented by tailors and furriers, blacksmiths, forgemen and hammermen, and by shoemakers and repairmen working outside factories, with percentages 65 and over ranging from 16.5 to 12.4 respectively. Among locomotive engineers, persons 65 and over were represented to the same degree as in the general population. At the other extreme, the proportion 65 and over for auto, radio and television, and airplane mechanics and repairmen, as well as for telegraph and telephone linemen and servicemen, was less than 1.0 percent.

Operatives as a group were somewhat younger than craftsmen, and the variability among the specific groups was less. The percentage 65 and over ranged from 8.3 for stationary firemen to 0.3 for apprentices. Among laborers there was somewhat more variability. The percentage 65 and over for "Other specified laborers"—a group including garage laborers, teamsters, carwashers, greasers, nonfarm gardeners, and groundskeepers— was 11.6. On the other hand, only 2.6 percent of the laborers in chemical and allied industries were 65 and over. The percentages for farm laborers, both paid and unpaid (6.0 and 4.2 respectively), were close to the percentage for laborers as a whole (5.4).

With respect to age, the occupations grouped under the heading of service workers fell into two rather distinct groups. Among guards, watchmen, elevator operators, charwomen, janitors, and porters the proportion of older persons was greater than for the general population. This was also true of private household workers, or servants, a group which under some circumstances has been subsumed under the general heading of service workers. At the other extreme, the proportions of elderly persons among workers in the field of police and fire protection, and employees of eating and drinking establishments, were relatively low.

Factors in occupational age structure

The fact that an occupation group contains a relatively high percentage aged 65 and over does not necessarily imply that the occupation is one in which the probability of retirement with increasing age is low; or, on the other hand, that it offers employment opportunities for older persons. Among blacksmiths, for example, the proportion 65 and over was 35 percent higher, and the proportion 55 to 64, 106 percent higher, than the corresponding proportion in the total male population 14 years old and over. Yet the number of blacksmiths 65 and over in 1950 constituted only about one-fourth of the number aged 55 and over in 1940, and only the most imaginative would list blacksmithing among the opportunities for postretirement employment.[4] In short, the concentration of older persons in a given occupation group is a function not only of low attrition rates or high entrance rates at the upper ages but also of past trends in the size of the group.

Occupational growth or decline as a factor in age structure. In examining trends in the size of occupation groups, the problem of comparability alluded to earlier is encountered, and, thus, such an examination cannot be made in any exhaustive fashion. There are, however, clear-cut examples of various types of relationships between rate of growth or decline and age structure. Table 27 presents figures for selected occupation groups, among them locomotive engineers and tailors. Both groups have a reasonably consistent pattern of decline since 1920, and both appear to represent occupations that are relatively "closed"; that is, in these occupations most of the workers enter when young and tend to remain until they die or retire. Contraction is largely through a decline in entrants at younger ages; thus, persons making up the larger entering classes of earlier decades, who by 1950 had aged through these decades, account for the major proportion of the group. Among locomotive engineers, for example, the ratio of the proportion 65 and over to that in the total population rose from .39 in 1920 to 1.00 in 1950; among tailors, from .56 to 1.74.

Conversely, of course, in occupations such as electrical engineering, which is relatively "closed" and has grown rapidly, the percentage 65 and over has remained low because the entering classes in recent decades have been so much larger than those of previous decades. Between 1920 and 1950, this group increased almost four times, and the ratio of the proportion 65 and over to the total remained relatively constant at about .15.

---

[4] See appendix tables D–2 and D–3.

TABLE **27.**—RATIO OF PROPORTION 65 YEARS OLD AND OVER IN SELECTED OCCUPATION TO
CORRESPONDING PROPORTION IN TOTAL POPULATION, 1920 TO 1950, AND SURVIVAL RATES,
1940 TO 1950, FOR MALES IN SELECTED OCCUPATIONS

Occupation	Percent change, 1920 to 1950	Percent 65 years and over in occupation as ratio to percent 65 years and over in population 14 years old and over				Survival rate--ratio of age group in 1950 to age group 10 years younger in 1940		
		1950	1940	1930	1920	45 to 54 years	55 to 64 years	65 and over
Total employed..................	+24	0.53	0.55	0.69	0.70	1.00	0.83	0.42
Locomotive engineers................	-34	1.00	0.67	0.65	0.39	2.52	1.15	0.28
Tailors............................	-58	[1]1.74	1.16	0.80	0.56	0.85	0.69	0.37
Clergymen..........................	+28	1.00	1.16	1.43	1.47	1.06	0.84	0.45
Lawyers and judges.................	+45	1.02	1.05	1.16	1.26	0.87	0.76	0.47
Physicians and surgeons............	+31	1.06	1.33	1.38	1.21	0.94	0.76	0.44
Farmers and farm managers..........	-29	1.19	1.37	1.47	1.30	0.84	0.67	0.34
State and local officials and inspectors......................	+87	[1]1.35	1.39	1.70	1.59	1.32	1.08	0.58
Real estate agents and brokers........	[2]-41	1.50	1.66	1.35	[3]	1.49	1.02	0.49
Guards and watchmen.................	[4]+25	1.90	1.91	[5]3.00	[5]2.92	1.65	1.62	0.57
Elevator operators..................	+87	1.53	0.74	1.27	1.59	1.06	1.59	0.88
Charwomen, janitors, and porters......	[4]+23	1.47	1.11	[5]1.54	[5]1.65	1.24	1.35	0.70
Electrical engineers................	+290	0.14	0.17	0.15	0.14	0.91	0.68	0.24
Electricians.......................	+54	0.18	0.15	0.11	0.08	1.06	0.80	0.36
Locomotive firemen.................	-41	0.14	0.08	0.09	0.06	0.56	0.29	0.18
Surveyors..........................	[4]+84	0.38	0.45	[3]	[3]	0.98	1.05	0.67
Mechanics, repairmen, and loom fixers.	[4]+102	0.25	0.17	[5]0.16	[5]0.23	1.22	1.11	0.64
Attendants, auto service, and parking.	[4]+6	0.19	0.11	[3]	[3]	0.70	0.91	0.62
Farm laborers, unpaid farm workers....	-45	0.40	0.11	0.15	0.11	0.49	1.36	1.32

[1] Estimated.
[2] Change, 1930 to 1950.
[3] Comparable figures not available.
[4] Change, 1940 to 1950.
[5] Figures not strictly comparable with those for 1940 and 1950.
Source: Appendix tables D-3 and D-4.

Career line and age structure. In addition to the effects of growth
and decline in the size of an occupation group on its age structure, some
groups tend by their very nature to be older than others. In certain professions, for example, an individual must have considerable training after
college before he is admitted as a full-fledged member of the profession.
Notable in this respect are the professions of clergymen, lawyers, and
physicians, which have relatively low proportions of persons under 35
years of age and relatively high proportions for ages 65 and over. To a
somewhat lesser degree, architects, dentists, and pharmacists seem to follow this same pattern.[5] Again, as it takes time for State and local officials
and inspectors to acquire sufficient stature in the public eye to be appointed
or elected to office, and in the case of civil service workers for the principle
of seniority to operate, the proportion of persons 65 and over among public
officials in 1950 was about 35 percent higher than for all males.

Farmers and farm managers might be included in this general category.
Time is required to inherit a farm—or amass capital to buy a farm—and
to acquire the "know-how" needed by tenant farmers or farm managers.
Traditionally, of course, the relatively high concentration of older farmers

[5] See appendix table D-2.

has been explained in terms of self-employment, and the possibility of the owner operating a farm (with a decreasing level of activity) well into advanced years. In Chapter 4 some questions were raised as to the adequacy of this hypothesis, and it seems probable that, in immediate terms, out-migration from farms has had its impact on the age structure of this occupation group. Heavy out-migration among young adults may account for the relatively low concentration at this age level, and the smaller but appreciable out-migration at the upper ages may account for the relatively low survival rate in the cohort of farmers becoming 65 and over.

At the other end of the scale, in occupations which provide preparatory experience for occupations of higher status, the proportion of older persons is low. Apprentices, on the average, were younger than craftsmen, farm laborers younger than farmers, and locomotive firemen younger than locomotive engineers. In short, in such "feeder" occupations, upward occupational mobility tends to keep the proportion of older persons low.

These differences in age, which appear to be related to the intrinsic character of certain occupations, are perhaps more closely related to the presence or absence of concentrations of younger persons in the occupation and imply little as to the probability of survival in the group at the older ages. That is, the high percentage 65 and over among professional and farm groups tends to reflect the general concentration in the middle and upper ages rather than the fact that these groups suffer little attrition in passing from the age group, say, 55 to 64, to the group 65 to 74.

Concentration at upper age levels and occupational longevity. Evidence on this point appears in table 27, in which the survival rates represent merely the figure for a given 10-year age group in 1950 as a ratio to the figure for the age group 10 years younger in 1940. In short, the figures relate to cohorts. The survival rates are of course not true survival rates, since they reflect both separations from and additions to the cohort in the 10-year interval. The rates do, however, give some indication as to the relative net gain or loss to the cohort considered.

These figures suggest that, although in 1950 there was a relatively high proportion 65 and over among clergymen, lawyers, physicians, farmers, and State and local officials, the survival rates based on the age group 55 and over in 1940 were not appreciably higher (with the possible exception of State and local officials) than the rates for all employed persons. Farmers and farm managers, in fact, had a rate appreciably below the total. On the other hand, certain groups with a relatively low proportion 65 and over—surveyors; mechanics, repairmen, and loom fixers; auto service and parking attendants; and unpaid family farm laborers—had relatively high survival rates.

The unpaid family farm workers—who actually showed cohort gains at ages 55 to 64 and 65 and over—represent perhaps the logical extreme of an occupation which is, on the one hand, unattractive but, on the other hand, demands little in the way of performance; such occupations contain heavy concentrations of the very young and the very old—their position in the labor market being unfavorable. The high survival rates for auto and parking service attendants are open to the same general type of interpretation.

The high survival rates at 65 and over in 1950 for mechanics, repairmen, and loom fixers appear to be related to the total increase in this group between 1940 and 1950. During this decade the number more than doubled and the increase appears to be spread throughout the age distribution. Thus, in 1950, there were more persons 55 to 64 in this group than there were persons 45 to 54 in 1940, and the cohort 45 to 54 in 1950 shows the same type of increase. Although there was no increase for the cohort becoming 65 and over in 1950, the high survival rate suggests that some addition to the cohort during the decade compensated for normal attrition. Figures for this cohort are of course materially affected by the higher death rates at this same age level, and, in theory, it would be desirable to account for loss through mortality. Unfortunately, although available data indicate large interoccupational differences in mortality, these data are not sufficiently detailed for use in the present context. However, the crude survival rate for this group (.64) is slightly higher than a similar rate for all males (.59), which suggests the possibility of some net gain in the cohort becoming 65 and over in 1950.

The net cohort gains in the occupation group under consideration (mechanics, repairmen, and loom fixers) can probably be explained by the fact that in 1940 there existed a pool of persons who had the necessary skills for the occupations in question but were either unemployed, on emergency work, or in other occupations; however, with the increased industrial activity of the 1940's, members of this pool at all ages were drawn back into the occupation. This phenomenon, in varying degrees, applies to many other occupation groups. The figures for locomotive engineers, for example, indicate net gains in the cohorts becoming 45 to 54 and 55 to 64 in 1950, but net losses for the cohorts reaching the same ages in 1940. These figures suggest that the 1950 increase represents the promotion of engineers who had been demoted to firemen during the depression, or of firemen who failed to receive normal promotions during this period. In short, the survival rates reflect changes in the level of economic activity, and conclusions drawn from the examination of 1940 to 1950 survival rates can be generalized to other periods only with extreme caution.[6]

[6] In 1940, there were approximately 2 million males on public emergency work and about 3.8 million seeking work. In 1950, there were approximately 2 million unemployed. These figures suggest that, in contrast to 1950, there was in 1940 a considerable number of workers from which persons with specialized occupational skills might have been drawn. See *1940 Census of Population*, Vol. III, *The Labor Force*, Part 1, table 1, and *1950 Census of Population*, Vol. II, *Characteristics of the Population*, Part 1, table 52.

Occupations with high survival rates and high proportions of older persons. Of the occupations with high proportions of persons 65 and over thus far examined, survival rates at 65 and over have tended to be less than for the total population. However, both the percentage 65 and over and the survival rates were relatively high among certain of the service occupation groups, specifically, among two groups: charwomen, janitors, and porters; and elevator operators.

Both groups showed increases between 1940 and 1950 in the cohorts reaching the age of 45 to 54 and 55 to 64, and the survival rates for those 65 and over were well above the rates for all males. Likewise, the percentages 65 and over were well above those for the total male population. These are clearly groups in which older persons found employment during the decade 1940 to 1950. Strictly comparable figures for 1930 to 1940 are available only for elevator operators, and these figures display little evidence of the net cohort gains of the decade 1940 to 1950. They do, however, indicate relatively low net cohort attrition, which suggests the existence of the same general pattern operating under adverse conditions. To these two groups (charwomen, janitors, and porters; and elevator operators) might be added watchmen and guards. This group showed appreciable net gains in the cohorts becoming 45 to 54 and 55 to 64 in 1950, but the survival rate at 65 and over was somewhat lower. Generally speaking, the gains in the number of older persons in these occupations reflect the downward occupational mobility incident to aging and suggest also the limited employment opportunities for older persons.

It is clear then that a high proportion of older persons in an occupation does not necessarily imply an unusual tendency to survive in the occupation, nor does it imply employment opportunities for older people. The occupation in question may be one which is contracting, or one which by its nature includes a relatively small number of younger persons. In the decade 1940 to 1950, high survival rates occurred in occupations with both low and high proportions of older persons. In general, the intermediate occupation groups with both high proportions of older persons and high survival rates fell in the service category and, in the main, their age structure reflected downward occupational mobility.

Self-employment and occupational longevity. The role of self-employment in perpetuating employment well into the later years was considered in general in Chapter 4. Although the farmer, as it was indicated, is by virtue of self-employment commonly held to be in a position to continue working indefinitely, the issue is clouded by out-migration from farms; as a matter of fact, the labor force survival rates in the cohorts entering the advanced years were lower in 1950 for the farm than the nonfarm population. Likewise, it was indicated in Chapter 4 that, among the nonagricultural self-employed, similar survival rates were slightly lower than among nonagricultural wage or salary workers. Since the self-employed are far from constituting a representative sample of the entire occupational distribution, it is possible that occupational longevity is greater among the self-employed in some occupations but not in others, and that the net effect is to reduce the general rates to approximately the level for all workers.

It is of interest, therefore, to examine the data on class of worker for individual occupations in which there were substantial numbers of self-employed and salaried workers. Ideally, the most adequate answer to the question of the effects of self-employment on occupational longevity would be found in an examination of the crude cohort survival rates considered in the foregoing discussion. Unfortunately, however, data by age, occupation, and class of worker are not available for 1940, and the examination must therefore be limited to 1950 age data and trends in the total numbers of salaried and self-employed workers in the decade 1940 to 1950.

Data of this type for occupation groups selected from among those occupations in which there were appreciable numbers of both self-employed and wage and salary workers are presented in table 28. These figures indicated that, with the exception of pharmacists, the percentage that persons 65 and over constitute of the total 14 years old and over, or of the number of persons 55 and over, was greater occupation by occupation for the self-employed than for the wage and salary workers.

This situation, however, does not necessarily imply a lower attrition rate among the self-employed than among wage and salary workers at the upper age levels. In the first place, there is generally some delay in achieving a self-employed status and thus a higher proportion of older persons among the self-employed might be normally expected.[7] In the second place, in the decade 1940 to 1950, the wage and salary segment of most of the occupations under consideration grew more rapidly, or declined less rapidly than the self-employed segments, which, other things being equal, would imply a higher proportion of older persons among the self-employed. Finally, the available evidence indicates that there has been, generally, a relative decline in the numbers of self-employed not only in the decade 1940 to 1950 but also in previous decades.

This situation would imply that there would be less difference between successive age cohorts as they reached the upper age levels in 1950 among the self-employed than among the wage and salary workers, and thus the percentage which persons 65 and over constituted of those 55 and over would be expected to be greater in the former than in the latter group. Thus, for example, among self-employed blacksmiths in 1950, persons 65 and over outnumbered persons 55 to 64. This relationship does not mean

---

[7] Generally speaking, self-employment as a professional worker, craftsman, or proprietor requires training, experience, and capital. Typically, the self-employed craftsman or proprietor begins as a wage or salary worker and becomes self-employed only after he has accumulated experience, capital, and potential clientele. This process is perhaps less characteristic of the professional group, but, here actual practice of the professional is delayed by a longer period of training. By and large the figure indicates many more younger persons among the salaried than among the self-employed and, conversely, proportionately fewer older persons.

that there was no attrition from this occupation, but rather suggests that the cohort becoming 65 to 74 in 1950 (and the residual cohorts becoming 75 and over) was initially much larger than the cohort reaching 55 to 64 in that year. The former cohorts were recruited in the heyday of blacksmithing, but the latter was recruited when the occupation had begun to contract.

TABLE **28.**—PERCENT OF OLDER PERSONS IN SELECTED OCCUPATIONS, BY CLASS OF WORKER: 1950

Occupation	Percent change, 1940 to 1950			Males 65 years old and over, 1950--			
	Males 14 years old and over			As percent of males 14 years old and over		As percent of males 55 years old and over	
	Total	Salaried	Self-employed	Salaried	Self-employed	Salaried	Self-employed
PROFESSIONAL							
Architects........................	+22.3	+43.2	+1.8	4.3	9.4	20.2	28.0
Artists and art teachers..........	+38.9	+54.7	+8.9	3.3	6.0	27.9	31.1
Dentists..........................	+5.7	+142.2	-1.7	9.9	11.2	40.6	39.1
Lawyers and judges................	+0.4	+44.2	-15.9	8.4	11.8	40.9	43.4
Musicians and music teachers......	+9.8	+22.7	-23.0	3.1	8.9	31.0	40.2
Pharmacists.......................	+8.4	+10.3	+6.2	9.1	7.2	39.6	27.7
Physicians and surgeons...........	+13.8	+90.3	-5.9	5.8	12.9	41.3	46.8
MANAGERS, OFFICIALS, AND PROPRIETORS, EXCEPT FARM							
Construction......................	+79.7	+127.3	+65.0	4.7	6.7	22.8	27.5
Eating and drinking places........	+32.5	+90.0	+23.9	2.9	4.4	19.1	20.2
Finance, insurance, and real estate	+29.3	+18.9	+70.4	6.8	15.7	28.7	38.1
Manufacturing.....................	+51.7	+50.2	+54.4	4.1	8.3	21.5	30.6
Retail trade, except eating and drinking places............................	+15.7	+62.7	+3.6	3.3	8.0	24.8	31.7
Wholesale trade...................	+51.7	+84.2	+31.6	4.9	7.9	26.9	29.9
CRAFTSMEN, FOREMEN, AND KINDRED WORKERS							
Blacksmiths, forgemen, and hammermen.....	-29.5	-13.9	-56.7	9.5	29.8	29.3	54.1
Carpenters........................	+67.1	+81.0	+22.9	6.4	14.0	27.1	37.9
Painters, construction and maintenance...	+21.7	+43.2	-9.4	5.3	9.9	24.9	32.3
Plasterers and cement finishers..........	+70.6	+90.0	+9.3	3.2	6.5	18.6	26.0
Plumbers and pipe fitters.........	+63.4	+90.2	-9.9	3.1	8.8	19.7	31.7
Shoemakers and repairers..........	-9.6	+43.3	-28.2	6.3	16.5	35.3	37.3
Tailors and furriers..............	-26.3	-11.9	-50.0	14.6	24.8	33.5	42.3
SERVICE WORKERS, EXCEPT PRIVATE HOUSEHOLD							
Barbers, beauticians, and manicurists....	-8.0	+19.3	-24.4	7.8	12.3	30.1	33.1
LABORERS, EXCEPT FARM AND MINE							
Fishermen and oystermen...........	+20.7	+75.3	-10.1	4.2	7.9	33.7	35.5

Source: Appendix table D–5.

It is clear then that, although higher survival rates (or lower attrition rates) among the self-employed would result in a higher proportion of persons aged 65 and over in this group, there are several other factors which might also account for these higher percentages. The use of the percentage which persons 65 and over constitute of the number 55 and over mitigates to some extent the effects of the general pattern by which self-employment is achieved and the effects of differential rates of growth in the past decade, but it is still affected by long-run trends.

The really critical test of the hypothesis that the self-employed continue in their occupations to more advanced years than do wage and salary workers would be in terms of survival rates within the same cohorts. Although, as indicated earlier in this discussion, the necessary 1940 occupational data are not available, data by age and industry are available for 1940 which permit the development of indirect evidence in the context of survival rates. Thus, for example, it is possible to develop survival rates for the self-employed in a given industry such as manufacturing. Operating on the not unreasonable assumption that the majority of the self-employed in manufacturing are proprietors, managers, or officials, survival rates for this occupation as a whole may be compared with the survival rates for the self-employed in the industry. The validity of inferences from such a comparison rests on the extent to which the self-employed in the given industry are to be found in the occupation group to which comparison is made. Some measure of this correspondence is possible in terms of a comparison of 1950 figures on the self-employed in the industry and the occupation.

Comparisons of survival rates for the limited number of groups for which a reasonable match of industry and occupation data are possible indicate that the survival rates for the self-employed in the industries are lower than, or about the same as, those for the corresponding occupations, with the exception of finance insurance and real estate.[8] Since these findings are limited to a small number of industries, and the self-employed groups are usually diluted in some degree with occupations not included in the matching occupations, the general results of this comparison do not provide a valid basis for the conclusion that occupational longevity among the self-employed is not greater than among wage and salary workers. The conclusion is simply that if such a difference exists in the industries considered, it is not sufficiently great to be detected by an analysis of such data as are available.

In the case of finance insurance and real estate, the self-employed in the industry appear to have a survival rate clearly higher than that for the matching occupations: proprietors, managers, and officials in this industry group and insurance and real estate agents and brokers. This is an occupational group in which there was a substantial increase between 1940 and 1950 and in which the increase was greater among the self-employed than among the wage and salary workers. It is also an occupation in which common knowledge suggests that occupational longevity may well be associated with self-employment.

---

[8] See Appendix D, section 1, and appendix table D–6.

Survival rates, 1940 to 1950, for major occupation groups

As previously indicated, the evidence implicit in survival rates is the most direct, if not completely adequate, evidence relating to the degree to which older persons survive in their present occupations, and the degree to which employment opportunities are available for older persons in a given occupation or group of occupations. Such survival rates reflect only the net effects of gains and losses to the occupation by age during a decade. The result is that a given rate may represent, on the one hand, the effect of small losses and gains, or, on the other hand, large losses and gains. Thus, if the survival rate is greater than one, it is clear that the cohort in the occupation in question has had gains in excess of losses; but if the rate is high but less than one, it is only possible to infer from other evidence whether the rate is the result of a high degree of persistence in the occupation or of large gains exceeded by slightly larger losses.

Likewise, because the rates reflect both gain and loss, they may delineate a sort of occupational life cycle; in the younger ages, when individuals are entering the labor force, the rates would be expected to be greater than one; this increase would continue to some peak age group (varying from occupation to occupation), and thereafter the rates would show progressive decline. If, as commonly assumed, employment difficulties are first encountered in the 40's, these gains—say in the cohort becoming 45 to 54 years old—may be evidence of upward mobility, as in the case of managers, officials, etc., or of downward mobility, as in the case of service workers. In short, in the middle-age range, there is some ambiguity as to the meaning of the rates.

Within this frame of reference, and in spite of considerable heterogeneity within the major occupation groups, these survival rates for the adjusted major occupation groupings[9] presented in table 29 give evidence of distinct age patterns. The professional group—usually regarded as a group of "closed" occupations in the sense that there are relatively few additions to the group after age 40—showed some gain in the age group 35 to 44 between 1940 and 1950, remained constant in the next older age group, and thereafter showed declines to about the same levels as the total employed for the age groups 55 to 64 and 65 and over. In short, at the older age levels, the survival rates for professional persons were not essentially different from those for craftsmen or operatives, although there was some indication of a higher survival rate at 65 and over.

Among farmers and farm managers, after a slight gain in the cohort becoming 35 to 44 in 1950, there were continued cohort decreases at the upper age levels, which in all probability reflected the long continued decline in this occupation group distributed over the entire age range. In any event, the relatively low rates at the terminal age groups (not essentially

---

[9] See appendix table D–2.

different from those for the decade 1930 to 1940) do not support the hypothesis that farming is an occupation actively carried on to a ripe old age.

The rates for the managerial group showed relatively large increases in cohorts becoming 35 to 44 and 45 to 54 in 1950, and thereafter showed declines of about the same level as those for the total employed. There was some suggestion of a greater mortality at 65 and over. Here it appears that the time required to attain a managerial position or establish a business of one's own results in continued gains well into middle age, but that there tends to be a fairly sharp cutoff at about age 65.

TABLE 29.—SURVIVAL RATES FOR MALES, 1940 TO 1950, BY ADJUSTED MAJOR OCCUPATION GROUP AND AGE

[Major occupation group classifications for both 1950 and 1940 adjusted to a comparable basis]

Occupation	35 to 44 years	45 to 54 years	55 to 64 years	65 years and over
All males.....................................	1.01	0.94	0.84	0.59
Employed, total................................	1.10	1.00	0.83	0.42
Professional, technical, and kindred workers.....	1.12	0.97	0.85	0.46
Farmers and farm managers.......................	1.02	0.84	0.67	0.34
Managers, officials, and proprietors, exc. farm..	1.92	1.25	0.84	0.39
Clerical and kindred workers.....................	0.92	1.02	1.00	0.51
Sales workers...................................	0.90	0.83	0.74	0.45
Craftsmen, foremen, and kindred workers..........	1.61	1.16	0.89	0.40
Operatives and kindred workers...................	1.00	0.95	0.86	0.42
Private household workers........................	0.54	0.64	0.62	0.40
Service workers, except private household........	1.07	1.07	1.07	0.60
Farm laborers, unpaid family workers.............	0.20	0.49	1.36	1.32
Farm laborers, except unpaid, and foremen........	0.46	0.64	0.63	0.39
Laborers, except farm and mine..................	0.80	0.89	0.82	0.44

Source: Appendix tables D-2 and D-3.

Between 1940 and 1950 the clerical occupation had already begun to show a decline in the age group 35 to 44, but thereafter seemed to show a high degree of persistence up to the age group 65 and over; here the decline was appreciably less than for the total employed. It seems probable that the decrease at the younger ages reflects upward mobility into other occupations; once this has tapered off, employment in the occupation tends to persist well into the upper ages. It is also probable that the increase in this occupation group occurred not only at the entering ages but was to some degree spread over the entire age range. As previously indicated, the available rates do not discriminate between these two factors.

Sales workers, who shared with clerical workers the early attrition to other occupation groups, did not display the same persistence at the upper ages. The rates showed substantial declines at each succeeding age level, although there was an appreciable increase in the entire group during the decade.

The pattern of survival rates for craftsmen and kindred workers is generally similar to that of the managerial group. The time required to attain a foothold in this occupation group is probably not seriously involved here; it is more likely that the great demand for their skills in the 1940's drew on a pool of craftsmen who were not employed during those years in the occupation involved. This generalization seems applicable to the age group 45 to 54, and to a lesser degree to the age group 55 to 64. As in the managerial group, the drop at age 65 and over is relatively sharp.

In contrast to craftsmen, the rates for operatives showed a continuous decline in survival rates from the age group 35 to 44 on. Operatives constitute the largest of the major occupation groups; although this group increased by about one-third between 1940 and 1950, it appeared to have a steady rate of attrition similar to that of the labor force as a whole.

Among service workers, cohort gains were about 7 percent in the cohorts becoming 35 to 44, 45 to 54, and 55 to 64 in 1950, and the survival rate for 65 and over (with the exception of the unpaid family farm workers) was the highest of any of the major occupation groups. It is reasonably clear that, during the decade 1940 to 1950, older persons found employment in the service occupations.

The survival rates for private household workers, farm laborers, and foremen, and for laborers except farm and mine, were less than one in each age interval from 35 to 44, to 65 and over. Moreover, the rates for the interval 35 to 44 were in each instance lower than those for the two succeeding intervals, and at 65 and over were not materially different from those of the total employed.

The pattern of rates suggests that these three occupation groups had peak employment in the age interval 25 to 34, with a rapid exodus into other occupations as this cohort moved on to ages 35 to 44. For those who remained, however, attrition was less marked at the next two age levels and until the cohort became 65 and over. Since both farm laborers and private household workers showed marked decreases between 1940 and 1950, the level of the survival rates was undoubtedly somewhat depressed. Statistics for laborers, which showed a slight increase during the decade, showed also, as previously indicated, the same general pattern but at a somewhat higher level.

Attention has been called to the fact that between 1940 and 1950 unpaid family farm workers showed net gains in the cohorts becoming 55 to 64 and 65 and over in 1950. In this occupation group, as in the three groups previously discussed, the period of peak employment is reached at an early age and the survival rate at 35 to 44 is less than the rates for succeeding age intervals. Here indeed, as indicated by the rates in excess of one in the last two age intervals, is a postretirement occupation among persons with farming experience—particularly in a period of acute shortages of farm labor. It can be considered as an opportunity for postretirement employment in only a very limited sense; it does not produce income for the elderly persons, and the great majority of the older persons in this group are there simply by virtue of the fact that they are living on a farm as relatives of a farm operator.

Age structure and occupation among women

Labor force participation among women, as previously noted, differs from that among men. Social values do not demand that women work; the labor force participation rate of women is considerably lower than that for men, and there are marked sex differences in the pattern of participation by age. In 1950, for example, the peak of labor force participation occurred among women 20 to 24 years old; and, after some decline, a secondary but lower peak occurred in the age group 40 to 44; thereafter there was a continuous decline with age. Among men, peak employment was reached in the age group 35 to 39, and thereafter the rate showed a continuous decline.

These differences are of course apparent in the age structure of employed women among the major occupation groups. With a few exceptions, group for group, women were younger than men. In 1950, for example, the proportion of women aged 14 to 24 was as great as or greater than the corresponding proportion for men in each major occupation group except those connected with agriculture—farmers and farm managers, farm laborers and foremen, and unpaid family farm workers (table 30). Among farmers and farm laborers, the differences were small; among unpaid family workers, more than three-fourths of the men, but less than one-fourth of the women, were 14 to 24 years of age. Of the typical differences in the opposite direction, the greatest relative difference occurred in the professional group in which only 8.1 percent of the men but 18.7 percent of the women were 14 to 24 years of age. Differences were also large for clerical and sales workers.

TABLE 30.—PERCENT DISTRIBUTION BY AGE OF FEMALES 14 YEARS OLD AND OVER, BY MAJOR OCCUPATION GROUP: 1950

Occupation	Total, 14 years old and over	14 to 24 years	25 to 34 years	35 to 44 years	45 to 54 years	55 to 64 years	65 years and over
Total............................	100.0	21.4	21.3	19.0	15.2	11.6	11.3
Employed................................	100.0	23.3	23.4	23.3	17.5	9.5	3.0
Professional, techn'l, & kindred wkrs...	100.0	18.7	22.9	25.1	19.9	10.3	3.0
Farmers and farm managers..............	100.0	5.1	10.4	20.3	25.5	23.1	15.6
Managers, off'ls, & propr's, exc. farm..	100.0	5.1	16.4	29.3	27.7	15.8	5.7
Clerical and kindred workers...........	100.0	35.1	26.5	19.5	13.0	5.0	1.0
Sales workers.........................	100.0	25.0	19.5	24.0	19.0	9.9	2.7
Craftsmen, foremen, and kindred wkrs....	100.0	13.4	23.3	27.9	21.1	11.1	3.1
Operatives and kindred workers.........	100.0	18.7	26.7	26.3	17.3	8.8	2.2
Private household workers..............	100.0	17.9	18.3	22.4	20.1	14.3	6.9
Service workers, exc. private hshld.....	100.0	19.2	22.3	23.4	18.5	12.6	4.1
Farm laborers, exc. unpaid, & foremen...	100.0	30.4	21.8	20.8	15.3	8.4	3.3
Farm laborers, unpaid family workers....	100.0	24.6	21.0	23.2	17.9	10.3	3.2
Laborers, except farm and mine.........	100.0	21.5	25.3	24.6	16.8	9.1	2.7
Occupation not reported................	100.0	23.3	21.2	21.0	16.8	10.9	6.8
Other[1]................................	100.0	20.8	20.5	17.4	14.4	12.4	14.5

[1] Includes Armed Forces, unemployed, and not in labor force.

Source: Same as table 26.

In the early middle years, 35 to 44, there were still heavier concentrations of women in most of the major occupation groups, although for the total employed the proportion of men was slightly higher. The differences in the proportion were not large, and in the atypical groups—professional workers, farmers, and clerical workers—the excesses in the proportions of men were not great. At this age level (35 to 44) the proportion of women exceeded that of men among both farm laborers and unpaid family farm workers. In the latter category, farmers' wives evidently replaced farmers' sons. In every major occupation group except farmers and farm managers, the percentage of persons 65 and over among women was less than among men. The typical differences were relatively large among laborers, service workers, and clerical workers. Generally speaking, then, the concentration of older women among the major occupation groups is less than the concentration of older men.

This conclusion is certainly to be expected in view of the general pattern of labor force participation of women. If, as indicated, housekeeping is regarded as a competing occupation, its character is such that the number of women who find their way into other occupations is restricted. Over the past years the labor force participation of women has increased, and the increase has in general been concentrated at the younger ages. Likewise, the increase in labor force participation among women and the concentration of this increase at the younger ages have served to keep the proportion of women in the labor force low at the older ages.

Although, in general, the major occupation groups include relatively fewer older women than older men, it does not necessarily follow that at ages, say, above 45, the attrition for these groups is greater for women than for men. Data relating to this question are presented in table 31 for some of the occupations in which relatively large numbers of women are engaged.

For each of these particular occupations (with the exception of farmers and farm managers), ratios between the percentage 65 and over and the percentage 65 and over in the total population of women were extremely low in comparison to the corresponding figures for men. In short, the figures for the past three decades confirm the general conclusion that in most occupations the concentration of older women is lower than the concentration of older men.

In terms of survival rates, however, women at the upper age levels showed roughly the same tendency as men to remain in or be drawn into the occupations examined. For all employed women the rates at ages 45 to 54, and 55 to 64, were greater than 1.00, and for ages 65 and over, .48 —whereas for men the two former rates were 1.00 and .83 respectively, and the rate for ages 65 and over was .42. For teachers the rates at ages 45 to 54 and 55 to 64 were higher for women than for men, but at ages 65 and over, slightly lower. Private household workers showed essentially the same pattern. Among waitresses, bartenders, and counter workers, at each of the terminal age groups, the rates for women were all higher than those for men. If any real difference exists between the rates for men and for women, it would appear to be that survival rates for the cohorts becoming 55 to 64 were somewhat higher for women than for men.

TABLE **31.**—RATIO OF PROPORTION 65 YEARS OLD AND OVER IN SELECTED OCCUPATION TO CORRESPONDING PROPORTION IN TOTAL POPULATION, 1920 TO 1950, AND SURVIVAL RATES, 1940 TO 1950, FOR FEMALES IN SELECTED OCCUPATIONS

Occupation	Percent change, 1920 to 1950	Percent 65 years and over in occupation as ratio to percent 65 years and over in population 14 years old and over				Survival rate--ratio of age group in 1950 to age group 10 years younger in 1940		
		1950	1940	1930	1920	45 to 54 years	55 to 64 years	65 and over
Total employed..................	+86.8	0.27	0.25	0.33	0.34	1.24	1.01	0.48
Nurses and student nurses, profess'l..	+223.9	0.19	0.11	0.11	0.10	1.16	0.98	0.55
Teachers (n.e.c.).....................	+32.8	0.21	0.16	0.15	0.10	1.11	0.88	0.32
Farmers and farm managers............	-54.1	1.38	1.81	2.29	2.24	1.01	0.62	0.29
Stenographers, typists, and secretaries......................	+166.1	0.06	0.03	0.01	0.01	0.94	0.89	0.53
Salesmen and sales clerks............	+138.9	0.22	0.13	0.12	0.07	1.56	1.22	0.62
Private household workers............	[1]-32.0	0.61	0.40	0.59	([2])	0.71	0.65	0.37
Waitresses, bartenders, counter wkrs..	+418.3	0.06	0.02	0.04	0.06	1.20	1.19	0.74

[1] Change, 1930 to 1950.
[2] Comparable figures not available.

Source: Appendix table D-7.

It should be noted, however, that the gains at the older ages among women in the occupations examined may well have been in large part a function of the expanding labor market during the 1940's. During the war years these occupation groups—nurses, teachers, secretaries, saleswomen, and waitresses—were in short supply and consequently drew on older women. Available survival rates for the decade 1930 to 1940 do not indicate the same pattern of gains.

As suggested earlier, the proportion of older women engaged in farming or farm management was extremely high, in sharp contrast to the other occupation groups. Although this situation may have resulted in part from the same factors which account for the concentration of older men in this occupation group, it is possible that the women in question, on the death of their husbands, continued to operate the family farm. The data on occupation by marital status tend to confirm this hypothesis. In 1950 approximately 40 percent of all women engaged in farming were widows, as compared with about 10 percent of all employed women. Among the other occupation groups, with high concentrations of older women, were dressmakers and seamstresses working outside factories, and housekeepers and stewards working outside private households. Here, again, the high proportion of widows suggests the use of a currently existing skill or resource as a means of earning a living.

This brief examination of the age structure of women among the various occupations suggests that, for obvious reasons, the concentration of older women among the employed, and in most major occupation groups, was less than that for men. However, for those occupational groups in which there were relatively large numbers of women, there seemed to be little difference between women and men in survival rates at the older ages.

CHAPTER 6

MARITAL STATUS, THE FAMILY CYCLE, LIVING ARRANGEMENTS, AND AGE

A knowledge of the living arrangements of older persons is indispensable in considering their welfare. The implications of low income for the widow who lives with a prosperous son-in-law, for example, are quite different from the implications for a widow without children, without social security benefits, and without a home inherited from her husband. Likewise, for an isolated elderly person, problems of adequate care in case of disability and illness are quite different from similar problems for an elderly person who is part of a family group. If one is concerned with improving the living arrangements of older persons, then for those living in the homes of relatives it may become a matter of improving the general adequacy of housing; for older persons maintaining their own households, a matter of special programs for such persons; and for older people with no family connections, possibly some venture into planning ideal congregate living quarters. In short, the ways in which the needs of elderly people can be met are determined to a great extent by their living arrangements.

Superficially at least, it would seem easier to meet the objective, physical needs of older people when they live with a family group than when they live alone, and this position is supported in the literature by nostalgic references to the three-generation family and its attendant advantages—not only in terms of physical welfare but also in terms of social and psychological well-being. In our current culture, however, the values point in the other direction; it is felt only right and proper that each married couple should set up and maintain its own household, and that as children reach adulthood they in turn should marry and establish their own households. Thus it is frequently with some reluctance that older people give up their autonomous status and become members of their children's families, and it is often with similar reluctance that they are received by their children. The statistics on living arrangements indicate something as to the relative numbers of older persons who by virtue of their isolation are relatively free to make their own decisions but do not have ready access to help from relatives in time of need, and the relative numbers of those who, with some loss of independence and privacy, are assured of immediate care in time of stress.

In a population such as that of the United States, the arrangements in which people live are varied. Some people live alone in hotels or in rooming houses; some people live as heads of small families or as "in-laws" in families in which membership extends to three generations; and other people live in institutions. It is clear that the type of living arrangement is, in a general way, related to age. Typically, an individual begins life as a child in the household of his parents; may as a young adult live alone or with partners in rooming houses, hotels, or apartments; marries and becomes the head or wife in his or her own household; with the advent of children becomes a parent; and, when children have left home, and with the death of the marriage partner, may live alone again continuing in the family residence or move to an apartment or lodginghouse, or may become a member of the household of a married child.

Although there are many variants of this sequence of events, it is apparent that this process of family formation and dissolution accounts to a considerable degree for changes in living arrangements. The operation of this process of family formation and dissolution in the population is reflected in data on marital status by age. Gains in the proportion married from adolescence to middle age indicate, in some measure, the formation of families and gains in the proportion widowed, the dissolution of families. For this reason it is proposed to examine the changes in marital status with age before considering age variations in living arrangements.

Marital status

The trend in the percentage married as age increases is perhaps the best single index of the cycle of family formation and dissolution. In terms of 1950 data, among men this percentage rises from less than 1 percent at age 15 to about 83 percent at ages 50 to 64 and then declines, first slowly and then rapidly, so that in the age group 85 and over the proportion married is about 30 percent (table 32).

TABLE 32.—PERCENT DISTRIBUTION BY MARITAL STATUS AND SEX, FOR SELECTED AGE GROUPS: 1950

Age	Male					Female				
	Total	Single	Married, spouse present	Widowed	Spouse absent and divorced	Total	Single	Married, spouse present	Widowed	Spouse absent and divorced
Total, 14 years and over.........	100.0	26.4	64.1	4.1	5.5	100.0	20.0	62.3	11.8	5.9
15 years...............	100.0	99.1	0.3	0.1	0.4	100.0	97.9	1.6	0.1	0.4
30 to 34 years........	100.0	13.2	80.5	0.4	6.0	100.0	9.3	82.2	1.6	6.9
35 to 39 years........	100.0	10.1	82.9	0.7	6.4	100.0	8.4	81.3	2.7	7.6
40 to 44 years........	100.0	9.0	83.1	1.2	6.7	100.0	8.3	78.9	5.0	7.8
50 to 54 years........	100.0	8.3	80.7	3.7	7.3	100.0	7.7	71.1	13.9	7.3
60 to 64 years........	100.0	8.6	75.4	9.6	6.4	100.0	8.2	56.9	29.7	5.3
65 years and over.....	100.0	8.4	62.1	24.1	5.5	100.0	8.9	33.2	54.3	3.6
65 to 69 years......	100.0	8.7	70.3	15.0	6.1	100.0	8.4	46.0	41.1	4.3
70 to 74 years......	100.0	8.3	64.0	22.2	5.4	100.0	9.0	34.2	53.3	3.6
75 to 79 years......	100.0	8.1	55.5	31.4	4.9	100.0	9.4	22.5	65.1	2.9
80 to 84 years......	100.0	7.4	44.8	43.3	4.4	100.0	9.4	12.3	75.9	2.4
85 years and over...	100.0	7.7	30.4	57.9	4.0	100.0	9.7	5.3	82.9	2.1

Source: *1950 Census of Population*, Vol. II, *Characteristics of the Population*, Part 1, U. S. Summary, table 104.

Marital status and age. Single men, who of course constitute the major pool from which married men are drawn, comprised in 1950 about 99 percent of the 15-year-olds but only 9 percent of those 40 to 44. At older ages this percentage remained relatively constant at something less than 10 percent. The proportion of men who were widowed, which gives some indication of the volume of family dissolution, rose from about 1 percent at ages 40 to 44 to nearly 60 percent at ages 85 and over. The percentage of men in the residual group—divorced and married, spouse absent—reached a peak of about 7 percent in the early 50's and thereafter declined.[1]

Although women have a similar pattern of change in marital status with age, there are notable differences. In 1950 the age group with the highest percentage married (30 to 34 years) was 10 years younger than the corresponding group for men, and the decline with increasing age was somewhat more precipitous. At 60 to 64, 75 percent of the men were still married but only about 57 percent of the women, and at 85 and over, only 5 percent of the women were married. On the other hand, at ages 30 and over the percentage widowed was greater among women than among men, and this difference increased with age. Thus at 85 and over, more than four-fifths of the women were widowed, as compared with slightly less than three-fifths of the men.

Although these differences in the proportions married and widowed between men and women increased most rapidly at the extreme upper ages, they were still clearly apparent for the entire population 65 and over. In this group the percentage married was 62.1 for men and 33.2 for women, and the corresponding percentages for widowed were 24.1 and 54.3, respectively. The 3.5 million widows 65 and over constituted more than one-fourth of the total population of this age group, and of the total population aged 85 and over, nearly one-half.

Sources of sex differences in marital status. The deficit of married women and the excess of widows relative to the corresponding categories among men at the upper age levels reflect the operation of several factors. Mortality among women is lower than among men and, therefore, larger numbers of women survive to advanced years; on the average, wives are younger than their husbands, and thus, even without sex differences in mortality, might be expected on the average to outlive their husbands. Finally, among the widowed and divorced, remarriage rates are lower for women than for men. Each of these factors, then, tends to produce proportions of married and widowed women which are, respectively, lower and higher than the corresponding proportions for men.

Although there are more male than female births (the sex ratio at birth is something like 105), mortality rates for males are higher than those for females at each age level. This is true not only in terms of current mor-

---

[1] See *1950 Census of Population*, Vol. II, *Characteristics of the Population*, Part 1, U. S. Summary, pp. 41–43, for definitions of marital status and relationship categories.

tality rates; the gap between the mortality rates for the two sexes has increased progressively during the century.   If, for example, the expectation of life at birth is taken as a convenient summary index, then in 1900 the expectation of life of white females was 51.1 years, or about 2.9 years higher than the corresponding figure for males—48.2 years.   By 1950, although life expectation had increased for both males and females, this difference had increased to 5.7 years.

The potential effects of this differential are reflected in the sex ratios in the stationary population of the 1950 life table (table 33).   According to mortality rates and sex ratio at birth of the period 1949 to 1951, the sex ratio in the age group 45 to 49 would have been approximately 100; that is, the number of men and women would have been approximately equal. For the group 65 and over, there would have been approximately 75 men to every 100 women, and by the time the group 85 and over was reached, about 54 men to every 100 women—nearly two women to every man.

TABLE **33.**—SEX RATIO FOR SELECTED POPULATIONS AND AGE GROUPS: 1950

Age	Life-table population	Total population	Native population
45 to 49 years.....................	100.5	99.6	98.7
65 years and over..................	74.6	89.6	85.8
65 to 69 years.................	84.5	94.0	89.2
70 to 74 years.................	77.9	91.3	87.9
75 to 79 years.................	71.0	87.1	84.2
80 to 84 years.................	63.9	81.4	78.4
85 years and over.............	54.0	69.6	66.7

Source: Appendix tables A-2 and A-3; National Office of Vital Statistics, *Vital Statistics—Special Reports*, Vol. 41, No. 1, tables 2 and 3.

The sex ratios in the actual population are not as low as those in the life table population for comparable age groups because the survivors in the actual population, in attaining the upper ages, have been subjected to earlier mortality schedules in which the sex difference was not so pronounced; for example, persons who were 65 in 1950 had been subject to the changing mortality schedules between 1885 and 1950, with the result that only in most recent years had they been affected by the large sex difference implied in the 1950 life tables.   In addition, the large-scale immigration of the early 1900's, in which men predominated, retarded the decline in the sex ratio implied by mortality rates.   The effects of this factor may be inferred from the difference between sex ratios for the total population and for the native population, which are presented in table 33.   Finally, the sex ratio is an extremely sensitive index, and it thus reflects the misreporting of age as well as other errors in the reporting and processing of data.   For this reason, the differences between the sex ratio in the life table population and the actual population must be regarded, in some small measure, as approximate.

It is clear, however, that in 1950 the population 65 and over contained some 700,000 more women than men; and, as suggested by a comparison of the differences in the number of men and women by marital status, a large proportion of the women in the group were widows. It is also clear that unless the trends in male and female mortality are sharply reversed, the excess of women over men at the upper ages will increase, and our older population will contain a larger and larger proportion of widows.

The common assumption that a man marries a woman younger than himself is generally supported by the statistics in this field. In 1950, the median age at marriage for men was 22.8 years, nearly 3 years higher than the corresponding 20.1 years for women.[2] An investigation of this relationship among married couples in the Current Population Survey of April 1948 indicates that this relationship was about the same.[3]

For the 33,274,000 married couples in which both husband and wife were over 18 and under 75 (about 97 percent of all married couples), husbands were on the average 2.96 years older than their wives.

This is of course an average figure and does not imply that all husbands are older than their wives. The data from this study indicate that approximately, in terms of single years of age, slightly more than three-fourths of the husbands were older than their wives, somewhat more than one-tenth younger than their wives, and, of course, a residual group the same age as their wives. Slightly more than 10 percent of the husbands were 10 or more years older than their wives, about 25 percent 5 to 9 years older, and about 40 percent less than 5 years older.

These figures, then, indicate something as to the potential contribution of age differences between husband and wife to the greater number of widows than widowers at the upper ages. However, figures on the median age at marriage going back to 1890 suggest that the age gap between husband and wife is decreasing, and, therefore, it seems probable that this factor may be of somewhat less importance in the future.

Once a marriage has been dissolved by death or divorce, men tend to remarry at a considerably higher rate than women do. Data on this point were obtained in the Current Population Survey of April 1953.[4] The data covering persons 14 years old and over married between January 1, 1950, and April 1953 indicate a remarriage rate for men more than twice as great as the comparable rate for women; and for those 55 and over, a remarriage rate about five times as great. For widowed persons, as such, the sex difference in the remarriage rate was roughly about the same. Moreover, the data previously mentioned on age of husband by age of wife suggest that, particularly at the upper ages, the age differential was greater among remarried persons than among those married only once. For example, among remarried couples in which the husbands were 60 to 64, nearly 30 percent

---

[2] Paul C. Glick, "The Life Cycle of the Family," *Marriage and Family Living*, Vol. XVII, No. 1, February 1955, table 1.

[3] U. S. Bureau of the Census, *Current Population Reports*, Series P–20, No. 26, table 10.

[4] U. S. Bureau of the Census, *Current Population Reports*, Series P–20, No. 50, table 4, and unpublished data.

of the wives were under 50, whereas for couples married only once the figure was only about 8 percent.[5]

Life cycle of the family

Marriage customs, then, operating in the context of differences in mortality between the sexes, make the process of family formation and dissolution one which in the end leaves disproportionately large numbers of women unattached. Although statistics on marital status provide the basis for an examination of family formation and dissolution in terms of the married couple, they indicate nothing as to the role of children in this process; that is, it is possible to conceive of family formation and dissolution as a cycle which begins with marriage, passes through phases in which children are born and reared and eventually leave home, and a phase which terminates with the death of husband or wife.

Glick, in his paper, "The Life Cycle of the Family,"[6] summarized in statistical terms the characteristics of the life history of the average family. The figures appear in table 34. In 1950, as previously indicated, on the average, men married at age 22.8 and women at age 20.1, and the last child was born some 6 years later when the husband was about 29 and the wife about 26. The period of child rearing—or more specifically the period between the birth of the last child and the marriage of the last child (assuming that children marry at the same age as their parents)—was slightly more than 20 years. After the marriage of the last child both husband and wife might be expected to live 13 or 14 years longer. When the marriage was ended by the death of the wife, the husband might be expected to live about 7 years longer, whereas for widows the expected average period of survival was about 15 years.

TABLE 34.—Median Age of Husband and Wife at Selected Stages of the Life Cycle of the Family: 1950, 1940, and 1890

Stage of the life cycle of the family	Median age of husband			Median age of wife		
	1950	1940	1890	1950	1940	1890
First marriage................	22.8	24.3	26.1	20.1	21.5	22.0
Birth of last child..........	28.8	29.9	36.0	26.1	27.1	31.9
Marriage of last child.......	50.3	52.8	59.4	47.6	50.0	55.3
Death of one spouse[1]........	64.1	63.6	57.4	61.4	60.9	53.3
Death of other spouse[2]......	71.6	69.7	66.4	77.2	73.5	67.7

[1] Husband and wife survive jointly from marriage to specified age.

[2] Husband (wife) survives separately from marriage to specified age.

Source: Paul C. Glick, "The Life Cycle of the Family," *Marriage and Family Living*, Vol. XVII, No. 1, February 1955, p. 4.

In 1890, couples married later and had more children, with the result that husbands and wives were appreciably older by the time all children had left home. In addition, the higher mortality rates of that time limited the

[5] U. S. Bureau of the Census, *Current Population Reports*, Series P–20, No. 26, table 9.

[6] Paul C. Glick, *op. cit.*, pp. 3–9.

period of survival after the children had left. In fact, on the average the death of one spouse occurred before the last child had left home. Thus, in 1890 the death of husband or wife and the marriage of the last child tended, on the average, to be simultaneous events occurring in the late 50's for men and the early 50's for women. In contrast, in 1950 both husband and wife survived jointly, on the average, for a decade or more after the marriage of the last child.

The period of widowhood was about the same in both years beginning in the 50's in 1890 but early 60's in 1950. In both years this period was considerably longer for women than for men. Thus the isolation and dependency frequently associated with widowhood which constitutes a major problem among older people began at older ages in 1950 than in 1900 but continued roughly for the same period of time.

As indicated earlier, the general pattern of living arrangements may be regarded as either a type of adjustment to the situations created by the processes of family formation and dissolution, or as the end result of these processes.

Living arrangements

The celebration of "home" in picture, song, and story reflects its central place in our value system. In census terminology the home becomes a colorless "dwelling unit," the term used to designate such ordinary living quarters as houses or apartments. Not regarded as dwelling units are, at one extreme, rooms occupied by lodgers, and, at the other extreme, such congregate living quarters as large lodginghouses, hotels, dormitories, and institutions.[7]

Household living. The term "household" refers to the group of persons living in a dwelling unit; that is, the group ordinarily regarded as a family living in a home. "Quasi household," in contrast, refers to the groups found in congregate living quarters.

Most people live in households, and in this respect the older population (persons 65 and over) is not materially different from the total population. Only at the extreme ages does appreciable variation appear. In 1950 some 96 percent of the total population lived in households (table 35). This figure was slightly less than 97 percent for persons in the 5-year age groups falling between the ages of 30 and 49, dropped to about 94 percent for persons 65 and over, and was about 88 percent for persons 85 and over. Thus, although advancing years bring some decline in the proportion of persons living in households, the decline is relatively small. The great majority of the population, including the very old, are living under conditions generally regarded as "normal."

Of the persons living in households, the question may be raised as to the degree of autonomy which their position within the household permits. Presumably, household heads, or wives of household heads, are better able

---

[7] See *1950 Census of Population*, Vol. IV, *Special Reports*, Part 2, Chapter D, Marital Status, pp. 5–7, for definitions of households, families, and family status. See also Appendix A, section 1.

to make and carry out their own decisions than are persons living as other, and sometimes dependent, relatives of the head. It is true, of course, that many factors affect the status relationships among household members. Nevertheless, and particularly among older persons, an individual's position in the household has a clear relationship to his ability to make and carry out his own decisions.

In the classification by household relationship the reference point is the head of the household. The "normal" household is probably most often thought of as consisting of a man and wife and their children. However, a household may include occasionally other relatives (such as aunts, uncles, grandparents), lodgers, or servants. On the other hand, it may comprise simply a husband and wife, or widow and child, or a single individual occupying a house or apartment. In the ordinary husband and wife household, the census somewhat arbitrarily defines the husband as the head. In households in which the membership does not permit this simple Victorian solution, the person whom others in the household regard as head is so designated.

TABLE **35.**—PERCENT DISTRIBUTION BY LIVING ARRANGEMENTS, FOR SELECTED AGE GROUPS: 1950

Age	All persons	Living in household--				Living in quasi household
		Total	As head or wife in own household	As relative of head of household	Not related to head of household	
Total, all ages...........	100.0	96.2	50.3	43.3	2.7	3.8
15 years......................	100.0	98.2	0.7	96.3	1.2	1.8
30 to 34 years...............	100.0	96.8	80.2	13.8	2.8	3.2
35 to 39 years...............	100.0	96.9	83.8	10.4	2.7	3.1
40 to 44 years...............	100.0	96.8	85.5	8.6	2.7	3.2
45 to 49 years...............	100.0	96.5	86.1	7.4	3.0	3.5
50 to 54 years...............	100.0	96.2	85.6	7.4	3.2	3.8
60 to 64 years...............	100.0	95.6	81.1	10.6	3.8	4.4
65 years and over............	100.0	94.3	68.9	21.0	4.3	5.7
65 to 69 years...............	100.0	95.5	77.0	14.4	4.2	4.5
70 to 74 years...............	100.0	94.9	71.3	19.4	4.2	5.1
75 to 79 years...............	100.0	93.6	63.2	26.0	4.4	6.4
80 to 84 years...............	100.0	91.3	52.8	33.9	4.6	8.7
85 years and over...........	100.0	87.8	38.3	44.4	5.1	12.2

Source: Appendix table E-1.

Own households. If persons who are heads of households or wives of household heads (including male heads without wives present and female heads without husbands present) may be regarded as maintaining their own households, then again the population 65 and over is not strikingly different from younger age groups. In 1950 the highest proportion of heads, including wives (86 percent), was in the age group 45 to 49 (table 35).[8] For

[8] The relative distribution of the population into heads and wives, on the one hand, and other persons, on the other, has different implications at the extremes of the age distribution. At the younger ages the proportion of heads is low because the proportion of children is high at these age levels. At the upper age levels, however, the contraction in the proportion of heads represents, in the main, shifts from the status of head or wives to that of relatives of head. Thus, it is in the middle years that the proportion of heads is highest.

the age group 65 and over the proportion was about 69 percent. Within this group, however, the proportion of persons living in their own households dropped off rapidly, so that by the time the age group 85 and over is reached slightly less than 40 percent were heads or wives.

In household of relatives. The complementary group, persons living in households as relatives of the head (other than wives), showed a complementary relationship with age. The proportion of this group was lowest (7.4 percent) for the age group 45 to 54, rose to 21 percent for persons 65 and over, and at 85 and over constituted nearly 45 percent of the total. To a very considerable extent, this increase with age in the proportion of persons living as relatives of the household head represented the entrance of parents into the households of their children. Among persons 85 and over living as relatives of the head of the household, about four-fifths were parents and the remainder were other relatives (table 36). The increase in the proportion of such persons with age was much greater for parents than for other relatives, and greater for women than for men.

TABLE 36.—RELATIVES OF HOUSEHOLD HEAD, BY RELATIONSHIP TO HEAD, AS PERCENT OF ALL PERSONS, FOR SELECTED AGE GROUPS: 1950

| Age | All persons | Relatives of household head | | | | | | | | All other |
| | | Total | Child | Parent | | | Other | | | |
				Total	Male	Female	Total	Male	Female	
Total, all ages...	100.0	43.3	35.6	1.8	0.5	1.4	5.8	2.9	3.0	56.7
15 years..............	100.0	96.3	89.7	...	...	...	6.6	3.3	3.3	3.7
30 to 34 years........	100.0	13.8	9.5	...	...	...	4.4	2.5	1.8	86.2
35 to 39 years........	100.0	10.4	6.6	0.1	...	0.1	3.8	2.1	1.7	89.6
40 to 44 years........	100.0	8.6	4.8	0.3	...	0.3	3.5	1.9	1.6	91.4
50 to 54 years........	100.0	7.4	1.9	1.9	0.3	1.5	3.6	1.6	1.9	92.6
60 to 64 years........	100.0	10.6	0.5	5.9	1.3	4.6	4.1	1.6	2.6	89.4
65 years and over.....	100.0	21.0	0.1	15.4	4.4	11.0	5.5	1.8	3.7	79.0
65 to 69 years......	100.0	14.4	0.3	9.4	2.3	7.1	4.7	1.6	3.0	85.6
70 to 74 years......	100.0	19.4	...	13.9	3.8	10.1	5.5	1.8	3.7	80.6
75 to 79 years......	100.0	26.0	...	20.0	6.0	14.0	6.1	1.9	4.1	74.0
80 to 84 years......	100.0	33.9	...	27.3	8.6	18.6	6.7	2.1	4.6	66.1
85 years and over...	100.0	44.4	...	35.9	11.6	24.3	8.5	2.5	6.0	55.6

Source: Appendix table E-1.

Other persons living as relatives of the household head may be considered as living in the three-generation family setting, a situation which has been of concern in much of the literature on aging, and such persons tend to have subsidiary and dependent roles in the household.

Although the term "three-generation family" has been used primarily to apply to the situation in which older parents live in the households of their adult children, the converse situation, in which adult children live in the household of their elderly parents, is perhaps as common. Thus, in April 1955, about 57 percent of the members of families headed by persons 65 and over were themselves 65 and over—heads, wives, and a few other relatives; about 30 percent of the members, however, were other relatives of the head under 65 years of age. Although the data do not permit an explicit answer to the question as to the proportion of all older persons living in families in which the head is 65 and over and in which there are also other relatives under 65 in the family, they do suggest that this proportion may be larger than that for persons living as other relatives.[9]

Among husband-and-wife families headed by persons 65 and over, other relatives under 65 constituted a minority of the membership; but in other types of families at this age level other relatives under 65 constituted a majority of the membership. These latter types of family, in which characteristically the head is a widowed person 65 and over and the other adult members are sons and daughters, most closely represent the analogue of the three-generation setting previously considered. Here, however, the older person is the head, and the younger members of the family are other relatives.

It seems probable that, as a family head rather than as an "other relative," the older person is in a somewhat more strategic position. Parent-child relationships of the past may carry over—particularly if there has been no break in the continuity of this relationship—and the family property may be in the name of the head. On the other hand, it seems probable that other relatives in these families make the major contribution to family income. A comparative study of the role of older persons in this situation or in the situation in which they are other relatives might serve to provide a more clear-cut answer to the implied question.

The foregoing discussion of younger persons in the families headed by older persons has been confined to families, whereas the discussion elsewhere in this chapter relates to households. Aside from the minor intrusion of lodgers, the households and families under consideration are identical since a consideration of the comparative roles of head and other relative involves only households in which there are two or more related persons present and such a group is by definition a family. The households which are not families, that is, households in which the head lives alone or with nonrelatives, are considered later in this chapter.

Type of own household. As indicated in the introductory discussion of living arrangements, a fundamental dilemma is involved in the process of aging. Independence is a basic value cherished by many older people. As the family contracts, and when the death of the spouse occurs, independence is often maintained at the expense of companionship and ready availability of assistance in time of need. The result may often be a good deal of psychological and physical deprivation. Some indication of this progressive isolation with age among older persons maintaining their own households is shown by statistics on the type of household (table 37).

---

[9] U. S. Bureau of the Census, *Current Population Reports*, Series P–20, No. 67, table 7. This table indicates that of the 14 million persons living in families headed by persons 65 and over, 37.5 percent were heads; 15.4 percent, wives 65 and over; 3.7 percent, other relatives 65 and over; 13.1 percent, wives under 65; and 30.2 percent, other relatives under 65. It should be noted that the term "three-generation family" is used loosely in this discussion and refers to the situation in which elderly parents live with adult sons or daughters or adult sons and daughters live with elderly parents; the adult sons and daughters may or may not have children living in the families under consideration so that by no means all of them are literally three-generation families.

TABLE **37.**—PERSONS LIVING IN OWN HOUSEHOLD, BY LIVING ARRANGEMENTS, AS PERCENT OF
ALL PERSONS, FOR SELECTED AGE GROUPS: 1950

Age	All persons	Living in own household--				All other
		Total	In married couple	As other male head	As female head	
30 to 34 years..............	100.0	80.2	76.0	1.5	2.7	19.8
35 to 39 years..............	100.0	83.8	78.2	1.9	3.8	16.2
40 to 44 years..............	100.0	85.5	78.0	2.4	5.1	14.5
45 to 49 years..............	100.0	86.1	76.3	3.1	6.6	13.9
50 to 54 years..............	100.0	85.6	73.6	3.8	8.2	14.4
60 to 64 years..............	100.0	81.1	63.7	5.6	11.8	18.9
65 years and over..........	100.0	68.9	44.0	8.1	16.9	31.1
65 to 69 years.............	100.0	77.0	55.0	6.9	15.1	23.0
70 to 74 years.............	100.0	71.3	45.4	8.2	17.7	28.7
75 to 79 years.............	100.0	63.2	34.7	9.3	19.1	36.8
80 to 84 years.............	100.0	52.8	23.9	9.9	18.9	47.2
85 years and over.........	100.0	38.3	13.1	9.1	16.2	61.7

Source: Appendix table E-1.

Although in 1950 the percentage of persons maintaining their own households declined from about 86 percent at ages 45 to 49 to 69 percent at age
65 and over, the decline in the proportion of persons living as married
couples was greater.   At ages 35 to 39, 78 percent of the total were living
in households headed by husband and wife; by 65 and over this proportion
had dropped to 44 percent, and by 85 and over to 13 percent.   This
decline was accompanied, of course, by complementary increases with
age in the proportion of older persons living as male heads (those who
were single, widowed, or divorced), and in the proportion of women
who were heads of households and who fell into the same marital status
categories.
   It is these figures which, of course, reflect the trends in marital status
considered earlier.   The highest proportion of husband-and-wife households
in the age group 35 to 39 fell between the peak age groups in the proportion married for men and women, and the marked and progressive attrition
of the proportion in husband-and-wife households paralleled the increase
in widowhood.   The sex difference in the proportions of male and female
heads reflects the higher mortality among males and their greater tendency
to remarry.
   The progressive increase with age in the numbers of male heads without
wives, and of female heads, does not necessarily mean complete isolation
for all the individuals involved, but it does mean progressive impairment
of the household as an agency of mutual aid.   It is significant, perhaps, that
for both the male heads without wives and the female heads the proportion
reached its maximum in the age group 75 to 84 and thereafter dropped
slightly.   This change suggests that in the late 70's and early 80's the increase in disabilities which make the maintenance of an independent household impractical is sufficiently great to halt and reverse the progressive
increase in the proportion of persons living as other male heads and as female heads, which begins at a relatively early age.

Other living arrangements

The remaining older persons fall into two categories of living arrangements: (1) those, mainly lodgers and servants, who live in households in which they are not related to the head, and (2) those who live in quasi households which include institutions, hotels, and large lodginghouses. In 1950, the over-all proportion of persons in these two categories rose from about 6 percent of those aged 30 to 34 to 10 percent of those aged 65 and over, and to a little more than 17 percent of those who had reached age 85 (table 35). The increase in both categories was gradual until ages 70 to 74, when a rather sharp increase appeared in the proportion living in quasi households.

The increase in the relative importance of the quasi household arrangement is accounted for largely by older persons who took up residence in homes for the aged (table 38). It is worth noting that, even for all persons aged 85 and over, only about 2 percent were in mental hospitals, whereas 38 percent were still maintaining their own households.

TABLE 38.—PERSONS IN QUASI HOUSEHOLDS, BY TYPE OF QUASI HOUSEHOLDS, AS PERCENT OF ALL PERSONS, FOR SELECTED AGE GROUPS: 1950

Age	All persons	In quasi households						All other
		Total	Institutions				Other	
			Total	Mental hospitals	Homes for aged	Other		
35 to 44 years...........	100.0	3.1	1.0	0.5	...	0.4	2.1	96.9
45 to 54 years...........	100.0	3.6	1.2	0.7	0.1	0.3	2.4	96.4
55 to 64 years...........	100.0	4.2	1.5	0.9	0.3	0.3	2.7	95.8
65 years and over........	100.0	5.7	3.1	1.2	1.8	0.2	2.6	94.3
65 to 69 years.........	100.0	4.5	1.8	1.0	0.6	0.2	2.7	95.5
70 to 74 years.........	100.0	5.1	2.6	1.1	1.2	0.2	2.6	94.9
75 to 79 years.........	100.0	6.4	4.0	1.3	2.4	0.2	2.4	93.6
80 to 84 years.........	100.0	8.7	6.2	1.5	4.5	0.3	2.5	91.3
85 years and over......	100.0	12.2	9.4	1.7	7.3	0.4	2.7	87.8

Source: Appendix table E–2.

The situation of this residual group with respect to both independence and isolation is varied. If the absence of relatives in their immediate living quarters is taken as evidence of isolation, then, obviously, in this entire group isolation is high and, generally speaking, genuine, for lodgers and for persons living in hotels, clubs, and the like. For people in institutions, professional care and visitors appear to take the place of immediate family members. Professional care, however, is certainly variable in both quantity and quality.

Living arrangements without relatives. Although only fragmentary data are available on the actual number of older persons living by themselves (see Chapter 7), data based on the 3⅓-percent sample on detailed marital and family status make it possible to examine various types of living arrangements with respect to the presence or absence of relatives. These data are presented in table 39.

TABLE **39.**—PERCENT DISTRIBUTION OF ALL PERSONS, BY LIVING ARRANGEMENTS AND PRESENCE
OR ABSENCE OF RELATIVES, FOR SELECTED AGE GROUPS: 1950

Living arrangements and presence or absence of relatives	35 to 44 years	45 to 54 years	55 to 64 years	65 years old and over		
				Total	65 to 74 years	75 years and over
All persons......................	100.0	100.0	100.0	100.0	100.0	100.0
Relatives present..............	92.9	89.7	85.2	76.5	78.4	72.2
No relatives present...........	7.1	10.3	14.8	23.5	21.6	27.8
In married couples.................	78.2	75.1	67.3	43.9	51.1	28.3
As other male head................	2.1	3.4	5.0	8.1	7.5	9.4
Relatives present..............	1.0	1.6	2.1	3.3	3.0	4.0
No relatives present...........	1.1	1.8	2.9	4.8	4.5	5.5
As female head......................	4.4	7.3	10.7	16.9	16.1	18.6
Relatives present..............	2.9	4.4	5.6	7.3	7.0	7.9
No relatives present...........	1.5	2.9	5.1	9.6	9.1	10.7
As relative of head................	9.5	7.4	9.2	21.1	16.4	31.3
Other living arrangements..........	5.9	6.7	7.8	10.0	8.9	12.4
Relatives present..............	1.3	1.2	1.1	0.9	0.9	0.8
No relatives present...........	4.6	5.6	6.7	9.1	7.9	11.6

Source: Appendix table E-3.

These figures indicate quite clearly the increasing isolation with age, if isolation is defined purely in terms of the presence or absence of relatives. For persons aged 35 to 44 in 1950, about 7 percent were not living with relatives. In the age group 65 to 74 this figure had increased to 22 percent, and for persons 75 and over, 28 percent. It seems reasonable to conclude, then, that from one-fifth to one-fourth of the older population was in a type of living arrangement in which no relative was present. Among persons 75 and over, something less than half of the men living as other male heads, and of the women living as female heads, were living with relatives. At this age level, among persons in living arrangements which by definition permit the presence or absence of relatives, few of those who were neither household heads nor relatives of household heads were living with relatives.

In short, as need for the care normally provided by relatives in the household increased, larger and larger proportions of older persons were living in circumstances in which such care was not available.

Living arrangements of widows. The clearest and most obvious situation in which the individual is faced with the loss of related household members is that of widowhood. This situation, of course, does not necessarily imply immediate isolation, but it does entail a sharp change in mode of living and, particularly at the upper ages, greatly increases the probability of isolation. It is a situation, moreover, which in some respects is typical of the older population. In 1950 the 3.5 million widows constituted more than one-fourth of the population 65 and over; among the other sex-marital status groups in this age group this number was exceeded only by the number of married men living with their wives. In the population 75 and over, widows constituted the largest sex-marital status group, and at 85 and over, nearly one-half of the entire population.

In 1950, about 70 percent of the widows aged 35 to 44 were heads of their own households; 20 percent were in the households of relatives; and the remaining 10 percent were in some other type of living arrangement (table 40). For the older widows the distribution by type of living arrangement was quite different. Among those 75 and over, only about 40 percent were living as heads of their own households, and nearly one-half lived in the homes of relatives.

TABLE **40.**—PERCENT DISTRIBUTION OF WIDOWS BY LIVING ARRANGEMENTS AND PRESENCE OR ABSENCE OF RELATIVES, FOR SELECTED AGE GROUPS: 1950

Living arrangements and presence or absence of relatives	35 to 44 years	45 to 54 years	55 to 64 years	65 years old and over		
				Total	65 to 74 years	75 years and over
All widows......................	100.0	100.0	100.0	100.0	100.0	100.0
Relatives present..............	76.9	68.5	63.0	62.5	60.4	65.3
No relatives present...........	23.1	31.5	37.0	37.5	39.6	34.7
As head.........................	69.5	69.9	62.5	49.5	55.3	41.5
Relatives present..............	54.6	47.2	34.6	21.8	24.6	18.1
No relatives present...........	14.9	22.7	28.0	27.6	30.7	23.5
As relative of head.............	20.2	20.0	27.5	40.0	35.1	46.6
Child...........................	10.4	3.8	1.2	0.1	0.2	...
Parent..........................	2.8	10.5	20.9	33.9	29.1	40.3
Other relative..................	7.0	5.7	5.3	6.1	5.9	6.3
Other living arrangements.........	10.3	10.1	9.9	10.5	9.5	11.8
Relatives present..............	2.0	1.3	0.8	0.6	0.6	0.6
No relatives present...........	8.3	8.8	9.1	9.9	8.9	11.2

Source: Appendix table E–4.

It is particularly interesting to note that, although widows have a marked tendency to abandon the status of household head and to move in with others, a good one-third of those 75 and over were living in situations with no relatives present, and two-thirds of this fraction—constituting one-fourth of the total number of widows aged 75 and over—were living as heads of households.

Increasing age also changes the character of the household relationship of widows living with relatives. One-half of the widows in the 35-to-44-year age group were living with their parents. Widows in the later years, however, being without parents, tend to join the households of their children when they live with other relatives. Thus more than four-fifths of the widows 75 and over living as relatives of the head were parents of the head.

Widows who are neither heads of households nor living as relatives of heads of households remain a relatively constant proportion of the total as age increases and, for the most part, live as lodgers or in congregate living quarters such as hotels, lodginghouses, and the like.

In general, then, as age increases, the proportion of widows maintaining their own households decreases, and, in this contracting group, the proportion with relatives in their households declines.

CHAPTER 7

HOUSING

In the preceding chapter living arrangements have been considered from an essentially sociological point of view; that is, the various kinds of groups in which people live have been examined, and the changes in these relationships with advancing years have been traced. In the present chapter we are concerned with the more tangible physical aspect of living arrangements. If housing is examined in its relation to the physical needs of older people, it is possible to develop tangible answers to the question, "What constitutes 'adequate' or 'good' housing for older persons?" This has been done. Whether or not "good" housing in this sense is attractive or even acceptable to older persons would seem to remain an open question. To be sure, a small apartment with all modern conveniences may be attractive; however, the cold, impersonal efficiency—and occasional recalcitrance —of air conditioners, dishwashers, and garbage disposal units may not compensate for the satisfactions derived from the assured and habitual mastery of a crotchety door latch or a familiar oven in a state of genteel decay. This statement perhaps oversimplifies the issue. Certainly some of the statistics on changes in housing characteristics with age reveal situations which may cause real physical and psychological deprivation. It is perhaps worth noting, in this context, that those who study the housing problems of older persons are considerably more sophisticated in this field than are the older people themselves.

Statistics from the 1950 Census of Housing which relate the age of persons to the conditions under which they are housed are limited, for the most part, to those derived from tabulations in which the housing characteristics of nonfarm dwelling units were classified by the age of the head of the household occupying these units.[1] It is clear, then, that the statistics relating housing characteristics to age refer explicitly only to heads of households in the nonfarm population. Actually the housing statistics for a given age group, such as 65 and over, may cover a larger number of persons than the number of heads since there may be other members of the household—wives, brothers, sisters, and the like—who fall into the same age group as the head. In this context it appears that the 1950 housing statistics considered in this chapter covered approximately 70 percent of

---

[1] See Appendix F, section 1, for sources of 1950 housing data available for households by age of head.

all persons 65 and over in the nonfarm population and 60 percent of this age group in the population of the country as a whole.[2]

In the housing statistics, dwelling units are classified by the living arrangements of the households occupying the unit—in much the same way as persons living in their own households were classified in the consideration of living arrangements in Chapter 6.   There are three major categories: male head with wife present, or married couples maintaining their own households; other male heads, or households headed by men with no wife present in the household; and female heads, or, as the designation implies, households headed by women with no husband present in the household. This classification differs from the previous one in that, to assure greater homogenity in the "normal" or husband-and-wife household category, households of this type which include nonrelatives (lodgers, servants, etc.) are excluded and combined with the "Other male head" category—an already rather heterogeneous group.   Husband-and-wife households which include nonrelatives are estimated to constitute about 30 percent of the "Other male head" households as they appear in the housing statistics.[3]

Changes in housing with age

If it can be assumed that home ownership, particularly of a detached single-family dwelling unit, is a major value in our society, and that over the years, as families became smaller and costs of construction increased, the size of houses has declined—then, given the family cycle described earlier, it should be possible to infer some of the changes in housing characteristics which occur as age increases.   In these terms, *increases* with age might be expected in the proportion of home owners, in the proportion occupying detached single-family dwelling units, and in the size of dwelling unit—and *decreases* might be expected in the number of persons in the dwelling unit.   The degree to which these expectations conform to the facts is indicated in table 41.

Home ownership.   With respect to home ownership the figures amply confirm the expectation.   In 1950 there were substantial increases in the proportion of home owners as the age of household heads increased, and this was true not only among husband-and-wife households but also among other types of households.   The increase among households headed by women was particularly striking—more than doubling between the age groups 14 to 44, and 65 and over.   These figures, then, appear to reflect the importance of home ownership in our national ethos, and the longer period of time in which older persons have been exposed to the possibility

[2] Appendix F, section 2.

[3] Quite apart from the difference in definition under consideration, the statistics on type of household from the housing tabulations are not in exact agreement with those from the population tabulation. If the population figures are adjusted to the housing level, it appears that of the 3.7 million households classified in the "Other male head" category 1.1 million, or approximately 30 percent, are husband-and-wife households in which nonrelatives are present.   For households of this type headed by persons aged 65 and over, the corresponding percentage is about 17.

of home ownership. This pattern is particularly noteworthy in view of the sharp increase in home ownership between 1940 and 1950, which might be expected to be concentrated in the younger age groups.

TABLE 41.—TENURE, NUMBER OF PERSONS, NUMBER OF ROOMS, AND TYPE OF STRUCTURE OF NONFARM DWELLING UNITS, BY AGE AND TYPE OF HOUSEHOLD HEAD: 1950

Age and type of household	Percent of all dwelling units--					
	Owner occupied	In 1-dwelling-unit detached structures		With 5 rooms or more	Occupied by 1 person	Occupied by 5 persons or more
		Owner occupied	Renter occupied			
ALL HOUSEHOLD HEADS						
Total, 14 years and over.......	52.9	81.3	31.3	52.0	9.9	19.2
14 to 44 years.....................	43.7	84.9	31.9	43.8	4.4	23.6
45 to 64 years.....................	60.4	79.7	29.3	60.8	10.9	18.0
65 years and over..................	64.7	77.1	33.4	57.3	25.3	8.1
MALE HEAD, WIFE PRESENT[1]						
Total, 14 years and over.......	54.8	83.2	33.2	54.1	...	21.5
14 to 44 years.....................	46.0	85.8	33.5	45.4	...	24.4
45 to 64 years.....................	64.6	81.4	31.9	65.6	...	20.1
65 years and over..................	70.5	79.7	36.4	63.8	...	9.4
OTHER MALE HEAD[2]						
Total, 14 years and over.......	49.8	77.9	32.5	48.9	34.2	18.2
14 to 44 years.....................	38.6	78.9	30.6	43.4	26.9	25.6
45 to 64 years.....................	52.5	77.5	30.7	52.0	33.8	17.6
65 years and over..................	60.0	77.5	39.4	51.2	44.2	9.5
FEMALE HEAD						
Total, 14 years and over.......	46.7	73.6	23.5	44.4	38.3	10.0
14 to 44 years.....................	26.0	77.5	22.5	28.8	27.9	14.2
45 to 64 years.....................	50.0	73.0	21.8	48.5	36.6	10.8
65 years and over..................	59.4	72.9	27.5	51.8	48.9	5.5

[1] Excludes households with nonrelatives present.
[2] Includes those households with male head, wife present, in which nonrelatives (i.e., lodgers, servants, etc.) are present. It is estimated that such households constitute approximately 30 percent of the "Other male head" category.

Source: Appendix tables F-1 to F-4.

Detached single-family dwelling unit. In contrast, however, to the expectation with respect to home ownership, the figures do not confirm the expectation with respect to type of unit occupied. In fact, the proportion of renters living in detached single-family dwelling units is greater for the age group 65 and over than for the group 14 to 44, and this is true for each type of household. On the other hand, for all owner-occupied dwelling units the proportion of detached single-family units tends to decrease with the age of the household head. These relationships probably reflect the unique character of the housing market during the 1940's rather than any enduring relationship between type of housing and age.

In the 1940's, and particularly in the postwar years, most families wishing to live in detached single-family dwelling units had to buy, regardless of their feeling with respect to home ownership; that is to say, generally speaking, single-family dwelling units were built for sale and not for rental, which meant that younger persons who established their household in detached single-family dwelling units became, by and large, home owners. This trend is, of course, dramatized in the "mass-produced" suburbs of our larger metropolitan areas.   In contrast, many older persons who were already renting detached single-family dwelling units at the beginning of the decade were in a strategic position to maintain the *status quo*. This hypothesis would seem to be supported by the experience of many who attempted to find housing during the 1940's. Whether or not this interpretation of the figures is valid, it still leaves open the question as to whether ownership of a detached single-family dwelling unit is a major goal in our culture.

Number of rooms.   The expectation that the number of rooms in a dwelling unit increases with the age of the household head rests on the assumption: that older people are disinclined to move, and that the older people of today established their households at a time when dwelling units were more generously supplied with rooms.

The figures confirm this expectation to the extent that, for all types of households, the proportion of dwelling units with five or more rooms is higher for household heads 65 and over than it is for those 14 to 44, and higher than the proportion for heads of all ages. This difference is more than a mere reflection of the higher incidence of home ownership among older persons, since—although the level of this percentage is lower for renter-occupied than for owner-occupied units—the same patterns appear among both types of units.[4]

If, however, the full age distribution of household heads is considered, there appears to be (on the basis of the percentages for the age group 45 to 64) a leveling off at ages 65 and over; for husband-and-wife households and other male head households, there is a drop of a few percentage points at ages 65 and over; but for households headed by women, a slight gain. This leveling off may reflect some tendency on the part of older people to readjust their living arrangements to fit their needs. The slight increase in the cases of households headed by women may reflect the heavy concentration of older widows who have inherited the family dwelling unit.   The differences are small, however, and the general pattern is not inconsistent with the hypothesis that, generally speaking, most older people continue living in the homes they have established in earlier phases of the family cycle.

Number of persons.   The fact that children leave home as they grow up is sufficiently commonplace to make the smaller number of persons in households headed by persons 65 and over a foregone conclusion. This conclusion is supported by the 1950 figures, either in terms of the proportion of single-person households, which increases with age, or in the proportion of households with five or more persons, which decreases with age. These gradients are characteristic of both owner-occupied and renter-

---

[4] Appendix table F–3.

occupied units and of each type of household—with the exception, of course, of husband-and-wife households, which by definition contain at least two persons (table 41).

In connection with the increase with age of one-person households, it is perhaps of interest to relate these figures to those for persons living in households with no relatives present (considered in the chapter on living arrangements). In 1950, nearly 1,000,000 men 65 and over were living as heads of households without wives. Of these men, 400,000 had one or more relatives living in the household, and another 100,000 had one or more nonrelated persons, but no relatives, living with them. The remaining 500,000 (one-half of these other male household heads) were living entirely alone. Among the 2,100,000 women 65 and over living as heads of households, about 900,000 were living with relatives, about 200,000 were living with persons who were not related to them, and 1,000,000 (nearly 50 percent) were living alone.[5]

Changes in quality of housing with age

If it is true that older persons tend to stay on in the homes which they established in earlier years, it might be expected that their housing would be older than the average and, by virtue of its age, of somewhat poorer quality. Also, since income declines with age,[6] older persons are at a disadvantage in buying the best quality of housing, in maintaining or improving the quality of homes which go back to an earlier and more prosperous period, and certainly in renting living quarters.

The data on quality of housing are derived from questions relating to plumbing facilities (the presence or absence of private toilet and bath, running water, and hot running water), and condition of the dwelling unit, that is, whether or not the unit is dilapidated. A dilapidated dwelling unit is one which, because of serious structural deficiencies resulting from neglect or from inadequate original construction, fails to provide adequate shelter from the elements or endangers the safety of the occupant.[7]

Substandard housing. The Public Housing Administration defines "standard" housing as housing which is not dilapidated, and in which dwelling units are characterized by the presence of private toilet and bath and hot running water. All other housing is by this definition substandard. Data on the proportion of "standard" and dilapidated dwelling units are presented in table 42, by age and sex of household head and by type of household.

In 1950, dwelling units occupied by husband-and-wife households in which the head was 65 or over showed a slightly lower proportion of units

[5] The figures on other male heads and females by presence or absence of relatives in the household appear in appendix table E–3. The corresponding figures on the numbers living alone are those for one-person households in the nonfarm population adjusted to the national level (see appendix table F–4).
[6] See Chapter 8.
[7] *1950 Census of Housing*, Vol. II, *Nonfarm Housing Characteristics*, Part 1, pp. XIV and XV.

of standard quality, and a slightly higher proportion of dilapidated units, than among the dwelling units of household heads of all ages. The highest proportions of standard housing and the lowest proportions of dilapidation were found, as might be expected, among persons in the middle years— that is, among household heads 45 to 64—and this pattern was characteristic of both owned and rented units.[8]

TABLE **42.**—CONDITION, VALUE, RENTAL, AND VALUE- AND RENT-INCOME RATIOS OF NONFARM DWELLING UNITS, BY AGE AND TYPE OF HOUSEHOLD HEAD: 1950

| Age and type of household | Percent of all dwelling units-- | | Median value of owner-occupied units | Median rental of renter-occupied units | Percent of owner-occupied units with value-income ratio of 3.0 or more | Percent of renter-occupied units with rent-income ratio of 0.3 or more |
	Of "standard"[1] quality	In dilapidated condition				
ALL HOUSEHOLD HEADS						
Total, 14 years and over...	70.7	7.9	$7,338	$42.41	27.4	20.2
14 to 44 years................	69.9	7.9	7,445	42.60	18.6	15.7
45 to 64 years................	74.3	7.2	7,772	43.85	26.9	20.3
65 years and over............	64.5	9.7	6,325	36.24	53.0	49.2
MALE HEAD, WIFE PRESENT[2]						
Total, 14 years and over...	73.6	6.5	$7,588	$44.04	22.7	13.6
14 to 44 years................	71.5	6.9	7,582	43.37	17.1	11.9
45 to 64 years................	77.9	5.6	8,074	46.34	22.7	13.2
65 years and over............	70.2	7.0	6,461	41.21	48.0	37.9
OTHER MALE HEAD[3]						
Total, 14 years and over...	60.7	13.8	$6,723	$36.78	34.5	27.0
14 to 44 years................	63.5	11.7	6,719	40.26	24.2	22.9
45 to 64 years................	62.5	13.3	7,164	36.70	29.3	22.8
65 years and over............	54.7	17.0	6,129	28.25	50.7	45.7
FEMALE HEAD						
Total, 14 years and over...	63.9	10.7	$6,423	$38.16	54.6	44.5
14 to 44 years................	59.7	14.0	6,103	38.18	44.6	40.2
45 to 64 years................	68.0	9.5	6,780	40.15	50.2	38.7
65 years and over............	62.1	9.6	6,167	34.30	64.2	63.7

[1] As defined by the Public Housing Administration, units not dilapidated and with private toilet and bath and with hot running water.

[2] Excludes households with nonrelatives present.

[3] Includes those households with male head, wife present, in which nonrelatives (i.e., lodgers, servants, etc.) are present. It is estimated that such households constitute approximately 30 percent of the "Other male head" category.

Source: Appendix tables F-5 to F-9.

Among the households of other male heads there appeared to be a clear age gradient, with the percentage of standard housing declining and the percentage of dilapidated housing increasing. The pattern again was characteristic of both owners and renters.[9]

Among households headed by women, the pattern is similar to that of the husband-and-wife household. The highest proportions of standard units and the lowest proportions of dilapidated units appeared in the middle years. Again this pattern appeared for both owners and renters, and the

---

[8] Appendix table F-5.
[9] Appendix table F-5.

improvement of the oldest group over the youngest may result partly from the sharp increase with age in home ownership in households headed by women.

The general pattern of variations in quality of housing with age suggests an economic interpretation. Among husband-and-wife households the period of best housing is also the period of peak income and, since in one sense housing is a commodity, such a relationship is to be expected. Among households headed by women the variation is open to the same interpretation. Although households headed by men without wives do not conform to the pattern of the two other types of households, the distribution by age does conform to the income distribution for this group.[10]

In terms of sharp contrasts, the differences in quality of housing among the three types of households headed by persons 65 and over are of more interest than are the differences by age of household head. Whereas about 30 percent of the dwelling units of husband-and-wife households were substandard, 38 percent of the households headed by women and about 45 percent of the "Other male head" household were substandard. The proportion of dilapidated dwelling units—about 7 percent for husband-and-wife households and 10 percent for households headed by women—was 17 percent for the "Other male" households. These figures again emphasize the inferior position of incomplete households headed by older persons.

Value and rental. Data on value and rental indicate the quality of housing only on the assumption that quality is correlated with cost. The patterns by type of household and age of head closely parallel those for the indexes of quality (table 42). Among husband-and-wife households and households headed by women, the highest median values and median rentals were found in the middle years, flanked on either side by somewhat lower values. Among incomplete households headed by men, this same pattern appeared in the value of dwelling unit, but the median rental declined steadily with age.

Value-and-rental-income ratios. Value-income and rental-income ratios indicate something as to the proportion of income expended on shelter—in the case of value, inferentially, and in the case of rental, directly. Among owner-occupied dwelling units, the proportion with value-income ratios of 3.0 or more increases considerably with age for each type of household, with the greatest increases between the age groups 45 to 64 and the group 65 and over (table 42). In most general terms, this trend seems to reflect the relationship between values geared to the peak income of the middle years and the reduced income of the later years. The financial position of the older person in this situation seems to depend on whether he owns the house outright or is still making payments on the mortgage. If he owns the house he may be reasonably well off; if he is still making mortgage payments he may be in acute financial straits. Without more in-

---

[10] See Chapter 8.

formation on this issue, it is hard to draw a definite conclusion as to the implication of high-value ratios for the welfare of older persons.

In the case of rent and income the implications are much more explicit. Here rental is, in effect, expressed as a percentage of income, and thus a high percentage implies an income consumed largely by paying rent. As with the income-value ratio, this rental-income ratio increases sharply from the middle to the later years—reflecting, again, contracting income and a constant or increasing rental level. It is significant here that, although approximately 38 percent of the husband-and-wife households in which the head was 65 and over had rental income ratios of .3 or more, the corresponding percentage was nearly twice as great (64 percent) for households headed by women.

Housing of other segments of the population

As stated in the introduction to this chapter, only limited data are available on the housing of older persons in the farm population. Such data as there are indicate trends with age similar to those in the nonfarm population. Specifically, the proportion of homes owned increases with age of head, as do the number of rooms. Although additional data by age of head are not available, it seems reasonable to infer that differences between farm and nonfarm housing, at the upper ages, reflect the differences observed in the population of all ages; that is, less adequate housing, lower values, and lower rentals. These indexes however, do not necessarily have the same implications for the farm population as for the nonfarm population. Although there has been convergence in the characteristics of these two populations, the way of life of the farm population is still reasonably distinct and not altogether amenable to evaluation by urban standards.

As previously indicated, older persons who are relatives of household heads under 65 live under the housing conditions of the latters' dwelling unit. Although in the absence of pertinent data we have no basis for firm conclusions, it can be inferred that high income levels make possible a variety of living arrangements for older people, whereas, at the lower levels, food and shelter are about all the younger generation has to offer its elders. It may follow, then, that in this situation the quality of the housing of older persons is somewhat below average.

In the absence of other data, statistics on incomplete households provide a clue to the housing conditions of older persons living as lodgers, and in quasi households other than institutions. As previously indicated, possibly one-third of the "Other male head" category actually represents husband-and-wife households in which there are nonrelatives. Assuming that characteristics of the total category are moderately descriptive of this special group, it seems reasonable to infer that the quality of the housing afforded to lodgers is somewhat below that of, say, husband-and-wife households. This tentative conclusion is supported by commonsense observation of households offering rooms for rent. If the majority of older persons in quasi households (other than institutions) are living in large lodginghouses (those with five or more lodgers), then it seems probable that their housing situation is even less desirable than that of lodgers in private households. Living conditions for older persons in institutions pose, of course, a special problem.

CHAPTER 8

AGE AND INCOME

Since ours is a money economy, income is generally regarded as the best single index to welfare. And in many senses it is. Food, shelter, clothing, medical care—in many contexts, self-respect—may all be had for a price. So long as we are concerned with relatively concrete and objective needs, income provides a measure of the degree to which they can be met. But in the field of more subtle values, social and psychological—which might be crudely subsumed under the heading of "happiness"—the relationship is by no means so clear, although, as suggested, adequate income may be helpful. However, because of the complex interplay of the potentialities of additional increments of income with the infinite variation in aspiration level, most inferences as to psychological gains from adequate income are of somewhat dubious validity. An adequate income, in short, may insure an elderly couple good housing and good food, but it does not necessarily insure happiness.

An examination of the data relating income to aging brings out two major problems: First, there are data which make possible the delineation of a sort of income cycle (analagous to the family cycle described in Chapter 6) indicating the typical pattern of shifting income level with age; second, there are data which provide some clue as to how adequately the income of older persons meets their needs.

The pattern of income change with age is perhaps most clearly revealed in figures on individual income, either in terms of measures of central tendency such as median income, or in terms of the variations with age of the proportion of persons receiving more or less than a given amount of income. The determination of how adequately the income of older persons meets their needs presents a more difficult problem. Although it is easy enough to say that higher incomes meet concrete tangible needs more adequately than do lower incomes, it is quite another matter to specify the exact point at which the income of an elderly couple becomes adequate or inadequate. What is really needed is a series of "adequate" budgets for households of various types and circumstances, and figures on the aggregate income of the members of these households. This ideal situation is approximated only rarely among the data that are currently available.

Individual income and age

The age-income cycle. The individual income cycle clearly follows the parabolic curve that describes a number of (though by no means all) age-associated phenomena. Figures from the 1950 Census[1] show that, for males with income, the median rises from $435 at ages 14 to 19 to $3,073 at ages 35 to 44, and thereafter drops to $1,128 at ages 65 and above (table 43). Thus, although the median income of older men is higher than that of teen-agers, it is something less than half that for men of all ages ($2,434), and equal to only slightly more than one-third of the median income at the age level of peak earnings.

TABLE 43.—MEDIAN INCOME OF PERSONS WITH INCOME IN 1949 AND PERCENT WITH INCOME OF LESS THAN $2,000, BY AGE AND SEX

Age	Male		Female	
	Median income	Percent less than $2,000	Median income	Percent less than $2,000
Total, 14 years and over........	$2,434	39.8	$1,029	74.7
14 to 19 years......................	435	93.6	419	95.3
20 to 24 years......................	1,669	59.4	1,276	75.8
25 to 34 years......................	2,737	29.4	1,309	69.1
35 to 44 years......................	3,073	24.7	1,358	67.2
45 to 54 years......................	2,979	28.3	1,316	67.5
55 to 64 years......................	2,551	37.0	1,006	75.0
65 years and over..................	1,128	68.0	602	89.1

Source: Appendix table G-1.

Figures on the proportion of men among income recipients with incomes of under $2,000 indicate that about 95 percent of the teen-age group received incomes of less than $2,000. At ages 35 to 44 this figure had dropped to about 25 percent, but by the time the age group 65 and over is reached, the figure had increased to nearly 70 percent. Although data by separate age periods above 65 are not available, figures from special tabulations of income by family and household status suggest that, among men 65 and over, income continues to decline with age. For example, among male heads of primary families aged 65 to 74, the proportion with income of less than $2,000 was approximately 60 percent, but among those 75 and over, this proportion was about 80 percent.[2]

Among women receiving income in 1950, the distribution of income by age was not essentially different from that for men—with the exception, of course, that the level of median income was considerably lower and the proportion with low income higher. Also, among women, there was less difference in the level of income between the very young and the very old.

For both men and women who received income, the general trend appears to be a progressive decline in income with advancing years. Although this pattern is certainly typical, there is evidence that it is not universal; that is, a small proportion of older men and women succeed in maintaining a high income level even with advancing years. The percentage distribution by income among the various age levels indicates that among the age groups under 45 there is a steady decline in the proportion

[1] See Appendix G-1, section 1, for a discussion of census income statistics.
[2] 1950 Census of Population, Vol. III, Special Reports, Part 2, Chapter D, Marital Status, table 6.

of persons in income classes above the modal class.   Among males 25 to 34, for example, 53 percent had incomes falling in the range $2,000 to $3,999; and in each subsequent income class this percentage declined, so that by the time the $10,000 level was reached, only 0.8 percent of the age group fell in this category.   In the three upper age groups, however—45 to 54, 55 to 64, and 65 and over—the proportion of each of these age groups with incomes of $10,000 or more was slightly greater than the proportion receiving $7,000 to $9,999.[3]

Since in the three upper age groups the proportion with incomes of $10,000 or more declined with age—but less rapidly than the proportions in the income level $7,000 to $9,999—it would appear that the attrition with age from the higher income levels was to some extent inversely related to size of income.   Thus, at age 65 and over there appeared a tendency toward concentrations of persons at the extremes of the income distribution.   In the high income extreme, it should be emphasized that the high concentration is relative only to other age groups, and that the proportion of men with incomes of $10,000 is small at any age level.

This tendency toward an increasing spread with age to the extremes of the income distribution is apparent in the data for the civilian noninstitutional population from the Current Population Survey of April 1954, presented in table 44.   Here, with data available for the upper income brackets, it appears that, at ages 45 to 54, the proportions of men in the highest income brackets reach a peak, which persists relatively unchanged in the succeeding age groups; whereas, in the income classes below $15,000, there is a progressive decline with age in all classes except the lowest, which shows a compensating increase.

TABLE 44.—PERCENT DISTRIBUTION BY INCOME CLASS, FOR PERSONS WITH INCOME IN 1953, BY AGE AND SEX

Income and sex	Total, 14 years and over	14 to 24 years	25 to 34 years	35 to 44 years	45 to 54 years	55 to 64 years	65 years and over
Male, total..............	100.0	100.0	100.0	100.0	100.0	100.0	100.0
Under $2,000.................	30.5	68.1	15.2	13.5	18.5	27.1	68.1
$2,000 to $4,999.............	49.1	29.3	62.5	55.4	52.7	54.1	24.3
$5,000 to $9,999.............	18.0	2.5	21.1	27.2	25.2	15.8	5.4
$10,000 to $14,999...........	1.5	...	0.8	2.7	2.5	1.7	1.0
$15,000 to $24,999...........	0.5	0.1	0.3	0.8	0.7	0.8	0.6
$25,000 and over.............	0.3	...	0.1	0.2	0.5	0.5	0.5
Female, total............	100.0	100.0	100.0	100.0	100.0	100.0	100.0
Under $2,000.................	67.6	75.5	58.2	59.5	55.9	69.8	90.1
$2,000 to $4,999.............	30.3	24.5	39.7	38.4	41.4	26.5	8.1
$5,000 to $9,999.............	1.5	...	2.0	1.7	2.2	3.1	1.2
$10,000 to $14,999...........	0.2	...	...	0.2	0.2	0.4	0.3
$15,000 to $24,999...........	0.1	...	0.1	0.1	0.2	...	...
$25,000 and over.............	0.1	...	0.1	...	0.2	...	0.3

Source: U. S. Bureau of the Census, *Current Population Reports*, Series P-60, No. 16, table 3.

---

[3] Appendix table G-2.

These figures suggest that although for most persons the normal trend is one of declining income with advancing years, some few individuals—by virtue of judicious investment, outstanding capacity, or inheritance—succeed in maintaining a high level of income well into advanced years. Again the small size of this group should be emphasized. In 1953, only 0.5 percent of the men 65 and over with income had incomes of $25,000 or more; in terms of actual numbers—20,000 to 30,000 persons in a population of nearly 6 million.

Among women, with the restrictions previously noted, the same pattern is evident. In 1953 the median income of women 65 and over with income was $659, but 0.3 percent, or a possible 12,000, had incomes of $25,000 or more. It is perhaps in this group that the wealthy widows, so frequently encountered in folklore but so rare in the statistics on income, are to be found.

So far, the relationship of income to age has been considered only among persons with income. Actually, in terms of individual income, an appreciable proportion of men 14 and over (12.5 percent) and a majority of women of the same age group (57.1 percent) reported no income in 1949 (table 45). This situation seems to follow, in a general way, from social arrangements which do not require that housewives produce money income, and which take for granted that parents may support adolescent children who are completing their education. There are no grounds, then, for assuming that lack of individual income *per se* necessarily implies a precarious economic situation.

Income and employment. In most general terms, the variation with age in the proportion of persons without income parallels the age variations in labor force participation rates. Among men, both the percentage without income and the percentage not in the labor force were high at the youngest ages, declined to a low point for the age group 35 to 44, and thereafter increased (table 45). Among women, although the pattern is more irregular, there was the same concomitant change, with the possible exception of the age group 65 and over.

TABLE 45.—PERSONS WITH NO INCOME IN 1949 AND PERSONS NOT IN LABOR FORCE IN 1950, AS PERCENT OF TOTAL POPULATION, BY AGE AND SEX

Age	Male		Female	
	Percent with no income	Percent not in labor force	Percent with no income	Percent not in labor force
Total, 14 years and over.......	12.5	21.0	57.1	71.0
14 to 19 years....................	55.4	60.5	68.4	77.4
20 to 24 years....................	10.7	18.1	44.6	57.1
25 to 34 years....................	3.9	7.9	58.7	68.2
35 to 44 years....................	3.4	5.4	57.3	65.0
45 to 54 years....................	4.7	8.0	56.9	67.1
55 to 64 years....................	7.6	16.6	60.3	76.5
65 years and over................	18.8	58.6	51.4	92.2

Source: Appendix tables C-1, C-8, and G-1.

This relationship follows from the fact that, in the aggregate, the major source of income is from employment, and thus persons without income might normally be expected to be outside the labor force. The fact that the percentages of persons not in the labor force are higher, age for age, than the percentages without income suggests that some income is derived from other sources. This situation is particularly evident at ages 65 and over; among men of this age group the increase in the proportion with no income fails to keep pace with the increase in the proportion not in the labor force; among women, the former percentage decreases, whereas the latter percentage rises sharply. These variations from the standard pattern obviously reflect the development of income maintenance systems for the retired in the form of pensions, old-age benefits, old-age assistance, and the like.

The positive relationship between income and employment is apparent not only in the case of persons with no income but it is also evident among persons with income. Data from the Current Population Survey for the civilian noninstitutional population indicate that for all men aged 14 and over the median income in 1951 for those in the labor force in April 1952 was $3,155, as compared with $718 for those not in the labor force (table 46). At ages 65 and over the corresponding figures were $2,121 and $774. The classification by labor force status is for the survey week, whereas the figures on income cover income for the calendar year 1951. It is quite possible that persons classified as not in the labor force in 1952 actually were employed in some part of 1951. In spite of this limitation, however, the contrast between the median income of persons in and out of the labor force remains sharp.

TABLE 46.—MEDIAN INCOME OF PERSONS WITH INCOME IN 1951, BY LABOR FORCE STATUS, AGE, AND SEX

Age	Male		Female	
	Labor force	Not in labor force	Labor force	Not in labor force
Total, 14 years and over.....	$3,155	$718	$1,695	$502
14 to 24 years..................	1,731	344	1,357	415
25 to 64 years..................	3,361	1,082	1,830	578
65 years and over...............	2,121	774	850	506

Source: U. S. Bureau of the Census, *Current Population Reports*, Series P-60, No. 11, table 4.

It appears, then, that a large part of the decline in individual income, and the decrease in the proportion of persons without income—which occur with advancing years—is traceable to the decline in labor force participation.[4] This is perhaps an obvious conclusion and validates the traditional belief that industry is rewarding. Although the data do reflect the effects of social measures to maintain the income of older persons, the size of such income shows clearly that it has not been raised to the level which

[4] See Melvin W. Reder, "Age and Income," *American Economic Review*, Vol. XLIV, No. 2, May 1950, pp. 661–670.

might be expected from continued employment. In short, in the aggregate at least, the financial rewards of retirement are extremely meager.

Adequacy of the income of older persons

Any attempt to specify how adequately the income of older persons meets their needs requires the answers to two questions: "How can the cost of meeting their needs be cast into a single figure to balance against available income?" And, given an answer to that question, "What kinds of data present the most realistic description of the financial resources available to older persons for meeting their needs?"

The problem of adequate budget determination. The problem of setting a dollar cost to goods and services required to meet the needs of an elderly person or couple is likewise somewhat involved. The Social Security Administration and the Bureau of Labor Statistics have worked out annual budgets for elderly persons and elderly couples. Such budgets implicitly define and enumerate the needs of the group for which the budget was worked out. It is always possible to quarrel with such budgets—since they are in the nature of averages—and to cite many examples of persons who have been living for years below the specified budget level. It can be argued also that the goods and services provided by the budget fall well below the standards dictated by common decency; or, on the contrary, that the same budget implies a level of living well above what could reasonably be expected. In short, the determination of the items that should go into any budget is a matter of judgment, and judgments vary.

Given a budget which includes a satisfactory list of items, there still remain such additional problems as variations in the cost of living between farm and nonfarm areas, by size of place, and by region. In the case of elderly persons, variations in assets accumulated over the years (such as home ownership) also enter the picture. Finally, in dealing with the adequacy of family income, variations in the size of family must be considered from the standpoint of both income and expenditure.

In view of these problems, the adoption of any set of budget standards would appear to be highly arbitrary. An examination of actual budget figures adjusted in various ways leads to the conclusion that no matter what refinements are introduced, the minimum figure for a single older person ranges from $500 to $1,000, and for an elderly couple from $1,000 to $2,000.[5] Although these ranges are, of course, too wide to determine the exact proportion of older persons living at various levels of adequacy or inadequacy, within this general frame of reference it is possible to examine the income distribution of the various groups under consideration and to make some rough inferences as to the proportion with inadequate income.

Income data requirements. If attention is focused on the resources available to meet the needs of the elderly, as it is here, then it becomes a

---

[5] See, for example, Peter O. Steiner, "The Size, Nature, and Adequacy of the Resources of the Aged," *American Economic Review*, Vol. XLIV, No. 2, pp. 647–49.

matter of the income level of the consuming units in which older persons are found rather than a matter of the individual income *per se* of older persons. For example, in the case of elderly couples, it is not the individual income of husband or wife, unrelated to the income of the other spouse, which provides the financial base for the couple's level of living, but rather their joint income and, in addition, the income of other members of the family, if any. There may be rare and unusual families whose bookkeeping establishes each member as a separate fiscal entity with an exact accounting of individual income and expenditure, but the vast majority operate as a single entity, and it is impossible to separate effectively their individual incomes or expenditures. It is clear that data on family income are needed for both husband-and-wife families and for other family groups not centered around a married couple.

Likewise, it is not the individual income of relatives (other than wives) of household heads which reflects their level of living, but rather the family income of the group as a whole. However, in the case of household heads living in the absence of relatives, or of individuals living as lodgers or members of quasi households, individual income obviously provides the most adequate index of their financial resources.

In view of this situation, it is proposed to examine available data on the income of older persons among the various types of living arrangements detailed in Chapter 6: persons living in their own households; persons living as relatives of the household head; and persons unrelated to the head living as lodgers, or in hotels, residence clubs, and the like.

Family income of older families. The family income data from the 1950 Census relate to all families in which the head was 65 and over. Obviously, not all the members of these families were 65 and over. Although relevant statistics are not available from the 1950 Census, tabulations from the Current Population Survey of April 1955 indicate that persons under 65 constituted about 43 percent of the total membership of these families. The family income reported for these families represents, of course, the aggregate income of all members—those 65 and over and those under 65.[6]

The persons 65 and over living in families headed by persons 65 and over constituted in 1955 about 57 percent of the total population 65 and over; they were for the most part either family heads or their wives, although there was a small residual group of other relatives of the head.[7] These statistics, of course, are for 1955 rather than 1950, but it seems not unreasonable to suppose that the 1950 statistics on family income indicate something as to the level of living of somewhat more than one-half of the total population 65 and over on that date.

The data on family income presented in table 47 suggest that if the minimum budget for families in which the head was 65 and over is set

[6] U. S. Bureau of the Census, *Current Population Reports*, Series P–20, No. 67, table 7.
[7] *Ibid.*, tables 1 and 7.

at $1,000 (certainly a low figure), then slightly more than one-third of these families have substandard incomes.   If the minimum budget is raised to $1,500 (a more reasonable figure, in view of estimates of $1,600 to $1,900 budgets for elderly couples in selected large cities at October 1950 price levels),[8] then the proportion of families with inadequate income jumps to about 45 percent.   The variations in these proportions by type of family are small.   The figures suggest that families with other male heads were slightly better off, and those with female heads were slightly worse off, than the husband-and-wife families.

TABLE 47.—INCOME IN 1949 OF FAMILIES WITH HEADS 65 YEARS OLD AND OVER,
BY TYPE OF FAMILY

Type of family	Percent of total population 65 years old and over	Income			
		Percent under $1,000	Percent under $1,500	Percent under $2,000	Median
All families..................	56.8	36.5	46.5	56.4	$1,677
Husband-wife families..............	43.6	34.7	45.3	55.9	1,721
Other families with male head......	4.1	34.1	42.7	51.3	1,924
Families with female head..........	9.1	44.6	52.5	60.5	1,341

Source: Appendix table F-10; *1950 Census of Population*, Vol. IV, *Special Reports*, Part 2, Chapter A, General Characteristics of Families, table 23.

Actually, these estimates of the proportions of families with inadequate income are conservative, since the budget figures are those developed for an elderly couple, whereas in the families covered by the income data the average number of persons per family was something greater than two.[9] Moreover, these additional family members contributed appreciably to family income, as indicated by a comparison of median family income with median income of the heads of the families under consideration.[10]

Income adequacy among elderly married couples in ten cities. Because of the difficulties implicit in the comparison of income with minimum budget, there is some virtue perhaps in making this comparison in a situation in which the ambiguities are further reduced.   Such a situation presents itself in the case of "modest" budgets for elderly couples prepared by the Bureau of Labor Statistics on the basis of the October 1950 price levels for a number of the larger cities, and on the basis of income data for elderly couples and members of their families from the 1950 Census of Housing for the same cities.

The results of comparing these two sets of figures are presented in table 48.   The cleanest comparison is that between the budget cost (which includes rent as the housing cost component) and the income of renters.

[8] Eunice M. Knapp and Mary T. Cooperman, "Estimating a Budget for an Elderly Couple," *Monthly Labor Review*, Vol. 73, No. 3, September 1951, pp. 304–6.

[9] U. S. Bureau of the Census, *op. cit.*, table 7.

[10] *1950 Census of Population*, Vol. IV, *Special Reports*, Part 2, Chapter A, General Characteristics of Families, tables 22 and 23.

In these terms, the percent of married couples with incomes below budget level ranged from about one-fourth, for Washington, D. C., to slightly more than one-half for Atlanta, Georgia. In general terms, these figures for selected cities tend to confirm the conclusions drawn from the data on the population of the country as a whole. The percentages with inadequate income among home owners in the group under consideration are lower, but probably still overstate the true percentage insofar as they own their homes outright. It seems doubtful, however, that a correction for housing cost would materially change the proportions observed.

TABLE 48.—COST OF ELDERLY COUPLE'S TOTAL BUDGET, OCTOBER 1950, AND FAMILY INCOME IN 1949 OF MARRIED COUPLES WITH HUSBAND 65 YEARS OLD AND OVER, BY TENURE, FOR SELECTED CITIES

City	Total budget cost	Percent with income below budget cost			Median income		
		Total	Owner	Renter	Total	Owner	Renter
Milwaukee, Wis..............	$1,908	31.9	30.7	34,1	$2,825	$3,035	$2,607
Boston, Mass................	1,880	35.4	30.6	38.6	2,672	3,020	2,462
Los Angeles, Calif..........	1,866	43.7	40.3	49.3	2,186	2,420	1,892
Washington, D. C............	1,863	24.5	23.6	25.8	3,546	3,715	3,374
Chicago, Ill................	1,818	28.4	26.1	30.5	3,140	3,404	2,917
Detroit, Mich...............	1,818	28.4	25.5	35.0	3,214	3,445	2,664
New York, N. Y..............	1,782	34.6	30.5	37.0	2,726	3,086	2,542
Atlanta, Ga.................	1,748	43.6	35.4	55.4	2,074	2,647	1,539
Portland, Maine[1]..........	1,733	34.8	29.1	42.8	2,475	2,762	2,026
New Orleans, La.............	1,602	38.6	30.7	46.2	2,091	2,071	1,730

[1] Standard metropolitan area.

Source: Eunice M. Knapp and Mary T. Cooperman, "Budget for Elderly Couple; Estimated Cost, October 1950," *Monthly Labor Review*, 73, 3, September 1951, table 1, p. 305; *1950 Census of Housing*, Vol. II, *Nonfarm Housing Characteristics*, Chapters 17, 26, 36, 49, 92, 100, and 152, table B–8; Chapter 84, table C–8; Chapter 101, table G–8; and Chapter 110, table A–8.

The relatively low proportion of couples in Washington, D. C., with inadequate income reflected in part the unusually high labor force participation rates in that city, and also the effects of the heavy concentration in a single area of beneficiaries of the various pension systems operated by the Federal Government. By virtue of this situation, the frequency with which residual income becomes available when retirement stops earned income was considerably greater in Washington than elsewhere.

Income of relatives of household heads. In 1950, persons other than wives living as relatives of household heads constituted about 20 percent of the total population 65 and over. It is clear from the figures presented in table 49 that their income was extremely low, which perhaps accounted for their presence in this type of living arrangement, for in the absence of the financial resources necessary to maintain independent living quarters the most ready solution is to move in with relatives. Although their personal income is low, their level of living is that determined by the family income in the households in which they live—usually those of their children. It is possible, as previously suggested, that a few live in households headed by persons 65 and over; for these, the family income at this age level may to some extent be applicable. Since the great majority of those with inadequate income live with their children, and since data on the family income of families with parents or other relatives 65 and over among their members are not available at present, little can be said as to the financial circumstances under which elderly relatives of household heads are living.

TABLE **49.**—INCOME IN 1949 OF INDIVIDUALS 65 YEARS OLD AND OVER, IN SELECTED TYPES OF LIVING ARRANGEMENTS

[Statistics cover noninstitutional population reporting income]

Type of living arrangements and sex	Percent of total population 65 years and over	Percent with--			Median income[1]
		No income	Income under $850	Income under $1,000	
RELATIVE OF HOUSEHOLD HEAD					
As male relative.............................	6.2	39.1	73.8	79.9	$268
As female relative other than wife..............	14.8	59.4	88.0	93.1	...
NO RELATIVE PRESENT IN HOUSEHOLD					
As male head of household.......................	4.8	15.3	60.8	68.8	649
As female head of household.....................	9.6	23.2	68.7	76.8	501
As male household or quasi-household member.....	3.4	20.5	58.5	65.3	659
As female household or quasi-household member...	1.7	32.5	71.0	77.7	386

[1] For all persons including those reporting no income.

Source: Appendix tables E-1, E-3, and G-3.

Income of unrelated individuals. In 1950, an additional 20 percent of the population 65 and over were unrelated individuals; that is, living in households with no relatives present. This group, in turn, falls into two subgroups: heads of households, who accounted for roughly 15 percent of the total; and other household members, who comprised the remaining 5 percent. Among the subdivisions of the total group the percentage with no income ranged from 15 to 30 percent (table 49). The percentage having incomes of less than $850 (a figure inferred from the $1,500 adequacy level for elderly couples) ranged roughly between 60 and 70 percent. Here, unequivocally, income is inadequate. As might be expected, men in this group fared better than women, and household heads better than household members.

Economic position of the older population. The evaluation of the economic position of older persons, purely in terms of reported income and standard budget, is calculated perhaps to paint the bleakest possible picture. A large proportion of this segment of the population apparently have available financial resources other than those reported as income. The University of California survey provides some evidence on this point.

In considering this evidence, however, it is necessary to recognize that the definitions of living arrangements or relationship are somewhat different from those which have been used in the foregoing discussion. The data from this survey relate to three categories of older persons: married couples, unrelated men, and unrelated women. For married couples the data on income and other financial resources relate only to those of the husband and wife, and a married couple is defined as a couple in which the husband is 65 and over.   Unrelated men represent all other men with no spouse or with spouse absent.   Unrelated women are similarly defined; that is, the only relationship recognized by the definition is the marital bond.   These definitions of relationship are obviously much more restricted than the corresponding definitions used in the preceding discussion.   For convenience and to avoid confusion, these two latter categories will be designated in the following discussion as unmarried men and unmarried women.

In the California survey, in addition to information on income, information was also obtained on "total receipts" which was defined as total receipts or expenditures, whichever is greater.   This amount included, in addition to income as defined in the census income surveys, use of savings, occasional cash gifts, and other resources used to meet living expenses.   A comparison of the income distribution with the total receipts distribution indicates that, whereas for married couples 38 percent had incomes of less than $1,000, 34 percent had total receipts of less than this amount.   The comparable percentages for unmarried men were 70 and 65, and for women, 87 and 83.[11]   Thus, these figures suggest that older persons do have available slightly larger amounts of money for living expenses than indicated by income figures.

Another aspect of the economic position of the elderly relates, of course, to the extent of their savings, or in broader terms, assets.   Information as to the extent and character of the assets of older persons was obtained in the University of California survey (table 50).   For more than 70 percent of the married couples, the net value of total assets was $3,000 or more, and more than 40 percent of both the unmarried men and women had assets of this value.   More than 60 percent of the married couples owned their homes free and clear and more than 30 percent of the unmarried men and women also owned homes unencumbered by mortgages.   Appreciable proportions of each of the three groups had life insurance, but the proportion with policies of $1,200 or more was relatively small except in the case of married couples; for this group, the percentage was about 25.

All of these figures suggest that, if assets are regarded as a supplement to income, income data *per se* overstate the financial stringency under which older people live.   If, however, assets are viewed as insurance against emergencies requiring large financial outlays such as, for example, protracted and serious illness, then they appear to be less adequate; particularly when it is recognized that a major element in the value of total assets is the value of owned homes.

The assessment of the economic position of older people is a complicated matter and does not lend itself to summary in a brief succinct statement.   It is not only a matter of the availability of income data for various types of

---

[11] Data for April 1952, from the University of California survey.

living arrangements and acceptable budget figures to match but it is also a matter, in part, of philosophy. The position implicit in the preceding discussion is perhaps naive in that it assumes "sharing" is an integral part of family life and that it is the duty, if not the privilege, of children to support their elderly parents; thus it is in terms of total family income—no matter who earns it—that adequacy is to be judged. In these terms, about 56 percent of the families headed by older persons had incomes of less than $2,000.

TABLE 50.—ASSETS OF MARRIED COUPLES WITH HEAD 65 YEARS OLD AND OVER, AND OF UN-RELATED MALES AND FEMALES 65 YEARS OLD AND OVER: 1952

[Numbers in thousands. Percent based on inflated figures]

Type of asset	Married couples		Unrelated males		Unrelated females	
	Number	Percent	Number	Percent	Number	Percent
NET VALUE OF TOTAL ASSETS						
Total.......................	3,763	100.0	1,810	100.0	4,230	100.0
No assets......................	488	13.0	622	34.4	1,101	26.0
Assets of less than $3,000.........	617	16.4	452	25.0	1,373	32.5
Assets of $3,000 or more...........	2,658	70.6	736	40.7	1,756	41.5
HOME OWNERSHIP						
Total.......................	3,763	100.0	1,810	100.0	4,230	100.0
Homes owned.....................	2,753	73.2	651	36.0	1,607	38.0
Free and clear.................	2,360	62.7	561	31.0	1,442	34.1
Still making payments...........	393	10.4	90	5.0	165	3.9
Homes rented....................	1,010	26.8	1,159	64.0	2,623	62.0
LIFE INSURANCE						
Total.......................	3,763	100.0	1,810	100.0	4,230	100.0
No life insurance...............	1,647	43.8	1,082	59.8	2,654	62.7
Coverage under $1,200.............	1,169	31.1	470	26.0	1,434	33.9
Coverage $1,200 or more...........	947	25.2	258	14.3	142	3.4

Source: Institute of Industrial Relations of the University of California supplement to Current Population Survey of April 1952.

In the University of California survey, family income is limited to the joint income of husbands 65 and over and their respective wives. It is possible to infer from this definition that it is wrong, if not intolerable, for elderly couples to be dependent on the income of sons and daughters or other relatives living in the household. In these terms some 64 percent of the elderly married couples had incomes of less than $2,000.[12]

Corson and McConnell examine the economic position of older persons in terms of the individual income of family heads. This is by all odds the simplest approach to the question and might be interpreted to imply that the family head has sole responsibility for income maintenance and, therefore, the adequacy of income of older persons can be judged purely in terms of family heads. In this frame of reference the percentage with incomes of less than $2,000 becomes about 70.[13]

[12] *Ibid.*

[13] John J. Corson and John W. McConnell, *Economic Needs of Older People*, The Twentieth Century Fund, New York, 1956, p. 36.

It is apparent, then, that conclusions as to the economic position of older persons in the form of a single concise statement as to the percentage receiving more or less than a given amount will depend on the particular series chosen for this type of analysis and will carry with it an implied philosophy as to the nature of the income expectation appropriate to older persons.   All of these statements are legitimate in terms of the assumptions under which they are developed, but an explicit statement of the given assumption and the recognition of competing assumptions would contribute substantially to a clearer understanding of the problem and minimize controversy.

C H A P T E R   9

SUMMARY AND COMMENT

The concluding chapter of this monograph will attempt to highlight some of the more salient facts which the 1950 Census data reveal about our older generation, and also offer such comment on the conclusions drawn as may help to give a somewhat broader perspective to the study as a whole.

The growth of our older population

The outstanding fact of any analysis of our changing age structure is, of course, the rapid increase in the number and proportion of older people in our population. This process has been continuous over at least the past century, though it has been considerably accelerated during the last 50 years. In 1850, persons 65 years of age or over constituted perhaps 2.5 percent of the total population, whereas by 1950 they accounted for approximately 8 percent. In terms of 60 years of age or over, the 1850 proportion was 4 percent, and by 1950 it had climbed to around 12 percent.

These changes in the age structure obviously reflect past trends in the number of births, deaths, and immigration: the increasing number of births, but declining birth rate; the decline in mortality; and the increase in volume of immigration rising to a peak in the decade 1900 to 1910 and dropping rapidly thereafter. An examination of these trends suggests that about 50 percent of the 1900 to 1950 increase in the *number* of persons 60 years of age or older derived from the increase in number of births, about 21 percent from the decline in mortality in this increase in the number of births, about 11 percent from the decline in mortality *per se,* and nearly 20 percent from immigration. The increase in the *proportion* of older persons was, in large part, a matter of declining birth rates.

To what extent this age shift in population structure will constitute a mounting "burden" on our economy is a question that has not as yet been resolved. It is apparent, however, that much of the concern voiced over the growing proportion of older persons is that the increase will continue at pretty much the same rate as in the past.

Actually, in terms of current information this expectation appears somewhat unlikely. An examination of the size of the age groups that will become 60 and over during the remainder of the 20th century indicates that the rate of growth of the *number* of older persons will decline. As to the *proportion* of older persons, much will depend on the fertility levels of the intervening years. If, for instance, the high birth rate of the 1950's holds through the succeeding decades, the proportion of older people in our population at the beginning of the next century will not be appreciably larger than in 1950. It is also apparent that any numerical increase in the number of older persons will not seriously reduce the proportion of those in the productive ages, since the postwar rise in the birth rate will bring a higher proportion of adults into the labor market.

The outstanding fact that emerges from an analysis of the composition of our older population is the disproportionate number of women. Present indications are that this disproportion will continue to increase. The large majority of these women (particularly in the age group 75 and over) are elderly widows who, in many ways, tend to personify dependent old age.

The geographic distribution of the older population

Wide differences in the proportion of older people exist among the States, counties, cities, and other geographic units. These differences reflect the effects of past trends in births, deaths, and migration, but, since the pattern of these trends has tended to be unique from area to area, generalizations are not easy. Generally speaking, States with low fertility have a higher proportion of older persons than those with high fertility. The expected effects of given fertility and mortality levels are, however, frequently obscured by the effect of migration.

The effects of migration have been variable. In broad terms it may be said that, for those States in which there has been a large and continued in-migration, the net result seems to have been to *reduce* the proportion of older people over that which might have been expected if there had been no migration. The Pacific Coast States especially appear to fall into this category. Conversely, and particularly in certain Midwestern States, continued out-migration seems to have *raised* the proportion of older people above expectation. In other words, despite much that we have heard about retired people leaving their homes to "move into sunnier climes," the bulk of the migrants are younger people. When they move *into* a State they, and their descendants, help to reduce the proportion of older persons; when they move *out* and have their children elsewhere, the older persons left at home assume, numerically, a higher relative importance.

The most notable exception to this general statement is Florida, where in-migration seems to have raised the proportion of older people within the State above expectation. Here, relatively high proportions of the in-migrants entered the State as older persons who had reared their families and, thus, the contribution to the younger population, characteristic of young adult migrants, tended to be minimized. This general situation lends support to the common assumption that Florida has long been the Mecca for "old folks." Although California has been similarly regarded, the data suggest that, in this State, in-migration has tended to lower the proportion of older persons.

At the national level in 1950, the highest proportion of older persons was found in the rural-nonfarm population. The proportion for the rural-farm population was lowest, and that for the urban population fell between the two extremes. This pattern, however, did not occur consistently from State to State. Generally speaking, the proportion of elderly persons tended to increase as the size of place decreased, and thus the highest percentages of persons aged 65 and over occurred in village population.

In general, there was a lower percentage of older people in the suburbs than in the central cities which the suburbs surround. However, this statement requires certain qualifications. For long-established suburban communities, especially those settled in the early part of the century or before, there was a relatively high proportion of older people, and those communities settled at a much later time had relatively smaller proportions of elderly persons. There were, of course, exceptions to this general rule. The figures for the Los Angeles area show that although the general effect of in-migration has been to lower the proportion of older people, there are some suburbs in which in-migration has served to increase the proportion.

Age and labor force participation

In 1950, the labor force participation rate among men reached a peak in the age group 35 to 39 years. In this age group, approximately 95 percent of all men were in the labor force. Thereafter these percentages declined; for men 60 to 64 it was about 79, for those 65 to 69, about 60, and for those 75 and over, it was approximately 19. This decline in labor force participation rate with age is, of course, not unique to 1950; it is also apparent in the 1940 statistics and in the statistics from the Monthly Report on the Labor Force for intervening and subsequent years.

A good deal of interest has developed in this country in identifying the factors presumed to be associated with this relationship between age and labor force participation. Unfortunately, efforts to isolate and measure them quickly meet with various complications and do not yield wholly satisfactory results. It is clear, however, that the increase in disability and loss of energy incident to aging are the major sources of attrition from the labor force. Thus, among retired men "poor health" looms large both as a reason for retirement and as a reason for inability to return to work. Other factors such as voluntary retirement, compulsory separation at a fixed age, and outmoded skills are present but appear to be less important than is often supposed. The importance of retirement as a normal conclusion to the working life, whether compulsory or voluntary, may be expected to increase with the large-scale development, continued operation, and rising benefits of industrial pension plans and government-operated programs for economic security.

The 1950 level of participation of older men in the labor force represented a culmination of a long-time decline extending at least as far back as 1890. In that year, 68 percent of the men 65 and over were in the labor force in contrast to 42 percent in 1950. Traditionally, this decline has been attributed to several factors: movement of farmers and farm workers to cities where their particular skills are not needed; the decline in the proportion of self-employed workers; the availability of retirement income in the form of Social Security and private pensions; and rising productivity along with a rising proportion of the population in the middle-age periods, which together have lessened the need for both very young and very old workers. None of these factors stands out as particularly compelling. It is likely that all of them have to some degree contributed to the decline.

How many potential workers are there in the current population of retired men? This question has been asked with increasing frequency as the size of the older population has increased and as serious shortages have developed in some occupations. Evidence available from the 1950 Census and from other studies indicates that the proportion of retired men (and women) who could return to work is small. Here again, there is some variability in the size of this proportion from study to study, but, all things considered, a figure of 10 percent seems reasonable. This figure is predicated upon hiring practices and conditions of employment in actual operation around 1950. It is quite probable however, that, if drastic changes in these institutional arrangements were made to create working conditions suitable to the tastes and physical capacities of older persons, this proportion might be increased substantially.

Among women the pattern of employment and age differs considerably. Peaks in the proportion of women employed appear in the early 20's and again in the 40's after the parental role has been completed. Withdrawal from the work force in the older ages occurs more rapidly for women than for men.

Age and occupation

Interest in the relationship between age and occupation centers largely around the implications for continued employment in the older years and around the degree to which certain occupations may offer new work opportunities to older persons who, for various reasons, have become unemployed. These implied questions are perhaps best answered for particular occupation groups in terms of the changes in the size of a given age cohort from one decade to the next. Thus, if in a given occupation the number of persons 65 and over in 1950 exceeded the number 55 and over in 1940, it is reasonable to infer that not only did the 1940 members of the occupation suffer little attrition from mortality and retirement but also that additional aging persons found employment in the occupation in the 10-year period. An occupation of this description would indeed be one that meets the employment needs of older persons.

Actually, of course, from occupation to occupation, the number of persons 65 and over in 1950 was generally less than the number 55 and over in 1940; there were, nevertheless, marked differences in the relation between these two numbers among the occupation groups. For the total employed, persons 65 and over in 1950 constituted about 42 percent of persons 55 and over in 1940; that is, the "survival rate" for employed males was .42. Occupations with survival rates appreciably higher than those for the total employed may be regarded as those in which the opportunities for continued and new employment are greatest. Among the occupation groups meeting this description were clerical workers; service occupations such as those of guards and watchmen, elevator operators, and janitors; State and local officials; surveyors; and mechanics, repairmen and loom fixers.

It has been commonly held that self-employment provides a setting favorable to occupational longevity. If this relationship exists in the occupation groups in which there were appreciable numbers of self-employed and salaried workers, it is not sufficiently great to be clearly apparent in the limited data available from the censuses of 1940 and 1950.

For women—because of their involvement with family responsibilities and the rapid growth in their labor force participation—the occupational age patterns differed considerably from those for men. In typically distaff occupations, however, the patterns were more nearly alike.

Family and living arrangements of older people

The data presented in Chapter 6 reveal a number of characteristics of older people which have important implications for both the individuals concerned and for community planning. First, it would seem that a new period is making its appearance in the life cycle of the individual and of the family. Whereas in 1890, adults tended to move directly from parental and household responsibilities into the status of old age, the data indicate that there is now coming to be an identifiable period of middle-age or transitional stage following the completion of the parental stage. The typical husband and wife may now expect as much as 14 years of life together after their last child has left home and before the appearance of other events and circumstances that mark the transition into old age.

The second conclusion from the analysis of marital status and family data is that disability, retirement, and death do eventually leave their marks on the family and living arrangements of the older population. It may seem surprising that nearly 95 percent of all persons 65 and over live in households and that the great majority (over two-thirds) live in households maintained by themselves. A closer analysis, however, shows that, as age increases, there is, on the one hand, a process of progressive isolation for the individual or, on the other hand, a progressive loss of independence. The fact that the average wife outlives her husband by several years makes this especially true in the case of women. Thus, for example, the woman who, in her middle years, was the mistress of her own household is likely to end as a widow living alone or "taking in roomers" in the family home, or living as a more or less dependent relative in the home of one of her children.

This same trend occurs among men, though because of their higher mortality and the greater tendency for widowers to remarry, there are fewer men to whom this description applies. For both men and women, the proportion living as relatives in someone else's household increases with age; in the age group 65 to 69 those who had given up their homes to live with their children or other relatives constituted about 14 percent of all older persons, whereas at ages 80 to 84, they constituted a full third and at 85 and over, at least 44 percent. Likewise, the proportion living alone, or with no relatives in the household, increased from about 22 percent at ages 65 to 74, to about 28 percent at 75 and over.

The proportion of older people living in quasi households is under 6 percent; slightly over half of these persons live in institutions, particularly in homes for the aged. It is only for the very oldest age groups that the curve rises appreciably and we find that over 12 percent of those 85 and older live in quasi households. Nearly 10 percent are in some sort of institution and of these roughly three-quarters are residents of homes for the aged.

The housing of older persons

Closely allied to the problem of living arrangements of older people is the matter of housing. Chapter 7 offers data on the type and quality of housing occupied by households classified by the age of the head of these households. In the course of the family cycle it would appear that the purchase of a home is generally made at the point of the family's maximum size and that the parents continue to live in it throughout their middle and later years when the children are gone. There is, therefore, a marked decline with age in the number of persons occupying a dwelling unit, and a very large increase in the proportion of dwellings occupied by one person. Comparatively few families, apparently, seek smaller accommodations after their children have left home. Roughly two-thirds of the heads of families 65 and over own their own homes, and a high proportion of these homes are free and clear of mortgages.

The quality of housing appears to be highest during those years in the family cycle when income is the greatest. As the family ages so does the home, and some measure of deterioration sets in. Thus, among households headed by persons 45 to 64 years old, possibly one-fourth had "substandard" housing, but among those 65 and over, the corresponding proportion was one-third. With the decline in income incident to aging, rent became a proportionally larger element of expenditures of older persons who rent their homes, and home owners who have not paid off their mortgages find themselves in a similar position.

The question of adequate housing for older people is becoming a matter of greater and greater interest among people concerned with the problem of aging. There is some evidence of a rising demand by both elderly couples and single men and women for living arrangements geared to their special needs and pocketbooks, and thus, it may well be that the apparent desire or willingness to remain in the family home in which they have reared their children reflects, in some degree, the lack of any practical alternative. The sentimental attachment to the "old home" perhaps, may not always compensate for its lack of modern conveniences, for stairs to climb, for the isolation, or for the sense of "rattling around" in a house that is much too large for their present needs.

Low rental public housing, with modernly equipped 2- and 3-room apartments especially designed for elderly people would seem to be one answer. Units already built in Massachusetts, New York, Rhode Island, Cleveland, Chicago, Denver, and elsewhere have proved to be enormously popular. The community retirement home or village, often with infirmary, central dining and recreation facilities, seems to have attracted an increasing number of older people. Such facilities have been developed by churches (Willammette View Manor in Oregon), labor organizations (Salhaven in Florida), teachers (in Washington, California, and Nebraska), fraternal orders (Moosehaven in Florida), charitable organizations (Community Service Society in New York City and The Farmer Foundation in Fort Worth), and by commercial interests (Ryderwood in Washington, Orange Gardens, Bradenton Trailer Park, and others in Florida, and the Lavin Hotels in Pennsylvania and Florida). This movement toward the development of congregate living facilities without the regulatory and protective atmosphere of old-age homes was given impetus by the 1956 Federal Housing Legislation, which made long-term federal mortgage insurance available for financing the construction or rehabilitation of rental housing for the elderly by public and nonprofit organizations.

Aging and income

Generally speaking, the 1950 data suggest that the age cycle of income is similar to that of the cycle of labor force participation. Income rises to a peak in the middle years and thereafter declines; and it declines sharply following retirement.

In spite of the various measures that may loosely be described as social security (public and private pension systems, old-age assistance and other programs), the income of retired workers is considerably below that of those older workers who are still in the active labor force. Since comparatively few reach the age of retirement with any substantial savings or income from investments, their chief resource is a form of deferred earnings; that is, benefits from old-age and survivors insurance supplemented, for those fortunate enough to be under both systems, by benefits from a private pension plan. These may, of course, be augmented by earnings from part-time employment provided the amount earned does not jeopardize the continued drawing of the retiree's OASI benefits. Those whose income from any of these sources is insufficient to provide for their minimum needs have usually little other recourse than to apply for old-age assistance. About one-fifth of the older population now receives part or all of its support from this source.

The data show that incomes are lowest among women who may be said to have been "displaced" in the operation of the family cycle. Thus, the smallest incomes are found among women living in the households of their children, suggesting a large measure of financial dependence. Incomes are somewhat higher among women maintaining their own households, though in the majority of cases these seem to be below subsistence levels. The highest levels are found in husband-and-wife households, though, here again, a large proportion are found to be below minimum standards.

One fact which emerges from the data is the great spread in the amount of income received by older persons. In 1953, the percentage, small as it may be, of men with incomes of $25,000 and over continued to be the same as in the 45 to 64 age group. On the other hand, the proportion of those with income of under $2,000 was nearly four times as great as those in the 45 to 64 age group, and approximately two and one-half times as great as those in the 55 to 64 age group.

These data on income do not, of course, give the entire picture of the resources of older people. No account is taken of accumulated savings, annuities or insurance policies, though, as previously noted, the average retired worker has very little of such resources to fall back on. A more important consideration is that of home ownership; a retired worker who owns his own home free and clear is more likely to be in a better financial position than one who must pay out a large part of his reduced income for rent. Also, many older people manage to eke out their slender incomes through gifts, from relatives and friends, of food, clothing, and other necessities.

Income data in themselves tell little about their adequacy for meeting needs. Measurement of income adequacy is a complicated undertaking and the proportion of older persons with incomes below that level depends in part upon how this level of adequacy is defined. Although precise measures were not used in the present analysis, it is clear that the level of income for the great majority of older persons is disturbingly low. Furthermore, an income which is technically adequate may still give little or no margin for anything beyond what is required to cover the ordinary costs of food, shelter, and clothing. It is likely, as we shall see later, to be wholly inadequate to meet the costs of serious illness. It also makes no provision for the "wherewithal" needed to make pleasant use of one's retirement leisure or to indulge in any of the so-called creative activities on which increasing stress is being laid and which serve so effectively to maintain the mental and physical health of an aging person.

Since these 1950 Census data were collected there has been a substantial rise in wages, an important increase in the amount of OASI benefits, together with an expansion of coverage, and also a very great increase in the number of private pension plans. These factors have, of course, been offset by a marked increase in the cost of living, but it is probable that the net effect has been to strengthen the income position of the older age group as a whole.

A further expansion of private pension systems to parallel the coverage that now obtains under the Federal system is obviously one answer to the problem of retirement income for older workers. In any event, since it is probable that the proportion of older persons in the labor market will continue to decrease, a much broader system for the support of the great bulk of older people who derive no income from employment is clearly indicated.

Health and the later years

Since the 1950 Census made no specific inquiry into the health status of the older population, no attempt has been made in this monograph to deal with health status *per se*. Yet the real significance of much of the data presented has been seen to lie in this relationship to age changes in the health of the individual.

We have seen that, for the majority of workers, poor health and declining energy are the decisive reasons given for withdrawal from the labor force. These are fairly broad terms. They can include a downright disability, ranging from the accidental loss of limb to the sudden onset of a serious heart condition which makes it impossible for a man any longer to hold down his job. Or they may apply to a chronic ailment which has been developing over the past several years and has reached a point where the man can no longer function effectively, or his doctor may have warned him to quit work. These terms may also refer to a progressive lowering of energy resources which cannot be pin-pointed to any specific disease but which makes a man feel he is simply "not up to the job any longer." Moreover, it is quite likely that for every man or woman who actually retires for health reasons there are others for whom encroaching ill health is progressively interfering with their ability to function on the job but who have put off retirement in the hope that they will be able to "keep going" for another year or two.

When we consider that one out of two persons over the age of 65 has one or more chronic ailments (though not necessarily of a disabling nature), it is obvious that the health factor, in the later years, assumes enormous significance. From merely a financial point of view, the increasingly high cost of medical care imposes a burden which practically no ordinary retirement income can successfully shoulder. And if most older people live in fear of serious illness, the question of how it is to be paid for often becomes a veritable nightmare. Some progress in meeting this problem has been made, but it has been slow. As of 1956, one out of three men and women over the age of 65 had some form of health insurance, usually restricted to short-term hospital and surgical expenses. The great majority of older persons find it impossible to obtain any effective health coverage, and it is quite likely that serious and long-term illness is the major factor which leads to an older person's loss of independence. For those receiving old-age assistance there are, in most States, special provisions to cover the cost of medical care after illness has set in. These programs are being improved in response to new Federal legislation but, thus far, few programs have been developed to provide for periodic health examinations and services which could postpone or prevent the onset of disabling illness.

Beyond this there is a pressing need for more chronic hospitals with rehabilitation facilities, more and better nursing homes, and more geriatric clinics to serve all older people. As recently as 1954, it was estimated that the country had less than 15 percent of the beds needed for geriatric hospital patients. Local awareness as well as recent amendments to the Hill-Burton health facilities act has led to stepped-up construction in some States, notably California, Connecticut, Massachusetts, Minnesota, and New York. Simultaneously, there was an upsurge of interest in providing community facilities in the form of home health care, housekeeping help, periodic visiting, and other services which have proved markedly effective in enabling older persons to remain in their own homes in the countries of northwestern Europe.

The role of the older person in our society

The foregoing conclusions have pointed to the rising longevity of our population, to the earlier completion of parental roles, to separation from the labor force, to infirmity and ill health, and to widowhood, social isolation, and dependency. Some aspects of this situation are depressing but nevertheless real. In spite of the actual or potential miracles of modern medicine, old age, at some point, would still appear to be a period of contracting physical powers and declining health, and a period in which there is a progressive loss of relatives and friends. Other aspects such as those relating to income maintenance, housing, and the like are subject to amelioration, and steps have been taken in this direction. The aspect of aging which presents the clearest challenge is the increased period of leisure incident to the increase in longevity on the one hand, and earlier retirement on the other. This period may be accepted with an unreflective passivity or cheerful stoicism, may be perceived as a time of frustration and boredom, or it may be seized upon as an opportunity for new and constructive activities.

There is considerable evidence that this challenge is being increasingly accepted and that many older people are beginning to look at leisure and retirement as an opportunity to develop new modes of life consistent with their new status. Indeed, it has been observed that the turning point of maturity may occur at around 50 years of age when parental responsibilities are all but completed and while the vigor of the earlier years is still largely intact. In any event, increasing numbers of people at this stage of life appear to be taking stock of themselves and to be developing new interests which may well represent setting new and positive goals for the later periods of life. Retirement preparation programs with emphasis on maintenance of health and continuing participation in community life are becoming increasingly popular in large employing organizations and there is a tendency to open them to workers in their 50's.

The new activities to which older people are turning are almost legion. Hundreds are patronizing full-time activity centers with programs in the fine arts and artcrafts, languages, poetry and drama, nutrition and rhythm classes, music, and social activities in such widely scattered places as

Menlo Park, Los Angeles, San Francisco, Seattle, Omaha, Minneapolis, South Bend, Detroit, Cleveland, Syracuse, and New York. Local school systems and university extension services in California, Florida, Michigan, New York, and elsewhere are finding new acceptance, among older people, of courses and particularly of discussion programs in such things as world affairs, world politics, art and music appreciation, and great books. The handicrafts are attracting more and more middle-aged and older persons in New England, the Southern Highlands, Denver, and Portland, Oregon. Libraries in Cleveland, Queens, and Boston have been offering high-level lectures, film, and discussion programs for more than a decade. Senior citizens clubs and recreation programs have sprung into being by the hundreds. North Carolina has a public recreation program for older people in every community of 8,000.

More recently older people have begun to create their own organizations to study and promote their own needs and to explore ways in which they can serve their communities. Prominent among these groups are the Sunset Clubs of New Hampshire, New Jersey's Old Guard, Experience, Inc., in Saint Louis, the Senior Council in Cleveland, the Los Angeles County Senior Citizens Association, and the Senior Citizens Association of the (San Francisco) Bay area.

Whether or not these examples are indications of an incipient redefinition of retirement roles by older persons themselves remains an open question. They do seem to indicate quite clearly that many persons who have completed their family and work roles are not satisfied with an extended life of rocking-chair reflection and protracted deterioration. Certainly, one answer to the question lies in whether or not society itself is willing to recognize the potentials of its senior citizens whose principal faults are that they have more leisure and more years of energetic life than their predecessors. Since the 1950 Census was taken, two Presidents of the United States have reiterated the words of Cicero that a good deal of experience and wisdom resides in old men and that no nation can afford to overlook this fact.

Conclusion

The 1950 Census data provide certain bench marks, and indicate certain trends that have been set in motion, which will, to some extent, enable us to gauge the weight and impact on our society of the growing number and proportion of older people in our population. Steadily increasing longevity, side by side with steadily increasing productive capacity, would indicate that the nation is undergoing important social and economic changes the final consequence of which cannot be accurately forecast. The developing awareness concerning the many and various problems involved has been most significant since the mid-century mark when these data were assembled. The 1960 Census may well provide data that will show far more clearly the general direction in which we are going.

APPENDIX A

CHANGING AGE STRUCTURE

Section 1: Age statistics from the 1950 Census

A discussion of the nature and quality of the age statistics from the 1950 Census appears in the introduction to Part I, Vol. II, of the 1950 Census of Population. As this discussion indicates, the Post Enumeration Survey indicated that the largest net undercounts occurred in the age group under 5, and in the 5-year age groups in the population 45 years old and over. This discussion further indicates that this finding was contrary to expectations for the group 65 and over, which has been commonly assumed to be overcounted. The evidence for this assumption is developed from a procedure whereby the population at a given census is brought forward to the next census by the addition of births and the subtraction of deaths at appropriate age intervals. The hypothetical population so derived is then compared with the enumerated population and the differences interpreted as evidence of age bias in enumeration. If the logic of this operation is accepted, then persons 65 to 74 years of age were overcounted in both 1940 and 1950, and persons 55 to 64 years of age were undercounted. These discrepancies appear both for the white and nonwhite population, but are particularly large for the nonwhite population.[1]

Data on age for the 1950 Census were, for various segments of the population, tabulated on a complete count basis, on a 20-percent sample basis, and on a 3⅓-sample basis. In addition, there were, in most cases, several tabulations at each of these levels and no attempt was made to reconcile small discrepancies which normally arise among several tabulations of the same deck of cards. The figures for 1950 presented in tables A–2 to A–4 represent a "rational" age distribution in which the discrepancies arising from both sampling error and serial tabulation have been eliminated. The over-all controls for the total population are based on the initial 100-percent tabulation. The statistics on age by nativity for the white population represent ratio estimates based on 20-percent data—the only data available for the nativity classes of the population. The data on nativity for the nonwhite population represent 100-percent data from a retabulation of the nonwhite population by nativity, adjusted to the controls established in the initial 100-percent tabulation. The net results of this operation rep-

---

[1] For a detailed analysis of this type of result in the 1950 Census, see U. S. Bureau of the Census, *Current Population Reports*, Series P–25, No. 98.

resent some small gain in accuracy and serve to eliminate the frustration involved in dealing with the small discrepancies which arise in using, in a single context, figures from the several sources mentioned.

The figures for 1900 which appear in tables A–2 to A–4 represent the published results of the 1900 Census with unknown age distributed in proportion to known age.

The figures used in Chapter 2 are based entirely on the adjusted figures. However, in subsequent chapters there has been little adjustment, and the age figures are those derived from the particular tabulation in which the subject matter under consideration was derived. There are, therefore, some explicit and implicit discrepancies in the figures for given age groups from chapter to chapter as well as within chapters.

Section 2: Estimates of births, 1810 to 1910

The estimates of births, which are used to evaluate the contributions of changes in the number of births and changes in mortality to the difference in the size of the population 60 and over between 1900 and 1950, begin with census statistics on children under 5 and children 5 to 9 years old from each decennial census between 1820 and 1910. Numbers in these exact age groups were estimated for the white population in 1820 and for the nonwhite population in 1820, 1830, and 1840. Allowance was also made for the obvious underenumeration in the Census of 1870. Allowances, however, were not made for possible children in these age groups for whom age was not reported, nor were the small number of foreign-born children in these age groups excluded. Children under 5 were adjusted for underenumeration but no adjustment was made in the age group 5 to 9. For the group under 5, the adjustment was made separately for whites and nonwhites, assuming a higher rate of underenumeration for nonwhites.

Survival factors were then developed from the United States life table for 1901–1910 and from the English life tables of 1838–1854, 1871–1880, 1881–1890, and 1891–1900. These rates were used to estimate births in the white population. For the nonwhite population, the relationship observed between the white and nonwhite survival rates in the 1900–1910 period was assumed to obtain throughout the entire period. The net result was a series of birth estimates by quinquennial periods for the period 1810 to 1910. For the period 1910 to 1950 the estimates of births developed by Whelpton for the National Office of Vital Statistics for the period 1910 to 1939 were used, and the subsequent revision of these estimates was used for the decade of the 1940's.[2]

These estimates for quinquennial periods are presented in table A–6; those for the nine decades prior to 1950 and to 1900 are presented in table A–7. These latter figures are adjusted to the census dates of these two years—April 1 and June 1, respectively.

---

[2] National Office of Vital Statistics, *Special Reports*, Vol. 33, No. 8, September 28, 1950; *Vital Statistics of the United States, 1953*, Vol. I, table K.

TABLE A-1.—MEDIAN AGE AND PERCENT 60 AND 65 YEARS OLD AND OVER, BY COLOR AND SEX: 1790 TO 1950

Year and color	Total			Male			Female		
	Median age	Percent of total population		Median age	Percent of total population		Median age	Percent of total population	
		60 years and over	65 years and over		60 years and over	65 years and over		60 years and over	65 years and over
ALL CLASSES									
1950	30.2	12.2	8.1	29.9	11.8	7.7	30.5	12.5	8.5
1940	29.0	10.4	6.8	29.1	10.3	6.7	29.0	10.6	7.0
1930	26.5	8.5	5.4	26.7	8.5	5.4	26.2	8.4	5.5
1920	25.3	7.5	4.7	25.8	7.6	4.6	24.7	7.4	4.7
1910	24.1	6.8	4.3	24.6	6.7	4.2	23.5	6.8	4.4
1900	22.9	6.4	4.1	23.3	6.4	4.0	22.4	6.5	4.1
1890	22.0	6.2	3.9	22.3	6.2	3.9	21.6	6.2	3.9
1880	20.9	5.6	3.4	21.2	5.7	3.4	20.7	5.6	3.5
1870	20.2	5.0	3.0	20.2	5.1	3.0	20.1	5.0	3.0
1860	19.4	4.3	...	19.8	4.2	...	19.1	4.4	...
1850	18.9	4.1	...	19.2	4.1	...	18.6	4.2	...
1840	17.8	...	...	17.8	...	...	17.7	...	...
1830	17.2	...	...	17.1	...	...	17.3	...	...
1820	16.7	...	...	16.6	...	...	16.7	...	...
WHITE									
1950	30.8	12.6	8.4	30.4	12.2	8.0	31.1	13.0	8.9
1940	29.5	10.8	7.1	29.5	10.6	6.9	29.5	11.0	7.3
1930	26.9	8.8	5.7	27.1	8.8	5.6	26.6	8.9	5.7
1920	25.6	7.8	4.8	26.1	7.8	4.8	25.1	7.8	4.9
1910	24.5	7.0	4.5	24.9	6.9	4.3	23.9	7.1	4.6
1900	23.4	6.6	4.2	23.8	6.6	4.2	22.9	6.7	4.3
1890	22.5	6.4	4.0	22.9	6.4	4.0	22.1	6.4	4.0
1880	21.4	5.8	3.6	21.6	5.8	3.5	21.1	5.8	3.6
1870	20.4	5.1	3.1	20.5	5.2	3.0	20.3	5.1	3.1
1860	19.7	4.4	...	20.1	4.3	...	19.3	4.5	...
1850	19.1	4.2	...	19.5	4.1	...	18.8	4.3	...
1840	17.9	3.9	...	17.9	3.8	...	17.8	4.1	...
1830	17.2	4.0	...	17.2	3.9	...	17.3	4.1	...
1820	16.5	...	...	16.5	...	...	16.6	...	...
1810	16.0	...	...	15.9	...	...	16.1	...	...
1800	16.0	...	...	15.7	...	...	16.3	...	...
1790	...	...	...	15.9	...	...	...	...	...
NONWHITE									
1950	26.1	8.3	5.7	25.9	8.4	5.7	26.2	8.2	5.7
1940	25.2	7.1	4.8	25.4	7.4	4.9	25.1	6.8	4.6
1930	23.5	5.2	3.2	23.9	5.5	3.3	23.1	4.9	3.1
1920	22.5	5.2	3.2	23.1	5.6	3.4	21.9	4.7	3.1
1910	21.1	5.0	3.0	21.5	5.3	3.1	20.6	4.7	2.9
1900	19.9	4.9	3.0	20.0	5.0	3.0	19.5	4.7	3.0
1890	18.5	4.6	2.8	18.5	4.7	2.9	18.3	4.5	2.8
1880	18.0	4.5	2.7	17.9	4.7	2.7	18.0	4.4	2.7
1870	18.5	4.3	2.5	18.5	4.4	2.4	18.8	4.3	2.5
1860	17.7	3.7	...	17.7	3.6	...	17.5	3.7	...
1850	17.3	3.8	...	17.3	3.6	...	17.4	3.9	...
1840	17.3	...	...	17.0	...	...	17.5	...	...
1830	16.7	...	...	16.7	...	...	17.1	...	...
1820	17.2	...	...	16.9	...	...	17.4	...	...

Source: *1950 Census*, Vol. II, *Characteristics of the Population*, Part 1, U. S. Summary, table 39, p. 93; *1940 Census of Population*, Vol. IV, *Characteristics of the Population*, Part 1, U. S. Summary, table III, p. 3; *1930 Census*, Vol. II, *Population*, Chapter 10, table 7, p. 576; *1840 Census*, p. 474; *1830 Census*, p. 162.

TABLE **A-2.**—TOTAL POPULATION BY AGE, COLOR, AND SEX: 1950 AND 1900

Age and color	Total		Male		Female	
	1950	1900	1950	1900	1950	1900
ALL CLASSES						
All ages.............	150,697,361	75,994,575	74,833,239	38,816,448	75,864,122	37,178,127
Under 5 years..............	16,163,571	9,194,905	8,236,164	4,648,894	7,927,407	4,546,011
5 to 9 years..............	13,199,685	8,897,733	6,714,555	4,494,226	6,485,130	4,403,507
10 to 14 years............	11,119,268	8,101,773	5,660,399	4,096,576	5,458,869	4,005,197
15 to 19 years............	10,616,598	7,576,162	5,311,342	3,762,877	5,305,256	3,813,285
20 to 24 years............	11,481,828	7,354,703	5,606,293	3,636,667	5,875,535	3,718,036
25 to 29 years............	12,242,260	6,546,728	5,972,078	3,334,488	6,270,182	3,212,240
30 to 34 years............	11,517,007	5,570,565	5,624,723	2,910,766	5,892,284	2,659,799
35 to 39 years............	11,246,386	4,977,942	5,517,544	2,625,467	5,728,842	2,352,475
40 to 44 years............	10,203,973	4,258,315	5,070,269	2,263,277	5,133,704	1,995,038
45 to 49 years............	9,070,465	3,463,793	4,526,366	1,843,900	4,544,099	1,619,893
50 to 54 years............	8,272,188	2,950,696	4,128,648	1,569,803	4,143,540	1,380,893
55 to 59 years............	7,235,120	2,216,863	3,630,046	1,148,966	3,605,074	1,067,897
60 to 64 years............	6,059,475	1,796,029	3,037,838	920,159	3,021,637	875,870
65 to 69 years............	5,002,936	1,306,243	2,424,561	669,803	2,578,375	636,440
70 to 74 years............	3,411,949	886,095	1,628,829	451,035	1,783,120	435,060
75 to 79 years............	2,152,393	521,165	1,001,788	262,404	1,150,605	258,761
80 to 84 years............	1,125,358	252,162	504,968	122,665	620,390	129,497
85 years and over.........	576,901	122,703	236,828	54,475	340,073	68,228
60 years and over.........	18,329,012	4,884,397	8,834,812	2,480,541	9,494,200	2,403,856
Percent of total........	12.2	6.4	11.8	6.4	12.5	6.5
65 years and over.........	12,269,537	3,088,368	5,796,974	1,560,382	6,472,563	1,527,986
Percent of total........	8.1	4.1	7.7	4.0	8.5	4.1
60 to 89 years............	18,181,454	4,850,523	8,777,514	2,466,941	9,403,940	2,383,582
WHITE						
All ages..............	134,942,028	66,809,196	67,129,192	34,201,735	67,812,836	32,607,461
Under 5 years..............	14,184,504	7,936,819	7,244,211	4,022,913	6,940,293	3,913,906
5 to 9 years..............	11,596,572	7,654,610	5,915,130	3,873,384	5,681,442	3,781,226
10 to 14 years............	9,694,529	6,974,125	4,944,535	3,529,366	4,749,994	3,444,759
15 to 19 years............	9,330,520	6,557,191	4,685,825	3,267,416	4,644,695	3,289,775
20 to 24 years............	10,179,187	6,348,691	5,002,782	3,154,500	5,176,405	3,194,191
25 to 29 years............	10,924,804	5,775,571	5,349,707	2,951,333	5,575,097	2,824,238
30 to 34 years............	10,356,331	5,015,519	5,080,610	2,626,979	5,275,721	2,388,540
35 to 39 years............	10,058,473	4,470,513	4,955,941	2,367,141	5,102,532	2,103,372
40 to 44 years............	9,190,290	3,860,735	4,573,529	2,061,089	4,616,761	1,799,646
45 to 49 years............	8,169,354	3,112,620	4,080,174	1,656,727	4,089,180	1,455,893
50 to 54 years............	7,535,439	2,639,887	3,756,125	1,400,056	3,779,314	1,239,831
55 to 59 years............	6,695,732	2,025,713	3,350,888	1,043,233	3,344,844	982,480
60 to 64 years............	5,652,606	1,624,261	2,829,399	827,593	2,823,207	796,668
65 to 69 years............	4,585,586	1,197,955	2,223,014	610,470	2,362,572	587,485
70 to 74 years............	3,181,575	809,896	1,513,308	412,845	1,668,267	397,051
75 to 79 years............	2,016,861	478,777	933,333	240,976	1,083,528	237,801
80 to 84 years............	1,057,549	225,209	472,521	110,404	585,028	114,805
85 years and over.........	532,116	101,104	218,160	45,310	313,956	55,794
60 years and over.........	17,026,293	4,437,202	8,189,735	2,247,598	8,836,558	2,189,604
Percent of total........	12.6	6.6	12.2	6.6	13.0	6.7
65 years and over.........	11,373,687	2,812,941	5,360,336	1,420,005	6,013,351	1,392,936
Percent of total........	8.4	4.2	8.0	4.2	8.9	4.3
60 to 89 years............	16,895,914	4,414,292	8,138,986	2,238,229	8,756,928	2,176,063
NONWHITE						
All ages..............	15,755,333	9,185,379	7,704,047	4,614,713	8,051,286	4,570,666
Under 5 years..............	1,979,067	1,258,086	991,953	625,981	987,114	632,105
5 to 9 years..............	1,603,113	1,243,123	799,425	620,842	803,688	622,281
10 to 14 years............	1,424,739	1,127,648	715,864	567,210	708,875	560,438
15 to 19 years............	1,286,078	1,018,971	625,517	495,461	660,561	523,510
20 to 24 years............	1,302,641	1,006,012	603,511	482,167	699,130	523,845
25 to 29 years............	1,317,456	771,157	622,371	383,155	695,085	388,002
30 to 34 years............	1,160,676	555,046	544,113	283,787	616,563	271,259
35 to 39 years............	1,187,913	507,429	561,603	258,326	626,310	249,103

TABLE A-2.—TOTAL POPULATION BY AGE, COLOR, AND SEX: 1950 AND 1900—Cont.

Age and color	Total		Male		Female	
	1950	1900	1950	1900	1950	1900
NONWHITE--Cont.						
40 to 44 years	1,013,683	397,580	496,740	202,188	516,943	195,392
45 to 49 years	901,111	351,173	446,192	187,173	454,919	164,000
50 to 54 years	736,749	310,809	372,523	169,747	364,226	141,062
55 to 59 years	539,388	191,150	279,158	105,733	260,230	85,417
60 to 64 years	406,869	171,768	208,439	92,566	198,430	79,202
65 to 69 years	417,350	108,288	201,547	59,333	215,803	48,955
70 to 74 years	230,374	76,199	115,521	38,190	114,853	38,009
75 to 79 years	135,532	42,388	68,455	21,428	67,077	20,960
80 to 84 years	67,809	26,953	32,447	12,261	35,362	14,692
85 years and over	44,785	21,599	18,668	9,165	26,117	12,434
60 years and over	1,302,719	447,195	645,077	232,943	657,642	214,252
Percent of total	8.3	4.9	8.4	5.0	8.2	4.7
65 years and over	895,850	275,427	436,638	140,377	459,212	135,050
Percent of total	5.7	3.0	5.7	3.0	5.7	3.0
60 to 89 years	1,285,540	436,231	638,528	228,712	647,012	207,519

Source: *1950 Census of Population*, Vol. II, *Characteristics of the Population*, Part 1, U. S. Summary, tables 38, 94, and 97.

TABLE A-3.—NATIVE POPULATION BY AGE, COLOR, AND SEX: 1950 AND 1900

Age and color	Total		Male		Female	
	1950	1900	1950	1900	1950	1900
ALL CLASSES						
All ages	140,275,616	65,653,299	69,490,737	33,186,258	70,784,879	32,467,041
Under 5 years	16,097,212	9,142,135	8,202,786	4,622,118	7,894,426	4,520,017
5 to 9 years	13,135,085	8,749,651	6,681,620	4,420,006	6,453,465	4,329,645
10 to 14 years	11,050,241	7,788,419	5,623,869	3,937,864	5,426,372	3,850,555
15 to 19 years	10,519,398	7,006,202	5,260,792	3,484,728	5,258,606	3,521,474
20 to 24 years	11,255,349	6,421,128	5,509,370	3,169,155	5,745,979	3,251,973
25 to 29 years	11,869,236	5,432,332	5,804,110	2,730,716	6,065,126	2,701,616
30 to 34 years	11,177,365	4,377,841	5,466,434	2,233,586	5,710,931	2,144,255
35 to 39 years	10,693,114	3,777,315	5,254,614	1,931,936	5,438,500	1,845,379
40 to 44 years	9,379,741	3,271,407	4,659,203	1,687,030	4,720,538	1,584,377
45 to 49 years	7,971,249	2,606,997	3,960,482	1,360,496	4,010,767	1,246,501
50 to 54 years	6,999,399	2,134,670	3,467,489	1,118,453	3,531,910	1,016,217
55 to 59 years	5,873,253	1,566,524	2,898,343	797,357	2,974,910	769,167
60 to 64 years	4,713,824	1,245,635	2,296,313	629,795	2,417,511	615,840
65 to 69 years	3,876,357	892,935	1,827,805	454,360	2,048,552	438,575
70 to 74 years	2,656,644	602,486	1,242,440	302,055	1,414,204	300,431
75 to 79 years	1,698,730	361,616	776,747	179,059	921,983	182,557
80 to 84 years	872,372	182,786	383,459	87,098	488,913	95,688
85 years and over	437,047	93,220	174,861	40,446	262,186	52,774
60 years and over	14,254,974	3,378,678	6,701,625	1,692,813	7,553,349	1,685,865
Percent of total	10.2	5.1	9.6	5.1	10.7	5.2
65 years and over	9,541,150	2,133,043	4,405,312	1,063,018	5,135,838	1,070,025
Percent of total	6.8	3.2	6.3	3.2	7.3	3.3
60 to 89 years	14,140,238	3,352,023	6,658,248	1,682,387	7,481,990	1,669,636
WHITE						
All ages	124,780,860	56,595,379	61,952,802	28,686,450	62,828,058	27,908,929
Under 5 years	14,121,355	7,884,324	7,212,700	3,996,268	6,908,655	3,888,056
5 to 9 years	11,534,820	7,507,065	5,883,853	3,799,441	5,650,967	3,707,624
10 to 14 years	9,631,751	6,661,810	4,911,888	3,371,271	4,719,863	3,290,539
15 to 19 years	9,238,697	5,994,108	4,638,452	2,995,239	4,600,245	2,998,869
20 to 24 years	9,971,178	5,427,006	4,916,082	2,696,975	5,055,096	2,730,031
25 to 29 years	10,571,020	4,675,665	5,193,772	2,360,082	5,377,248	2,315,583
30 to 34 years	10,033,091	3,838,940	4,932,045	1,964,338	5,101,046	1,874,602
35 to 39 years	9,527,185	3,290,031	4,707,973	1,692,363	4,819,212	1,597,668

TABLE **A-3.**—NATIVE POPULATION BY AGE, COLOR, AND SEX: 1950 AND 1900—Cont.

Age and color	Total		Male		Female	
	1950	1900	1950	1900	1950	1900
WHITE--Cont.						
40 to 44 years............	8,394,897	2,892,226	4,182,551	1,502,154	4,212,346	1,390,072
45 to 49 years............	7,103,437	2,270,332	3,536,173	1,186,886	3,567,264	1,083,446
50 to 54 years............	6,295,406	1,834,527	3,115,350	958,686	3,180,056	875,841
55 to 59 years............	5,356,799	1,381,142	2,633,240	696,979	2,723,559	684,163
60 to 64 years............	4,326,631	1,077,908	2,100,922	540,971	2,225,709	536,937
65 to 69 years............	3,472,850	786,221	1,635,715	396,403	1,837,135	389,818
70 to 74 years............	2,434,385	526,887	1,132,364	264,343	1,302,021	262,544
75 to 79 years............	1,567,068	319,476	710,671	157,800	856,397	161,676
80 to 84 years............	805,954	155,967	351,895	74,910	454,059	81,057
85 years and over..........	394,336	71,744	157,156	31,341	237,180	40,403
60 years and over..........	13,001,224	2,938,203	6,088,723	1,465,768	6,912,501	1,472,435
Percent of total.........	10.4	5.2	9.8	5.1	11.0	5.3
65 years and over..........	8,674,593	1,860,295	3,987,801	924,797	4,686,792	935,498
Percent of total.........	7.0	3.3	6.4	3.2	7.5	3.4
60 to 89 years............	12,902,877	2,922,433	6,051,557	1,459,534	6,851,320	1,462,899
NONWHITE						
All ages...............	15,494,756	9,057,920	7,537,935	4,499,808	7,956,821	4,558,112
Under 5 years..............	1,975,857	1,257,811	990,086	625,850	985,771	631,961
5 to 9 years..............	1,600,265	1,242,586	797,767	620,565	802,498	622,021
10 to 14 years............	1,418,490	1,126,609	711,981	566,593	706,509	560,016
15 to 19 years............	1,280,701	1,012,094	622,340	489,489	658,361	522,605
20 to 24 years............	1,284,171	994,122	593,288	472,180	690,883	521,942
25 to 29 years............	1,298,216	756,667	610,338	370,634	687,878	386,033
30 to 34 years............	1,144,274	538,901	534,389	269,248	609,885	269,653
35 to 39 years............	1,165,929	487,284	546,641	239,573	619,288	247,711
40 to 44 years............	984,844	379,181	476,652	184,876	508,192	194,305
45 to 49 years............	867,812	336,665	424,309	173,610	443,503	163,055
50 to 54 years............	703,993	300,143	352,139	159,767	351,854	140,376
55 to 59 years............	516,454	185,382	265,103	100,378	251,351	85,004
60 to 64 years............	387,193	167,727	195,391	88,824	191,802	78,903
65 to 69 years............	403,507	106,714	192,090	57,957	211,417	48,757
70 to 74 years............	222,259	75,599	110,076	37,712	112,183	37,887
75 to 79 years............	131,662	42,140	66,076	21,259	65,586	20,881
80 to 84 years............	66,418	26,819	31,564	12,188	34,854	14,631
85 years and over..........	42,711	21,476	17,705	9,105	25,006	12,371
60 years and over..........	1,253,750	440,475	612,902	227,045	640,848	213,430
Percent of total.........	8.1	4.9	8.1	5.0	8.1	4.7
65 years and over..........	866,557	272,748	417,511	138,221	449,046	134,527
Percent of total.........	5.6	3.0	5.5	3.1	5.6	3.0
60 to 89 years............	1,237,361	429,590	606,691	222,853	630,670	206,737

Source: *1950 Census of Population,* Vol. II, *Characteristics of the Population,* Part 1, U. S. Summary, tables 36, 38, 39, 94, and 97; and Vol. IV, *Special Reports,* Part 3, Chapter B, Nonwhite Population by Race, tables 25 and 26.

TABLE A-4.—FOREIGN-BORN POPULATION BY AGE, COLOR, AND SEX: 1950 AND 1900

Age and color	Total		Male		Female	
	1950	1900	1950	1900	1950	1900
ALL CLASSES						
All ages.............	10,421,745	10,341,276	5,342,502	5,630,190	5,079,243	4,711,086
Under 5 years..............	66,359	52,770	33,378	26,776	32,981	25,994
5 to 9 years...............	64,600	148,082	32,935	74,220	31,665	73,862
10 to 14 years.............	69,027	313,354	36,530	158,712	32,497	154,642
15 to 19 years.............	97,200	569,960	50,550	278,149	46,650	291,811
20 to 24 years.............	226,479	933,575	96,923	467,512	129,556	466,063
25 to 29 years.............	373,024	1,114,396	167,968	603,772	205,056	510,624
30 to 34 years.............	339,642	1,192,724	158,289	677,180	181,353	515,544
35 to 39 years.............	553,272	1,200,627	262,930	693,531	290,342	507,096
40 to 44 years.............	824,232	986,908	411,066	576,247	413,166	410,661
45 to 49 years.............	1,099,216	856,796	565,884	483,404	533,332	373,392
50 to 54 years.............	1,272,789	816,026	661,159	451,350	611,630	364,676
55 to 59 years.............	1,361,867	650,339	731,703	351,609	630,164	298,730
60 to 64 years.............	1,345,651	550,394	741,525	290,364	604,126	260,030
65 to 69 years.............	1,126,579	413,308	596,756	215,443	529,823	197,865
70 to 74 years.............	755,305	283,609	386,389	148,980	368,916	134,629
75 to 79 years.............	453,663	159,549	225,041	83,345	228,622	76,204
80 to 84 years.............	252,986	69,376	121,509	35,567	131,477	33,809
85 years and over..........	139,854	29,483	61,967	14,029	77,887	15,454
60 years and over..........	4,074,038	1,505,719	2,133,187	787,728	1,940,851	717,991
Percent of total.........	39.1	14.6	39.9	14.0	38.2	15.2
65 years and over..........	2,728,387	955,325	1,391,662	497,364	1,336,725	457,961
Percent of total.........	26.2	9.2	26.0	8.8	26.3	9.7
60 to 89 years.............	4,041,216	1,498,500	2,119,266	784,554	1,921,950	713,946
WHITE						
All ages.............	10,161,168	10,213,817	5,176,390	5,515,285	4,984,778	4,698,532
Under 5 years..............	63,149	52,495	31,511	26,645	31,638	25,850
5 to 9 years..............	61,752	147,545	31,277	73,943	30,475	73,602
10 to 14 years.............	62,778	312,315	32,647	158,095	30,131	154,220
15 to 19 years.............	91,823	563,083	47,373	272,177	44,450	290,906
20 to 24 years.............	208,009	921,685	86,700	457,525	121,309	464,160
25 to 29 years.............	353,784	1,099,906	155,935	591,251	197,849	508,655
30 to 34 years.............	323,240	1,176,579	148,565	662,641	174,675	513,938
35 to 39 years.............	531,288	1,180,482	247,968	674,778	283,320	505,704
40 to 44 years.............	795,393	968,509	390,978	558,935	404,415	409,574
45 to 49 years.............	1,065,917	842,288	544,001	469,841	521,916	372,447
50 to 54 years.............	1,240,033	805,360	640,775	441,370	599,258	363,990
55 to 59 years.............	1,338,933	644,571	717,648	346,254	621,285	298,317
60 to 64 years.............	1,325,975	546,353	728,477	286,622	597,498	259,731
65 to 69 years.............	1,112,736	411,734	587,299	214,067	525,437	197,667
70 to 74 years.............	747,190	283,009	380,944	148,502	366,246	134,507
75 to 79 years.............	449,793	159,301	222,662	83,176	227,131	76,125
80 to 84 years.............	251,595	69,242	120,626	35,494	130,969	33,748
85 years and over..........	137,780	29,360	61,004	13,969	76,776	15,391
60 years and over..........	4,025,069	1,498,999	2,101,012	781,830	1,924,057	717,169
Percent of total.........	39.6	14.7	40.6	14.2	38.6	15.3
65 years and over..........	2,699,094	952,646	1,372,535	495,208	1,326,559	457,438
Percent of total.........	26.6	9.3	26.5	9.0	26.6	9.7
60 to 89 years.............	3,993,037	1,491,859	2,087,429	778,695	1,905,608	713,164
NONWHITE						
All ages.............	260,577	127,459	166,112	114,905	94,465	12,554
Under 5 years..............	3,210	275	1,867	131	1,343	144
5 to 9 years..............	2,848	537	1,658	277	1,190	260
10 to 14 years.............	6,249	1,039	3,883	617	2,366	422
15 to 19 years.............	5,377	6,877	3,177	5,972	2,200	905
20 to 24 years.............	18,470	11,890	10,223	9,987	8,247	1,903
25 to 29 years.............	19,240	14,490	12,033	12,521	7,207	1,969
30 to 34 years.............	16,402	16,145	9,724	14,539	6,678	1,606
35 to 39 years.............	21,984	20,145	14,962	18,753	7,022	1,392

TABLE **A–4.**—FOREIGN-BORN POPULATION BY AGE, COLOR, AND SEX: 1950 AND 1900—Cont.

Age and color	Total		Male		Female	
	1950	1900	1950	1900	1950	1900
NONWHITE--Cont.						
40 to 44 years..............	28,839	18,399	20,088	17,312	8,751	1,087
45 to 49 years..............	33,299	14,508	21,883	13,563	11,416	945
50 to 54 years..............	32,756	10,666	20,384	9,980	12,372	686
55 to 59 years..............	22,934	5,768	14,055	5,355	8,879	413
60 to 64 years..............	19,676	4,041	13,048	3,742	6,628	299
65 to 69 years..............	13,843	1,574	9,457	1,376	4,386	198
70 to 74 years..............	8,115	600	5,445	478	2,670	122
75 to 79 years..............	3,870	248	2,379	169	1,491	79
80 to 84 years..............	1,391	134	883	73	508	61
85 years and over..........	2,074	123	963	60	1,111	63
60 years and over..........	48,969	6,720	32,175	5,898	16,794	822
Percent of total........	18.8	5.3	19.4	5.1	17.8	6.5
65 years and over..........	29,293	2,679	19,127	2,156	10,166	523
Percent of total........	11.2	2.1	11.5	1.9	10.8	4.2
60 to 89 years..............	48,179	6,641	31,837	5,859	16,342	782

Source: Same as table A-3.

The limitations of these estimates are obvious—the factors used in correcting for underenumeration are reasonable but only remotely based on empirical observation, and the results obtained from the use of the interpolation of survival rates derived from English life tables are legitimately open to question. In view of this situation, it is perhaps of some interest to find that crude rates based on these estimates for the total population show a reasonably close relationship in the expected direction to similar estimates developed by Thompson and Whelpton for the white population (table A–8).[3] The latter estimates were made by essentially the same procedure except reliance was placed on the fragmentary native mortality data rather than on the English experience. Moreover, in terms of the purpose for which the estimates presented here were made—the development of a rough evaluation of the relative contribution of the increase in the number of births and the decrease in mortality to the increase, between 1900 and 1950, in the size of the native population 60 to 89 years old—it appears that essentially the same results are obtained by using the unadjusted census figures for children under 10 as are obtained by using the estimated births (table A–10).

In estimating the relative contribution to the increase in the population 60 to 89 between 1900 and 1950 of the increase in number of births and the decline in mortality, births in the periods 1810 to 1840 and 1860 to 1890 are related to the population 60 to 89 in 1900 and in 1950 respectively to obtain crude survival rates for 1900 and 1950. If the 1900 survival rate is applied to the 1860–1890 births, an estimate of 10.0 million persons 60 to 89 in 1950 is obtained—about 6.6 million more than the 3.4 million of the same age group observed in 1900; the 6.6 million

[3] Warren S. Thompson and P. K. Whelpton, *Population Trends in the United States*, McGraw-Hill Book Company, New York, 1933, table 74, p. 263.

therefore represents the gain attributable solely to the increase in number of births, since it was calculated on the assumption of no improvement in mortality. If the 1950 survival rate is applied to the 1810–1840 births, an estimate of 4.8 million persons 60 to 89 in 1900 is obtained—1.4 million greater than the observed 3.4 million; the 1.4 million represents the gain attributable solely to declining mortality—that is, the increase which would have occurred if the number of births between 1860 and 1890 had been the same as that between 1810 and 1840 but if the observed improvement in mortality had obtained. The residual increase, 2.8 million, represents the increase attributable to the effects of improved mortality on the number by which the 1860–1890 births exceeded the 1810–1840 births. These figures appear in tabular form in table A–9. Table A–10 summarizes these figures and, with the addition of a figure representing the increase in the foreign born 60 to 89 years old, provides an indication of the relative contributions of the increased number of births, the decline in mortality, and immigration to the increase in the population 60 to 89 between 1900 and 1950.

TABLE **A–5.**—FOREIGN-BORN POPULATION AND IMMIGRATION, FOR THE UNITED STATES: 1840 TO 1950

Year	Foreign-born population	Change from preceding census	Immigration during preceding decade
1950............................	10,421,745	-1,173,151	1,035,039
1940............................	11,594,896	-2,609,253	528,431
1930............................	14,204,149	+283,457	4,107,209
1920............................	13,920,692	+404,806	5,735,811
1910............................	13,515,886	+3,174,610	8,795,386
1900............................	10,341,276	+1,091,716	3,687,564
1890............................	9,249,560	+2,569,617	5,246,613
1880............................	6,679,943	+1,112,714	2,812,191
1870............................	5,567,229	+1,428,532	2,314,824
1860............................	4,138,697	+1,894,095	2,598,214
1850............................	2,244,602	...	1,713,251
1840............................	(1)	...	599,125

[1] Not available.

Source: Table A-4; *1940 Census of Population*, Vol. II, *Characteristics of the Population*, Part 1, U. S. Summary, tables 4 and 15; U. S. Bureau of the Census, *Historical Statistics of the United States, 1820–1945*, Series B 304–330, p. 33.

TABLE **A–6.**—ESTIMATED BIRTHS FOR TOTAL POPULATION: 1810 TO 1910

Year	Births (thousands)	Year	Births (thousands)	Year	Births (thousands)
1905 to 1910..........	13,589	1870 to 1885...........	9,179	1835 to 1840..........	4,140
1900 to 1905..........	12,213	1865 to 1870...........	8,095	1830 to 1835..........	3,616
1895 to 1900..........	12,295	1860 to 1865...........	7,062	1825 to 1830..........	3,242
1890 to 1895..........	11,776	1855 to 1860...........	6,864	1820 to 1825..........	2,836
1885 to 1890..........	10,727	1850 to 1855...........	5,992	1815 to 1820..........	2,469
1880 to 1885..........	10,369	1845 to 1850...........	5,107	1810 to 1815..........	2,170
1875 to 1880..........	9,580	1840 to 1845...........	4,705		

Source: Derived from data on children under 10 years old from decennial censuses, 1820 to 1910; English life tables for 1838-54, 1870-71, 1880-91, and 1890-91; United States life tables for 1901-1910; unpublished data of the Bureau of the Census.

TABLE A-7.—ESTIMATED BIRTHS, BY DECADES: 1810 TO 1950

Decade	Estimated births adjusted to April 1 (thousands)	Decade	Estimated births adjusted to June 1 (thousands)
Total, 1860 to 1950..........	218,350	Total, 1810 to 1900..........	120,213
1890 to 1950.......................	163,467	1840 to 1900.......................	101,750
1940 to 1950....................	31,934	1890 to 1900....................	24,070
1930 to 1940....................	24,360	1880 to 1890....................	21,096
1920 to 1930....................	28,500	1870 to 1880....................	18,759
1910 to 1920....................	28,866	1860 to 1870....................	15,158
1900 to 1910....................	25,789	1850 to 1860....................	12,856
1890 to 1900....................	24,018	1840 to 1850....................	9,812
1860 to 1890.......................	54,884	1810 to 1840.......................	18,463
1880 to 1890....................	21,057	1830 to 1840....................	7,757
1870 to 1880....................	18,710	1820 to 1830....................	6,078
1860 to 1870....................	15,117	1810 to 1820....................	4,629

Source: Same as table A-6.

TABLE A-8.—ESTIMATED CRUDE BIRTH RATE FOR THE TOTAL POPULATION: 1820 TO 1900

[Estimates of births for each year represent annual averages for the quinquennia adjacent to each year]

Year	Total population			White population
	Population (thousands)	Estimated births (annual average in thousands)	Crude rate	Crude rate as estimated by Thompson and Whelpton
1900................................	75,995	2,455	32.3	30.1
1880................................	50,156	1,995	39.8	35.2
1860................................	31,443	1,393	44.3	41.4
1840................................	17,069	885	51.8	48.3
1820................................	9,638	532	55.2	52.8

Source: Table A-6; Warren S. Thompson and P. K. Whelpton, *Population Trends in United States*, McGraw-Hill, New York, 1933, table 74.

TABLE A-9.—SURVIVORS 60 TO 89 YEARS OLD EXPECTED IN 1950 AND 1900 FROM 1950 AND 1900 SURVIVAL RATES, AND BIRTHS, 1860 TO 1890 AND 1810 TO 1840

[In thousands]

Number of births	1860 to 1890	1810 to 1840	Increase
Births................................	54,884	18,463	36,421

Mortality assumption	Expected survivors (native population)		
	1950	1900	Gain from increase in births
Survival rate for 1950.......................	14,140	4,757	9,383
Survival rate for 1900.......................	9,964	3,352	6,612
Gain from decrease in mortality.............	4,176	1,405	2,771

Source: Same as tables A-3 and A-6.

TABLE **A-10.**—INCREASE IN POPULATION 60 TO 89 YEARS OLD, 1900 TO 1950,
BY COMPONENTS OF INCREASE

Components of increase	Based on estimates of births		Based on population under 10 years	
	Number (thousands)	Percent	Number (thousands)	Percent
Total increase..........................	13,331	100.0	13,331	100.0
In native population,.....................	10,788	80.9	10,788	80.9
From increase in number of births..........	6,612	49.6	6,782	50.9
From decrease in mortality.................	1,405	10.5	1,325	9.9
From increase in births and decrease in mortality...............................	2,771	20.8	2,681	20.1
In foreign-born population (immigration).....	2,543	19.1	2,543	19.1

Source: Tables A-3, A-4, and A-9; figures on children under 10 years old derived from decennial census reports, 1820 to 1950.

APPENDIX   B

GEOGRAPHIC DISTRIBUTION

Section 1: Age data from the 1950 Census

The principle source of data on age for geographic subdivisions of the United States are the initial 100-percent tabulations, on which the statistics presented in Chapter B, Vol. II, of the States reports are based; the initial 20-percent tabulation, on which the statistics presented in Chapter C of the same reports are based; and the 3⅓-percent sample tabulation, on which the statistics on size of place are based.   The statistics on persons 60 and over and 65 and over for States and the urban and rural parts of States, presented in tables B–4 and B–7, are from the 100-percent tabulation, as are the statistics on suburban communities presented in tables B–8 and B–9. The statistics presented in table B–6 on the nativity and State of birth are based on the 20-percent sample, and those in table B–10, on the 3⅓-percent sample; therefore, comparable numbers and percentages will not agree precisely with those presented in table B–4.

Section 2: State indexes of fertility, mortality, and migration

Any systematic consideration of interstate differences in the proportion of older persons in relation to interstate differences in fertility, mortality, and migration requires indexes summarizing these latter factors.   The selection of indexes was determined by the availability of appropriate data supplemented by "reasonable" assumptions.   The classification of States on the basis of these indexes did not appear to be particularly illuminating and, therefore, in an attempt to obtain a clearer picture of the relationships involved, estimates of the age structure expected in the State in the absence of migration in the period 1890 to 1950 were developed.   The methods by which the indexes of fertility, mortality, and migration, and the estimates of expected population were developed are as follows:

Fertility ratio.   The index of fertility developed simply represents the average of a figure for each census between 1900 and 1950 representing the number of children under 5 per 100 women 15 to 49 years of age. The ratios are based directly on published census figures and are not adjusted for underenumeration on the hypothesis that estimates of State-to-State variations in underenumeration would not be sufficiently accurate to

147

improve the ratios as an index of State-to-State variations in fertility. In short, it was felt that there was no assurance that a correction for under-enumeration would really improve the adequacy of the index.

Index of mortality. Here the State figures on the expectation of life at birth from the 1929–1931 life tables were used. The year 1930 was the first year in which the vital statistics necessary for developing life tables were available for most of the States. Even in this year it was necessary to estimate a figure for the State of Texas. These figures then were taken to approximate the mid-point of the period between 1890 and 1950. The scattered State figures prior to 1930 and the subsequent complete State figures since 1930 suggest that there has been some convergence in the mortality schedules among the States, and that many States have not necessarily maintained the same rank throughout the entire period 1890 to 1950. Here again, however, the structure of assumptions necessary to take these established generalizations into consideration would have been so elaborate as to create a reasonable doubt that any genuine improvement had been made in the index.

The final figures used as indexes represent the mean expectation of the figures for each sex-color group weighted by the proportion of each sex-color group in the total population. Since individual State figures for non-white males and nonwhite females were not available, the State figures were developed on the assumption that the relationship observed between the white and the nonwhite population at the national level obtained in each State. The approximate nature of the final index is apparent from this description.

Index of migration. The migration rates were developed from the estimates of net interstate migration prepared in connection with the University of Pennsylvania Studies of Population Redistribution and Economic Growth. The figures relate to the population 10 years old and over. In computing the rates, the aggregate net migration for the periods 1890 to 1920 and 1920 to 1950 was expressed as a percentage of the population expected at the end of each period. Here, again, there are a number of methodological problems. The estimates of net migration will vary appreciably with variations in the methods used, the use of the sheer decade aggregates ignores variation in the direction of migration within the two time periods, and also the variation in direction with age. It is therefore apparent that the index used is relatively crude, and significance can be attached only to relatively high migration rates.

Estimates of the population expected in the absence of migration, 1890 to 1950. These estimates merely represent an extension of the technique of calculating intercensal net migration to a 60-year period. They begin with the observed population of 1890 which, by the application of estimates of numbers of births and deaths, is brought forward to 1950.

Estimates of the additions to the population from births were obtained by computing the ratios of the number of observed children under 5 and children 5 to 9 to the observed number of women 15 to 49 at each census date. In these computations a correction was made for underenumeration in the group under 5, since the nature of the over-all calculation was such that understatements at this point cumulated throughout the entire calculation. These ratios were then applied to the expected number of women 15 to 49 at each census date to obtain an estimate for the two age groups at that date. The estimates of the loss to the population through mortality were made by applying age specific survival rates for the white population of each sex first to the 1890 population and then to the population at subsequent census dates as estimated. These survival rates were derived initially from the United States life tables for the appropriate years, and then the rates at the beginning and end of each decade were averaged to provide decade survival rates. Except for the age groups under 5 and 5 to 9 years, these rates were computed on a 10-year basis to the age group 70 and over. Rates for the decade 1890 to 1900 were developed on the assumption that the improvement observed in mortality between 1900 and 1910 had also occurred between 1890 and 1900.

In order to approximate the variations in mortality among the States, the 1930 United States rates were related to the 1930 rates for Kansas, Oregon, and Arizona, and the whole United States series was adjusted to this level. In addition, special adjustments were made for the States of Colorado and Nevada. The remaining States were then classified into four survival rate levels: (a) the Kansas level (highest); (b) the Oregon level (relative high); (c) the United States level (medium); and (d) the Arizona level (low). The appropriate rates were applied to each group of States. For States in which, in 1930, 10 percent or more of the population were nonwhite, calculations were made separately for the white and nonwhite population. In making estimates for the nonwhite population, United States rates, developed in the same way as those for the white population, were used. These various procedures then serve as a means of roughly approximating variations in mortality levels among the States.

The difficulties encountered with the procedure outlined are obvious. The estimates of the population increase from births would obviously have been better had they been based on age specific birth rates for the entire period. In the absence of such data, however, it seemed an open question as to whether the assumptions involved in estimating such rates would lead to results with a level of accuracy higher than that of the cruder procedure used. In either procedure, no recognition is given to the possibility of differential levels among migratory and nonmigratory populations. Likewise, the estimates of age specific losses through deaths are of necessity rough approximations and rest on a structure of reasonable but unproved assumptions. In addition, the use of 10-year survival rates yields results which fail to reflect precisely some of the abnormalities in the initial age distributions. It is, therefore, clear that the final estimates of the population expected in the absence of migration are rough approximations. They do, however, give some indication of the general effects of large-scale in-migration or of out-migration, as well as illustrate the role of fertility and mortality differences in determining age structure.

Section 3: Data on suburban age structure

The statistics presented in table B–8 are based on the 100-percent age tabulations for urbanized areas and urban places, and on 20-percent housing data on the year in which dwelling units were built. Suburbs were defined as urban places of 2,500 or more in the urban fringe. For each of these places the number of decades prior to 1950 necessary to account for the building of 50 percent or more of the 1950 dwelling units was determined and, on this basis, the suburbs were classified as follows: those in which 50 percent or more of the dwellings were built prior to 1920, and those in which 50 percent or more were built between 1920 and 1950, between 1930 and 1950, and between 1940 and 1950. Figures on the total population and the population 65 and over were then summarized for each of these classes.

The materials presented in table B–9 on the observed and expected population of Los Angeles suburbs are based on 100-percent data from the 1950 Census. The estimates of the population expected in 1950 on the assumption of no migration since 1930 were developed by applying 20-year survival rates (based on 1939–1941 California life tables for the white population) to the 1930 population to obtain an estimate of the number of survivors 20 years old and over in 1950. The expected population under 20 in 1950 was then estimated on the assumption that it bore the same relationship to the observed population under 20 as the expected population 20 to 54 bore to the observed population 20 to 54 years old—that is, that the size of the population under 20 was in large part a function of the size of the total population passing through, and in, the child-bearing ages between 1930 and 1950. It is obvious that this is an assumption calculated to produce reasonably rough estimates of the expected population under 20. It was found, however, that the use of more refined and elaborate methods for several of the suburbs under consideration produced estimates of the expected population in which the percentages 65 and over did not differ materially from those obtained by the cruder method.

TABLE **B-1.**—FERTILITY RATIO, BY STATES: 1900 TO 1950

[Ratio expressed as number of children under 5 years old per 100 women 15 to 49 years old.
Data for children under 5 years not adjusted for underenumeration]

State	Mean ratio, 1900 to 1950	1950	1940	1930	1920	1910	1900
United States............	40.0	41.7	29.2	35.1	42.2	44.6	47.4
New England:							
Maine.....................	38.9	45.4	33.2	39.0	39.8	38.6	37.2
New Hampshire.............	35.4	42.0	28.2	34.2	37.0	35.6	35.2
Vermont...................	39.7	46.8	34.2	39.1	40.5	39.1	38.6
Massachusetts.............	32.6	37.1	23.4	30.1	36.3	34.0	34.7
Rhode Island..............	33.4	37.3	23.1	31.8	37.7	35.3	35.4
Connecticut...............	34.3	36.9	22.4	30.6	42.2	36.8	37.0
Middle Atlantic:							
New York..................	31.6	34.0	21.2	27.6	35.0	34.7	37.0
New Jersey................	34.0	35.5	21.2	29.5	39.9	38.0	40.0
Pennsylvania..............	38.8	37.1	26.5	35.5	45.0	44.1	44.3
East North Central:							
Ohio......................	36.2	41.6	26.9	32.6	39.2	37.7	39.3
Indiana...................	37.8	42.9	29.7	34.3	38.5	39.2	42.3
Illinois..................	35.2	37.2	24.4	29.1	37.7	39.3	43.7
Michigan..................	39.8	43.1	30.4	37.0	44.2	41.5	42.5
Wisconsin.................	41.7	44.5	31.0	36.3	43.2	43.7	51.4
West North Central:							
Minnesota.................	42.5	46.3	31.1	34.7	43.1	44.0	55.6
Iowa......................	40.4	45.1	31.7	35.2	40.8	41.7	47.7
Missouri..................	36.8	38.5	27.3	31.4	36.2	41.4	46.0
North Dakota..............	55.0	52.6	38.8	46.0	60.3	62.3	69.9
South Dakota..............	49.1	50.7	35.6	41.8	52.0	53.1	61.5
Nebraska..................	42.4	44.0	30.4	36.6	43.7	47.0	52.6
Kansas....................	40.6	43.2	29.4	35.7	41.8	45.5	48.2
South Atlantic:							
Delaware..................	36.2	39.8	26.7	31.4	40.0	37.8	41.3
Maryland..................	37.0	41.5	27.1	33.5	38.0	39.1	42.5
District of Columbia......	23.4	29.0	18.6	21.3	20.3	25.2	26.0
Virginia..................	45.7	44.3	34.0	41.6	47.7	52.1	54.3
West Virginia.............	51.7	47.6	39.6	49.0	56.3	58.1	59.4
North Carolina...........	52.6	47.2	38.5	48.0	57.5	62.1	62.2
South Carolina...........	52.5	51.4	40.7	45.0	54.0	60.8	62.9
Georgia...................	48.3	46.9	35.9	40.3	48.8	57.8	60.3
Florida...................	42.2	39.9	28.2	35.0	41.6	51.1	57.3
East South Central:							
Kentucky..................	47.6	48.3	39.2	45.3	48.6	51.0	53.4
Tennessee.................	45.8	44.2	34.9	40.7	46.8	53.2	55.0
Alabama...................	50.1	48.1	38.6	44.7	50.3	58.7	60.2
Mississippi...............	50.7	52.6	40.3	44.1	47.2	58.4	61.4
West South Central:							
Arkansas..................	50.6	49.0	38.4	43.6	50.7	60.4	61.5
Louisiana.................	46.6	48.1	34.9	40.3	44.1	53.4	58.9
Oklahoma..................	50.2	43.2	35.3	42.6	50.8	62.1	67.2
Texas.....................	46.8	44.9	32.2	38.9	44.6	56.6	63.6
Mountain:							
Montana...................	45.2	49.8	34.7	37.9	50.6	45.1	52.9
Idaho.....................	51.4	52.1	39.8	43.1	53.9	55.1	64.4
Wyoming...................	47.3	49.2	35.3	41.0	48.9	50.6	58.5
Colorado..................	39.2	44.8	32.8	35.8	40.6	39.5	41.6
New Mexico................	55.0	56.1	47.1	52.2	54.5	59.1	61.1
Arizona...................	49.4	48.9	41.0	45.7	50.5	53.8	56.5
Utah......................	54.4	55.4	41.5	47.5	57.2	59.7	64.9
Nevada....................	37.5	41.4	32.7	33.7	38.5	36.5	42.4
Pacific:							
Washington................	37.3	45.5	26.8	28.3	36.8	39.3	46.9
Oregon....................	35.5	43.7	26.5	27.7	35.6	36.8	42.5
California................	31.1	40.1	24.0	26.5	30.4	31.5	34.0

Source: *1950 Census of Population*, Vol. II, *Characteristics of the Population*, Parts 2 to 50, table 16.

TABLE **B-2.**—EXPECTATION OF LIFE AT BIRTH, BY COLOR AND SEX, BY STATES: 1929 TO 1931

[Average future lifetime in years]

State	Total[1]	White		Nonwhite[2]	
		Male	Female	Male	Female
United States............	59.62	59.12	62.67	47.55	49.51
New England:					
Maine.....................	59.49	58.70	61.85	47.21	48.86
New Hampshire.............	61.38	60.24	62.56	48.45	49.42
Vermont...................	61.31	59.97	62.74	48.23	49.57
Massachusetts.............	60.84	59.29	62.63	47.69	49.48
Rhode Island..............	59.58	58.06	61.39	46.70	48.50
Connecticut...............	61.33	59.77	63.35	48.07	50.05
Middle Atlantic:					
New York..................	59.36	57.84	61.72	46.52	48.76
New Jersey................	60.18	58.96	62.72	47.42	49.55
Pennsylvania..............	58.96	57.68	61.35	46.39	48.47
East North Central:					
Ohio......................	60.81	59.78	63.04	48.08	49.80
Indiana...................	60.96	60.04	62.79	48.29	49.60
Illinois..................	60.35	59.02	62.82	47.47	49.63
Michigan..................	60.76	59.80	62.76	48.10	49.58
Wisconsin.................	62.91	61.51	64.60	49.47	51.03
West North Central:					
Minnesota.................	63.44	61.97	65.22	49.84	51.52
Iowa......................	64.35	63.04	65.90	50.70	52.06
Missouri..................	60.79	59.76	63.38	48.06	50.07
North Dakota..............	64.35	63.24	65.95	50.86	52.10
South Dakota..............	65.10	64.38	66.81	51.78	52.78
Nebraska..................	64.16	62.92	65.82	50.61	52.00
Kansas....................	64.14	63.24	66.06	50.86	52.19
South Atlantic:					
Delaware..................	58.51	58.25	62.18	46.85	49.12
Maryland..................	57.55	57.72	61.51	46.42	48.59
District of Columbia......	56.24	56.35	62.46	45.32	49.34
Virginia..................	57.26	58.69	62.46	47.20	49.34
West Virginia.............	58.86	58.14	61.28	46.76	48.41
North Carolina............	56.62	58.95	61.51	47.41	48.59
South Carolina............	53.98	57.64	61.32	46.36	48.44
Georgia...................	56.25	58.92	62.65	47.39	49.49
Florida...................	57.69	58.99	63.77	47.45	50.38
East South Central:					
Kentucky..................	59.40	59.37	61.57	47.75	48.64
Tennessee.................	58.12	58.76	61.96	47.26	48.95
Alabama...................	56.23	59.37	61.88	47.75	48.89
Mississippi...............	55.49	60.34	63.28	48.53	49.99
West South Central:					
Arkansas..................	58.73	60.43	63.58	48.60	50.23
Louisiana.................	56.10	58.42	62.92	46.99	49.71
Oklahoma..................	62.59	62.72	65.42	50.45	51.68
Texas.....................	57.64	[3]57.48	[3]61.43	46.23	48.53
Mountain:					
Montana...................	61.20	59.40	64.26	47.78	50.77
Idaho.....................	62.82	61.44	64.78	49.42	51.18
Wyoming...................	61.24	59.78	63.57	48.08	50.22
Colorado..................	57.26	55.40	59.60	44.56	47.08
New Mexico................	50.01	49.46	52.22	39.78	41.25
Arizona...................	50.03	48.08	55.15	38.67	43.57
Utah......................	60.74	58.42	63.57	46.99	50.22
Nevada....................	57.97	55.77	63.13	44.86	49.87
Pacific:					
Washington................	62.94	61.37	65.41	49.36	51.67
Oregon....................	63.01	61.17	65.45	49.20	51.71
California................	60.45	58.56	63.68	47.10	50.31

[1] Weighted mean of sex-color groups.

[2] State values estimated on the basis of relationship between white and Negro values at the United States level, and on the assumption that life table values for Negroes are adequately representative of the nonwhite population as a whole.

[3] Estimated.

Source: *1950 Census of Population*, Vol. II, *Characteristics of the Population*, Parts 2 to 50, table 16; U. S. Bureau of the Census, *United States Life Tables and Actuarial Tables, 1939 to 1941*, table J; National Resources Committee, "State Data—Life Tables for White Population, by States, 1929 to 1931," *Population Statistics.*

TABLE **B–3.**—AGGREGATE NET MIGRATION, 1920–1950 AND 1890–1920, BY STATES

[Data for persons of "Other races" are excluded with the exception of the 1890-1900 component of the net migration figures for 1890 to 1920 which cover the total population. Minus sign (−) indicates net out-migration]

State	1920 to 1950				1890 to 1920			
	Population, 1950		Net migration[2]		Population, 1920		Net migration[2]	
	Observed	Expected[1]	Number	Rate[3]	Observed	Expected[1]	Number	Rate[3]
United States..	149,984,314	146,866,348	3,117,966	2.1	105,284,046	95,135,901	10,148,145	10.7
New England:								
Maine...........	912,067	988,378	-76,311	-7.7	767,005	761,607	5,398	0.7
New Hampshire....	533,006	543,470	-10,464	-1.9	442,952	423,200	19,752	4.7
Vermont.........	377,631	440,867	-63,236	-14.3	352,389	376,484	-24,095	-6.4
Massachusetts....	4,684,674	4,760,704	-76,030	-1.6	3,848,990	3,016,727	832,263	27.6
Rhode Island.....	790,918	778,992	11,926	1.5	604,016	479,379	124,637	26.0
Connecticut......	2,005,801	1,812,995	192,806	10.6	1,379,778	1,054,596	325,182	30.8
Middle Atlantic:								
New York........	14,790,286	13,245,341	1,544,945	11.7	10,370,510	8,238,756	2,131,754	25.9
New Jersey.......	4,830,150	4,214,569	615,581	14.6	3,154,219	2,282,119	872,100	38.2
Pennsylvania.....	10,492,333	11,492,718	-1,000,385	-8.7	8,717,294	7,963,515	753,779	9.5
East North Central:								
Ohio............	7,941,294	7,630,941	310,353	4.1	5,758,080	4,976,586	781,494	15.7
Indiana.........	3,932,680	3,866,413	66,267	1.7	2,929,881	2,936,541	-6,660	-0.2
Illinois........	8,692,038	8,256,709	435,329	5.3	6,481,607	5,660,009	821,598	14.5
Michigan........	6,360,121	5,541,500	818,621	14.8	3,661,709	3,018,330	643,379	21.3
Wisconsin.......	3,420,872	3,544,936	-124,064	-3.5	2,622,139	2,491,154	130,985	5.3
West North Central:								
Minnesota.......	2,967,719	3,199,348	-231,629	-7.2	2,377,745	2,098,243	279,502	13.3
Iowa............	2,619,238	3,036,824	-417,586	-13.8	2,403,186	2,605,705	-202,519	-7.8
Missouri........	3,952,681	4,240,826	-288,145	-6.8	3,403,285	3,723,610	-320,325	-8.6
North Dakota.....	608,705	900,492	-291,787	-32.4	640,421	484,438	155,983	32.2
South Dakota.....	629,231	847,329	-218,098	-25.7	619,979	563,233	56,746	10.1
Nebraska........	1,320,562	1,662,034	-341,472	-20.5	1,292,461	1,508,706	-216,245	-14.3
Kansas..........	1,902,119	2,231,293	-329,174	-14.8	1,766,831	1,969,930	-203,099	-10.3
South Atlantic:								
Delaware........	317,476	290,850	26,626	9.2	222,950	216,981	5,969	2.8
Maryland........	2,340,947	2,027,647	313,300	15.5	1,449,216	1,408,548	40,668	2.9
Dist. of Col.....	798,668	534,420	264,248	49.4	436,826	264,909	171,917	64.9
Virginia........	3,315,766	3,395,951	-80,185	-2.4	2,307,926	2,506,307	-198,381	-7.9
West Virginia....	2,005,149	2,344,379	-339,230	-14.5	1,463,580	1,401,584	61,996	4.4
North Carolina...	4,030,474	4,326,420	-295,946	-6.8	2,547,186	2,794,745	-247,559	-8.9
South Carolina...	2,115,482	2,647,582	-532,100	-20.1	1,683,257	1,925,730	-242,473	-12.6
Georgia..........	3,443,339	4,216,594	-773,255	-18.3	2,895,479	3,097,220	-201,741	-6.5
Florida..........	2,769,152	1,680,632	1,088,520	64.8	967,640	724,937	242,703	33.5
East South Central:								
Kentucky........	2,944,011	3,562,697	-618,686	-17.4	2,416,498	2,832,033	-415,535	-14.7
Tennessee.......	3,290,860	3,520,104	-229,244	-6.5	2,337,751	2,728,878	-391,127	-14.3
Alabama.........	3,059,208	3,645,036	-585,828	-16.1	2,347,684	2,554,609	-206,925	-8.1
Mississippi......	2,175,126	2,718,088	-542,962	-20.0	1,789,146	2,084,451	-295,305	-14.2
West South Central:								
Arkansas........	1,908,146	2,548,892	-640,746	-25.1	1,751,977	1,940,514	-188,537	-9.7
Louisiana.......	2,679,111	2,810,559	-131,448	-4.7	1,796,868	1,850,333	-53,465	-2.9
Oklahoma........	2,178,029	2,856,109	-678,080	-23.7	1,970,602	910,489	1,060,113	116.4
Texas...........	7,703,992	7,402,262	301,730	4.1	4,659,859	4,269,296	390,563	9.1
Mountain:								
Montana.........	573,270	708,487	-135,217	-19.1	535,918	285,498	250,420	87.7
Idaho...........	582,445	642,258	-59,813	-9.3	426,588	241,004	185,584	77.0
Wyoming.........	286,566	292,694	-6,128	-2.1	191,521	119,955	71,566	59.7
Colorado........	1,316,830	1,298,059	18,771	1.4	935,421	677,295	258,126	38.1
New Mexico.......	638,619	633,203	5,416	0.9	340,406	293,987	46,419	15.8
Arizona.........	680,485	504,312	176,173	34.9	299,454	132,142	167,312	126.6
Utah............	679,638	734,564	-54,926	-7.5	443,347	408,006	35,341	8.7
Nevada..........	154,210	106,118	48,092	45.3	71,045	49,541	21,504	43.4
Pacific:								
Washington......	2,347,187	1,805,977	541,210	30.0	1,326,660	670,515	656,145	97.9
Oregon..........	1,508,657	1,074,121	434,536	40.5	771,290	475,389	295,901	62.2
California......	10,377,345	5,301,654	5,075,691	95.7	3,303,474	1,638,137	1,665,337	101.7

[1] Difference between observed population and net migration.

[2] For persons 10 years old and over.

[3] Net migration as percent of expected population.

Source: *1950 Census of Population,* Vol. II, *Characteristics of the Population,* Parts 2 to 50, table 14; Everett S. Lee, Daniel O. Price, and others, *Net Intercensal Migration, 1870-1950,* Studies of Population Redistribution and Economic Growth, University of Pennsylvania, Philadelphia, 1954, tables I, II, IIa, and III.

Table **B-4.**—Population 60 and 65 Years Old and Over, by States: 1950 and 1900

State	1950					1900				
	All ages	60 years old and over	65 years old and over	Percent of all ages		All ages	60 years old and over[1]	65 years old and over[1]	Percent of all ages	
				60 and over	65 and over				60 and over	65 and over
United States......	150,697,361	18,029,012	12,269,537	12.2	8.1	75,994,575	4,871,861	3,080,498	6.4	4.1
New England:										
Maine.........	913,774	131,955	93,562	14.4	10.2	694,466	81,861	55,122	11.8	7.9
New Hampshire..	533,242	82,009	57,793	15.4	10.8	411,588	47,368	32,344	11.5	7.9
Vermont........	377,747	55,467	39,534	14.7	10.5	343,641	40,598	27,771	11.8	8.1
Massachusetts..	4,690,514	689,334	468,436	14.7	10.0	2,805,346	223,345	143,107	8.0	5.1
Rhode Island...	791,896	105,331	70,418	13.3	8.9	428,556	31,770	19,798	7.4	4.6
Connecticut....	2,007,280	268,349	176,824	13.4	8.8	908,420	78,004	50,850	8.6	5.6
Middle Atlantic:										
New York.......	14,830,192	1,943,142	1,258,457	13.1	8.5	7,268,894	546,464	347,905	7.5	4.8
New Jersey.....	4,835,329	609,535	393,989	12.6	8.1	1,883,669	128,843	79,617	6.8	4.2
Pennsylvania...	10,498,012	1,339,097	886,825	12.8	8.4	6,302,115	415,958	261,817	6.6	4.2
E. North Central:										
Ohio...........	7,946,627	1,053,805	708,975	13.3	8.9	4,157,545	323,249	209,563	7.8	5.0
Indiana........	3,934,224	528,002	361,026	13.4	9.2	2,516,462	183,813	117,861	7.3	4.7
Illinois.......	8,712,176	1,155,449	754,301	13.3	8.7	4,821,550	300,161	190,639	6.2	4.0
Michigan.......	6,371,766	715,426	461,650	11.2	7.2	2,420,982	188,045	121,160	7.8	5.0
Wisconsin......	3,434,575	464,406	309,917	13.5	9.0	2,069,042	151,761	103,192	7.3	5.0
W. North Central:										
Minnesota......	2,982,483	403,984	269,130	13.5	9.0	1,751,394	101,908	66,771	5.8	3.8
Iowa...........	2,621,073	393,241	272,998	15.0	10.4	2,231,853	161,070	105,916	7.2	4.7
Missouri.......	3,954,653	588,188	407,388	14.9	10.3	3,106,665	183,220	112,682	5.9	3.6
North Dakota...	619,636	72,050	48,196	11.6	7.8	319,146	11,776	7,357	3.7	2.3
South Dakota...	652,740	83,628	55,296	12.8	8.5	401,570	20,759	12,836	5.2	3.2
Nebraska.......	1,325,510	191,954	130,379	14.5	9.8	1,066,300	56,882	34,754	5.3	3.3
Kansas.........	1,905,299	279,722	194,218	14.7	10.2	1,470,495	97,878	60,373	6.7	4.1
South Atlantic:										
Delaware.......	318,085	39,000	26,320	12.3	8.3	184,735	13,525	8,468	7.3	4.6
Maryland.......	2,343,001	246,084	163,514	10.5	7.0	1,188,044	80,483	49,983	6.8	4.2
Dist. of Col...	802,178	86,512	56,687	10.8	7.1	278,718	19,935	11,734	7.2	4.2
Virginia.......	3,318,680	317,180	214,524	9.6	6.5	1,854,184	115,442	72,846	6.2	3.9
West Virginia..	2,005,552	204,474	138,526	10.2	6.9	958,800	50,572	32,236	5.3	3.4
North Carolina.	4,061,929	335,438	225,297	8.3	5.5	1,893,810	103,206	66,148	5.4	3.5
South Carolina.	2,117,027	169,560	115,005	8.0	5.4	1,340,316	66,148	39,623	4.9	3.0
Georgia........	3,444,578	319,751	219,655	9.3	6.4	2,216,331	109,239	66,376	4.9	3.0
Florida........	2,771,305	345,981	237,474	12.5	8.6	528,542	23,086	13,941	4.4	2.6
E. South Central:										
Kentucky.......	2,944,806	339,398	235,243	11.5	8.0	2,147,174	121,628	77,127	5.7	3.6
Tennessee......	3,291,718	341,253	234,884	10.4	7.1	2,020,616	106,456	66,441	5.3	3.3
Alabama........	3,061,743	287,881	198,648	9.4	6.5	1,828,697	86,938	54,306	4.8	3.0
Mississippi....	2,178,914	217,223	152,964	10.0	7.0	1,551,270	74,221	45,029	4.8	2.9
W. South Central:										
Arkansas.......	1,909,511	216,402	148,995	11.3	7.8	1,311,564	52,960	31,344	4.0	2.4
Louisiana......	2,683,516	258,232	176,849	9.6	6.6	1,381,625	65,277	40,223	4.7	2.9
Oklahoma.......	2,233,351	278,625	193,922	12.5	8.7	790,391	27,610	15,379	3.5	1.9
Texas..........	7,711,194	766,592	513,420	9.9	6.7	3,048,710	124,295	74,037	4.1	2.4
Mountain:										
Montana........	591,024	78,804	50,864	13.3	8.6	243,329	8,935	4,845	3.7	2.0
Idaho..........	588,637	65,707	43,537	11.2	7.4	161,772	7,626	4,425	4.7	2.7
Wyoming........	290,529	28,715	18,165	9.9	6.3	92,531	2,672	1,407	2.9	1.5
Colorado.......	1,325,089	169,118	115,592	12.8	8.7	539,700	24,217	13,646	4.5	2.5
New Mexico.....	681,187	51,231	33,064	7.5	4.9	195,310	10,062	5,846	5.2	3.0
Arizona........	749,587	68,200	44,241	9.1	5.9	122,931	5,908	3,328	4.8	2.7
Utah...........	688,862	64,163	42,418	9.3	6.2	276,749	15,348	10,055	5.5	3.6
Nevada.........	160,083	17,201	10,986	10.7	6.9	42,335	3,863	2,268	9.1	5.4
Pacific:										
Washington.....	2,378,963	315,321	211,405	13.3	8.9	518,103	25,088	14,681	4.8	2.8
Oregon.........	1,521,341	201,251	133,021	13.2	8.7	413,536	26,654	16,475	6.4	4.0
California.....	10,586,223	1,345,641	895,005	12.7	8.5	1,485,053	125,734	76,846	8.5	5.2

[1] As reported in the census; not adjusted for unknown age.

Source: *1950 Census of Population*, Vol. II, *Characteristics of the Population*, Parts 2 to 50, table 16.

TABLE **B-5.**—POPULATION 60 YEARS OLD AND OVER, OBSERVED AND EXPECTED IF NO
MIGRATION SINCE 1890, FOR STATES: 1950

[Minus sign (−) indicates net effective out-migration]

State	Total population			Population 60 years old and over					
				Number			Percent of total		
	Observed	Expected if no migration	Difference (net effective migration)	Observed	Expected if no migration	Difference (net effective migration)	Ob-served	Ex-pected	Dif-fer-ence
New England:									
Maine...........	913,774	1,066,390	−152,616	131,955	127,909	4,046	14.4	12.0	(¹)
New Hampshire....	533,242	506,957	26,285	82,009	68,401	13,608	15.4	13.5	51.8
Vermont.........	377,747	545,778	−168,031	55,467	64,648	−9,181	14.7	11.8	5.5
Massachusetts....	4,690,514	2,888,958	1,801,556	689,334	432,360	256,974	14.7	15.0	14.3
Rhode Island.....	791,896	479,830	312,066	105,331	69,094	36,237	13.3	14.4	11.6
Connecticut......	2,007,280	1,051,857	955,423	268,349	146,710	121,639	13.4	13.9	12.7
Middle Atlantic:									
New York........	14,830,192	7,862,645	6,967,547	1,943,142	1,235,191	707,951	13.1	15.7	10.2
New Jersey.......	4,835,329	2,191,538	2,643,791	609,535	303,646	305,889	12.6	13.9	11.6
Pennsylvania.....	10,498,012	10,022,201	475,811	1,339,097	1,194,155	144,942	12.8	11.9	30.5
East North Central:									
Ohio............	7,946,627	6,126,260	1,820,367	1,053,805	830,156	223,649	13.3	13.6	12.3
Indiana.........	3,934,224	4,077,798	−143,574	528,002	516,530	11,472	13.4	12.7	(¹)
Illinois........	8,712,176	6,511,963	2,200,213	1,155,449	907,096	248,353	13.3	13.9	11.3
Michigan........	6,371,766	3,971,345	2,400,421	715,426	474,468	240,958	11.2	11.9	10.0
Wisconsin.......	3,434,575	3,856,078	−421,503	464,406	444,474	19,932	13.5	11.5	(¹)
West North Central:									
Minnesota.......	2,982,483	3,044,828	−62,345	403,984	348,865	55,119	13.5	11.5	(¹)
Iowa............	2,621,073	4,164,625	−1,543,552	393,241	539,231	−145,990	15.0	12.9	9.5
Missouri........	3,954,653	5,164,866	−1,210,213	588,188	668,509	−80,321	14.9	12.9	6.6
North Dakota.....	619,636	659,472	−39,836	72,050	55,347	16,703	11.6	8.4	(¹)
South Dakota.....	652,740	991,871	−339,131	83,628	98,275	−14,647	12.8	9.9	4.3
Nebraska........	1,325,510	2,587,594	−1,262,084	191,954	315,476	−123,522	14.5	12.2	9.8
Kansas..........	1,905,299	3,282,646	−1,377,347	279,722	417,431	−137,709	14.7	12.7	10.0
South Atlantic:									
Delaware........	318,085	279,945	38,140	39,000	35,197	3,803	12.3	12.6	10.0
Maryland........	2,343,001	1,885,864	457,137	246,084	224,740	21,344	10.5	11.9	4.7
Dist. of Col.....	802,178	182,724	619,454	86,512	40,060	46,452	10.8	21.9	7.5
Virginia........	3,318,680	4,564,496	−1,245,816	317,180	362,932	−45,752	9.6	8.0	3.7
West Virginia....	2,005,552	2,659,014	−653,462	204,474	204,331	143	10.2	7.7	(¹)
North Carolina...	4,061,929	5,811,942	−1,750,013	335,438	380,135	−44,697	8.3	6.5	2.6
South Carolina...	2,117,027	4,178,345	−2,061,318	169,560	234,472	−64,912	8.0	5.6	3.1
Georgia.........	3,444,578	5,684,637	−2,240,059	319,751	410,806	−91,055	9.3	7.2	4.1
Florida.........	2,771,305	895,846	1,875,459	345,981	82,510	263,471	12.5	9.2	14.0
East South Central:									
Kentucky........	2,944,806	5,685,773	−2,740,967	339,398	485,136	−145,738	11.5	8.5	5.3
Tennessee.......	3,291,718	4,958,361	−1,666,643	341,253	426,889	−85,636	10.4	8.6	5.1
Alabama.........	3,061,743	4,981,156	−1,919,413	287,881	344,023	−56,142	9.4	6.9	2.9
Mississippi.....	2,178,914	4,299,982	−2,121,068	217,223	279,589	−62,366	10.0	6.5	2.9
West South Central:									
Arkansas........	1,909,511	3,976,778	−2,067,267	216,402	284,711	−68,309	11.3	7.2	3.3
Louisiana.......	2,683,516	3,165,116	−481,600	258,232	243,185	15,047	9.6	7.7	(¹)
Oklahoma........	2,233,351	204,315	2,029,036	278,625	18,176	260,449	12.5	8.9	12.8
Texas..........	7,711,194	6,694,485	1,016,709	766,592	569,413	197,179	9.9	8.5	19.3
Mountain:									
Montana.........	591,024	234,658	356,366	78,804	25,324	53,480	13.3	10.8	15.0
Idaho...........	588,637	244,834	343,803	65,707	21,678	44,029	11.2	8.9	12.8
Wyoming.........	290,529	126,893	163,636	28,715	12,937	15,778	9.9	10.2	9.6
Colorado........	1,325,089	636,270	688,819	169,118	79,768	89,350	12.8	12.5	13.0
New Mexico......	681,187	454,786	226,401	51,231	31,688	19,543	7.5	7.0	8.6
Arizona.........	749,587	121,759	627,828	68,200	11,039	57,161	9.1	9.1	9.1
Utah...........	688,862	741,090	−52,228	64,163	55,475	8,688	9.3	7.5	(¹)
Nevada..........	160,083	55,463	104,620	17,201	7,659	9,542	10.7	13.8	9.1
Pacific:									
Washington.......	2,378,963	553,747	1,825,216	315,321	80,184	235,137	13.3	14.5	12.9
Oregon..........	1,521,341	508,717	1,012,624	201,251	75,783	125,468	13.2	14.9	12.4
California......	10,586,223	1,378,563	9,207,660	1,345,641	233,807	1,111,834	12.7	17.0	12.1

¹ Not computed.

Source: *1950 Census of Population*, Vol. II, *Characteristics of the Population*, Parts 2 to 50, table 16; National Office of Vital Statistics, "Abridged Life Tables, United States, 1950," *Vital Statistics—Special Reports*, Vol. 37, No. 12, table 2; U. S. Bureau of the Census, *United States Life Tables and Actuarial Tables, 1939 to 1941*, tables 5, 6, 8, and 9; *United States Life Tables, 1930*, tables I, IV, VI, and VIII; *United States Life Tables, 1890, 1901, 1910, and 1901 to 1910*, tables 13, 15, 16, and 18; National Resources Committee, "State Data—Life Tables for White Population, by States, 1929 to 1931," *Population Statistics*.

TABLE B-6.—Total Population and Population 60 Years Old and Over, for Nativity and State-of-Birth Classes, by States: 1950

State	Total population living in State, all ages					
	All classes	Total native	Born in State[1]	Born outside State		
				Total	Native[2]	Foreign born
United States	150,216,110	129,868,715	104,158,170	46,057,940	35,710,545	10,347,395
New England:						
Maine	908,850	834,375	730,060	178,790	104,315	74,475
New Hampshire	529,330	471,855	328,995	200,335	142,860	57,475
Vermont	375,335	346,935	272,135	103,200	74,800	28,400
Massachusetts	4,672,020	3,950,790	3,341,940	1,330,080	608,850	721,230
Rhode Island	788,170	674,775	513,730	274,440	161,045	113,395
Connecticut	1,996,050	1,700,010	1,224,025	772,025	475,985	296,040
Middle Atlantic:						
New York	14,788,960	12,211,855	10,039,180	4,749,780	2,172,675	2,577,105
New Jersey	4,816,435	4,181,355	2,853,815	1,962,620	1,327,540	635,080
Pennsylvania	10,466,460	9,682,495	8,524,735	1,941,725	1,157,760	783,965
East North Central:						
Ohio	7,908,250	7,467,775	5,689,105	2,219,145	1,778,670	440,475
Indiana	3,917,640	3,818,365	2,873,990	1,043,650	944,375	99,275
Illinois	8,680,600	7,894,310	5,959,420	2,721,180	1,934,890	786,290
Michigan	6,342,590	5,738,765	4,158,225	2,184,365	1,580,540	603,825
Wisconsin	3,420,435	3,203,470	2,722,580	697,855	480,890	216,965
West North Central:						
Minnesota	2,972,150	2,761,580	2,190,920	781,230	570,660	210,570
Iowa	2,611,540	2,527,570	2,056,030	555,510	471,540	83,970
Missouri	3,943,310	3,851,890	2,895,395	1,047,915	956,495	91,420
North Dakota	617,705	569,500	437,735	179,970	131,765	48,205
South Dakota	649,710	619,000	437,800	211,910	181,200	30,710
Nebraska	1,319,015	1,261,415	954,265	364,750	307,150	57,600
Kansas	1,898,230	1,860,145	1,262,540	635,690	597,605	38,085
South Atlantic:						
Delaware	315,735	302,680	196,855	118,880	105,825	13,055
Maryland	2,333,245	2,248,080	1,482,445	850,800	765,635	85,165
District of Columbia	800,830	758,090	277,855	522,975	480,235	42,740
Virginia	3,312,565	3,276,875	2,461,490	851,075	815,385	35,690
West Virginia	1,999,835	1,965,925	1,630,665	369,170	335,260	33,910
North Carolina	4,052,795	4,037,545	3,560,045	492,750	477,500	15,250
South Carolina	2,114,355	2,107,235	1,870,255	244,100	236,980	7,120
Georgia	3,438,680	3,422,280	2,945,110	493,570	477,170	16,400
Florida	2,762,865	2,631,800	1,225,800	1,537,065	1,406,000	131,065
East South Central:						
Kentucky	2,936,630	2,921,105	2,568,515	368,115	352,590	15,525
Tennessee	3,286,285	3,271,980	2,633,200	653,085	638,780	14,305
Alabama	3,056,210	3,042,805	2,697,955	358,255	344,850	13,405
Mississippi	2,177,445	2,168,710	1,941,825	235,620	226,885	8,735
West South Central:						
Arkansas	1,905,705	1,896,210	1,474,570	431,135	421,640	9,495
Louisiana	2,677,370	2,647,695	2,257,910	419,460	389,785	29,675
Oklahoma	2,229,665	2,211,395	1,363,140	866,525	848,255	18,270
Texas	7,685,665	7,408,150	5,875,025	1,810,640	1,533,125	277,515
Mountain:						
Montana	587,940	544,555	308,925	279,015	235,630	43,385
Idaho	587,440	567,595	291,405	296,035	276,190	19,845
Wyoming	289,315	275,925	112,110	177,205	163,815	13,390
Colorado	1,320,905	1,260,340	634,245	686,660	626,095	60,565
New Mexico	679,425	661,990	375,300	304,125	286,690	17,435
Arizona	746,655	699,280	296,885	449,770	402,395	47,375
Utah	687,400	656,375	516,265	171,135	140,110	31,025
Nevada	159,390	148,670	48,915	110,475	99,755	10,720
Pacific:						
Washington	2,373,870	2,177,340	1,012,680	1,361,190	1,164,660	196,530
Oregon	1,516,180	1,431,305	621,005	895,175	810,300	84,875
California	10,558,925	9,498,550	4,011,155	6,547,770	5,487,395	1,060,375

[1] Includes persons for whom State of birth was not reported.
[2] Includes persons born in Territories and possessions and born abroad of American parents.

TABLE **B-6.**—TOTAL POPULATION AND POPULATION 60 YEARS OLD AND OVER, FOR NATIVITY
AND STATE-OF-BIRTH CLASSES, BY STATES: 1950—Cont.

State	Population 60 years old and over living in State					
	All classes	Total native	Born in State[1]	Born outside State		
				Total	Native[2]	Foreign born
United States.........	18,267,605	14,208,565	9,024,205	9,243,400	5,184,360	4,059,040
New England:						
Maine...................	130,640	102,585	88,280	42,360	14,305	28,055
New Hampshire...........	80,085	54,625	31,760	48,325	22,865	25,460
Vermont.................	54,625	44,505	33,200	21,425	11,305	10,120
Massachusetts...........	686,755	371,900	266,650	420,105	105,250	314,855
Rhode Island............	104,190	55,425	34,260	69,930	21,165	48,765
Connecticut.............	266,835	144,650	87,065	179,770	57,585	122,185
Middle Atlantic:						
New York................	1,952,855	1,076,625	848,040	1,104,815	228,585	876,230
New Jersey..............	608,775	361,265	190,985	417,790	170,280	247,510
Pennsylvania............	1,339,145	990,405	838,980	500,165	151,425	348,740
East North Central:						
Ohio....................	1,044,055	860,850	635,345	408,710	225,505	183,205
Indiana.................	524,050	483,355	352,840	171,210	130,515	40,695
Illinois................	1,148,790	815,650	553,275	595,515	262,375	333,140
Michigan................	705,530	486,365	318,950	386,580	167,415	219,165
Wisconsin...............	460,705	344,370	280,365	180,340	64,005	116,335
West North Central:						
Minnesota...............	401,705	272,995	171,300	230,405	101,695	128,710
Iowa....................	389,495	340,865	245,285	144,210	95,580	48,630
Missouri................	589,350	547,135	366,920	222,430	180,215	42,215
North Dakota............	71,595	42,260	11,700	59,895	30,560	29,335
South Dakota............	83,645	64,475	22,620	61,025	41,855	19,170
Nebraska................	189,850	155,565	77,930	111,920	77,635	34,285
Kansas..................	278,200	257,310	124,880	153,320	132,430	20,890
South Atlantic:						
Delaware................	38,330	33,435	19,890	18,440	13,545	4,895
Maryland................	243,065	213,285	150,250	92,815	63,035	29,780
District of Columbia....	87,855	76,720	18,165	69,690	58,555	11,135
Virginia................	318,105	309,065	243,485	74,620	65,580	9,040
West Virginia...........	202,025	188,005	138,460	63,565	49,545	14,020
North Carolina.........	335,735	332,450	289,565	46,170	42,885	3,285
South Carolina.........	170,010	168,390	146,310	23,700	22,080	1,620
Georgia.................	320,315	316,235	267,100	53,215	49,135	4,080
Florida.................	343,940	291,905	68,410	275,530	223,495	52,035
East South Central:						
Kentucky................	338,590	333,285	288,855	49,735	44,430	5,305
Tennessee...............	339,610	335,245	259,950	79,660	75,295	4,365
Alabama.................	286,360	281,435	229,710	56,650	51,725	4,925
Mississippi.............	217,355	215,040	182,485	34,870	32,555	2,315
West South Central:						
Arkansas................	215,940	212,125	122,865	93,075	89,260	3,815
Louisiana...............	258,525	247,435	197,415	61,110	50,020	11,090
Oklahoma................	278,755	271,100	26,720	252,035	244,380	7,655
Texas...................	764,315	697,850	447,295	317,020	250,555	66,465
Mountain:						
Montana.................	77,590	55,140	6,950	70,640	48,190	22,450
Idaho...................	64,895	55,455	6,515	58,380	48,940	9,440
Wyoming.................	28,165	22,470	2,015	26,150	20,455	5,695
Colorado................	168,370	138,695	21,230	147,140	117,465	29,675
New Mexico..............	51,415	47,065	18,045	33,370	29,020	4,350
Arizona.................	68,065	54,820	8,565	59,500	46,255	13,245
Utah....................	63,600	50,560	37,315	26,285	13,245	13,040
Nevada..................	16,985	13,100	2,855	14,130	10,245	3,885
Pacific:						
Washington..............	314,435	227,860	22,640	291,795	205,220	86,575
Oregon..................	200,205	162,930	34,660	165,545	128,270	37,275
California..............	1,344,175	984,285	185,855	1,158,320	798,430	359,890

[1] Includes persons for whom State of birth was not reported.
[2] Includes persons born in Territories and possessions and born abroad of American parents.

TABLE **B–6.**—TOTAL POPULATION AND POPULATION 60 YEARS OLD AND OVER, FOR NATIVITY AND STATE-OF-BIRTH CLASSES, BY STATES: 1950—Cont.

State	Population 60 years and over as percent of all ages, by class						Population 60 years and over as percent of all classes				
	All classes	Total native	Born in State	Born outside State			Native	Born in State	Born outside State		
				Total	Native	Foreign born			Total	Native	Foreign born
United States..	12.1	10.2	8.7	20.1	14.5	39.2	77.8	49.4	50.6	28.4	22.2
New England:											
Maine............	14.4	12.3	12.1	23.7	13.7	37.7	78.5	67.6	32.4	10.9	21.5
New Hampshire....	15.1	11.6	9.7	24.1	16.0	44.3	68.2	39.7	60.3	28.6	31.8
Vermont..........	14.6	12.8	12.2	20.8	15.1	35.6	81.5	60.7	39.2	20.7	18.5
Massachusetts....	14.7	9.4	8.0	31.6	17.3	43.7	54.2	38.8	61.2	15.3	45.8
Rhode Island.....	13.2	8.2	6.7	25.5	13.1	43.0	53.2	32.9	67.1	20.3	46.8
Connecticut......	13.4	8.5	7.1	23.3	12.1	41.3	54.2	32.6	67.4	21.6	45.8
Middle Atlantic:											
New York.........	13.2	8.8	8.4	23.3	10.5	34.0	55.1	43.4	56.6	11.7	44.9
New Jersey.......	12.6	8.6	6.7	21.3	12.8	39.0	59.3	31.4	68.6	28.0	40.7
Pennsylvania.....	12.8	10.2	9.8	25.8	13.1	44.5	74.0	62.7	37.3	11.3	26.0
East North Central:											
Ohio.............	13.2	11.5	11.2	18.4	12.7	41.6	82.5	60.9	39.1	21.6	17.5
Indiana..........	13.4	12.7	12.3	16.4	13.8	41.0	92.2	67.3	32.7	24.9	7.8
Illinois.........	13.2	10.3	9.3	21.9	13.6	42.4	71.0	48.2	51.8	22.8	29.0
Michigan.........	11.1	8.5	7.7	17.7	10.6	36.3	68.9	45.2	54.8	23.7	31.1
Wisconsin........	13.5	10.7	10.3	25.8	13.3	53.6	74.7	60.9	39.1	13.9	25.3
West North Central:											
Minnesota........	13.5	9.9	7.8	29.5	17.8	61.1	68.0	42.6	57.4	25.3	32.0
Iowa.............	14.9	13.5	11.9	26.0	20.3	57.9	87.5	63.0	37.0	24.5	12.5
Missouri.........	14.9	14.2	12.7	21.2	18.8	46.2	92.8	62.3	37.7	30.6	7.2
North Dakota.....	11.6	7.4	2.7	33.3	23.2	60.9	59.0	16.3	83.7	42.7	41.0
South Dakota.....	12.9	10.4	5.2	28.8	23.1	62.4	77.1	27.0	73.0	50.0	22.9
Nebraska.........	14.4	12.3	8.2	30.7	25.3	59.5	81.9	41.0	59.0	40.9	18.1
Kansas...........	14.7	13.8	9.9	24.1	22.2	54.9	92.5	44.9	55.1	47.6	7.5
South Atlantic:											
Delaware.........	12.1	11.0	10.1	15.5	12.8	37.5	87.2	51.9	48.1	35.3	12.8
Maryland.........	10.4	9.5	10.1	10.9	8.2	35.0	87.7	61.8	38.2	25.9	12.3
Dist. of Col....	11.0	10.1	6.5	13.3	12.2	26.1	87.3	20.7	79.3	66.6	12.7
Virginia.........	9.6	9.4	9.9	8.8	8.0	25.3	97.2	76.5	23.5	20.6	2.8
West Virginia...	10.1	9.6	8.5	17.2	14.8	41.3	93.1	68.5	31.5	24.5	6.9
North Carolina...	8.3	8.2	8.1	9.4	9.0	21.5	99.0	86.2	13.8	12.8	1.0
South Carolina...	8.0	8.0	7.8	9.7	9.3	22.8	99.0	86.1	13.9	13.0	1.0
Georgia..........	9.3	9.2	9.1	10.8	10.3	24.9	98.7	83.4	16.6	15.3	1.3
Florida..........	12.4	11.1	5.6	17.9	15.9	39.7	84.9	19.9	80.1	65.0	15.1
East South Central:											
Kentucky.........	11.5	11.4	11.2	13.5	12.6	34.2	98.4	85.3	14.7	13.1	1.6
Tennessee........	10.3	10.2	9.9	12.2	11.8	30.5	98.7	76.5	23.5	22.2	1.3
Alabama..........	9.4	9.2	8.5	15.8	15.0	36.7	98.3	80.2	19.8	18.1	1.7
Mississippi......	10.0	9.9	9.4	14.8	14.3	26.5	98.9	84.0	16.0	15.0	1.1
West South Central:											
Arkansas.........	11.3	11.2	8.3	21.6	21.2	40.2	98.2	56.9	43.1	41.3	1.8
Louisiana........	9.7	9.3	8.7	14.6	12.8	37.4	95.7	76.4	23.6	19.3	4.3
Oklahoma.........	12.5	12.3	2.0	29.1	28.8	41.9	97.3	9.6	90.4	87.7	2.7
Texas............	9.9	9.4	7.6	17.5	16.3	24.0	91.3	58.5	41.5	32.8	8.7
Mountain:											
Montana..........	13.2	10.1	2.2	25.3	20.5	51.7	71.1	9.0	91.0	62.1	28.9
Idaho............	11.0	9.8	2.2	19.7	17.7	47.6	85.5	10.0	90.0	75.4	14.5
Wyoming..........	9.7	8.1	1.8	14.8	12.5	42.5	79.8	7.2	92.8	72.6	20.2
Colorado.........	12.7	11.0	3.3	21.4	18.8	49.0	82.4	12.6	87.4	69.8	17.6
New Mexico.......	7.6	7.1	4.8	11.0	10.1	24.9	91.5	35.1	64.9	56.4	8.5
Arizona..........	9.1	7.8	2.9	13.2	11.5	28.0	80.5	12.6	87.4	68.0	19.5
Utah.............	9.3	7.7	7.2	15.4	9.5	42.0	79.5	58.7	41.3	20.8	20.5
Nevada...........	10.7	8.8	5.8	12.8	10.3	36.2	77.1	16.8	83.2	60.3	22.9
Pacific:											
Washington.......	13.2	10.5	2.2	21.4	17.6	44.1	72.5	7.2	92.8	65.3	27.5
Oregon...........	13.2	11.4	5.6	18.5	15.8	43.9	81.4	17.3	82.7	64.1	18.6
California.......	12.7	10.4	4.6	17.7	14.6	33.9	73.2	13.8	86.2	59.4	26.8

Source: *1950 Census of Population*, Vol. II, *Characteristics of the Population*, Parts 2 to 50, table 54, and Vol. IV, *Special Reports*, Part 4, Chapter A, State of Birth, table 18.

TABLE B-7.—POPULATION 60 AND 65 YEARS OLD AND OVER, BY STATES, URBAN AND RURAL: 1950

State	Urban					Rural nonfarm					Rural farm				
	All ages	60 years old and over	65 years old and over	Percent 60	Percent 65	All ages	60 years old and over	65 years old and over	Percent 60	Percent 65	All ages	60 years old and over	65 years old and over	Percent 60	Percent 65
United States.....	96,467,686	11,854,927	7,826,279	12.3	8.1	31,181,325	3,824,906	2,692,742	12.3	8.6	23,048,350	2,649,179	1,750,516	11.5	7.6
New England:															
Maine............	472,000	67,209	46,940	14.2	9.9	319,946	46,080	33,411	14.4	10.4	121,828	18,666	13,211	15.3	10.8
New Hampshire....	306,806	44,508	30,821	14.5	10.5	179,266	29,149	21,069	16.3	11.8	47,170	8,352	5,903	17.7	12.5
Vermont..........	137,612	20,431	14,387	14.8	10.5	159,003	24,436	17,857	15.4	11.2	81,132	10,600	7,290	13.1	9.0
Massachusetts....	3,959,239	584,612	395,817	14.8	10.0	651,299	91,119	63,472	14.0	9.7	79,976	13,603	9,147	17.0	11.4
Rhode Island.....	667,212	90,984	60,540	13.6	9.1	114,346	12,655	8,705	11.1	7.6	10,338	1,692	1,173	16.4	11.3
Connecticut......	1,558,642	207,898	135,660	13.3	8.7	385,982	49,462	33,843	12.8	8.8	62,656	10,989	7,321	17.5	11.7
Middle Atlantic:															
New York.........	12,682,446	1,619,258	1,034,042	12.8	8.2	1,570,092	237,943	166,552	15.2	10.6	577,654	85,941	57,863	14.9	10.0
New Jersey.......	4,186,207	522,575	335,185	12.5	8.0	543,822	71,263	48,701	13.1	9.0	105,300	15,697	10,103	14.9	9.6
Pennsylvania.....	7,403,036	955,832	625,008	12.9	8.4	2,389,769	289,916	198,845	12.1	8.3	705,207	93,349	62,972	13.2	8.9
East North Central:															
Ohio.............	5,578,274	730,131	482,593	13.1	8.7	1,515,265	199,732	142,845	13.2	9.4	853,088	123,942	83,537	14.5	9.8
Indiana..........	2,357,196	300,765	203,036	12.8	8.6	909,874	126,840	91,472	13.9	10.1	667,154	100,397	66,518	15.0	10.0
Illinois.........	6,759,271	867,706	556,118	12.8	8.2	1,189,709	187,506	133,996	15.8	11.3	763,196	100,237	64,187	13.1	8.4
Michigan.........	4,503,084	471,937	295,660	10.5	6.6	1,173,940	144,024	100,948	12.3	8.6	694,742	99,465	65,042	14.3	9.4
Wisconsin........	1,987,888	265,612	174,907	13.4	8.8	721,453	113,854	80,447	15.8	11.2	725,234	84,940	54,563	11.7	7.5
West North Central:															
Minnesota........	1,624,914	226,194	149,014	13.9	9.2	617,770	99,952	70,759	16.2	11.5	739,799	77,838	49,357	10.5	6.7
Iowa.............	1,250,938	192,414	133,515	15.4	10.7	587,485	123,755	91,332	21.1	15.5	782,650	77,072	48,151	9.8	6.2
Missouri.........	2,432,715	340,748	232,134	14.0	9.5	658,442	122,091	91,841	18.5	13.9	863,496	125,349	83,413	14.5	9.7
North Dakota.....	164,817	19,325	12,706	11.7	7.7	200,332	31,589	22,385	15.8	11.2	254,487	21,136	13,105	8.3	5.1
South Dakota.....	216,710	28,361	18,888	13.1	8.7	182,485	32,062	22,537	17.6	12.4	253,545	23,205	13,871	9.2	5.5
Nebraska.........	621,905	88,559	59,761	14.2	9.6	312,170	65,020	47,336	20.8	15.2	391,435	38,375	23,282	9.8	5.9
Kansas...........	993,220	134,693	93,251	13.6	9.4	468,340	85,962	63,237	18.4	13.5	443,739	59,067	37,730	13.3	8.5
South Atlantic:															
Delaware.........	199,122	23,837	15,907	12.0	8.0	84,738	10,282	7,214	12.1	8.5	34,225	4,881	3,199	14.3	9.3
Maryland.........	1,615,902	165,449	108,005	10.2	6.7	543,623	57,894	40,188	10.6	7.4	183,476	22,741	15,321	12.4	8.4
Dist. of Columbia..	802,178	86,512	56,687	10.8	7.1	...	...	...	...	...	...	...	...	...	...
Virginia.........	1,560,115	140,060	92,849	9.0	6.0	1,026,604	85,764	58,770	8.4	5.7	731,961	91,356	62,905	12.5	8.6
West Virginia....	694,487	79,519	53,081	11.5	7.6	900,143	72,293	48,438	8.0	5.4	410,922	52,662	37,007	12.8	9.0
North Carolina...	1,368,101	112,014	73,881	8.2	5.4	1,317,268	99,958	68,767	7.6	5.2	1,376,560	123,466	82,649	9.0	6.0
South Carolina...	777,921	63,023	41,681	8.1	5.4	638,495	49,776	34,969	7.8	5.5	700,611	56,761	38,355	8.1	5.5
Georgia..........	1,559,447	144,184	97,485	9.2	6.3	922,696	83,843	59,366	9.1	6.4	962,435	91,724	62,804	9.5	6.5
Florida..........	1,813,890	240,609	165,086	13.3	9.1	724,609	78,826	54,632	10.9	7.5	232,806	26,546	17,756	11.4	7.6

TABLE **B-7.**—POPULATION 60 AND 65 YEARS OLD AND OVER, BY STATES, URBAN AND RURAL: 1950—Cont.

State	Urban					Rural nonfarm					Rural farm				
	All ages	60 years old and over	65 years old and over	Percent of all ages 60 years and over	Percent of all ages 65 years and over	All ages	60 years old and over	65 years old and over	Percent of all ages 60 years and over	Percent of all ages 65 years and over	All ages	60 years old and over	65 years old and over	Percent of all ages 60 years and over	Percent of all ages 65 years and over
East South Central:															
Kentucky	1,084,070	136,335	93,652	12.6	8.6	886,566	88,414	63,459	10.0	7.2	974,170	114,649	78,132	11.8	8.0
Tennessee	1,452,602	147,022	99,615	10.1	6.9	822,912	79,672	56,953	9.7	6.9	1,016,204	114,559	78,316	11.3	7.7
Alabama	1,340,937	119,119	80,086	8.9	6.0	760,313	74,827	53,861	9.8	7.1	960,493	93,935	64,701	9.8	6.7
Mississippi	607,162	59,512	41,011	9.8	6.8	474,545	53,616	39,187	11.3	8.3	1,097,207	104,035	72,766	9.5	6.6
West South Central:															
Arkansas	630,591	74,599	51,275	11.8	8.1	477,093	59,563	42,815	12.5	9.0	801,827	82,240	54,905	10.3	6.8
Louisiana	1,471,696	139,185	93,822	9.5	6.4	644,365	66,226	47,398	10.3	7.4	567,455	52,621	35,629	9.3	6.3
Oklahoma	1,139,481	138,102	96,323	12.1	8.5	540,804	81,025	59,540	15.0	11.0	553,066	59,498	38,059	10.8	6.9
Texas	4,838,060	442,093	293,343	9.1	6.1	1,580,867	169,335	119,297	10.7	7.5	1,292,267	155,164	100,780	12.0	7.8
Mountain:															
Montana	258,034	36,272	23,800	14.1	9.2	197,051	26,459	17,621	13.4	8.9	135,939	16,073	9,443	11.8	6.9
Idaho	252,549	31,077	21,234	12.3	8.4	171,128	19,406	13,014	11.3	7.6	164,960	15,324	9,289	9.2	5.6
Wyoming	144,618	15,029	9,670	10.4	6.7	89,207	8,167	5,223	9.2	5.9	56,704	5,319	3,272	9.7	5.8
Colorado	831,318	115,965	80,515	13.9	9.7	295,590	35,354	24,323	12.0	8.2	198,181	17,299	10,754	9.0	5.4
New Mexico	341,889	25,737	16,629	7.5	4.9	207,475	14,515	9,614	7.0	4.6	131,823	10,379	6,821	8.3	5.2
Arizona	416,000	41,634	27,212	10.0	6.5	256,673	19,891	12,777	7.7	5.0	76,914	6,575	4,252	8.7	5.5
Utah	449,855	43,984	29,281	9.8	6.5	158,387	13,549	9,232	8.6	5.8	80,620	6,530	3,905	8.2	4.8
Nevada	91,625	9,754	6,199	10.6	6.8	54,997	5,793	3,748	10.5	6.8	13,461	1,554	1,039	12.3	7.7
Pacific:															
Washington	1,503,166	206,914	139,564	13.8	9.3	602,026	74,994	51,265	12.5	8.5	273,771	33,413	20,576	12.2	7.5
Oregon	819,318	121,535	81,631	14.8	10.0	473,788	50,113	33,167	10.6	7.0	228,235	29,603	18,223	13.0	8.0
California	8,539,420	1,116,100	746,772	13.1	8.7	1,478,572	160,941	106,314	10.9	7.2	568,231	68,600	41,919	12.1	7.4

Source: *1950 Census of Population*, Vol. II, *Characteristics of the Population*, Parts 2 to 50, table 15.

TABLE **B-8.**—POPULATION 65 YEARS OLD AND OVER IN SUBURBS BY PERIOD IN WHICH 50 PERCENT OR MORE OF TOTAL DWELLING UNITS WERE BUILT, FOR SELECTED URBANIZED AREAS: 1950

Urbanized area, component of urbanized area, and age of suburb	Number of urban places	Population		
		Total, all ages	65 years old and over	
			Number	Percent
NEW YORK-NORTHEASTERN NEW JERSEY				
Total urbanized area......................	169	12,296,117	937,240	7.6
Central cities...............................	3	8,629,750	658,482	7.6
Suburbs[1]......................................	166	2,809,991	225,823	8.0
50 percent or more of dwelling units built--				
1940 to 1950.............................	8	75,125	3,798	5.1
1930 to 1950.............................	19	183,108	11,169	6.1
1920 to 1950.............................	91	1,293,093	103,533	8.0
Before 1920..............................	48	1,258,665	107,323	8.5
Remainder of area............................	...	856,376	52,935	6.2
CHICAGO				
Total urbanized area......................	81	4,920,816	358,073	7.3
Central cities...............................	1	3,620,962	273,724	7.6
Suburb[1]..	80	1,168,813	77,527	6.6
50 percent or more of dwelling units built--				
1940 to 1950.............................	21	125,882	4,758	3.8
1930 to 1950.............................	8	42,002	2,295	5.5
1920 to 1950.............................	41	766,579	50,447	6.6
Before 1920..............................	10	234,350	20,027	8.5
Remainder of area............................	...	131,041	6,822	5.2
LOS ANGELES				
Total urbanized area......................	38	3,996,946	364,552	9.1
Central cities...............................	1	1,970,358	189,603	9.6
Suburbs[1]......................................	37	1,255,584	123,515	9.8
50 percent or more of dwelling units built--				
1940 to 1950.............................	13	357,940	21,256	5.9
1930 to 1950.............................	15	598,899	61,984	10.3
1920 to 1950.............................	9	298,745	40,275	13.5
Before 1920..............................	...	...	...	...
Remainder of area............................	...	771,004	51,434	6.7

[1] Urban places of 2,500 or more in the urban fringe.

Source: *1950 Census of Population*, Vol. II, *Characteristics of the Population*, Parts 5, 13, and 32, tables 33 and 38; *1950 Census of Housing*, Vol. I, *General Characteristics*, Part 2, California, Part 3, Illinois, Part 4, New York, tables 20 and 23.

TABLE **B-9.**—OBSERVED AND EXPECTED POPULATION 65 YEARS OLD AND OVER, FOR LOS ANGELES SUBURBS: 1950

Suburbs	Observed population, 1950			Population, 1950, expected if no migration since 1930			Difference between observed and expected population			Percent 65 years old and over, 1930
	All ages	65 years and over		All ages	65 years and over		All ages	65 years and over		
		Number	Per-cent		Number	Per-cent		Number	Per-cent	
Alhambra..........	51,359	5,904	11.5	29,805	3,320	11.1	21,554	2,584	12.0	8.0
Arcadia...........	23,066	2,165	9.4	5,103	774	15.2	17,963	1,391	7.7	8.7
Azusa.............	11,042	644	5.8	6,349	475	7.5	4,693	169	3.6	5.2
Bell..............	15,430	1,176	7.6	8,624	721	8.4	6,806	455	6.7	5.6
Beverly Hills.....	29,032	3,033	10.4	16,441	1,968	12.0	12,591	1,065	8.5	4.4
Burbank...........	78,577	4,557	5.8	18,697	1,652	8.8	59,880	2,905	4.9	5.8
Compton...........	47,991	2,437	5.1	15,150	1,109	7.3	32,841	1,328	4.0	4.7
Covina............	3,956	550	13.9	2,747	328	11.9	1,209	222	18.4	11.1
Culver City.......	19,720	1,110	5.6	6,290	540	8.6	13,430	570	4.2	4.3
El Monte..........	8,101	689	8.5	4,281	297	6.9	3,820	392	10.3	4.9
El Segundo........	8,011	397	5.0	4,315	246	5.7	3,696	151	4.1	3.5
Glendale..........	95,702	11,266	11.8	63,594	7,173	11.3	32,108	4,093	12.7	7.5
Hawthorne.........	16,316	1,086	6.7	7,558	699	9.2	8,758	387	4.4	6.7
Hermosa Beach.....	11,826	1,100	9.3	4,791	579	12.1	7,035	521	7.4	10.1
Huntington Park....	29,450	3,224	10.9	24,105	2,559	10.6	5,345	665	12.4	5.5
Inglewood.........	46,185	3,920	8.5	20,905	1,942	9.3	25,280	1,978	7.8	5.7
Long Beach........	250,767	28,085	11.2	139,118	17,299	12.4	111,649	10,786	9.7	9.2
Lynwood...........	25,823	1,408	5.5	8,484	629	7.4	17,339	779	4.5	6.0
Maywood...........	13,292	971	7.3	7,557	557	7.4	5,735	414	7.2	4.0
Monrovia..........	20,186	2,799	13.9	10,815	1,388	12.8	9,371	1,411	15.1	11.1
Montebello........	21,735	1,282	5.9	6,415	520	8.1	15,320	762	5.0	5.0
Monterey Park.....	20,395	1,538	7.5	6,778	739	10.9	13,617	799	5.9	7.1
Pasadena..........	104,577	17,525	16.8	68,917	10,919	15.8	35,660	6,606	18.5	12.2
Redondo Beach.....	25,226	2,167	8.6	10,516	1,128	10.7	14,710	1,039	7.1	8.6
San Fernando......	12,992	1,003	7.7	9,485	682	7.2	3,507	321	9.2	4.9
San Gabriel.......	20,343	1,556	7.6	8,598	684	8.0	11,745	872	7.4	4.7
San Marino........	11,230	983	8.8	3,895	456	11.7	7,335	527	7.2	5.9
Santa Monica......	71,595	8,118	11.3	35,439	4,799	13.5	36,156	3,319	9.2	8.8
Sierra Madre......	7,273	1,006	13.8	3,460	516	14.9	3,813	490	12.9	11.2
Signal Hill.......	4,040	352	8.7	3,139	292	9.3	901	60	6.7	5.7
South Gate........	51,116	2,969	5.8	23,068	1,602	6.9	28,048	1,367	4.9	4.0
South Pasadena.....	16,935	2,450	14.5	12,827	1,911	14.9	4,108	539	13.1	8.9
Torrance..........	22,241	1,002	4.5	8,903	710	8.0	13,338	292	2.2	3.1
Whittier..........	23,820	2,899	12.2	15,595	1,673	10.7	8,225	1,226	14.9	8.3

Source: *1950 Census of Population*, Vol. II, *Characteristics of the Population*, Part 5, tables 33 and 38; *1930 Census of Population*, Vol. III, *Population*, Part 1, California, tables 12 and 16; National Office of Vital Statistics, State and Regional Life Tables, 1939–41, California.

TABLE **B-10**.—POPULATION 65 YEARS OLD AND OVER, BY SIZE OF PLACE, BY REGIONS: 1950

Size of place	United States All ages	United States 65 years and over Number	United States 65 years and over Per-cent	Northeast All ages	Northeast 65 years and over Number	Northeast 65 years and over Per-cent	North Central All ages	North Central 65 years and over Number	North Central 65 years and over Per-cent	South All ages	South 65 years and over Number	South 65 years and over Per-cent	West All ages	West 65 years and over Number	West 65 years and over Per-cent
Total	150,288,630	12,245,040	8.1	39,351,660	3,443,430	8.8	44,279,490	3,953,760	8.9	47,103,450	3,252,600	6.9	19,554,030	1,595,250	8.2
In urbanized areas	69,114,600	5,413,410	7.8	26,161,710	2,165,610	8.3	19,942,470	1,529,190	7.7	13,271,310	860,100	6.5	9,739,110	858,510	8.8
Central cities	48,303,720	3,944,490	8.2	17,153,340	1,451,520	8.5	14,775,510	1,201,980	8.1	10,505,490	725,760	6.9	5,869,380	565,230	9.6
Urban fringe	20,810,880	1,468,920	7.1	9,008,370	714,090	7.9	5,166,960	327,210	6.3	2,765,820	134,340	4.9	3,869,730	293,280	7.6
Areas of 3,000,000 or more	21,184,020	1,670,040	7.9	12,287,910	945,270	7.7	4,907,550	360,390	7.3	...	...	...	3,988,560	364,380	9.1
Central cities	14,208,750	1,135,050	8.0	8,630,730	668,550	7.7	3,613,290	276,570	7.7	...	...	...	1,964,730	189,930	9.7
Urban fringe	6,975,270	534,990	7.7	3,657,180	276,720	7.6	1,294,260	83,820	6.5	...	...	...	2,023,830	174,450	8.6
Areas of 1,000,000 to 3,000,000	16,608,450	1,262,700	7.6	6,674,040	571,650	8.6	5,428,740	365,790	6.7	2,441,730	156,930	6.4	2,063,940	168,330	8.2
Central cities	10,106,460	803,790	8.0	3,544,350	308,130	8.7	3,613,080	254,760	7.1	1,746,330	128,310	7.3	1,202,700	112,590	9.4
Urban fringe	6,501,990	458,910	7.1	3,129,690	263,520	8.4	1,815,660	111,030	6.1	695,400	28,620	4.1	861,240	55,740	6.5
Areas of 250,000 to 1,000,000	17,380,080	1,359,000	7.8	3,280,890	286,530	8.7	5,827,290	482,010	8.3	6,208,530	401,130	6.5	2,063,370	189,330	9.2
Central cities	12,991,920	1,075,440	8.3	2,064,450	195,090	9.4	4,450,440	390,510	8.8	4,887,900	331,860	6.8	1,589,130	157,980	9.9
Urban fringe	4,388,160	283,560	6.5	1,216,440	91,440	7.5	1,376,850	91,500	6.6	1,320,630	69,270	5.2	474,240	31,350	6.6
Areas of less than 250,000	13,942,050	1,121,670	8.0	3,918,870	362,160	9.2	3,778,890	321,000	8.5	4,621,050	302,040	6.5	1,623,240	136,470	8.4
Central cities	10,996,990	930,210	8.5	2,913,810	279,750	9.6	3,098,700	280,140	9.0	3,871,260	265,590	6.9	1,112,820	104,730	9.4
Urban fringe	2,945,460	191,460	6.5	1,005,060	82,410	8.2	680,190	40,860	6.0	749,790	36,450	4.9	510,420	31,740	6.2
Outside urbanized areas	81,174,030	6,831,630	8.4	13,189,950	1,277,820	9.7	24,337,020	2,424,570	10.0	33,832,140	2,392,500	7.1	9,814,920	736,740	7.5
Places of 25,000 or more	7,108,050	603,090	8.5	1,272,870	130,830	10.3	2,469,360	227,790	9.2	2,346,060	158,100	6.7	1,019,760	86,370	8.5
Places of 10,000 to 25,000	8,204,070	721,710	8.8	1,685,100	166,740	9.9	2,517,870	255,720	10.2	2,768,550	197,460	7.1	1,232,550	101,790	8.3
Places of 2,500 to 10,000	11,822,340	1,091,910	9.2	2,196,570	227,040	10.3	3,446,130	393,870	11.4	4,499,130	335,760	7.5	1,680,510	135,240	8.0
Places of 1,000 to 2,500	6,440,550	662,190	10.3	1,234,380	129,900	10.5	2,122,350	274,560	12.9	2,290,140	190,020	8.3	793,680	67,710	8.5
Nonfarm	6,311,310	647,820	10.3	1,214,910	127,920	10.5	2,090,850	270,390	12.9	2,242,290	184,320	8.2	763,260	65,190	8.5
Farm	129,240	14,370	11.1	19,470	1,980	10.2	31,500	4,170	13.2	47,850	5,700	11.9	30,420	2,520	8.3
Incorporated places of less than 1,000	4,010,580	539,790	13.5	356,160	42,780	12.0	2,069,550	323,970	15.7	1,212,900	137,250	11.3	371,970	35,790	9.6
Nonfarm	3,795,630	515,880	13.6	340,920	40,590	11.9	1,987,050	312,660	15.7	1,125,960	128,700	11.4	341,700	33,930	9.9
Farm	214,950	23,910	11.1	15,240	2,190	14.4	82,500	11,310	13.7	86,940	8,550	9.8	30,270	1,860	6.1
Other rural territory	43,588,440	3,212,940	7.4	6,444,870	580,530	9.0	11,711,760	948,660	8.1	20,715,360	1,373,910	6.6	4,716,450	309,840	6.6
Nonfarm	20,929,410	1,512,780	7.2	4,704,390	410,820	8.7	4,414,680	371,790	8.4	8,955,150	543,510	6.1	2,855,190	186,660	6.5
Farm	22,659,030	1,700,160	7.5	1,740,480	169,710	9.8	7,297,080	576,870	7.9	11,760,210	830,400	7.1	1,861,260	123,180	6.6

Source: *1950 Census of Population*, Vol. IV, *Special Reports*, Part 5, Chapter A, Characteristics by Size of Place, tables 1 and 6.

APPENDIX   C

LABOR FORCE

Section 1: Concepts and nature of data

The concepts, definitions, procedures, and problems involved in the collection of census data on labor force participation are perhaps most fully described in the introduction to the special report on employment and personal characteristics.[1]   Although the labor force concepts are reasonably uncomplicated and well understood, it appears useful, in view of the importance of health as a factor in retirement, to supply additional detail on the concept "unable to work."   The standard definition of this category as it appears in the special report on employment and personal characteristics is as follows:

> Persons who cannot work because of a long-term physical or mental illness or disability.   There is some evidence, however, that some persons were included as "unable to work" who were only temporarily ill or who, although elderly, were not permanently disabled.

The instructions to enumerators on this category indicate in detail the classes of persons who are properly classified as unable to work:[2]

> Count as unable to work a person who, because of his own long-term physical or mental illness or disability, is unable to do any kind of "work" as defined under "working."   Long-term physical or mental illness includes such conditions as blindness, loss of limbs, serious heart trouble, tuberculosis, mental disorders.
>
> Note that this code is not confined to older persons.   It is applicable to both young and old persons of both sexes.   It should not be used, however, for an elderly person who is able to work but believes he is too old to find work.   Do not count an elderly person as unable to work unless he is suffering from a definite illness or disability of long duration.
>
> Do not count as unable to work a person who is only temporarily ill or disabled and who expects to be able to work within 6 months from the time of enumeration.

The 1950 data on employment status are available by age from the 20-percent sample and the 3⅓-percent sample.   With the exception of the discussion of labor force participation rates in the farm and the nonfarm population, which relates to the 20-percent data for 1950, the analysis of census data in Chapter 4 relates to the 3⅓-percent sample data.   Occasional reference is also made to employment data from the Current Population

---

[1] *1950 Census of Population,* Vol. IV, *Special Reports,* Part 1, Chapter A, Employment and Personal Characteristics, pp. 5–7.

[2] *1950 Census, Enumerator's Reference Manual,* p. 37.

Survey. In general, these data tend to indicate a slightly higher level of labor force participation than those from the decennial census.

Summary figures on the employment status of men by age are presented in table C–1, and a comparison of the 1950 Census and Current Population Survey data for the same group of persons in April 1950 are shown in table C–2.

TABLE **C–1.**—LABOR FORCE STATUS OF MALES, BY AGE: 1950

Age	Total population	Labor force	Not in labor force					
			Total	Keeping house	Unable to work	In institutions	Other	Not reported
Total.........	54,610,050	43,117,500	11,492,550	262,800	2,756,670	869,700	7,027,530	575,850
14 to 19 years....	6,443,040	2,542,650	3,900,390	22,260	37,260	75,390	3,605,430	160,050
20 to 24 years....	5,540,520	4,537,140	1,003,380	18,390	46,020	77,700	803,370	57,900
25 to 29 years....	5,900,970	5,333,940	567,030	18,480	56,880	83,070	359,520	49,080
30 to 34 years....	5,553,210	5,218,740	334,470	13,230	54,750	74,370	144,240	47,880
35 to 39 years....	5,453,430	5,165,070	288,360	14,340	60,840	69,810	99,420	43,950
40 to 44 years....	4,945,290	4,671,420	273,870	13,200	70,290	63,660	91,350	35,370
45 to 49 years....	4,463,310	4,162,380	300,930	16,350	88,800	62,670	96,630	36,480
50 to 54 years....	4,032,810	3,650,940	381,870	17,100	139,470	67,200	128,700	29,400
55 to 59 years....	3,577,470	3,103,410	474,060	19,770	193,770	63,960	169,860	26,700
60 to 64 years....	2,969,790	2,358,600	611,190	22,110	264,840	60,480	238,890	24,870
65 to 69 years....	2,396,430	1,431,180	965,250	29,820	440,580	49,740	421,890	23,220
70 to 74 years....	1,599,450	618,420	981,030	26,100	484,230	38,490	411,810	20,400
75 and over.......	1,734,330	323,610	1,410,720	31,650	818,940	83,160	456,420	20,550
PERCENT DISTRIBUTION								
Total.........	100.0	79.0	21.0	0.5	5.0	1.6	12.9	1.1
14 to 19 years....	100.0	39.5	60.5	0.3	0.6	1.2	56.0	2.5
20 to 24 years....	100.0	81.9	18.1	0.3	0.8	1.4	14.5	1.0
25 to 29 years....	100.0	90.4	9.6	0.3	1.0	1.4	6.1	0.8
30 to 34 years....	100.0	94.0	6.0	0.2	1.0	1.3	2.6	0.9
35 to 39 years....	100.0	94.7	5.3	0.3	1.1	1.3	1.8	0.8
40 to 44 years....	100.0	94.5	5.5	0.3	1.4	1.3	1.8	0.7
45 to 49 years....	100.0	93.3	6.7	0.4	2.0	1.4	2.2	0.8
50 to 54 years....	100.0	90.5	9.5	0.4	3.5	1.7	3.2	0.7
55 to 59 years....	100.0	86.7	13.3	0.6	5.4	1.8	4.7	0.7
60 to 64 years....	100.0	79.4	20.6	0.7	8.9	2.0	8.0	0.8
65 to 69 years....	100.0	59.7	40.3	1.2	18.4	2.1	17.6	1.0
70 to 74 years....	100.0	38.7	61.3	1.6	30.3	2.4	25.7	1.3
75 and over.......	100.0	18.7	81.3	1.8	47.2	4.8	26.3	1.2

Source: *1950 Census of Population*, Vol. IV, *Special Reports*, Part 1, Chapter A, Employment and Personal Characteristics, tables 1 and 3.

Section 2: Survey data on the economic position of older persons

The whole issue relating to age discrimination, fixed retirement ages, and potential workers among the retired has been the subject of widespread and lively discussion, all too frequently in the absence of concrete evidence or on the basis of fragmentary data. Late in 1951 and early in 1952, two surveys designed to collect information on the economic position of older persons roughly within the same frame of reference were conducted. Within the wide range of information obtained in both surveys, there was a considerable body of data relating to the issue described above.

TABLE C-2.—LABOR FORCE PARTICIPATION RATES BASED ON REPORTS FOR IDENTICAL PERSONS OBTAINED BY CENSUS AND BY CURRENT POPULATION SURVEY ENUMERATORS, BY AGE, COLOR, AND SEX

[Data for approximately 51,000 persons enumerated in both the Population Census and the Current Population Survey for April 1950]

Age, color, and sex	Labor force participation rates based on--		Census rate as percent of CPS rate	Age, color, and sex	Labor force participation rates based on--		Census rate as percent of CPS rate
	Census enumeration	CPS enumeration			Census enumeration	CPS enumeration	
TOTAL				WHITE--Cont.			
Male............	81.5	84.0	97.0	Female.........	28.3	30.6	92.5
14 to 17 years......	27.0	35.0	77.1	14 to 17 years......	13.2	16.7	79.0
18 to 24 years......	83.1	86.2	96.4	18 to 24 years......	45.0	46.4	97.0
25 to 44 years......	95.1	96.9	98.1	25 to 44 years......	31.1	33.5	92.8
45 to 64 years......	90.1	92.1	97.8	45 to 64 years......	28.4	30.8	92.2
65 and over.........	44.4	45.9	96.7	65 and over.........	6.7	8.4	79.8
Female.........	29.2	31.7	92.1	NONWHITE			
14 to 17 years......	13.2	17.1	77.2				
18 to 24 years......	44.0	45.5	96.7	Male............	79.5	84.2	94.4
25 to 44 years......	32.4	35.1	92.3	14 to 17 years......	37.5	46.1	81.3
45 to 64 years......	29.5	32.1	91.9	18 to 24 years......	82.6	89.5	92.2
65 and over.........	7.0	8.9	78.7	25 to 44 years......	90.9	94.2	96.5
				45 to 64 years......	88.3	93.2	94.7
WHITE				65 and over.........	43.9	43.9	100.0
Male............	81.7	84.0	97.3	Female.........	37.0	41.7	88.7
14 to 17 years......	25.6	33.6	76.2	14 to 17 years......	13.0	20.0	65.0
18 to 24 years......	83.2	85.9	96.9	18 to 24 years......	35.9	37.9	94.7
25 to 44 years......	95.5	97.1	98.4	25 to 44 years......	44.7	50.0	89.4
45 to 64 years......	90.3	92.0	98.2	45 to 64 years......	42.0	46.5	90.3
65 and over.........	44.5	46.0	96.7	65 and over.........	11.1	15.1	73.5

Source: *1950 Census of Population*, Vol. IV, *Special Reports*, Part 1, Chapter A, Employment and Personal Characteristics, table B.

The first of these surveys, that of the Bureau of Old-Age and Survivors Insurance of the Social Security Administration, was conducted in the last quarter of 1951 and covered a national sample of OASI beneficiaries. Since it was limited to persons who had retired from covered employment, the results of the survey cannot be generalized to the entire older population of the country, but they would seem to be reasonably representative for nonagricultural employment, a substantial part of the total. The results of this survey as they relate to retirement have been published in an article by Margaret L. Stecker,[3] and additional information is to be found in various intra-agency memoranda.

The second of these surveys was conducted in connection with the April 1952 Current Population Survey for the Institute of Industrial Relations of the University of California as a part of a larger study of the economic implications of an aging population. In this survey a battery of additional questions relating to the economic position of older persons were asked of persons 65 and over who fell in the Current Population Survey sample. Here, again, there was a group of questions relating to reasons for retirement and ability and inclination to return to work.

---

[3] Margaret L. Stecker, "Why Do Beneficiaries Retire? Who Among Them Return to Work?" *Social Security Bulletin*, 18, 5, May 1955, p. 3ff.

Preliminary analyses of the data from this survey were presented in a series of papers presented at the 1953 meetings of the American Economic Association,[4] and the final analysis appears in a recently published volume.[5] Since not all of the relevant data are available in published form, the data on reasons for retirement and labor force availability are presented in table C-3.

TABLE C-3.—PERSONS 65 YEARS OLD AND OVER WITH WORK EXPERIENCE BY LABOR FORCE STATUS, BY REASON FOR LEAVING LAST JOB AND LABOR FORCE AVAILABILITY: APRIL 1952

Labor force status, reason for leaving last job, and labor force availability	Male			Female		
	Number (thousands)	Percent of total	Percent not in labor force	Number (thousands)	Percent of total	Percent not in labor force
REASON FOR LEAVING LAST JOB						
Total............................	5,562	100.0	...	2,445	100.0	...
Labor force...........................	2,259	40.6	...	575	23.5	...
Not in labor force....................	3,303	59.4	100.0	1,870	76.5	100.0
Involuntary retirement...............	797	14.3	24.1	333	13.6	17.8
Age--compulsory system.............	453	8.1	13.7	89	3.6	4.8
Other involuntary...................	344	6.2	10.4	244	10.0	13.0
Age--employer's decision.........	47	0.8	1.4	34	1.4	1.8
Laid off, work unavailable.......	141	2.5	4.3	63	2.6	3.4
Miscellaneous....................	156	2.8	4.7	147	6.0	7.9
Voluntary retirement.................	2,506	45.1	75.9	1,537	62.9	82.2
Health...........................	1,959	35.2	59.3	932	38.1	49.8
Other voluntary...................	547	9.8	16.6	605	24.7	32.4
Age..............................	195	3.5	5.9	127	5.2	6.8
Family decision..................	28	0.5	0.8	233	9.5	12.5
Other............................	324	5.8	9.8	245	10.0	13.1
LABOR FORCE AVAILABILITY						
Total............................	5,562	100.0	...	2,445	100.0	...
Labor force...........................	2,259	40.6	...	575	23.5	...
Not in labor force....................	3,303	59.4	100.0	1,870	76.5	100.0
Unable or not well enough to work....	2,612	47.0	79.1	1,488	60.9	79.6
Able to work.........................	691	12.4	20.9	382	15.6	20.4
Interested in working..............	438	7.9	13.3	208	8.5	11.1
Full time.......................	104	1.9	3.1	35	1.4	1.9
Part time.......................	117	2.1	3.5	46	1.9	2.5
Occasionally....................	217	3.9	6.6	127	5.2	6.8
Not interested in working..........	253	4.5	7.7	174	7.1	9.3

Source: Institute of Industrial Relations of the University of California supplement to Current Population Survey of April 1952.

Section 3: Migration and farm-nonfarm labor force participation rates

The hypothesis under consideration here is that the observed differences in the labor force participation rates between farm and nonfarm males at the upper age level do not reflect intrinsic differences in occupational longevity but are simply a by-product of the out-migration from farms; that is, out-migrants from the farm population at these age levels are drawn heavily

[4] Robert Dorfman, "The Labor Force Status of Persons Aged Sixty-Five and Over"; Peter O. Steiner, "The Size, Nature, and Adequacy of the Resources of the Aged"; and Melvin W. Reder, "Age and Income," *American Economics Review*, Vol. XLIV, No. 2, May 1954, pp. 634–670.

[5] Peter O. Steiner and Robert Dorfman, *The Economic Status of the Aged*, The University of California Press, Berkeley and Los Angeles, 1957.

from retired or retiring males, and labor force participation rates in farm areas are "artificially" high. As indicated in the main body of the text, this hypothesis is not susceptible to proof, which would involve the determination of what the labor force rates among out-migrants from farms would have been at the end of a decade if they had not been out-migrants. It is possible, however, to estimate the labor force participation rates at the end of a decade for the members of this hypothetical group required to equalize the farm-nonfarm rates at the end of a decade on the assumption that the group had remained in the farm population.

This calculation involves the use of estimates of net out-migration from farms for appropriate cohorts and labor force survival ratios for these same cohorts, and is based on figures from the 1940 and 1950 Census.

The basic data are presented in table C–4a, which presents, for the appropriate cohorts total population, data on persons in the labor force for the farm and nonfarm populations in 1940 and 1950. For simplicity it is assumed that the rural-farm population is, in effect, the farm population, and that the remaining population is the nonfarm population. This assumption is not a particularly bold one since the urban farm population, misplaced by this assumption, constituted something like 1 percent of the total farm population in both 1940 and 1950. Likewise, the 1950 figures are based on the new urban-rural definition, whereas the 1940 figures are based obviously on the old definition; however, since the 1950 figures for the rural-farm population under the new definition differ from those under the old definition by less than one-tenth of 1 percent, there is little loss in comparability. The 1950 figures for the farm population have been adjusted to include institutional population, which was, by definition, excluded from the farm population in 1950 on the assumption that the proportion in 1950 was the same as that in 1940. Here, again, the numbers involved are small, but since they bear directly on the classification by employment status, there seemed to be some virtue in making this gesture in the direction of comparability.

No adjustment was made for the other definitional differences[6] which, if the Current Population Survey figure for April 1950 is taken as a standard, resulted in an understatement approaching 2 million—a difference, of course, subject to sampling error. The particular class of persons excluded by the definitional changes, such as persons living in motor courts located on farms or living in rented houses located on farms, would seem to have been largely peripheral to the farm population and, thus, is characterized by labor force rates more closely akin to those for the nonfarm population than those for the farm population. Thus, this lack of comparability would tend to overstate the farm-nonfarm difference in 1950, relative to 1940. On the other hand, the elimination of the peripheral group from the farm population maximizes the estimate of net migration and may give undue

---

[6] See *1950 Census of Population*, Vol. II, *Characteristics of the Population*, Part 1, U. S. Summary, pp. 33 and 34.

weight to the migration factor; that is, given farm and nonfarm rates for a particular age group, the greater the volume of out-migration, the smaller the difference from farm and nonfarm rates in the rates among out-migrants necessary to equalize the farm and nonfarm rates. The two biases which arise from the lack of exact comparability of the 1940 and the 1950 definitions thus appear to work in opposite directions, but it is not possible to affirm that they cancel each other out.

The estimates of net migration were derived from census survival rates or ratios based on the total population, rather than on the native population, on the assumption that the contribution of immigration to the cohorts involved was negligible in the decade of 1940 to 1950. (Survival rates computed on the two bases differ by only fractions of 1 percent.) The use of this assumption permits the calculation of net migration within a closed system, insures comparability between the over-all survival ratios and the labor force survival ratios, and obviates the necessity of estimating an age distribution for the total native population of 1940. The over-all survival ratios or rates, the estimates of net migration, and the labor force survival ratios or rates—the number of men in the labor force in the specified age groups in 1950 expressed as a decimal fraction of the corresponding number of males, 10 years younger in 1940—appear in table C–4b.

At the upper age levels, a part of the farm-nonfarm difference in labor force participation rates in 1950 is attributable to the differences which already existed in the same cohorts in 1940 (table C–4a). Thus, for example, a part of the difference between the farm and nonfarm rate for the cohort reaching age 65 to 74 in 1950 (69.8 versus 47.5) is attributable to the fact that 10 years earlier the rates in this same cohort were 90.9 and 81.6 for the farm and nonfarm populations respectively. In order to control this factor, and to examine the relationship between migration and labor force participation only in the decade of 1940 to 1950, 1940 figures for the farm and the nonfarm labor force for each cohort were adjusted in such a way as to make each rate equal the rate for the country as a whole. The labor force survival ratios were then applied to the adjusted figures to obtain estimates of the size of the farm and the nonfarm labor force in 1950 on the assumption that, cohort by cohort, there were no differences between the farm and nonfarm rates in 1940, but that the observed survival ratios of 1940–1950 had obtained. These figures are presented in table C–4a.

With these standardized figures for 1950 and estimates of total net out-migration from the farm population at hand, simple algebraic manipulation makes possible the determination of the size of the labor force among the out-migrants necessary to equalize the 1950 farm-nonfarm rates on the assumption that these out-migrants had remained in the farm population. In short, the numbers and rates presented in the last two columns of table C–4b are those which would have had to obtain among potential net out-migrants if there was to have been no difference between the farm and the nonfarm rates.

These rates, of course, do not answer the question as to whether or not heavy concentrations of retired or retiring persons among out-migrants from farms account for the higher labor force participation rates in the older farm population. They do, however, provide a basis for making some inferences as to the answer. The sharp drop in the rates between the cohort reaching age 55 to 64 in 1950 and the one becoming 65 to 74 in the same year seems to place a good deal of strain on the hypothesis that the differences in question are purely a function of migration. It may well be that agricultural occupations permit intrinsically a higher rate of survival in the labor force than do nonagricultural occupations, particularly as cohorts pass through the critical age of 65.

TABLE C-4.—LABOR FORCE STATUS OF MALES, BY AGE AND FARM RESIDENCE: 1950 AND 1940

[Figures for nonfarm population include urban-farm population—283,338 in 1950 and 330,723 in 1940. Farm figures for 1950 adjusted to include institutional population]

Year and age	United States			Farm			Nonfarm		
	Total	Labor force		Total	Labor force		Total	Labor force	
		Number	Rate		Number	Rate		Number	Rate
1950									
35 to 44 years....	10,402,195	9,828,295	94.5	1,481,144	1,424,450	96.2	8,921,051	8,403,845	94.2
45 to 54 years....	8,484,515	7,801,905	92.0	1,292,557	1,223,460	94.7	7,191,958	6,578,445	91.5
55 to 64 years....	6,540,100	5,452,135	83.4	1,084,026	964,130	88.9	5,456,074	4,488,005	82.3
65 to 74 years....	4,006,830	2,057,650	51.4	698,297	487,635	69.8	3,308,533	1,570,015	47.5
75 to 84 years....	1,492,990	305,740	20.5	249,486	95,240	38.2	1,243,504	210,500	16.9
85 and over.......	234,430	16,155	6.9	41,156	5,235	12.7	193,274	10,920	5.7
1940									
35 to 44 years....	9,164,794	8,678,280	94.7	1,728,290	1,662,243	96.2	7,436,504	7,016,037	94.3
45 to 54 years....	7,962,019	7,329,310	92.1	1,674,190	1,594,159	95.2	6,287,829	5,735,151	91.2
55 to 64 years....	5,409,180	4,533,909	83.8	1,311,537	1,191,878	90.9	4,097,643	3,342,031	81.6
65 to 74 years....	3,167,055	1,608,211	50.8	824,862	576,221	69.9	2,342,193	1,031,990	44.1
75 and over.......	1,239,065	220,998	17.8	309,655	98,848	31.9	929,410	122,150	13.1

Source: *1950 Census of Population*, Vol. II, *Characteristics of the Population*, Part 1, U. S. Summary, table 118, and Vol. IV, *Special Reports*, Part 2, Chapter C, Institutional Population, table 3; *1940 Census of Population*, Vol. IV, *Characteristics by Age*, Part 1, U. S. Summary, table 24, and *Institutional Population*, table 4.

TABLE C-4a.—SURVIVAL RATIOS FOR ALL MALES AND FOR THE MALE LABOR FORCE, FARM AND NONFARM, WITH ESTIMATED NET OUT-MIGRATION FROM FARMS, BY AGE: 1940 TO 1950

Age in 1950	Survival rate,[1] total population	Estimated net migration from farm population	Survival rate,[1] labor force	
			Farm	Nonfarm
45 to 54 years.....................	.9257726	307,446	.7360296	.9376297
55 to 64 years.....................	.8214123	291,174	.6047891	.7825435
65 to 74 years.....................	.7407463	273,219	.4091316	.4697787
75 to 84 years.....................	.4714127	139,364	.1652838	.2039748
85 years and over..................	.1891991	17,430	.0529601	.0893983

[1] Ratio of age group in 1950 to age group 10 years younger in 1940.

Source: Table C-4.

TABLE **C-4b.**—STANDARDIZED LABOR FORCE PARTICIPATION RATES BY FARM RESIDENCE AND PARTICIPATION RATE AMONG NET MIGRANTS REQUIRED TO EQUALIZE FARM AND NONFARM RATES, BY AGE: 1950

[Rates standardized for farm-nonfarm differences within cohorts in 1940]

Age	Farm			Nonfarm			Net migrants		
	Total	Labor force		Total	Labor force		Total	Labor force	
		Number	Rate		Number	Rate		Number	Rate
45 to 54 years.......	1,292,557	1,204,545	93.2	7,191,958	6,602,541	91.8	307,446	267,709	87.1
55 to 64 years.......	1,084,026	932,070	86.0	5,456,074	4,529,488	83.0	291,174	216,343	74.3
65 to 74 years.......	698,297	449,764	64.4	3,308,533	1,613,500	48.8	273,219	50,505	18.5
75 to 84 years.......	249,486	69,231	27.7	1,243,504	242,598	19.5	139,364	11,985	8.6
85 years and over....	41,156	2,925	7.1	193,274	14,819	7.7	17,430	1,509	8.7

Source: Tables C-4 and C-4a.

Section 4: Trends in nonagricultural self-employment

The folklore relating to the growth of corporations, the rise of chain stores, and the increasing "bigness" of business carries as a corollary the assumption that, in the course of this century, there has been a sharp decline in the independent self-employed businessman. All too frequently the statistics cited to demonstrate this proposition include farmers, and the inclusion of this group automatically insures a resounding decline. Statistics published by the Office of Business Economics of the Department of Commerce on full-time equivalent employees and number of persons engaged in production indicate for the period 1929 to 1950 an unspectacular decline in the proportion of nonagricultural self-employed not essentially different from that suggested by the census figures.[7] The fact that the survival ratio for the nonagricultural self-employed is perhaps slightly lower than that for wage and salary workers is not necessarily surprising. In 1950, nearly one-half of the nonagricultural self-employed were proprietors. It is reasonable to assume that a large proportion of the men were proprietors of small businesses, and, since the mortality of small businesses is high, a low survival ratio is to be expected. Likewise, studies of occupational mobility indicate that among craftsmen and operatives there is a considerable movement into, and out of, self-employment which suggests that self-employment does not necessarily insure occupational longevity. It is possible that the notion that self-employment insures a long occupational life represents a generalization based on specific cases of professional men, or craftsmen, for whom self-employment has, in fact, meant the continuation of employment well into the later years.

The data on nonagricultural self-employed are presented in table C-5. In this table the distinction between agricultural and nonagricultural employment is based on occupation rather than industry; that is, persons employed as farmers, farm managers, farm laborers, and foremen are as-

[7] Office of Business Economics; *National Income, 1954 Edition,* U. S. Government Printing Office, Washington 1954, tables 25 and 28.

TABLE C-5.—EMPLOYED AGRICULTURAL AND NONAGRICULTURAL MALE WORKERS, BY CLASS OF WORKER AND AGE: 1950, 1940, AND 1910

Year and age	All workers			Agricultural workers[1]			Nonagricultural workers[3]		
	Total	Self-employed	Other	Total	Self-employed[2]	Other	Total	Self-employed[4]	Other
1950..............	40,019,100	8,490,270	31,528,830	6,118,950	4,165,260	1,953,690	33,900,150	4,325,010	29,575,140
14 and 15 years.....	309,060	11,760	297,300	142,350	6,420	135,930	166,710	5,340	161,370
16 and 17 years.....	634,290	29,610	604,680	243,930	17,310	226,620	390,360	12,300	378,060
18 and 19 years.....	1,116,840	61,530	1,055,310	263,520	40,260	223,260	853,320	21,270	832,050
20 to 24 years......	3,887,160	346,230	3,540,930	555,180	219,120	336,060	3,331,980	127,110	3,204,870
25 to 29 years......	4,895,880	667,890	4,227,990	561,720	361,650	200,070	4,334,160	306,240	4,027,920
30 to 34 years......	4,889,700	885,030	4,004,670	561,090	420,720	140,370	4,328,610	464,310	3,864,300
35 to 44 years......	9,382,320	2,119,320	7,263,000	1,191,210	941,430	249,750	8,191,110	1,177,860	7,013,250
45 to 54 years......	7,465,500	1,947,630	5,517,870	1,063,350	870,300	190,050	6,405,150	1,077,330	5,327,820
55 to 59 years......	2,954,730	850,290	2,104,440	489,090	415,260	73,830	2,465,640	435,030	2,030,610
60 to 64 years......	2,231,070	670,380	1,560,690	421,770	352,020	69,750	1,809,300	318,360	1,490,940
65 years and over...	2,252,550	900,600	1,351,950	628,740	520,740	108,000	1,623,810	379,860	1,243,950
1940..............	34,102,440	8,910,740	25,191,700	7,750,340	4,996,780	2,733,563	26,372,100	3,913,960	22,458,140
14 and 15 years.....	170,280	7,180	163,100	120,600	1,160	119,440	49,680	6,020	43,660
16 and 17 years.....	482,940	23,140	459,800	277,500	6,640	270,860	205,440	16,500	188,940
18 and 19 years.....	1,113,000	76,720	1,036,280	393,180	41,500	351,680	719,820	35,220	684,600
20 to 24 years......	3,996,700	437,240	3,559,460	930,040	283,360	646,680	3,066,660	153,880	2,912,780
25 to 29 years......	4,466,180	741,500	3,724,680	818,200	447,440	370,760	3,647,980	294,060	3,353,920
30 to 34 years......	4,283,020	895,720	3,387,300	720,560	485,500	235,060	3,562,460	410,220	3,152,240
35 to 39 years......	4,019,140	990,840	3,028,300	692,820	516,280	176,540	3,326,320	474,560	2,851,760
40 to 44 years......	3,689,620	1,061,780	2,627,840	654,700	539,560	125,040	3,024,920	522,120	2,502,800
45 to 49 years......	3,419,920	1,108,000	2,311,920	685,340	575,280	110,060	2,734,580	532,720	2,201,860
50 to 54 years......	2,953,440	1,061,040	1,892,400	679,000	578,880	100,120	2,274,440	482,160	1,792,280
55 to 59 years......	2,243,660	887,120	1,356,540	595,760	508,540	87,220	1,647,900	378,580	1,269,320
60 to 64 years......	1,610,480	710,660	899,820	492,560	425,060	67,500	1,117,920	285,600	832,320
65 years and over...	1,654,060	909,800	744,260	660,080	587,480	72,600	993,980	322,320	671,660
1910, total..............	28,738,425	8,802,770	19,935,655	9,591,529	5,861,302	3,730,227	19,146,896	2,941,468	16,205,428

[1] Farmers and farm managers, farm laborers and foremen.
[2] For 1950 and 1940, includes farm managers; about 33,000 and 36,000, respectively.
[3] All other workers.
[4] For 1950 and 1940, includes nonfarm unpaid family workers; about 43,000 and 75,000, respectively.

Source: 1950 Census of Population, Vol. IV, Special Reports, Part 1, Chapter B, Occupational Characteristics, table 6, and Chapter D, Industrial Characteristics, table 4; 1940 Census of Population, Occupational Characteristics, table 1, and Industrial Characteristics, table 3; 1910 Census of Population, special compilation from unpublished tabulations of data on class of worker.

sumed to comprise agricultural workers, and persons employed in all other occupations, nonagricultural workers. The differences between these figures and those for persons employed in the industry, agriculture, are not large; in 1950, for example, the total number of males employed in agriculture (6,260,550) was only about 2 percent higher than the figure presented here.

In order to obtain figures in the desired categories by age for 1940 and 1950, it was necessary to approximate the self-employed group. This approximation involved the assumptions that the total self-employed is represented by the difference between the total employed and the sum of figures for wage or salary workers (from industry tabulations) and unpaid family farm workers, and that farm managers are self-employed. The net result of these assumptions is the inclusion of nonfarm unpaid family workers among the nonagricultural self-employed and farm managers among the agricultural self-employed. In both cases the numbers involved are small and do not appreciably distort the results.

Section 5: Changing age structure and the decline of labor force participation of older persons

Changing age structure among males 65 and over. As a part of the general aging of the population in the course of this century some shift toward the upper age level in the population 65 years old and over might be expected. The figures presented in table C–6 for 1950 and 1890 indicate that some such change did occur but that it was not large. The table presents the results of a calculation of the labor force participation rate to have been expected in 1950 for men 65 and over had the percentage age distribution within the group been identical with that of 1890, and had the age specific labor force rates observed in 1950 obtained. The figures suggest that the changes in age structure between 1890 and 1950 may have reduced the percent in the labor force at this level by about one percentage point.

TABLE **C–6.**—Observed and Expected Male Labor Force 65 Years Old and Over: 1950

[Data for 1890 exclude figures for age not reported]

Age	Total, 1890		Observed, 1950				Expected, 1950[1]		
			Total		Labor force			Labor force	
	Number	Per-cent	Number	Per-cent	Number	Per-cent	Total	Number	Per-cent
Total..............	1,233,719	100.0	5,734,250	100.0	2,379,545	41.5	5,734,250	2,414,487	42.1
65 to 69 years.........	525,627	42.6	2,399,645	41.8	1,435,050	59.8	2,443,082	1,461,027	59.8
70 to 74 years.........	363,642	29.5	1,607,185	28.0	622,600	38.7	1,690,185	654,753	38.7
75 to 79 years.........	199,093	16.1	992,645	17.3	239,830	24.2	925,372	223,576	24.2
80 to 84 years.........	97,862	7.9	500,345	8.7	65,910	13.2	454,857	59,918	13.2
85 years and over......	47,495	3.8	234,430	4.1	16,155	6.9	220,754	15,213	6.9

[1] On the basis of the observed age-specific labor force participation rates of 1950 and the percentage age distribution of 1890.

Source: *1950 Census of Population*, Vol. II, *Characteristics of the Population*, Part 1, U. S. Summary, table 118; *1930 Census of Population*, Vol. II, *General Report—Statistics by Subjects*, Chapter 10, Age Distribution, table 7.

General changes in age structure.   In assessing the potential productive capacity of a population from a demographic point of view, recourse is sometimes had to dependency ratios, that is, to the number of children and older persons per 100 or 1,000 of the population of working age.   High ratios imply a relative shortage of productive manpower and lead to concern as to whether there is sufficient manpower to support the economy, whereas low ratios imply a relative excess of productive manpower and lead to concern as to whether or not full employment can be maintained.   A ratio of this sort then provides a crude index of the number of nonproducing consumers relative to the size of the working or producing population or, conversely, an index of the intensity of the need for manpower.   In this context, the percentage which the working population constitutes of the total is perhaps the more direct index since members of the working population as well as members of the dependent population are consumers.

The crudity of such indexes is obvious; any definition of the working population in terms of sheer age fails to allow for age differences in labor force participation and, whatever the specified upper and lower limits are, they are bound to be arbitrary.   Likewise, the failure to allow for sex differences in labor force participation, and to take per capita productivity into consideration blunt the precision of the index.   In spite of these limitations, however, large differences in the proportion which the population of working age constitutes of the total reflect in a general way the need for manpower.

In compiling the data presented in table C–7, the population of working age was defined as that between the ages 20 and 64, and in these terms there was a substantial increase between 1890 and 1950 in the proportion which this population constituted of the total.   In more concrete terms, if the 1890 percentage had obtained in 1950, there would have been some 12

TABLE **C–7.**—WORKING POPULATION AND DEPENDENCY RATIOS: 1890 TO 1950

[Totals for 1890 and 1920 include figures for age not reported]

Year	Total population, all ages	"Working" population (20 to 64 years)		"Dependent" population					
				Number			Per 1,000 working population		
		Number	Percent of total	Total	Under 20 years	65 years and over	Total	Under 20 years	65 years and over
1950..................	150,697,361	87,328,702	57.9	63,368,659	51,099,122	12,269,537	726	585	140
1940..................	131,669,275	77,344,357	58.7	54,324,918	45,305,604	9,019,314	702	586	117
1920..................	105,710,620	57,734,407	54.6	47,976,213	43,042,998	4,933,215	831	746	85
1890..................	62,622,250	31,405,199	50.2	31,217,051	28,799,763	2,417,288	994	917	77

Source: *1950 Census of Population,* Vol. II, *Characteristics of the Population,* Part 1, U. S. Summary, table 39.

million fewer persons in the population of working age. This number is sufficiently large to serve as presumptive evidence that in 1950 there was less need for productive manpower than in 1890. If this was the case, then it seems plausible to assume that a part of the decline in the labor force participation rate among persons 65 and over is attributable to this situation.

Section 6: Marital status, employment, and age among women

Standard employment status data are presented for women in table C–8. Tables C–9 and C–10 bring together and rearrange data on age, marital status, and household relationship from the special report on employment and personal characteristics.

TABLE **C–8.**—LABOR FORCE STATUS OF FEMALES, BY AGE: 1950

Age	Total population	Labor force	Not in labor force					
			Total	Keeping house	Unable to work	In institutions	Other	Not reported
Total.........	57,083,190	16,553,040	40,530,150	32,073,180	1,866,750	564,120	5,371,770	654,330
14 to 19 years....	6,369,330	1,441,050	4,928,280	907,530	34,560	44,550	3,776,160	165,480
20 to 24 years....	5,869,860	2,520,840	3,349,020	2,832,090	31,320	22,980	375,510	87,120
25 to 29 years....	6,283,110	2,047,470	4,235,640	3,975,270	34,560	29,310	137,880	58,620
30 to 34 years....	5,874,930	1,819,830	4,055,100	3,840,390	32,280	33,300	96,720	52,410
35 to 39 years....	5,720,010	1,934,040	3,785,970	3,580,950	38,340	35,490	85,980	45,210
40 to 44 years....	5,127,480	1,864,680	3,262,800	3,068,340	39,450	39,330	74,370	41,310
45 to 49 years....	4,562,760	1,587,510	2,975,250	2,775,690	51,210	36,750	74,160	37,440
50 to 54 years....	4,125,060	1,271,220	2,853,840	2,633,760	68,790	39,090	79,110	33,090
55 to 59 years....	3,614,720	935,130	2,679,590	2,430,860	89,910	37,620	90,660	30,540
60 to 64 years....	3,021,430	622,170	2,399,260	2,077,720	147,150	39,060	106,260	29,070
65 to 69 years....	2,605,600	339,690	2,265,910	1,799,160	260,050	39,540	141,330	25,830
70 to 74 years....	1,790,120	114,210	1,675,910	1,164,750	315,740	45,060	130,020	20,340
75 and over.......	2,118,780	55,200	2,063,580	986,670	723,390	122,040	203,610	27,870
PERCENT DISTRIBUTION								
Total.........	100.0	29.0	71.0	56.2	3.3	1.0	9.4	1.1
14 to 19 years....	100.0	22.6	77.4	14.2	0.5	0.7	59.3	2.6
20 to 24 years....	100.0	42.9	57.1	48.2	0.5	0.4	6.4	1.5
25 to 29 years....	100.0	32.6	67.4	63.3	0.6	0.5	2.2	0.9
30 to 34 years....	100.0	31.0	69.0	65.4	0.5	0.6	1.6	0.9
35 to 39 years....	100.0	33.8	66.2	62.6	0.7	0.6	1.5	0.8
40 to 44 years....	100.0	36.4	63.6	59.8	0.8	0.8	1.5	0.8
45 to 49 years....	100.0	34.8	65.2	60.8	1.1	0.8	1.6	0.8
50 to 54 years....	100.0	30.8	69.2	63.8	1.7	0.9	1.9	0.8
55 to 59 years....	100.0	25.9	74.1	67.2	2.5	1.0	2.5	0.8
60 to 64 years....	100.0	20.6	79.4	68.8	4.9	1.3	3.5	1.0
65 to 69 years....	100.0	13.0	87.0	69.0	10.0	1.5	5.4	1.0
70 to 74 years....	100.0	6.4	93.6	65.1	17.6	2.5	7.3	1.1
75 and over.......	100.0	2.6	97.4	46.6	34.1	5.8	9.6	1.3

Source: *1950 Census of Population*, Vol. IV, *Special Reports*, Part 1, Chapter A, Employment and Personal Characteristics, tables 1 and 3.

TABLE C-9.—LABOR FORCE STATUS OF FEMALES 35 YEARS OLD AND OVER, BY MARITAL
STATUS AND AGE: 1950

Marital status	35 to 44 years	45 to 54 years	55 to 64 years	65 to 74 years	75 years and over
Total........................	10,847,490	8,687,820	6,636,150	4,395,720	2,118,780
Single........................	887,700	674,370	517,260	379,320	214,020
Wife of household head...........	8,381,670	6,210,930	3,951,360	1,709,340	321,840
Widowed or divorced..............	795,160	1,267,800	1,805,080	2,090,520	1,503,630
Other[1].......................	782,960	534,720	362,450	216,540	79,290
Labor force..................	3,798,720	2,858,730	1,557,300	453,900	55,200
Single........................	671,790	476,820	295,680	102,180	15,000
Wife of household head...........	2,177,070	1,405,560	510,090	84,720	5,190
Widowed or divorced..............	559,450	732,690	647,610	244,740	32,970
Other[1].......................	390,410	243,660	103,920	22,260	2,040
PERCENT IN LABOR FORCE					
Total........................	35.0	32.9	23.5	10.3	2.6
Single........................	75.7	70.7	57.2	26.9	7.0
Wife of household head...........	26.0	22.6	12.9	5.0	1.6
Widowed or divorced..............	70.4	57.8	35.9	11.7	2.2
Other[1].......................	49.9	45.6	28.7	10.3	2.6

[1] Married, husband absent, and married, husband present but not head of household.

Source: *1950 Census of Population*, Vol. IV, *Special Reports*, Part 1, Chapter A, Employment and Personal Characteristics, tables 6 and 10.

TABLE C-10.—LABOR FORCE STATUS OF SINGLE AND WIDOWED OR DIVORCED FEMALES 35
YEARS OLD AND OVER, BY HOUSEHOLD RELATIONSHIP AND AGE: 1950

[Statistics exclude institutional population]

Age and household relationship	Single			Widowed or divorced		
	Total	Labor force		Total	Labor force	
		Number	Per-cent		Number	Per-cent
All classes.................	2,534,490	1,561,470	61.6	7,295,840	2,217,460	30.4
35 to 44 years....................	853,290	671,790	78.7	787,030	559,450	71.1
45 to 54 years....................	646,110	476,820	73.8	1,254,030	732,690	58.4
55 to 64 years....................	492,870	295,680	60.0	1,783,750	647,610	36.3
65 to 74 years....................	355,380	102,180	28.8	2,050,350	244,740	11.9
75 years and over................	186,840	15,000	8.0	1,420,680	32,970	2.3
Head of household............	802,710	514,440	64.1	4,264,430	1,471,810	34.5
35 to 44 years....................	183,300	163,620	89.3	510,610	361,120	70.7
45 to 54 years....................	207,780	174,750	84.1	859,800	514,290	59.8
55 to 64 years....................	188,040	127,680	67.9	1,117,930	427,770	38.3
65 to 74 years....................	147,360	42,840	29.1	1,155,810	149,220	12.9
75 years and over................	76,230	5,550	7.3	620,280	19,410	3.1
Relative of head.............	1,218,270	657,990	54.0	2,370,210	404,220	17.1
35 to 44 years....................	504,570	362,250	71.8	182,250	123,120	67.6
45 to 54 years....................	303,390	185,130	61.0	261,810	121,050	46.2
55 to 64 years....................	196,830	84,060	42.7	493,290	112,980	22.9
65 to 74 years....................	137,520	23,880	17.4	730,650	40,860	5.6
75 years and over................	75,960	2,670	3.5	702,210	6,210	0.9
Other[1].......................	513,510	389,040	75.8	661,200	341,430	51.6
35 to 44 years....................	165,420	145,920	88.2	94,170	75,210	79.9
45 to 54 years....................	134,940	116,940	86.7	132,420	97,350	73.5
55 to 64 years....................	108,000	83,940	77.7	172,530	106,860	61.9
65 to 74 years....................	70,500	35,460	50.3	163,890	54,660	33.4
75 years and over................	34,650	6,780	19.6	98,190	7,350	7.5

[1] Unrelated persons in households and persons in quasi households other than institutions.

Source: *1950 Census of Population*, Vol. IV, *Special Reports*, Part 1, Chapter A, Employment and Personal Characteristics, table 6, and Part 2, Chapter D, Marital Status, table 1.

A P P E N D I X   D

OCCUPATION

Section 1: Data on occupation and age

The occupation classification used in the 1950 Census is described in the introduction to the U. S. Summary, Vol. II, of the 1950 Census reports on population. Briefly, the system consists of 469 items from which a detailed classification of 446 categories, an intermediate classification of 158 categories for males and 67 categories for females, and a major occupation group classification of 12 categories are developed. The composition of each of the detailed categories is presented in the publication, U. S. Bureau of the Census, *1950 Census of Population, Classified Index of Occupations and Industries*. For the most part, the discussion of age and occupation relates to the intermediate level of classification.

Summary figures on the age of males in each of the intermediate occupation groups are presented for 1950 in table D–1. Within each major occupation group the intermediate occupations are ranked on the basis of the percentage which persons 65 years old and over constitute of the totals. The summary figures are based directly on the data presented in table 127 of the U. S. Summary, Vol. II, of the 1950 Census population reports.

The intermediate occupation classification in table D–2 was designed to produce comparable figures by age for 1940 and 1950. The basic data for 1950 were derived from table 127 of the U. S. Summary, Vol. II, of the 1950 Census population reports, and those for 1940 from the U. S. Summary, Vol. III, of the 1940 Census population reports. For those occupation groups which were not comparable, reference was made to table 125 of the 1950 Census report which presents comparable 1940 and 1950 totals for the detailed classification. Using these figures as controls and data on age for detailed occupation groups from the 3⅓-percent special report on occupational characteristics, the 1950 categories were, generally speaking, adjusted to comparability with the 1940 categories. In some instances, of course, there was sufficient detail presented in the initial 1940 age data to make possible adjustment to a 1950 basis, and minor adjustments of the 1940 data were made in a large number of groups on the basis of the "comparable" 1940 totals presented in the 1950 report. The data presented in table D–2 represent, therefore, a unique set of figures developed for the purpose of establishing comparability between 1940 and 1950 in so far as possible. Table D–3 presents summary figures derived from table D–2.

The occupations for which data are presented in table D–4 were selected from among those for which a series of comparable figures were available in the period 1920 to 1950 to illustrate something as to the range of variation in the ratio of the percentage for persons aged 65 and over in the occupation to the percentage 65 and over in the total population and in survival rates, and the relationship between these two indexes. The data for 1950 and 1940 in table D–4 is, in the main, derived from table D–2 and from appropriate occupation data from the 1930 and 1920 Census reports.

The statistics presented in table D–5 on the self-employed and wage and salary workers are based on 3⅓-percent sample age and occupation data for the experienced labor force and for wage and salary workers in the experienced labor force. With the exception of several of the managerial groups for which age data for either the self-employed or salary workers were available for employed persons, the sample data for the experienced labor force were adjusted to the level for the total employed in each occupation. The 1940–1950 rates of change for males of all ages in the self-employed and wage and salary segments of the selected occupations are, therefore, calculated in terms of employed persons; on the other hand, the age data for 1950 are in error to the extent that the relative age distribution of the experienced labor force differed from that of the employed from occupation to occupation. The use of the alternative procedure—converting the 1940 figures to an experienced labor force basis—involved similar and probably larger errors in making allowances for persons on emergency work in 1940.

The statistics presented in table D–6 are based on 3⅓-percent sample data from the special reports on occupational characteristics and industrial characteristics and the 5-percent sample data from the special report on industrial characteristics of 1940. Since data on all employed workers and on wage and salary workers are available by industry for both 1950 and 1940, it is possible to develop survival rates for the self-employed in given industries. In a few industries, it is possible to specify an occupation group in which the self-employed approximate the self-employed in the industry group. A comparison of the survival rates for the total occupation group with the self-employed group which it approximates in the industry makes possible some inferences as to differences in survival rates between self-employed and wage and salary workers in roughly the same occupation groups. The data on the self-employed which appear in the last column of table D–6 give some indication as to the overlap between the two categories. These figures, as in the case of table D–5, are for workers in the experienced labor force adjusted to an "employed" level.

Table D–7 presents for selected occupations historical data on females of essentially the same character as those presented for males in table D–4.

TABLE **D-1.**—PERCENT OF EMPLOYED MALES 45 AND 65 YEARS OLD AND OVER WITH MEDIAN AGE, BY OCCUPATION: 1950

[Within major occupation groups, intermediate occupations ranked by percent 65 and over.
"N.e.c." means not elsewhere classified]

Occupation	Percent 65 years old and over	Percent 45 years old and over	Median age	Total, 14 years old and over
Professional, technical, and kindred workers.....	4.9	34.1	39.0	2,970,256
Physicians and surgeons................................	11.1	43.9	42.9	180,233
Lawyers and judges.....................................	10.7	48.6	44.5	174,205
Clergymen..	10.5	48.4	44.4	160,694
Dentists...	10.1	54.4	46.6	72,810
Pharmacists..	8.4	51.1	45.4	80,855
Architects...	7.9	46.5	43.7	23,823
Authors, editors, and reporters.......................	5.2	33.9	39.2	70,322
Social, welfare, and recreation workers...............	4.7	32.7	38.8	32,616
Engineers, civil......................................	4.6	41.3	41.8	121,386
Artists and art teachers..............................	4.5	29.8	37.3	47,907
Other professional, technical, and kindred workers.....	4.0	27.4	35.1	505,930
Musicians and music teachers..........................	4.0	26.5	35.1	75,612
Surveyors...	4.0	22.9	32.3	24,375
College presidents, prof'rs, & instructors (n.e.c.)....	3.9	32.3	38.5	95,779
Accountants and auditors..............................	3.5	34.8	39.3	320,799
Engineers, mechanical.................................	3.2	34.1	38.7	109,588
Social scientists.....................................	2.8	30.0	38.4	23,828
Other technical engineers.............................	2.3	28.9	37.7	165,225
Teachers (n.e.c.).....................................	2.3	30.6	38.4	285,609
Designers and draftsmen...............................	2.3	21.8	32.8	141,815
Natural scientists (n.e.c.)...........................	2.1	22.3	35.1	34,229
Chemists..	1.9	21.8	34.9	66,982
Technicians, medical and dental.......................	1.6	19.9	32.9	33,052
Engineers, electrical.................................	1.5	30.0	37.6	105,278
Engineers, aeronautical...............................	0.4	10.8	32.9	17,304
Farmers and farm managers......................	12.5	51.9	45.1	4,189,882
Managers, officials, & proprietors, exc. farm....	6.5	49.2	44.7	4,340,687
Officials & inspectors, State & local administration...	14.2	62.4	49.9	110,951
Managers, off'ls, & propr's (n.e.c.)--self-employed....	7.6	52.3	45.9	2,181,961
Manufacturing...	8.3	54.5	46.4	222,977
Other industries (including not reported)............	8.1	54.1	46.5	418,688
Retail trade, exc. eating & drinking places..........	8.0	51.4	45.5	960,114
Wholesale trade.......................................	7.9	54.5	46.6	170,574
Construction..	6.7	51.0	45.4	196,837
Eating and drinking places...........................	4.4	50.6	45.2	212,771
Other specified managers and officials...............	6.3	50.2	45.1	474,161
Managers, officials, & proprietors (n.e.c.)--salaried..	4.4	43.5	42.8	1,573,614
Finance, insurance, and real estate..................	6.8	52.5	45.9	164,922
Other industries (including not reported)............	4.9	47.8	44.2	439,090
Manufacturing...	4.1	46.0	43.7	386,146
Wholesale and retail trade...........................	3.6	36.1	40.4	583,456
Clerical and kindred workers....................	4.0	31.9	36.4	2,602,610
Bookkeepers...	5.3	28.4	34.0	164,748
Other clerical and kindred workers...................	4.0	31.6	36.3	2,276,160
Mail carriers...	3.2	39.3	40.4	161,702
Sales workers..................................	5.0	32.7	37.1	2,596,786
Real estate agents and brokers.......................	15.8	64.8	50.9	120,325
Insurance agents and brokers.........................	6.1	39.0	40.4	278,120
Salesmen and sales clerks (n.e.c.)...................	4.3	30.8	36.6	2,042,229
Other industries (including not reported)............	4.9	35.5	38.9	99,092
Retail trade...	4.5	28.5	34.6	1,253,109
Wholesale trade......................................	4.0	34.0	39.2	391,757
Manufacturing..	3.9	34.3	39.1	298,271
Other specified sales workers........................	3.8	21.5	18.7	156,112
Craftsmen, foremen, and kindred workers..........	4.4	39.2	40.8	7,537,016
Tailors and furriers.................................	16.5	67.7	53.4	75,864
Blacksmiths, forgemen, and hammermen.................	14.1	59.6	49.7	56,159
Shoemakers and repairers, except factory.............	12.4	55.9	47.7	54,969
Locomotive engineers.................................	10.5	80.7	55.2	72,412
Cabinetmakers and patternmakers......................	9.1	44.7	42.4	106,887
Carpenters...	7.5	46.7	43.6	907,728
Painters (construction), paperhangers, and glaziers....	6.6	46.6	43.6	409,947
Stationary engineers.................................	6.4	51.5	45.6	212,504
Masons, tile setters, and stone cutters..............	5.8	40.3	40.5	172,876

TABLE **D-1.**—PERCENT OF EMPLOYED MALES 45 AND 65 YEARS OLD AND OVER WITH MEDIAN AGE, BY OCCUPATION: 1950—Cont.

[Within major occupation groups, intermediate occupations ranked by percent 65 and over.
"N.e.c." means not elsewhere classified]

Occupation	Percent 65 years old and over	Percent 45 years old and over	Median age	Total, 14 years old and over
Craftsmen, foremen, and kindred workers--Cont.				
Other craftsmen and kindred workers.....................	4.5	37.1	39.7	476,199
Compositors and typesetters.........................	4.5	37.0	40.0	164,366
Plasterers and cement finishers.......................	4.2	40.6	41.1	89,112
Bakers...	4.1	36.6	39.5	105,790
Other mechanics & repairmen, and loom fixers..........	4.1	37.4	40.2	926,581
Millwrights.......................................	4.1	44.3	43.1	57,705
Machinists and job setters............................	3.9	40.0	41.1	529,242
Toolmakers, and die makers and setters................	3.8	39.3	40.8	151,587
Molders, metal.....................................	3.7	37.8	40.3	59,879
Plumbers and pipe fitters............................	3.7	39.7	41.3	275,892
Boilermakers.......................................	3.6	48.8	44.5	35,178
Printing craftsmen, except compositors & typesetters...	3.6	34.9	39.3	85,764
Foremen (n.e.c.)....................................	3.3	46.0	43.8	775,114
Nonmanufacturing industries (incl. not reported).....	3.9	50.7	45.2	314,812
Manufacturing, durable goods......................	2.8	43.3	43.1	276,032
Mfg., nondurable goods (incl. not spec. mfg.).....	2.8	41.8	42.7	184,270
Tinsmiths, coppersmiths, and sheet metal workers.......	3.2	30.8	37.2	121,660
Structural metal workers............................	2.1	33.5	39.2	48,963
Electricians.......................................	1.9	34.4	39.3	307,013
Cranemen, hoistmen, construction machinery operators...	1.5	31.6	39.1	207,043
Locomotive firemen.................................	1.5	28.1	37.3	53,944
Mechanics and repairmen, automobile.................	0.9	22.5	35.2	646,525
Mechanics and repairmen, radio and television.........	0.5	11.5	30.5	72,794
Linemen & servicemen, telegraph, telephone, & power....	0.5	20.0	31.0	207,752
Mechanics and repairmen, airplane...................	0.5	15.1	33.2	69,567
Operatives and kindred workers....................	2.7	28.4	36.1	8,127,433
Stationary firemen.................................	8.3	54.1	46.7	120,742
Meat cutters, except slaughter and packing house.......	4.4	33.2	38.4	167,153
Filers, grinders, and polishers, metal...............	4.3	33.9	38.6	141,021
Sawyers...	4.1	33.4	38.1	91,835
Spinners and weavers, textile.......................	3.7	34.6	38.4	79,555
Motormen, street, subway, and elevated railway........	3.7	44.2	42.8	26,190
Painters, except construction and maintenance.........	3.6	31.3	37.0	103,325
Operatives and kindred workers (n.e.c.)................	3.4	30.7	36.6	3,741,370
Nonmanufacturing industries (incl. not reported).....	4.5	34.9	37.1	550,853
Wholesale and retail trade......................	4.9	31.0	35.4	176,654
Other industries (including not reported).........	4.6	32.7	37.1	208,242
Transportation, commun., & other public utilities..	3.8	41.7	41.4	165,957
Manufacturing.....................................	3.2	30.0	36.4	3,190,517
Nondurable goods................................	3.4	30.8	36.8	1,397,664
Apparel and other fabricated textile products....	6.2	41.7	40.7	156,498
Leather and leather products....................	5.5	37.5	39.0	143,690
Knitting, and other textile mill products........	3.2	26.9	36.0	88,941
Yarn, thread, and fabric mills..................	3.1	29.1	36.4	221,354
Food and kindred products......................	3.0	29.2	35.7	303,469
Paper and allied products......................	2.7	26.4	34.9	147,559
Other nondurable goods.........................	2.4	30.8	37.2	194,295
Chemical and allied products...................	1.7	25.1	35.1	141,858
Not specified manufacturing industries.............	3.3	27.9	35.4	19,744
Durable goods...................................	3.1	29.4	36.2	1,773,109
Furniture and fixtures.........................	4.4	29.6	35.0	97,561
Other durable goods...........................	4.3	29.7	35.2	141,653
Sawmills, planing mills, & misc. wood products...	3.8	29.5	35.4	169,200
Stone, clay, and glass products................	3.5	30.5	36.7	135,397
Machinery, except electrical...................	3.3	31.0	37.0	282,084
Fabricated metal ind. (incl. not spec. metal)....	3.2	28.9	35.7	191,766
Primary metal industries......................	2.7	32.8	38.5	239,586
Motor vehicles and motor vehicle equipment.......	2.5	27.9	35.2	280,218
Transportation equipment, except motor vehicle...	2.0	27.5	36.5	81,029
Electrical machinery, equipment, and supplies....	1.6	24.1	34.2	154,615
Other specified operatives and kindred workers	3.3	33.5	38.2	188,139
Laundry and dry cleaning operatives	3.3	28.3	35.6	140,802
Brakemen and switchmen, railroad....................	3.2	39.1	40.6	138,960
Furnacemen, smeltermen, and heaters.................	2.5	35.3	39.7	63,007
Attendants, auto service and parking.................	2.0	14.2	27.3	229,381
Power station operators............................	2.0	43.1	42.0	20,642
Taxicab drivers and chauffeurs......................	1.9	32.8	38.8	198,681
Sailors and deck hands.............................	1.8	25.6	34.1	39,533
Mine operatives and laborers (n.e.c.)................	1.7	31.0	37.7	568,684
Bus drivers..	1.7	29.9	38.5	150,058

TABLE **D-1.**—PERCENT OF EMPLOYED MALES 45 AND 65 YEARS OLD AND OVER WITH MEDIAN AGE, BY OCCUPATION: 1950—Cont.

[Within major occupation groups, intermediate occupations ranked by percent 65 and over. "N.e.c." means not elsewhere classified]

Occupation	Percent 65 years old and over	Percent 45 years old and over	Median age	Total, 14 years old and over
Operatives and kindred workers--Cont.				
Truck drivers and deliverymen.........................	1.1	20.0	34.0	1,555,412
Welders and flame-cutters.............................	0.8	21.6	36.4	250,890
Apprentices...	0.3	2.6	23.8	112,053
Private household workers........................	11.7	52.0	45.9	73,156
Service workers, except private household........	9.6	48.0	44.0	2,373,410
Guards and watchmen...................................	19.9	72.6	55.1	243,031
Elevator operators...................................	16.1	61.8	50.5	62,160
Charwomen, janitors, and porters.....................	15.4	59.0	49.4	606,784
Barbers, beauticians, and manicurists................	9.6	57.0	47.7	192,595
Other service workers, except private household......	6.3	33.9	34.5	412,980
Policemen, sheriffs, and marshals....................	4.4	39.6	41.1	212,685
Waiters, bartenders, and counter workers.............	3.7	34.1	38.4	341,419
Cooks, except private household......................	3.5	41.9	41.9	192,340
Firemen, fire protection.............................	1.5	31.6	38.9	109,416
Farm laborers and foremen........................	5.4	22.7	26.6	1,950,458
Farm laborers, except unpaid, and farm foremen........	6.0	28.4	32.3	1,357,680
Farm laborers, unpaid family workers..................	4.2	9.7	19.2	592,778
Laborers, except farm and mine..................	5.0	34.1	37.4	3,290,253
Other specified laborers.............................	11.6	43.3	41.2	225,937
Fishermen and oystermen..............................	5.6	37.9	40.1	66,572
Laborers (n.e.c.)....................................	4.7	33.4	37.0	2,765,246
Nonmanufacturing (including not reported)...........	5.2	34.8	37.6	1,741,260
Other industries (including not reported)..........	10.8	44.4	41.9	313,847
Telecommunications, utilities, & sanitary services.	6.5	39.2	39.7	124,132
Construction.......................................	3.9	31.9	36.8	649,341
Wholesale and retail trade.........................	3.9	26.3	31.6	295,363
Railroads and railway express service..............	3.5	40.3	40.9	256,389
Transportation, except railroad....................	3.0	29.4	35.6	102,188
Manufacturing.......................................	3.7	31.1	35.9	1,023,986
Durable goods......................................	3.9	32.1	36.4	656,618
Other durable goods..............................	5.1	32.5	34.6	16,264
Machinery, including electrical..................	4.9	34.5	36.9	76,056
Fabricated metal ind. (incl. not spec. metal)....	4.7	32.3	36.0	51,282
Transportation equipment.........................	4.1	33.7	35.6	63,481
Stone, clay, and glass products..................	3.9	29.2	34.9	74,662
Primary metal industries.........................	3.7	34.7	38.1	204,266
Furniture, saw & planing mills, misc. wood prod..	3.3	28.6	34.7	170,607
Not specified manufacturing industries.............	3.5	29.8	35.4	8,031
Nondurable goods...................................	3.4	29.2	35.1	359,337
Textile mill products and apparel................	4.8	30.7	35.2	58,323
Food and kindred products........................	3.3	29.4	35.0	130,616
Other nondurable goods...........................	3.2	28.8	35.0	109,872
Chemical and allied products.....................	2.6	28.1	35.4	60,526

Source: *1950 Census of Population*, Vol. II, *Characteristics of the Population*, Part 1, U. S. Summary, table 127.

TABLE D-2.—OCCUPATION OF MALES, BY AGE: 1950 AND 1940

[Occupational classifications of 1950 and 1940 recombined to produce comparable groups; see text.
"N.e.c." means not elsewhere classified]

Year and occupation	Total, 14 years and over	14 to 34 years	35 to 44 years	45 to 54 years	55 to 64 years	65 years and over
Total population:						
1950............................	55,311,617	23,603,932	10,587,813	8,655,014	6,667,884	5,796,974
1940............................	50,553,748	23,611,635	9,164,794	7,962,019	5,409,180	4,406,120
Total employed:						
1950............................	40,510,176	15,806,757	9,534,985	7,605,816	5,278,911	2,283,707
1940............................	33,749,905	14,304,164	7,635,196	6,345,449	3,826,985	1,638,111
Profess'l, tech., & kindred wkrs.:						
1950............................	3,229,480	1,279,643	844,888	588,877	355,845	160,227
1940............................	2,340,747	968,612	606,216	419,166	239,309	107,444
Accountants and auditors:[1]						
1950............................	580,023	242,324	133,493	106,718	71,620	25,868
1940............................	455,956	211,268	113,937	78,531	39,179	13,041
Architects:						
1950............................	23,823	6,331	6,420	5,080	4,114	1,878
1940............................	19,479	5,581	5,229	5,083	2,469	1,117
Artists and art teachers:						
1950............................	47,907	21,129	12,481	7,586	4,578	2,133
1940............................	34,478	16,702	8,176	5,539	2,838	1,223
Authors, editors, and reporters:						
1950............................	70,322	26,937	19,580	12,919	7,232	3,654
1940............................	52,123	22,662	13,205	8,473	4,984	2,799
Chemists:						
1950............................	66,982	33,792	18,609	8,950	4,376	1,255
1940............................	52,191	29,258	12,651	6,741	2,753	788
Clergymen:						
1950............................	160,694	39,553	43,330	34,612	26,397	16,802
1940............................	133,307	31,694	32,574	31,575	24,050	13,414
College presidents, professors, instructors (n.e.c.):						
1950............................	95,779	38,872	25,962	17,099	10,127	3,719
1940............................	55,123	18,048	16,464	11,475	6,494	2,642
Dentists:						
1950............................	72,810	15,872	17,329	19,827	12,443	7,339
1940............................	68,874	15,618	21,803	16,094	10,386	4,973
Designers and draftsmen:						
1950............................	141,815	81,537	29,424	17,564	10,056	3,234
1940............................	91,820	47,850	23,538	13,374	5,658	1,400
Engineers, civil:						
1950............................	121,386	38,050	33,156	27,397	17,147	5,636
1940............................	85,684	23,629	27,755	21,265	10,472	2,563
Engineers, electrical:						
1950............................	105,278	45,127	28,618	21,069	8,890	1,574
1940............................	61,203	18,363	23,249	13,145	5,544	902
Other technical engineers:						
1950............................	292,117	125,003	80,104	51,446	28,137	7,427
1940............................	127,708	42,908	39,530	28,913	13,175	3,182
Lawyers and judges:						
1950............................	174,205	35,985	53,583	40,867	25,091	18,679
1940............................	173,456	53,897	46,858	33,182	23,660	15,859
Musicians and music teachers:						
1950............................	75,612	36,017	19,541	10,983	6,076	2,995
1940............................	68,892	38,328	15,106	8,931	4,627	1,900
Pharmacists:						
1950............................	80,855	16,900	22,625	21,015	13,500	6,815
1940............................	74,563	23,753	21,577	15,827	9,163	4,243
Physicians and surgeons:						
1950............................	180,233	48,892	52,255	35,894	23,237	19,955
1940............................	158,381	44,540	38,028	30,452	26,969	18,392
Social, welfare, & recreation wkrs.:						
1950............................	32,616	12,784	9,157	5,589	3,544	1,542
1940............................	25,188	11,091	6,008	4,464	2,542	1,083
Surveyors:						
1950............................	24,375	13,841	4,950	2,967	1,653	964
1940............................	13,243	7,210	3,024	1,569	920	520
Teachers (n.e.c.):						
1950............................	285,609	114,754	83,373	54,236	26,693	6,553
1940............................	248,141	131,075	64,022	33,633	14,875	4,536
Other profess'l, tech., & kind. wkrs.:						
1950............................	597,039	285,943	150,898	87,059	50,934	22,205
1940............................	340,937	175,137	73,482	50,900	28,551	12,867

[1] Includes bookkeepers, cashiers, and ticket, station, and express agents—groups combined with accountants and auditors and classified as clerical workers in the 1940 age data.

TABLE **D-2.**—OCCUPATION OF MALES, BY AGE: 1950 AND 1940—Cont.

[Occupational classifications of 1950 and 1940 recombined to produce comparable groups; see text.
"N.e.c." means not elsewhere classified]

Year and occupation	Total, 14 years and over	14 to 34 years	35 to 44 years	45 to 54 years	55 to 64 years	65 years and over
Farmers and farm managers:						
1950..............................	4,189,882	1,063,841	950,682	879,570	771,092	524,697
1940..............................	4,991,715	1,262,151	1,047,634	1,153,762	934,481	593,687
Mgrs., offs., & props., exc. farm:						
1950..............................	4,368,500	983,257	1,241,634	1,134,149	727,484	281,976
1940..............................	3,260,857	767,006	905,459	868,981	507,888	211,523
Offs. & inspectors, State & local:[1]						
1950..............................	203,206	37,317	47,346	53,074	44,563	20,906
1940..............................	162,758	32,993	42,319	44,821	28,563	14,062
Other specified managers and offs.:[2]						
1950..............................	409,719	104,203	107,176	98,050	74,406	25,884
1940..............................	323,692	82,783	85,975	83,935	53,998	17,001
Mgrs., offs., & props. (n.e.c.):						
Manufacturing:						
1950..............................	609,123	126,477	183,593	164,173	100,369	34,511
1940..............................	401,511	81,385	116,650	116,640	61,955	24,881
Wholesale trade:						
1950..............................	318,671	70,331	92,574	83,928	51,158	20,680
1940..............................	210,009	47,569	60,376	56,893	32,434	12,737
Retail trade, exc. eat'g & drink'g:						
1950..............................	1,346,136	330,921	391,563	330,589	203,624	89,439
1940..............................	1,163,878	310,346	308,764	283,397	176,228	85,143
Finance, insurance, & real estate:						
1950..............................	224,767	37,737	57,649	65,402	43,298	20,681
1940..............................	173,848	32,868	53,848	46,450	26,735	13,947
Eating and drinking places:						
1950..............................	262,108	58,635	78,609	70,771	43,268	10,825
1940..............................	197,744	44,888	56,602	60,061	28,341	7,852
Other industries (incl. not rptd.):						
1950..............................	994,770	217,636	283,124	268,162	166,798	59,050
1940..............................	627,417	134,174	180,925	176,784	99,634	35,900
Clerical and kindred workers:						
1950..............................	2,343,386	1,105,741	500,375	387,010	260,267	89,993
1940..............................	1,766,105	948,333	380,372	260,147	136,479	40,774
Mail carriers:						
1950..............................	161,702	60,738	37,453	33,616	24,686	5,209
1940..............................	119,246	29,991	36,524	33,958	16,631	2,142
Other clerical and kindred workers:[3]						
1950..............................	2,181,684	1,045,003	462,922	353,394	235,581	84,784
1940..............................	1,646,859	918,342	343,848	226,189	119,848	38,632
Sales workers:						
1950..............................	2,568,973	1,167,436	562,717	430,021	279,901	128,898
1940..............................	2,238,095	1,051,705	520,489	380,657	204,479	80,765
Insurance agents and brokers:						
1950..............................	278,120	103,447	66,290	56,071	35,387	16,925
1940..............................	226,561	73,998	64,920	48,060	26,349	13,234
Real estate agents and brokers:						
1950..............................	120,325	20,054	22,286	30,021	28,899	19,065
1940..............................	100,856	13,053	20,114	28,390	24,817	14,482
Other sales workers:[4]						
1950..............................	2,170,528	1,043,935	474,141	343,929	215,615	92,908
1940..............................	1,910,678	964,654	435,455	304,207	153,313	53,049
Craftsmen, foremen, & kind. wkrs.:						
1950..............................	7,628,851	2,674,290	1,970,851	1,590,146	1,058,088	335,476
1940..............................	5,082,028	1,679,172	1,373,530	1,186,943	650,009	192,374
Bakers:						
1950..............................	105,790	41,112	25,921	19,633	14,741	4,383
1940..............................	112,643	51,990	25,324	21,563	11,050	2,716
Blacksmiths, forgemen, & hammermen:						
1950..............................	56,159	11,944	10,763	11,541	13,985	7,926
1940..............................	79,634	11,926	13,980	23,022	20,603	10,103

[1] Includes Federal officials and postmasters—groups combined with State and local officials and inspectors in the 1940 age data.
[2] Excludes Federal officials and postmasters; includes advertising agents and railroad conductors.
[3] Excludes bookkeepers, cashiers, and ticket agents.
[4] Excludes advertising agents and salesmen.

TABLE **D-2.**—OCCUPATION OF MALES, BY AGE: 1950 AND 1940—Cont.

[Occupational classifications of 1950 and 1940 recombined to produce comparable groups; see text.
"N.e.c." means not elsewhere classified]

Year and occupation	Total, 14 years and over	14 to 34 years	35 to 44 years	45 to 54 years	55 to 64 years	65 years and over
Craftsmen, foremen, and kindred workers--Cont.						
Boilermakers:						
1950	35,178	9,359	8,657	8,803	7,079	1,280
1940	27,039	5,212	7,511	8,998	4,717	601
Cabinetmakers and patternmakers:						
1950	106,887	37,133	21,939	19,447	18,603	9,765
1940	77,943	25,062	17,558	17,687	12,260	5,376
Carpenters:						
1950	907,728	274,793	208,781	192,986	163,048	68,120
1940	543,246	132,220	122,133	148,435	104,798	35,660
Compositors and typesetters:						
1950	164,366	60,938	42,665	31,983	21,448	7,332
1940	153,347	66,690	37,739	28,291	14,170	6,457
Cranemen, hoistmen, construction mach. oper., & stationary engineers:						
1950	419,547	126,760	118,083	97,515	60,507	16,682
1940	282,332	81,773	84,040	68,134	37,010	11,375
Electricians:						
1950	307,013	117,179	84,238	87,641	91,998	5,957
1940	187,321	66,695	63,639	40,218	14,341	2,428
Foremen (n.e.c.)--manufacturing:						
1950	460,302	101,532	162,116	120,379	63,226	13,049
1940	265,366	74,609	83,885	67,238	31,363	8,271
Foremen (n.e.c.)--nonmanufacturing:						
1950	314,812	59,965	95,127	92,650	54,884	12,186
1940	218,348	44,564	68,419	62,333	34,985	8,047
Linemen & servicemen, t'graph, etc.:[1]						
1950	207,752	128,587	37,703	28,732	11,685	1,045
1940	106,501	46,733	37,034	16,469	5,774	491
Locomotive engineers:						
1950	72,412	5,608	8,364	21,604	29,252	7,584
1940	63,496	2,135	8,576	25,412	23,695	3,678
Locomotive firemen:						
1950	53,944	23,381	15,402	9,684	4,684	793
1940	43,851	6,130	17,179	16,239	3,992	311
Machinists & job setters, millwrights & toolmakers, & die makers & setters:						
1950	738,534	249,973	191,825	159,085	109,059	28,592
1940	610,192	210,757	166,801	144,647	70,710	17,277
Masons, tile setters, & stone cutters:						
1950	172,876	66,237	36,970	33,991	25,653	10,025
1940	97,689	26,757	26,068	24,963	15,372	4,529
Mechanics, repairmen and loom fixers:						
1950	1,715,467	745,100	459,560	304,069	162,026	44,712
1940	850,392	384,365	250,249	145,532	57,105	13,141
Molders, metal:						
1950	59,879	21,690	15,525	10,898	9,533	2,233
1940	72,784	24,087	17,394	20,079	9,551	1,673
Painters (const.), paperhgrs., glazrs:						
1950	409,947	116,048	102,968	95,904	67,805	27,222
1940	344,372	110,413	87,389	80,382	49,950	16,238
Plasterers and cement finishers:						
1950	89,112	31,649	21,286	20,041	12,436	3,700
1940	52,226	15,302	15,416	13,108	6,702	1,698
Plumbers and pipe fitters:						
1950	275,892	90,032	76,363	60,768	38,487	10,242
1940	168,885	49,083	47,647	44,662	21,495	5,998
Printing craftsmen, exc. compositors and typesetters:						
1950	85,764	33,034	22,816	16,488	10,316	3,110
1940	60,830	24,461	16,468	12,441	5,770	1,690
Shoemakers & repairers, exc. factory:						
1950	54,969	13,332	10,910	11,823	12,071	6,833
1940	60,809	14,162	12,700	16,526	11,732	5,689
Structural metal workers:						
1950	48,963	18,626	13,936	10,072	5,286	1,043
1940	32,739	11,399	10,192	7,753	2,956	439
Tailors and furriers:						
1950	75,864	13,315	11,192	15,981	22,834	12,542
1940	102,922	15,076	20,566	34,040	24,017	9,223

[1] Classified as operatives in 1940.

TABLE **D-2.**—OCCUPATION OF MALES, BY AGE: 1950 AND 1940—Cont.

[Occupational classifications of 1950 and 1940 recombined to produce comparable groups; see text.
"N.e.c." means not elsewhere classified]

Year and occupation	Total, 14 years and over	14 to 34 years	35 to 44 years	45 to 54 years	55 to 64 years	65 years and over
Craftsmen, foremen, and kindred workers--Cont.						
Tinsmiths, coppersmiths, and sheet metal workers:						
1950	165,786	74,812	41,031	27,807	17,312	4,824
1940	100,742	41,470	25,059	20,571	10,395	3,247
Other craftsmen and kindred wkrs.:[1]						
1950	523,908	202,151	126,710	100,621	70,130	24,296
1940	366,379	136,101	90,564	78,200	45,496	16,018
Operatives and kindred workers:						
1950	8,035,598	3,809,542	1,950,214	1,282,721	777,225	215,896
1940	5,960,783	3,179,189	1,353,882	907,998	414,906	104,808
Apprentices:						
1950	112,053	103,484	5,680	1,682	884	323
1940	79,407	77,200	1,529	478	155	45
Attendants, auto service and parking:						
1950	229,381	161,776	34,961	18,204	9,743	4,697
1940	215,849	171,444	26,154	10,687	5,435	2,129
Brakemen and switchmen, railroad:						
1950	138,960	50,304	34,282	27,879	22,056	4,439
1940	115,532	20,515	34,790	39,646	18,613	1,968
Bus, taxicab drivers, chauffeurs, and deliverymen:						
1950	1,904,151	965,726	516,599	287,544	111,485	22,797
1940	1,487,982	873,816	372,365	174,025	56,340	11,436
Mine operatives & laborers (n.e.c.):						
1950	568,684	243,887	148,736	103,387	62,956	9,718
1940	645,226	303,447	153,296	119,476	57,305	11,702
Painters, exc. const. & maintenance:						
1950	103,325	46,732	24,226	17,301	11,355	3,711
1940	82,568	42,530	19,243	13,156	6,051	1,588
Power station operators:						
1950	20,642	5,735	6,010	5,450	3,034	413
1940	20,805	6,939	7,167	4,275	1,977	447
Sailors and deck hands:						
1950	39,533	20,632	8,787	6,467	2,931	716
1940	34,728	18,774	8,495	4,878	2,115	466
Stationary firemen:						
1950	120,742	29,160	26,300	29,008	26,228	10,046
1940	110,512	30,317	28,444	28,645	17,624	5,482
Welders and flame-cutters:						
1950	250,890	113,585	83,059	38,622	13,617	2,007
1940	118,688	65,326	34,108	15,427	3,398	429
Other operatives & kindred wkrs.:						
1950	4,547,237	2,068,521	1,061,574	747,177	512,936	157,029
1940	3,049,486	1,568,881	668,291	497,305	245,893	69,116
Private household workers:						
1950	73,156	20,338	14,798	16,626	12,836	8,558
1940	116,531	48,538	26,179	20,553	13,362	7,899
Service wkrs., exc. priv. hshld.:						
1950	2,373,410	758,222	477,118	483,782	427,216	227,072
1940	1,963,184	729,438	453,496	398,965	261,409	119,876
Barbers, beauticians, & manicurists:						
1950	192,595	39,411	43,340	50,343	40,980	18,521
1940	209,259	53,909	58,654	55,246	30,379	11,071
Charwomen, janitors, and porters:						
1950	606,784	147,779	101,202	124,043	140,235	93,525
1940	491,519	153,733	100,293	103,999	85,807	47,687
Cooks, except private household:						
1950	192,340	62,075	49,725	45,495	28,299	6,746
1940	160,206	66,132	43,600	34,169	13,637	2,668
Elevator operators:						
1950	62,160	13,350	10,386	13,358	15,051	10,015
1940	64,120	30,724	12,596	9,451	7,222	4,127
Firemen, fire protection:						
1950	109,416	41,725	33,151	22,214	10,644	1,682
1940	80,682	20,964	28,997	22,279	7,210	1,232

[1] Includes sawyers, classified as operatives in 1950.

TABLE **D-2.**—OCCUPATION OF MALES, BY AGE: 1950 AND 1940—Cont.

[Occupational classifications of 1950 and 1940 recombined to produce comparable groups; see text.
"N.e.c." means not elsewhere classified]

Year and occupation	Total, 14 years and over	14 to 34 years	35 to 44 years	45 to 54 years	55 to 64 years	65 years and over
Service workers, except private household--Cont.						
Guards and watchmen:						
1950............................	243,031	30,787	35,818	54,395	73,554	48,477
1940............................	194,892	31,430	32,920	45,519	52,892	32,031
Policemen, sheriffs, and marshals:						
1950............................	212,685	71,208	57,188	48,700	26,170	9,419
1940............................	172,172	39,397	62,477	42,898	20,724	6,676
Waiters, bartenders, & counter wkrs.:						
1950............................	341,419	142,424	82,647	63,587	40,113	12,648
1940............................	283,374	149,189	62,883	46,228	20,403	4,671
Other service workers, except private household:						
1950............................	412,980	209,463	63,661	61,647	52,170	26,039
1940............................	306,960	183,960	51,076	39,176	23,335	9,413
Farm laborers and foremen:						
1950............................	1,950,458	1,254,478	253,010	190,332	146,358	106,280
1940............................	2,784,380	2,031,091	306,060	216,544	155,697	74,988
Farm laborers, unpaid family workers:						
1950............................	592,778	510,177	25,378	15,951	16,669	24,603
1940............................	941,841	878,483	32,431	12,289	9,582	9,056
Farm labor., exc. unpaid, & foremen:						
1950............................	1,357,680	744,301	227,632	174,381	129,689	81,677
1940............................	1,842,539	1,152,608	273,629	204,255	146,115	65,932
Laborers, except farm and mine:						
1950............................	3,290,253	1,483,917	683,135	550,753	406,548	165,900
1940............................	3,000,926	1,510,573	618,397	496,149	285,827	89,980
Fishermen and oystermen:						
1950............................	66,572	24,931	16,409	13,151	8,339	3,742
1940............................	55,176	22,972	11,943	10,601	6,910	2,750
Longshoremen and stevedores:						
1950............................	62,003	17,266	18,257	15,670	8,905	1,905
1940............................	60,441	20,339	18,012	14,511	6,441	1,138
Lumbermen, raftsmen, & wood choppers:						
1950............................	170,495	84,067	37,684	27,401	16,226	5,117
1940............................	126,947	67,200	24,853	20,078	11,463	3,353
Other specified laborers:						
1950............................	225,937	88,213	39,854	37,197	34,488	26,185
1940............................	209,294	83,094	40,878	37,543	30,704	17,075
Laborers (n.e.c.):						
1950............................	2,765,246	1,269,440	570,931	457,334	338,590	128,951
1940............................	2,549,068	1,316,968	522,711	413,416	230,309	65,664
Occupation not reported:						
1950............................	458,229	206,052	85,563	71,829	56,051	38,734
1940............................	244,554	128,356	43,482	35,584	23,139	13,993

Source: *1950 Census of Population*, Vol. II, *Characteristics of the Population*, Part 1, tables 125 and 127, and Vol. IV, *Special Reports*, Part 1, Chapter B, Occupational Characteristics, tables 4 and 6; *1940 Census of Population*, Vol. III, The Labor Force, Part 1, table 65.

TABLE **D–3.**—SURVIVAL RATES, 1940 TO 1950, FOR MALES 14 YEARS OLD AND OVER BY AGE IN 1950, BY OCCUPATION

["N.e.c." means not elsewhere classified. Minus sign (−) denotes decrease]

Occupation	Total, 14 years and over — Percent increase, 1940 to 1950	Percent 65 years old and over		Survival rate--ratio of age group in 1950 to age group 10 years younger in 1940		
		1950	1940	45 to 54 years	55 to 64 years	65 years and over
Total population.....................	9.4	10.5	8.7	0.9444	0.8375	0.5906
Total employed.......................	20.0	5.6	4.9	0.9962	0.8319	0.4179
Profess'l, techn'l, and kindred wkrs......	38.0	5.0	4.6	0.9714	0.8489	0.4621
Accountants and auditors[1]................	27.2	4.5	2.9	0.9366	0.9120	0.4954
Architects...........................	22.3	7.9	5.7	0.9715	0.8094	0.5237
Artists and art teachers..............	38.9	4.5	3.5	0.9278	0.8265	0.5252
Authors, editors, and reporters.......	34.9	5.2	5.4	0.9783	0.8535	0.4695
Chemists.............................	28.3	1.9	1.5	0.7075	0.6492	0.3544
Clergymen............................	20.5	10.5	10.1	1.0626	0.8360	0.4485
College pres., prof'rs, and instr's (n.e.c.)..	73.8	3.9	4.8	1.0386	0.8825	0.4071
Dentists.............................	5.7	10.1	7.2	0.9094	0.7731	0.4778
Designers and draftsmen...............	54.4	2.3	1.5	0.7462	0.7519	0.4582
Engineers, civil.....................	41.7	4.6	3.0	0.9871	0.8063	0.4324
Engineers, electrical................	72.0	1.5	1.5	0.9062	0.6763	0.2442
Other technical engineers............	128.7	2.5	2.5	1.3014	0.9732	0.4541
Lawyers and judges...................	0.4	10.7	9.1	0.8721	0.7562	0.4727
Musicians and music teachers.........	9.8	4.0	2.8	0.7271	0.6803	0.4589
Pharmacists..........................	8.4	8.4	5.7	0.9740	0.8530	0.5084
Physicians and surgeons..............	13.8	11.1	11.6	0.9439	0.7631	0.4399
Social, welfare, and recreation workers.......	29.5	4.7	4.3	0.9303	0.7939	0.4254
Surveyors............................	84.1	4.0	3.9	0.9812	1.0535	0.6694
Teachers (n.e.c.)....................	15.1	2.3	1.8	0.8471	0.7937	0.3376
Other profess'l, techn'l, and kindred wkrs....	75.1	3.7	3.8	1.1848	1.0007	0.5361
Farmers and farm managers.................	-16.1	12.5	11.9	0.8396	0.6683	0.3434
Mgrs., offs., and propr's, exc. farm.......	34.0	6.5	6.5	1.2526	0.8372	0.3920
Officials and inspectors, State and local[2]....	24.9	10.3	8.6	1.2541	0.9942	0.4905
Other specified managers and officals[3]........	26.6	6.3	5.3	1.1404	0.8865	0.3646
Managers, officials, & proprietors (n.e.c.):						
Manufacturing.............................	51.7	5.7	6.2	1.4074	0.8605	0.3974
Wholesale trade...........................	51.7	6.5	6.1	1.3901	0.8992	0.4578
Retail trade, except eating and drinking....	15.7	6.6	7.3	1.0707	0.7185	0.3422
Finance, insurance, and real estate.........	29.3	9.2	8.0	1.2146	0.9321	0.5084
Eating and drinking places...............	32.5	4.1	4.0	1.2503	0.7204	0.2991
Other industries (including not reported)...	58.6	5.9	5.7	1.4822	0.9435	0.4357
Clerical and kindred workers..............	32.7	3.8	2.3	1.0175	1.0005	0.5077
Mail carriers.............................	35.6	3.2	1.8	0.9204	0.7270	0.2775
Other clerical and kindred workers[4]..........	32.5	3.9	2.3	1.0278	1.0415	0.5350
Sales workers.............................	14.8	5.0	3.6	0.8262	0.7353	0.4519
Insurance agents and brokers..................	22.8	6.1	5.8	0.8637	0.7363	0.4276
Real estate agents and brokers..............	19.3	15.8	14.4	1.4925	1.0179	0.4851
Other sales workers[5].........................	13.6	4.3	2.8	0.7898	0.7088	0.4502
Craftsmen, foremen, and kindred workers...	50.1	4.4	3.8	1.1577	0.8914	0.3982
Bakers..................................	-6.1	4.1	2.4	0.7753	0.6836	0.3184
Blacksmiths, forgemen, and hammermen..........	-29.5	14.1	12.7	0.8255	0.6075	0.2581
Boilermakers...........................	30.1	3.6	2.2	1.1720	0.7867	0.2407
Cabinetmakers and patternmakers..............	37.1	9.1	6.9	1.1076	1.0518	0.5537
Carpenters.............................	67.1	7.5	6.6	1.5801	1.0984	0.4850
Compositors and typesetters..............	7.2	4.5	4.2	0.8475	0.7581	0.3555
Cranemen, hoistmen, construction machinery operators, and stationary engineers..........	48.6	4.0	4.0	1.1603	0.8881	0.3448
Electricians...........................	63.9	1.9	1.3	1.0629	0.7956	0.3552
Foremen (n.e.c.)--manufacturing..............	73.5	2.8	3.1	1.4350	0.9403	0.3292
Foremen (n.e.c.)--nonmanufacturing..........	44.2	3.9	3.7	1.3542	0.8805	0.2832

[1] Includes bookkeepers, cashiers, and ticket, station, and express agents—groups combined with accountants and auditors and classified as clerical workers in the 1940 age data.

[2] Includes Federal officials and postmasters—groups combined with State and local officials and inspectors in the 1940 age data.

[3] Excludes Federal officials and postmasters; includes advertising agents and railroad conductors.

[4] Excludes bookkeepers, cashiers, and ticket agents.

[5] Excludes advertising agents and salesmen.

TABLE **D-3.**—SURVIVAL RATES, 1940 TO 1950, FOR MALES 14 YEARS OLD AND OVER BY AGE
IN 1950, BY OCCUPATION—Cont.

["N.e.c." means not elsewhere classified. Minus sign (−) denotes decrease]

Occupation	Total, 14 years and over — Percent increase, 1940 to 1950	Percent 65 years old and over		Survival rate--ratio of age group in 1950 to age group 10 years younger in 1940		
		1950	1940	45 to 54 years	55 to 64 years	65 years and over
Craftsmen, foremen, and kindred workers--Continued						
Linemen and servicemen, telegraph, etc.[1]	95.1	0.5	0.5	0.7758	0.7095	0.1668
Locomotive engineers	14.0	10.5	5.8	2.5191	1.1511	0.2771
Locomotive firemen	23.0	1.5	0.7	0.5637	0.2884	0.1843
Machinists and job setters, millwrights and toolmakers, and die makers and setters	21.0	3.9	2.8	0.9537	0.7540	0.3250
Masons, tile setters, and stone cutters	77.0	5.8	4.6	1.3039	1.0276	0.5037
Mechanics, repairmen, and loom fixers	101.7	2.6	1.5	1.2151	1.1133	0.6365
Molders, metal	-17.7	3.7	2.3	0.6265	0.4748	0.1989
Painters (const.), paperhgrs., & glaziers	19.0	6.6	4.7	1.0974	0.8435	0.4113
Plasterers and cement finishers	70.6	4.2	3.3	1.3000	0.9487	0.4405
Plumbers and pipe fitters	63.4	3.7	3.6	1.2754	0.8617	0.3725
Printing craftsmen, exc. compos. & typeset.	41.0	3.6	2.8	1.0012	0.8292	0.4169
Shoemakers and repairers, except factory	-9.6	12.4	9.4	0.9309	0.7304	0.3922
Structural metal workers	49.6	2.1	1.3	0.9882	0.6818	0.3072
Tailors and furriers	-26.3	16.5	9.0	0.7771	0.6708	0.3773
Tinsmiths, coppersmiths, & sheet metal wkrs.	64.6	2.9	3.2	1.1097	0.8416	0.3536
Other craftsmen and kindred workers[2]	43.0	4.6	4.4	1.1110	0.8968	0.3950
Operatives and kindred workers	34.8	2.7	1.8	0.9474	0.8560	0.4154
Apprentices	41.1	0.3	0.1	1.1001	1.8494	1.6150
Attendants, auto service and parking	6.3	2.0	1.0	0.6960	0.9117	0.6210
Brakemen and switchmen, railroad	20.3	3.2	1.7	0.8014	0.5563	0.2157
Bus, taxicab dr., chauffeurs, & deliverymen	28.0	1.2	0.8	0.7722	0.6406	0.3364
Mine operatives and laborers (n.e.c.)	-11.9	1.7	1.8	0.6744	0.5269	0.1408
Painters, exc. construction & maintenance	25.1	3.6	1.9	0.8991	0.8631	0.4858
Power station operators	-0.8	2.0	2.1	0.7604	0.7097	0.1704
Sailors and deck hands	13.8	1.8	1.3	0.7613	0.6009	0.2774
Stationary firemen	9.3	8.3	5.0	1.0198	0.9156	0.4348
Welders and flame-cutters	111.4	0.8	0.4	1.1323	0.8827	0.5244
Other operatives and kindred workers	49.1	3.5	2.3	1.1180	1.0314	0.4985
Private household workers	-37.2	11.7	6.8	0.6351	0.6245	0.4025
Service workers, exc. private household	20.9	9.6	6.1	1.0668	1.0708	0.5955
Barbers, beauticians, and manicurists	-8.0	9.6	5.3	0.8583	0.7418	0.4468
Charwomen, janitors, and porters	23.5	15.4	9.7	1.2368	1.3484	0.7006
Cooks, except private household	20.1	3.5	1.7	1.0435	0.8282	0.4137
Elevator operators	-3.1	16.1	6.4	1.0605	1.5925	0.8825
Firemen, fire protection	35.6	1.5	1.5	0.7661	0.4778	0.1992
Guards and watchmen	24.7	19.9	16.6	1.6523	1.6159	0.5702
Policemen, sheriffs, and marshals	23.5	4.4	3.9	0.7795	0.6101	0.3438
Waiters, bartenders, and counter workers	20.5	3.7	1.6	1.0112	0.8677	0.5044
Other service workers, exc. priv. household	34.5	6.3	3.1	1.2070	1.3317	0.7951
Farm laborers and foremen	-30.0	5.4	2.7	0.6219	0.6759	0.4607
Farm laborers, unpaid family workers	-37.1	4.2	1.0	0.4918	1.3564	1.3200
Farm laborers, exc. unpaid, & foremen	-26.3	6.0	3.6	0.6373	0.6349	0.3852
Laborers, except farm and mine	9.6	5.0	3.0	0.8906	0.8194	0.4414
Fishermen and oystermen	20.7	5.6	5.0	1.1011	0.7866	0.3874
Longshoremen and stevedores	2.6	3.1	1.9	0.8700	0.6137	0.2514
Lumbermen, raftsmen, and wood choppers	34.3	3.0	2.6	1.1025	0.8081	0.3454
Other specified laborers	8.0	11.6	8.2	0.9100	0.9186	0.5480
Laborers (n.e.c.)	8.5	4.7	2.6	0.8749	0.8190	0.4357
Occupation not reported	87.4	8.5	5.7	1.6519	1.5752	1.0431

[1] Classified as operatives in 1940.
[2] Includes sawyers, classified as operatives in 1950.

Source: Table D-2.

TABLE **D-4.**—AGE OF MALES IN SELECTED OCCUPATIONS: 1920 TO 1950

Year and occupation	Total, 14 years and over	14 to 34 years	35 to 44 years	45 to 54 years	55 to 64 years	65 years and over
TOTAL						
Number:						
1950	55,311,617	23,603,932	10,587,813	8,655,014	6,667,884	5,796,974
1940	50,553,748	23,611,635	9,164,794	7,962,019	5,409,180	4,406,120
1930	45,035,691	21,723,092	8,816,319	6,803,569	4,367,500	3,325,211
1920	37,861,085	18,903,150	7,359,904	5,653,095	3,461,865	2,483,071
Percent distribution:						
1950	100.0	42.7	19.1	15.6	12.1	10.5
1940	100.0	46.7	18.1	15.7	10.7	8.7
1930	100.0	48.2	19.6	15.1	9.7	7.4
1920	100.0	49.9	19.4	14.9	9.1	6.6
TOTAL EMPLOYED						
Number:						
1950	40,510,176	15,806,812	9,534,991	7,605,784	5,278,894	2,283,695
1940	33,749,905	14,304,164	7,635,196	6,345,449	3,826,985	1,638,111
1930	37,884,515	16,830,915	8,608,202	6,565,135	3,941,514	1,938,749
1920	32,749,403	(1)	(1)	(1)	(1)	1,492,837
Percent distribution:						
1950	100.0	39.0	23.5	18.8	13.0	5.6
1940	100.0	42.4	22.6	18.8	11.3	4.9
1930	100.0	44.4	22.7	17.3	10.4	5.1
1920	100.0	...	...	...	...	4.6
Ratio to total:						
1950	...	0.91	1.23	1.21	1.07	0.53
1940	...	0.91	1.25	1.20	1.06	0.56
1930	...	0.92	1.16	1.15	1.07	0.69
1920	...	...	...	...	...	0.70
LOCOMOTIVE ENGINEERS						
Number:						
1950	72,412	5,608	8,364	21,604	29,252	7,584
1940	63,496	2,135	8,576	25,412	23,695	3,678
1930	101,135	10,804	31,779	35,533	18,158	4,861
1920	109,698	(1)	(1)	(1)	(1)	2,882
Percent distribution:						
1950	100.0	7.7	11.6	29.8	40.4	10.5
1940	100.0	3.4	13.5	40.0	37.3	5.8
1930	100.0	10.7	31.4	35.1	18.0	4.8
1920	100.0	...	...	...	...	2.6
Ratio to total:						
1950	...	0.18	0.61	1.91	3.34	1.00
1940	...	0.07	0.75	2.55	3.49	0.67
1930	...	0.22	1.60	2.32	1.86	0.65
1920	...	...	...	...	...	0.39
TAILORS						
Number:						
1950	66,435	10,521	8,572	13,915	21,292	12,135
1940	91,980	12,359	16,349	30,765	23,245	9,262
1930	147,357	32,087	45,721	38,899	21,937	8,713
1920	160,197	(1)	(1)	(1)	(1)	5,925
Percent distribution:						
1950	100.0	15.8	12.9	20.9	32.0	18.3
1940	100.0	13.4	17.8	33.4	25.3	10.1
1930	100.0	21.8	31.0	26.4	14.9	5.9
1920	100.0	...	...	...	...	3.7
Ratio to total:						
1950	...	0.37	0.68	1.34	2.64	1.74
1940	...	0.29	0.98	2.13	2.36	1.16
1930	...	0.45	1.58	1.75	1.54	0.80
1920	...	...	...	...	...	0.56

[1] Not available.

TABLE **D-4.**—AGE OF MALES IN SELECTED OCCUPATIONS: 1920 TO 1950—Cont.

Year and occupation	Total, 14 years and over	14 to 34 years	35 to 44 years	45 to 54 years	55 to 64 years	65 years and over
CLERGYMEN						
Number:						
1950.....................	160,694	39,553	43,330	34,612	26,397	16,802
1940.....................	133,307	31,694	32,574	31,575	24,050	13,414
1930.....................	145,445	27,557	36,556	37,337	28,608	15,387
1920.....................	125,285	(1)	(1)	(1)	(1)	12,182
Percent distribution:						
1950.....................	100.0	24.6	27.0	21.5	16.4	10.5
1940.....................	100.0	23.8	24.4	23.7	18.0	10.1
1930.....................	100.0	18.9	25.1	25.7	19.7	10.6
1920.....................	100.0	...	...	...	...	9.7
Ratio to total:						
1950.....................	...	0.58	1.41	1.38	1.36	1.00
1940.....................	...	0.51	1.35	1.51	1.68	1.16
1930.....................	...	0.39	1.28	1.70	2.03	1.43
1920.....................	...	...	...	...	...	1.47
LAWYERS AND JUDGES						
Number:						
1950.....................	174,205	35,985	53,583	40,867	25,091	18,679
1940.....................	173,456	53,897	46,858	33,182	23,660	15,859
1930.....................	157,048	50,264	37,964	32,474	22,770	13,576
1920.....................	120,503	(1)	(1)	(1)	(1)	10,059
Percent distribution:						
1950.....................	100.0	20.7	30.8	23.5	14.4	10.7
1940.....................	100.0	31.1	27.0	19.1	13.6	9.1
1930.....................	100.0	32.0	24.2	20.7	14.5	8.6
1920.....................	100.0	...	...	...	...	8.3
Ratio to total:						
1950.....................	...	0.48	1.61	1.51	1.19	1.02
1940.....................	...	0.67	1.49	1.22	1.27	1.05
1930.....................	...	0.66	1.23	1.37	1.49	1.16
1920.....................	...	...	...	...	...	1.26
PHYSICIANS AND SURGEONS						
Number:						
1950.....................	180,233	48,892	52,255	35,894	23,237	19,955
1940.....................	158,381	44,540	38,028	30,452	26,969	18,392
1930.....................	146,809	32,237	33,476	37,636	28,545	14,915
1920.....................	137,522	(1)	(1)	(1)	(1)	10,942
Percent distribution:						
1950.....................	100.0	27.1	29.0	19.9	12.9	11.1
1940.....................	100.0	28.1	24.0	19.2	17.0	11.6
1930.....................	100.0	22.0	22.8	25.6	19.4	10.2
1920.....................	100.0	...	...	...	...	8.0
Ratio to total:						
1950.....................	...	0.63	1.52	1.28	1.07	1.06
1940.....................	...	0.60	1.33	1.22	1.59	1.33
1930.....................	...	0.46	1.16	1.70	2.00	1.38
1920.....................	...	...	...	...	...	1.21
FARMERS AND FARM MANAGERS						
Number:						
1950.....................	4,189,882	1,063,841	950,682	879,570	771,092	524,697
1940.....................	4,991,715	1,262,151	1,047,634	1,153,762	934,481	593,687
1930.....................	5,813,244	1,467,025	1,374,030	1,348,270	990,192	633,727
1920.....................	5,942,891	(1)	(1)	(1)	(1)	509,098
Percent distribution:						
1950.....................	100.0	25.4	22.7	21.0	18.4	12.5
1940.....................	100.0	25.3	21.0	23.1	18.7	11.9
1930.....................	100.0	25.2	23.6	23.2	17.0	10.9
1920.....................	100.0	...	...	...	...	8.6
Ratio to total:						
1950.....................	...	0.59	1.19	1.35	1.52	1.19
1940.....................	...	0.54	1.16	1.47	1.75	1.37
1930.....................	...	0.52	1.20	1.54	1.75	1.47
1920.....................	...	...	...	...	...	1.30

[1] Not available.

TABLE **D-4.**—AGE OF MALES IN SELECTED OCCUPATIONS: 1920 TO 1950—Cont.

Year and occupation	Total, 14 years and over	14 to 34 years	35 to 44 years	45 to 54 years	55 to 64 years	65 years and over
REAL ESTATE AGENTS AND BROKERS						
Number:						
1950.....................	120,325	20,054	22,286	30,021	28,899	19,065
1940.....................	100,856	13,053	20,114	28,390	24,817	14,482
1930.....................	202,949	35,613	51,606	55,252	40,136	20,342
1920.....................	139,661	(1)	(1)	(1)	(1)	12,566
Percent distribution:						
1950.....................	100.0	16.7	18.5	24.9	24.0	15.8
1940.....................	100.0	12.9	19.9	28.1	24.6	14.4
1930.....................	100.0	17.5	25.4	27.2	19.8	10.0
1920.....................	100.0	...	...	...	...	9.0
Ratio to total:						
1950.....................	...	0.39	0.97	1.60	1.98	1.50
1940.....................	...	0.28	1.10	1.79	2.30	1.66
1930.....................	...	0.36	1.30	1.80	2.04	1.35
1920.....................	...	...	...	...	...	1.36
STATE AND LOCAL OFFICIALS AND INSPECTORS						
Number:						
1950.....................	110,951	18,008	23,716	27,981	25,537	15,709
1940.....................	87,492	15,866	21,157	23,585	16,337	10,547
1930.....................	83,623	14,614	19,541	20,765	18,148	10,555
1920.....................	59,268	(1)	(1)	(1)	(1)	6,202
Percent distribution:						
1950.....................	100.0	16.2	21.4	25.2	23.0	14.2
1940.....................	100.0	18.1	24.2	27.0	18.7	12.1
1930.....................	100.0	17.5	23.4	24.8	21.7	12.6
1920.....................	100.0	...	...	...	...	10.5
Ratio to total:						
1950.....................	...	0.38	1.12	1.62	1.90	1.35
1940.....................	...	0.39	1.34	1.72	1.75	1.39
1930.....................	...	0.36	1.19	1.64	2.24	1.70
1920.....................	...	...	...	...	...	1.59
WATCHMEN AND GUARDS						
Number:						
1950.....................	243,031	30,787	35,818	54,395	73,554	48,477
1940.....................	194,892	31,430	32,920	45,519	52,692	32,331
1930.....................	146,986	16,793	20,314	33,468	43,792	32,619
1920.....................	114,968	(1)	(1)	(1)	(1)	22,202
Percent distribution:						
1950.....................	100.0	12.7	14.7	22.4	30.3	19.9
1940.....................	100.0	16.1	16.9	23.4	27.0	16.6
1930.....................	100.0	11.4	13.8	22.8	29.8	22.2
1920.....................	100.0	...	...	...	...	19.3
Ratio to total:						
1950.....................	...	0.30	0.77	1.44	2.50	1.90
1940.....................	...	0.34	0.93	1.49	2.52	1.91
1930.....................	...	0.24	0.70	1.51	3.07	3.00
1920.....................	...	...	...	...	...	2.92
ELEVATOR OPERATORS						
Number:						
1950.....................	62,160	13,350	10,386	13,358	15,051	10,015
1940.....................	64,120	30,724	12,596	9,451	7,222	4,127
1930.....................	55,211	27,197	8,794	7,376	6,644	5,200
1920.....................	33,297	(1)	(1)	(1)	(1)	3,498
Percent distribution:						
1950.....................	100.0	21.5	16.7	21.5	24.2	16.1
1940.....................	100.0	47.9	19.6	14.7	11.3	6.4
1930.....................	100.0	49.3	15.9	13.4	12.0	9.4
1920.....................	100.0	...	...	...	...	10.5
Ratio to total:						
1950.....................	...	0.50	0.87	1.38	2.00	1.53
1940.....................	...	1.03	1.08	0.94	1.06	0.74
1930.....................	...	1.02	0.81	0.89	1.24	1.27
1920.....................	...	...	...	...	...	1.59

[1] Not available.

TABLE **D-4.**—AGE OF MALES IN SELECTED OCCUPATIONS: 1920 TO 1950—Cont.

Year and occupation	Total, 14 years and over	14 to 34 years	35 to 44 years	45 to 54 years	55 to 64 years	65 years and over
CHARWOMEN, JANITORS, AND PORTERS						
Number:						
1950.....................	606,784	147,779	101,202	124,043	140,235	93,525
1940.....................	491,519	153,733	100,293	103,999	85,807	47,687
1930.....................	421,548	125,941	88,739	88,458	70,417	47,993
1920.....................	247,900	(1)	(1)	(1)	(1)	26,923
Percent distribution:						
1950.....................	100.0	24.4	16.7	20.4	23.1	15.4
1940.....................	100.0	31.3	20.4	21.2	17.5	9.7
1930.....................	100.0	29.9	21.1	21.0	16.7	11.4
1920.....................	100.0	...	...	...	...	10.9
Ratio to total:						
1950.....................	...	0.57	0.87	1.31	1.91	1.47
1940.....................	...	0.67	1.13	1.35	1.64	1.11
1930.....................	...	0.62	1.08	1.39	1.72	1.54
1920.....................	...	...	...	...	...	1.65
ELECTRICAL ENGINEERS						
Number:						
1950.....................	105,278	45,127	28,618	21,069	8,890	1,574
1940.....................	61,203	18,363	23,249	13,145	5,544	902
1930.....................	57,730	30,551	15,140	8,568	2,839	632
1920.....................	27,029	(1)	(1)	(1)	(1)	238
Percent distribution:						
1950.....................	100.0	42.9	27.2	20.0	8.4	1.5
1940.....................	100.0	30.0	38.0	21.5	9.1	1.5
1930.....................	100.0	52.9	26.2	14.8	4.9	1.1
1920.....................	100.0	...	...	...	...	0.9
Ratio to total:						
1950.....................	...	1.00	1.42	1.28	0.69	0.14
1940.....................	...	0.64	2.10	1.37	0.85	0.17
1930.....................	...	1.10	1.34	0.98	0.51	0.15
1920.....................	...	...	...	...	...	0.14
ELECTRICIANS						
Number:						
1950.....................	327,655	122,914	90,248	73,091	35,032	6,370
1940.....................	208,126	73,634	70,806	44,493	16,318	2,875
1930.....................	280,097	159,368	73,577	33,935	10,924	2,293
1920.....................	212,703	(1)	(1)	(1)	(1)	1,114
Percent distribution:						
1950.....................	100.0	37.5	27.5	22.3	10.7	1.9
1940.....................	100.0	35.4	34.0	21.4	7.8	1.4
1930.....................	100.0	56.9	26.3	12.1	3.9	0.8
1920.....................	100.0	...	...	...	...	0.5
Ratio to total:						
1950.....................	...	0.88	1.44	1.43	0.88	0.18
1940.....................	...	0.76	1.88	1.36	0.73	0.16
1930.....................	...	1.18	1.34	0.80	0.40	0.11
1920.....................	...	...	...	...	...	0.08
LOCOMOTIVE FIREMEN						
Number:						
1950.....................	53,944	23,381	15,402	9,684	4,684	793
1940.....................	43,851	6,130	17,179	16,239	3,992	311
1930.....................	67,045	33,603	24,070	7,039	1,833	500
1920.....................	91,088	(1)	(1)	(1)	(1)	371
Percent distribution:						
1950.....................	100.0	43.3	28.6	18.0	8.7	1.5
1940.....................	100.0	14.0	39.2	37.0	9.1	0.7
1930.....................	100.0	50.1	35.9	10.5	2.7	0.7
1920.....................	100.0	...	...	...	...	0.4
Ratio to total:						
1950.....................	...	1.01	1.50	1.15	0.72	0.14
1940.....................	...	0.30	2.17	2.36	0.85	0.08
1930.....................	...	1.04	1.83	0.70	0.28	0.09
1920.....................	...	...	...	...	...	0.06

[1] Not available.

TABLE **D-4.**—AGE OF MALES IN SELECTED OCCUPATIONS: 1920 TO 1950—Cont.

Year and occupation	Total, 14 years and over	14 to 34 years	35 to 44 years	45 to 54 years	55 to 64 years .	65 years and over
SURVEYORS						
Number:						
1950......................	24,375	13,841	4,950	2,967	1,653	964
1940......................	13,243	7,210	3,024	1,569	920	520
1930......................	(1)	(1)	(1)	(1)	(1)	(1)
1920......................	(1)	(1)	(1)	(1)	(1)	(1)
Percent distribution:						
1950......................	100.0	56.8	20.3	12.2	6.8	4.0
1940......................	100.0	54.4	22.8	11.8	6.9	3.9
1930......................	...	...	...	...	...	...
1920......................	...	...	...	...	...	...
Ratio to total:						
1950......................	...	1.33	1.06	0.78	0.56	0.38
1940......................	...	1.16	1.26	0.75	0.64	0.45
1930......................	...	...	...	...	...	...
1920......................	...	...	...	...	...	...
MECHANICS, REPAIRMEN, AND LOOM FIXERS						
Number:						
1950......................	1,715,467	745,100	459,560	304,069	162,026	44,712
1940......................	850,392	384,365	250,249	145,532	57,105	13,141
1930......................	656,883	391,723	163,064	69,206	25,037	7,853
1920......................	297,197	(1)	(1)	(1)	(1)	4,358
Percent distribution:						
1950......................	100.0	43.4	26.8	17.7	9.4	2.6
1940......................	100.0	45.2	29.4	17.1	6.7	1.5
1930......................	100.0	59.6	24.8	10.5	3.8	1.2
1920......................	100.0	...	...	...	...	1.5
Ratio to total:						
1950......................	...	1.02	1.40	1.13	0.78	0.25
1940......................	...	0.97	1.62	1.09	0.63	0.17
1930......................	...	1.24	1.27	0.70	0.39	0.16
1920......................	...	...	...	...	...	0.23
ATTENDANTS, AUTO SERVICE AND PARKING						
Number:						
1950......................	229,381	161,776	34,961	18,204	9,743	4,697
1940......................	215,849	171,444	26,154	10,687	5,435	2,129
1930......................	(1)	(1)	(1)	(1)	(1)	(1)
1920......................	(1)	(1)	(1)	(1)	(1)	(1)
Percent distribution:						
1950......................	100.0	70.5	15.2	7.9	4.2	2.0
1940......................	100.0	79.4	12.1	5.0	2.5	1.0
1930......................	...	...	...	...	...	...
1920......................	...	...	...	...	...	...
Ratio to total:						
1950......................	...	1.65	0.80	0.51	0.35	0.19
1940......................	...	1.70	0.67	0.32	0.23	0.11
1930......................	...	...	...	...	...	...
1920......................	...	...	...	...	...	...
FARM LABORERS, UNPAID FAMILY WORKERS						
Number:						
1950......................	592,778	510,177	25,378	15,951	16,669	24,603
1940......................	941,841	878,483	32,431	12,289	9,582	9,056
1930......................	1,058,362	1,005,389	22,452	10,216	8,137	12,168
1920......................	1,071,696	(1)	(1)	(1)	(1)	7,665
Percent distribution:						
1950......................	100.0	86.1	4.3	2.7	2.8	4.2
1940......................	100.0	93.3	3.4	1.3	1.0	1.0
1930......................	100.0	95.0	2.1	1.0	0.8	1.1
1920......................	100.0	...	...	...	...	0.7
Ratio to total:						
1950......................	...	2.02	0.23	0.17	0.23	0.40
1940......................	...	2.00	0.19	0.08	0.09	0.11
1930......................	...	1.97	0.11	0.07	0.08	0.15
1920......................	...	...	...	...	...	0.11

[1] Not available.

Source: Table D-2; *1950 Census of Population*, Vol. II, *Characteristics of the Population*, Part 1, table 125, and Vol. IV, *Special Reports*, Part 1, Chapter B, Occupational Characteristics, table 4; *1930 Census of Population*, Vol. IV, *Occupations by States*, Part 1, table 22; *1920 Census of Population*, Vol. IV, *Occupations*, Chapter IV, table 6.

TABLE **D-5.**—MALES IN SELECTED OCCUPATIONS, BY CLASS OF WORKER AND AGE: 1950

Occupation and class of worker	14 years old and over			55 years old and over, 1950	65 years old and over, 1950
	1950	1940	Percent change, 1940 to 1950		
PROFESSIONAL					
Architects.........................	23,823	19,479	+22.3	6,292	1,534
Salaried...........................	13,805	9,640	+43.2	2,943	595
Self-employed......................	10,018	9,839	+1.8	3,349	939
Artists and art teachers...........	47,907	34,478	+38.9	6,594	1,920
Salaried...........................	34,998	22,625	+54.7	4,090	1,141
Self-employed......................	12,909	11,853	+8.9	2,504	779
Dentists...........................	72,810	68,874	+5.7	20,582	8,075
Salaried...........................	8,601	3,551	+142.2	2,100	853
Self-employed......................	64,209	65,323	-1.7	18,482	7,222
Lawyers and judges.................	174,205	173,456	+0.4	42,809	18,243
Salaried...........................	68,038	47,194	+44.2	13,911	5,691
Self-employed......................	106,167	126,262	-15.9	28,898	12,552
Musicians and music teachers.......	75,612	68,892	+9.8	9,473	3,243
Salaried...........................	60,592	49,391	+22.7	6,145	1,906
Self-employed......................	15,020	19,501	-23.0	3,328	1,337
Pharmacists........................	80,855	74,563	+8.4	19,630	6,657
Salaried...........................	44,487	40,318	+10.3	10,204	4,044
Self-employed......................	36,368	34,245	+6.2	9,426	2,613
Physicians and surgeons............	180,233	158,381	+13.8	41,421	18,892
Salaried...........................	61,665	32,409	+90.3	8,657	3,572
Self-employed......................	118,568	125,972	-5.9	32,764	15,320
MANAGERS, OFFICIALS, AND PROPRIETORS, EXCEPT FARM					
Construction.......................	280,439	156,088	+79.7	65,350	17,150
Salaried...........................	83,602	36,777	+127.3	17,329	3,956
Self-employed......................	196,837	119,311	+65.0	48,021	13,194
Eating and drinking places.........	262,108	197,744	+32.5	54,128	10,833
Salaried...........................	49,337	25,962	+90.0	7,606	1,450
Self-employed......................	212,771	171,782	+23.9	46,522	9,383
Finance, insurance, and real estate...........	224,767	173,848	+29.3	63,979	20,681
Salaried...........................	164,922	138,719	+18.9	39,285	11,261
Self-employed......................	59,845	35,129	+70.4	24,694	9,420
Manufacturing......................	609,123	401,511	+51.7	134,880	34,511
Salaried...........................	386,146	257,058	+50.2	74,419	15,995
Self-employed......................	222,977	144,453	+54.4	60,461	18,516
Retail trade, exc. eating and drink'g places..	1,346,136	1,163,878	+15.7	293,243	89,510
Salaried...........................	386,022	237,229	+62.7	51,069	12,680
Self-employed......................	960,114	926,649	+3.6	242,174	76,830
Wholesale trade....................	318,671	210,009	+51.7	71,713	20,635
Salaried...........................	148,097	80,393	+84.2	26,691	7,185
Self-employed......................	170,574	129,616	+31.6	45,022	13,450
CRAFTSMEN, FOREMEN, AND KINDRED WORKERS					
Blacksmiths, forgemen, and hammermen..........	56,159	79,634	-29.5	21,018	7,878
Salaried...........................	43,583	50,598	-13.9	14,091	4,132
Self-employed......................	12,576	29,036	-56.7	6,927	3,746
Carpenters.........................	907,728	543,246	+67.1	235,516	70,187
Salaried...........................	748,140	413,436	+81.0	176,672	47,865
Self-employed......................	159,588	129,810	+22.9	58,844	22,322
Painters, construction and maintenance........	381,994	313,948	+21.7	91,757	25,522
Salaried...........................	265,549	185,471	+43.2	56,015	13,969
Self-employed......................	116,445	128,477	-9.4	35,742	11,553
Plasterers and cement finishers....	89,112	52,226	+70.6	16,425	3,302
Salaried...........................	75,379	39,663	+90.0	13,012	2,414
Self-employed......................	13,733	12,563	+9.3	3,413	888
Plumbers and pipe fitters..........	275,892	168,885	+63.4	48,520	10,906
Salaried...........................	235,129	123,627	+90.2	37,127	7,299
Self-employed......................	40,763	45,258	-9.9	11,393	3,607
Shoemakers and repairers...........	54,969	60,809	-9.6	18,333	6,764
Salaried...........................	22,649	15,801	+43.3	4,070	1,438
Self-employed......................	32,320	45,008	-28.2	14,263	5,326

TABLE **D-5.**—MALES IN SELECTED OCCUPATIONS, BY CLASS OF WORKER AND AGE: 1950—Cont.

Occupation and class of worker	14 years old and over			55 years old and over, 1950	65 years old and over, 1950
	1950	1940	Percent change, 1940 to 1950		
CRAFTSMEN, FOREMEN, AND KINDRED WORKERS--Cont.					
Tailors and furriers..........................	75,864	102,922	-26.3	35,940	13,041
Salaried..	56,432	64,069	-11.9	24,562	8,226
Self-employed...................................	19,432	38,853	-50.0	11,378	4,815
SERVICE WORKERS, EXCEPT PRIVATE HOUSEHOLD					
Barbers, beauticians, and manicurists..........	192,595	209,259	-8.0	60,988	19,469
Salaried..	93,860	78,678	+19.3	24,227	7,283
Self-employed...................................	98,735	130,581	-24.4	36,761	12,186
LABORERS, EXCEPT FARM AND MINE					
Fishermen and oystermen.......................	66,572	55,176	+20.7	11,396	3,972
Salaried..	34,848	19,881	+75.3	4,383	1,479
Self-employed...................................	31,724	35,295	-10.1	7,013	2,493

Source: Table D-2; *1950 Census of Population*, Vol. IV, *Special Reports*, Part 1, Chapter B, Occupational Characteristics, tables 4 and 5; *1940 Census of Population, Occupational Characteristics*, table 6.

TABLE **D-6.**—SURVIVAL RATES, 1940 TO 1950, FOR SELF-EMPLOYED MALES IN SELECTED INDUSTRIES AND FOR ALL EMPLOYED MALES IN COMPARABLE OCCUPATION GROUPS

Industry and occupation containing majority of self-employment in industry	55 years old and over, 1940	65 years old and over, 1950	Survival rate	Self-employed 65 and over in comparable occupation, 1950
Medical and other health services:				
Self-employed in industry........................	65,646	24,030	.37	...
All physicians, surgeons, and dentists....................	60,720	27,294	.45	22,542
Manufacturing:				
Self-employed in industry........................	70,415	28,380	.40	...
All managers, officials, and proprietors..................	86,836	34,511	.40	18,516
Wholesale trade:				
Self-employed in industry........................	43,396	19,050	.44	...
All managers, officials, and proprietors..................	45,171	20,680	.46	13,450
Eating and drinking places:				
Self-employed in industry........................	38,470	11,850	.31	...
All managers, officials, and proprietors..................	36,193	10,825	.30	9,383
Retail trade, except eating and drinking places:				
Self-employed in industry........................	315,277	105,480	.33	...
All managers, officials, and proprietors..................	261,371	89,439	.34	76,830
Drug stores:				
Self-employed in industry........................	12,512	3,180	.25	...
All pharmacists..................................	13,406	6,815	.51	2,613
Finance, insurance, and real estate:				
Self-employed in industry........................	60,098	32,730	.54	...
Total comparable occupations.....................	119,564	56,671	.47	27,110
All managers, officials, and proprietors............	40,682	20,681	.51	9,420
All insurance and real estate agents and brokers.......	78,882	35,990	.46	17,690

Source: Tables D-2 and D-5; *1950 Census of Population*, Vol. IV, *Special Reports*, Part 1, Chapter D, Industrial Characteristics, tables 3 and 4; *1940 Census of Population*, Vol. III, *The Labor Force*, Part 1, table 80, and *Industrial Characteristics*, table 3.

APPENDIX D

TABLE D-7.—AGE OF FEMALES IN SELECTED OCCUPATIONS: 1920 TO 1950

Year and occupation	Total, 14 years old and over	14 to 34 years	35 to 44 years	45 to 54 years	55 to 64 years	65 years and over
TOTAL						
Number:						
1950..........................	57,042,417	24,392,958	10,862,546	8,687,639	6,626,711	6,472,563
1940..........................	50,549,176	24,054,479	9,168,426	7,550,052	5,163,025	4,613,194
1930..........................	43,970,842	22,035,815	8,382,521	6,214,514	4,029,398	3,308,594
1920..........................	36,134,659	19,008,376	6,760,934	4,845,398	3,069,807	2,450,144
Percent distribution:						
1950..........................	100.0	42.8	19.0	15.2	11.6	11.3
1940..........................	100.0	47.6	18.1	14.9	10.2	9.1
1930..........................	100.0	50.1	19.1	14.1	9.2	7.5
1920..........................	100.0	52.6	18.7	13.4	8.5	6.8
TOTAL EMPLOYED						
Number:						
1950..........................	15,715,164	7,337,002	3,659,820	2,752,650	1,490,272	475,420
1940..........................	11,138,178	6,433,979	2,224,251	1,481,907	744,813	253,228
1930..........................	10,665,646	6,591,986	1,892,338	1,266,026	649,078	266,218
1920..........................	8,414,060	(1)	(1)	(1)	(1)	196,900
Percent distribution:						
1950..........................	100.0	46.7	23.3	17.5	9.5	3.0
1940..........................	100.0	57.8	20.0	13.3	6.7	2.3
1930..........................	100.0	61.8	17.7	11.9	6.1	2.5
1920..........................	100.0	...	...	...	...	2.3
Ratio to total:						
1950..........................	...	1.09	1.23	1.15	0.82	0.27
1940..........................	...	1.21	1.10	0.89	0.66	0.25
1930..........................	...	1.23	0.93	0.84	0.66	0.33
1920..........................	...	...	...	...	...	0.34
NURSES, PROFESSIONAL AND STUDENT PROFESSIONAL						
Number:						
1950..........................	463,495	259,765	95,082	63,669	34,647	10,332
1940..........................	344,977	236,037	54,894	35,229	15,235	3,582
1930..........................	288,173	203,471	46,719	25,783	9,952	2,248
1920..........................	143,097	(1)	(1)	(1)	(1)	968
Percent distribution:						
1950..........................	100.0	56.0	20.5	13.7	7.5	2.2
1940..........................	100.0	68.4	15.9	10.2	4.4	1.0
1930..........................	100.0	70.6	16.2	8.9	3.5	0.8
1920..........................	100.0	...	...	...	...	0.7
Ratio to total:						
1950..........................	...	1.31	1.08	0.90	0.65	0.19
1940..........................	...	1.44	0.88	0.68	0.43	0.11
1930..........................	...	1.41	0.85	0.63	0.38	0.11
1920..........................	...	...	...	...	...	0.10
TEACHERS (N.E.C.) AND FARM AND HOME MANAGEMENT ADVISORS						
Number:						
1950..........................	841,028	269,111	247,001	206,079	98,304	20,533
1940..........................	776,440	415,841	184,865	111,936	52,134	11,664
1930..........................	853,549	577,232	146,888	83,387	37,056	8,986
1920..........................	633,457	(1)	(1)	(1)	(1)	4,519
Percent distribution:						
1950..........................	100.0	32.0	29.4	24.5	11.7	2.4
1940..........................	100.0	53.6	23.8	14.4	6.7	1.5
1930..........................	100.0	67.6	17.2	9.8	4.3	1.1
1920..........................	100.0	...	...	...	...	0.7
Ratio to total:						
1950..........................	...	0.75	1.55	1.61	1.01	0.21
1940..........................	...	1.13	1.31	0.97	0.66	0.16
1930..........................	...	1.35	0.90	0.70	0.47	0.15
1920..........................	...	...	...	...	...	0.10

[1] Not available.

TABLE **D-7.**—AGE OF FEMALES IN SELECTED OCCUPATIONS: 1920 TO 1950—Cont.

Year and occupation	Total, 14 years old and over	14 to 34 years	35 to 44 years	45 to 54 years	55 to 64 years	65 years and over
FARMERS AND FARM MANAGERS						
Number:						
1950...........................	116,371	17,986	23,659	29,666	26,935	18,125
1940...........................	151,899	15,952	29,239	43,526	38,085	25,097
1930...........................	263,436	25,955	54,064	75,620	62,427	45,370
1920...........................	253,502	(1)	(1)	(1)	(1)	38,459
Percent distribution:						
1950...........................	100.0	15.5	20.3	25.5	23.1	15.6
1940...........................	100.0	10.5	19.2	28.7	25.1	16.5
1930...........................	100.0	9.9	20.5	28.7	23.7	17.2
1920...........................	100.0	...	...	...	...	15.2
Ratio to total:						
1950...........................	...	0.36	1.07	1.68	1.99	1.38
1940...........................	...	0.22	1.06	1.93	2.46	1.81
1930...........................	...	0.20	1.07	2.04	2.58	2.29
1920...........................	...	...	...	...	...	2.24
STENOGRAPHERS AND TYPISTS						
Number:						
1950...........................	1,501,090	1,015,955	263,031	158,020	53,503	10,581
1940...........................	988,081	740,568	167,789	59,825	16,744	3,155
1930...........................	774,521	683,183	67,246	18,963	4,420	709
1920...........................	564,118	(1)	(1)	(1)	(1)	286
Percent distribution:						
1950...........................	100.0	67.7	17.5	10.5	3.6	0.7
1940...........................	100.0	75.0	17.0	6.1	1.7	0.3
1930...........................	100.0	88.2	8.7	2.4	0.6	0.1
1920...........................	100.0	...	...	...	...	0.1
Ratio to total:						
1950...........................	...	1.58	0.92	0.69	0.31	0.06
1940...........................	...	1.58	0.94	0.41	0.17	0.03
1930...........................	...	1.76	0.46	0.17	0.07	0.01
1920...........................	...	...	...	...	...	0.01
SALESMEN AND SALES CLERKS						
Number:						
1950...........................	1,283,534	580,303	307,477	239,730	124,028	31,996
1940...........................	775,944	469,491	153,624	101,335	42,409	9,085
1930...........................	728,652	462,039	145,643	85,139	29,417	6,414
1920...........................	537,205	(1)	(1)	(1)	(1)	2,647
Percent distribution:						
1950...........................	100.0	45.2	24.0	18.7	9.7	2.5
1940...........................	100.0	60.5	19.8	13.1	5.5	1.2
1930...........................	100.0	63.4	20.0	11.7	4.0	0.9
1920...........................	100.0	...	...	...	...	0.5
Ratio to total:						
1950...........................	...	1.06	1.26	1.23	0.84	0.22
1940...........................	...	1.27	1.09	0.88	0.54	0.13
1930...........................	...	1.27	1.05	0.83	0.43	0.12
1920...........................	...	...	...	...	...	0.07
PRIVATE HOUSEHOLD WORKERS						
Number:						
1950...........................	1,334,310	483,526	299,492	268,559	190,752	91,981
1940...........................	1,971,483	1,051,304	376,094	292,237	180,299	71,549
1930...........................	1,962,595	1,005,472	387,778	305,493	177,592	86,260
1920...........................		(1)	(1)	(1)	(1)	...
Percent distribution:						
1950...........................	100.0	36.2	22.4	20.1	14.3	6.9
1940...........................	100.0	53.3	19.1	14.8	9.1	3.6
1930...........................	100.0	51.2	19.8	15.6	9.0	4.4
1920...........................		...	...	...	...	...
Ratio to total:						
1950...........................	...	0.85	1.18	1.32	1.23	0.61
1940...........................	...	1.12	1.06	0.99	0.89	0.40
1930...........................	...	1.02	1.04	1.11	0.98	0.59
1920...........................	...	...	...	...	...	...

[1] Not available.

APPENDIX D

Table **D-7.**—Age of Females in Selected Occupations: 1920 to 1950—Cont.

Year and occupation	Total, 14 years old and over	14 to 34 years	35 to 44 years	45 to 54 years	55 to 64 years	65 years and over
WAITRESSES, BARTENDERS, AND COUNTER WORKERS						
Number:						
1950............................	603,419	376,699	138,148	61,661	22,510	4,401
1940............................	364,036	287,731	51,487	18,903	5,098	817
1930............................	231,708	180,679	34,444	12,466	3,442	677
1920............................	116,424	(¹)	(¹)	(¹)	(¹)	409
Percent distribution:						
1950............................	100.0	62.4	22.9	10.2	3.7	0.7
1940............................	100.0	79.0	14.1	5.2	1.4	0.2
1930............................	100.0	78.0	14.9	5.4	1.5	0.3
1920............................	100.0	...	...	...	...	0.4
Ratio to total:						
1950............................	...	1.46	1.21	0.67	0.32	0.06
1940............................	...	1.66	0.78	0.35	0.14	0.02
1930............................	...	1.56	0.78	0.38	0.16	0.04
1920............................	...	...	...	...	...	0.06

¹ Not available.

Source: Same as table D-4.

APPENDIX E

LIVING ARRANGEMENTS

Section 1: Sources of data on living arrangements

The basic data on living arrangements presented in tables E–1 and E–2 are based on 20-percent tabulations and 3⅓-percent tabulations respectively. There are, therefore, some slight discrepancies between the figures for comparable categories.

The data on living arrangements presented in table E–1 are derived, for the most part, from the statistics on relationship which appear in table 108 of the U. S. Summary, Vol. II, of the 1950 Census reports. In the case of persons living as head or wife in their own households, however, use is made of statistics from table 105 on the marital and household status of males which make it possible to determine the number of married males whose spouse is present in the household and who are also heads of households. The difference between this number and the total number of male heads of households provides a figure for "Other male heads." The statistics on quasi households are derived from table 108 and those for institutions from table 118 for the population 14 years old and over. For the population of all ages, these figures are supplemented by the statistics from the special report on the institutional population. The figures presented for quasi households other than institutions represent the difference between the total for quasi households and the figures for institutions.

The statistics presented in table E–3 on presence or absence of relatives are taken from the special report on marital status. In this report the statistics for the category "Primary individual" refer to a household head with no relatives in his household, and those for the category "Secondary individual" refer to persons living in households or quasi households in a status of other than that of head, but with no relatives present. In table E–3, persons in institutions are assumed to be living in the absence of relatives. This is certainly true, but the implications for the welfare of such persons are somewhat different in this situation than in the case of the elderly person living alone as a lodger.

The data presented in table E–2 on persons in institutions are derived for the institutional population from the special report on institutions, and the residual "Other quasi households" represent the difference between the 100-percent institutional figures and the 20-percent figures presented in table E–1.

In all of these tables the unit of classification is the individual. Thus, for example, the number of persons classified as living as a spouse in a married couple represents the number of male household heads 65 and over who are married with spouse present, plus the number of wives (for

TABLE **E-1**.—LIVING ARRANGEMENTS OF

	Living arrangements	All ages	Under 25 years	25 to 29 years	30 to 34 years	35 to 39 years	40 to 44 years	45 to 49 years
1	Total..............	150,216,110	62,732,630	12,182,455	11,458,940	11,145,185	10,094,660	8,997,450
2	In households..........	144,551,805	60,515,340	11,659,570	11,088,895	10,801,425	9,774,400	8,679,815
3	As head or wife in own household............	75,527,290	5,665,390	8,579,285	9,186,915	9,344,745	8,630,045	7,744,730
4	As spouse in married couple.............	65,954,710	5,355,305	8,177,240	8,707,895	8,712,915	7,872,790	6,866,765
5	As other male head..	3,184,065	146,095	168,915	170,785	208,945	245,010	283,140
6	As female head......	6,388,515	163,990	233,130	308,235	422,885	512,245	594,825
7	As relative of head of household.............	64,978,190	53,670,540	2,625,505	1,585,920	1,160,160	870,330	668,590
8	Parent..............	2,756,015	...	...	2,560	8,895	31,170	73,670
9	Male...............	715,280	...	...	815	1,730	4,845	12,710
10	Female.............	2,040,735	...	...	1,745	7,165	26,325	60,960
11	Child..............	53,471,470	48,700,295	1,907,585	1,083,845	731,545	484,510	284,170
12	Male..............	27,626,005	25,241,215	1,048,620	542,435	346,035	219,375	123,830
13	Female.............	25,845,465	23,459,080	858,965	541,410	385,510	265,135	160,340
14	Other relative......	8,750,705	4,970,245	717,920	499,515	419,720	354,650	310,750
15	Male..............	4,309,620	2,471,875	408,935	289,330	234,945	188,855	155,240
16	Female.............	4,441,085	2,498,370	308,985	210,185	184,775	165,795	155,510
17	Not related to head of household............	4,046,325	1,179,410	454,780	316,060	296,520	274,025	266,495
18	In quasi households.....	5,664,305	2,217,290	522,885	370,045	343,760	320,260	317,635
19	Institutions[1]........	1,558,800	344,675	112,080	105,495	106,075	102,585	102,330
20	Other................	4,105,505	1,872,615	410,805	264,550	237,685	217,675	215,305
	PERCENT DISTRIBUTION							
21	Total.............	100.0	100.0	100.0	100.0	100.0	100.0	100.0
22	In households..........	96.2	96.5	95.7	96.8	96.9	96.8	96.5
23	As head or wife in own household............	50.3	9.0	70.4	80.2	83.8	85.5	86.1
24	As spouse in married couple.............	43.9	8.5	67.1	76.0	78.2	78.0	76.3
25	As other male head..	2.1	0.2	1.4	1.5	1.9	2.4	3.1
26	As female head......	4.3	0.3	1.9	2.7	3.8	5.1	6.6
27	As relative of head of household............	43.3	85.6	21.6	13.8	10.4	8.6	7.4
28	Parent..............	1.8	...	...	(2)	0.1	0.3	0.8
29	Male...............	0.5	...	...	(2)	(2)	(2)	0.1
30	Female.............	1.4	...	...	(2)	0.1	0.3	0.7
31	Child..............	35.6	77.6	15.7	9.5	6.6	4.8	3.2
32	Male..............	18.4	40.2	8.6	4.7	3.1	2.2	1.4
33	Female.............	17.2	37.4	7.1	4.7	3.5	2.6	1.8
34	Other relative......	5.8	7.9	5.9	4.4	3.8	3.5	3.5
35	Male..............	2.9	3.9	3.4	2.5	2.1	1.9	1.7
36	Female.............	3.0	4.0	2.5	1.8	1.7	1.6	1.7
37	Not related to head of household............	2.7	1.9	3.7	2.8	2.7	2.7	3.0
38	In quasi households.....	3.8	3.5	4.3	3.2	3.1	3.2	3.5
39	Institutions.........	1.0	0.5	0.9	0.9	1.0	1.0	1.1
40	Other................	2.7	3.0	3.4	2.3	2.1	2.2	2.4

[1] Data for ages 14 and over are from 20-percent labor force tabulations; for ages under 14 they are derived from the 100-percent institutional tabulations.

[2] Less than 0.1 percent.

whom, by definition, the spouse is present) 65 and over. Thus, although in the majority of cases (in which both husband and wife are 65 and over) both members fall in this category, in those cases in which one spouse is under 65 and the other 65 and over, the spouse under 65 is excluded.

THE POPULATION, BY AGE: 1950

50 to 54 years	55 to 59 years	60 to 64 years	65 years old and over						15 years	
			Total, 65 and over	65 to 69 years	70 to 74 years	75 to 79 years	80 to 84 years	85 years and over		
8,174,670	7,162,515	6,010,755	12,256,850	4,997,790	3,406,665	2,150,375	1,124,570	577,450	2,130,055	1
7,861,535	6,872,415	5,743,345	11,555,065	4,775,130	3,232,420	2,013,080	1,027,150	507,285	2,092,625	2
6,995,180	6,054,085	4,876,140	8,450,775	3,849,455	2,427,890	1,358,665	593,400	221,365	15,795	3
6,017,250	5,029,855	3,827,035	5,387,660	2,750,335	1,545,935	746,835	269,115	75,440	10,325	4
309,225	325,225	337,805	988,920	344,700	280,170	200,320	111,245	52,485	4,125	5
668,705	699,005	711,300	2,074,195	754,420	601,785	411,510	213,040	93,440	1,345	6
603,010	580,210	637,225	2,576,700	717,325	661,290	560,125	381,705	256,255	2,052,295	7
152,240	242,950	357,520	1,887,010	468,665	475,105	429,500	306,520	207,220	...	8
28,035	48,670	80,130	538,345	115,275	129,870	128,880	97,160	67,160	...	9
124,205	194,280	277,390	1,348,665	353,390	345,235	300,620	209,360	140,060	...	10
157,595	75,595	31,965	14,365	14,365	...	...	...	...	1,911,065	11
62,300	27,015	10,400	4,780	4,780	...	...	...	...	970,185	12
95,295	48,580	21,565	9,585	9,585	...	...	...	...	940,880	13
293,175	261,665	247,740	675,325	234,295	186,185	130,625	75,185	49,035	141,230	14
134,140	109,525	94,430	222,345	82,215	60,930	41,385	23,165	14,650	70,095	15
159,035	152,140	153,310	452,980	152,080	125,255	89,240	52,020	34,385	71,135	16
263,345	238,120	229,980	527,590	208,350	143,240	94,290	·52,045	29,665	24,535	17
313,135	290,100	267,410	701,785	222,660	174,245	137,295	97,420	70,165	37,430	18
104,575	102,725	98,505	379,755	87,925	86,425	83,685	68,340	53,380	20,637	19
208,560	187,375	168,905	322,030	134,735	87,820	53,610	29,080	16,785	16,793	20
100.0	100.0	100.0	100.0	100.0	100.0	100.0	100.0	100.0	100.0	21
96.2	95.9	95.6	94.3	95.5	94.9	93.6	91.3	87.8	98.2	22
85.6	84.5	81.1	68.9	77.0	71.3	63.2	52.8	38.3	0.7	23
73.6	70.2	63.7	44.0	55.0	45.4	34.7	23.9	13.1	0.5	24
3.8	4.5	5.6	8.1	6.9	8.2	9.3	9.9	9.1	0.2	25
8.2	9.8	11.8	16.9	15.1	17.7	19.1	18.9	16.2	0.1	26
7.4	8.1	10.6	21.0	14.4	19.4	26.0	33.9	44.4	96.3	27
1.9	3.4	5.9	15.4	9.4	13.9	20.0	27.3	35.9	...	28
0.3	0.7	1.3	4.4	2.3	3.8	6.0	8.6	11.6	...	29
1.5	2.7	4.6	11.0	7.1	10.1	14.0	18.6	24.3	...	30
1.9	1.1	0.5	0.1	0.3	...	...	...	...	89.7	31
0.8	0.4	0.2	(2)	0.1	...	...	...	...	45.5	32
1.2	0.7	0.4	0.1	0.2	...	...	...	...	44.2	33
3.6	3.7	4.1	5.5	4.7	5.5	6.1	6.7	8.5	6.6	34
1.6	1.5	1.6	1.8	1.6	1.8	1.9	2.1	2.5	3.3	35
1.9	2.1	2.6	3.7	3.0	3.7	4.1	4.6	6.0	3.3	36
3.2	3.3	3.8	4.3	4.2	4.2	4.4	4.6	5.1	1.2	37
3.8	4.1	4.4	5.7	4.5	5.1	6.4	8.7	12.2	1.8	38
1.3	1.4	1.6	3.1	1.8	2.5	3.9	6.1	9.2	1.0	39
2.6	2.6	2.8	2.6	2.7	2.6	2.5	2.6	2.9	0.8	40

Source: *1950 Census of Population*, Vol. II, *Characteristics of the Population*, Part 1, U. S. Summary, tables 105, 107, 108, and 118.

TABLE E-2.—PERSONS IN QUASI HOUSEHOLDS, BY TYPE OF QUASI HOUSEHOLD, FOR SELECTED AGE GROUPS: 1950

Age	All persons	In quasi households						All other
		Total	Institutions				Other	
			Total	Mental hospitals	Homes for aged	Other		
35 to 44 years	21,450,359	664,020	210,106	111,740	7,012	91,354	453,914	20,786,339
45 to 54 years	17,342,653	630,770	206,032	127,292	19,125	59,615	424,790	16,711,883
55 to 64 years	13,294,595	557,510	203,566	125,678	43,817	34,071	353,944	12,737,085
65 years and over	12,269,537	701,785	385,419	141,346	217,536	26,537	316,366	11,567,752
65 to 69 years	5,002,936	222,660	88,671	48,723	29,745	10,203	133,989	4,780,276
70 to 74 years	3,411,949	174,245	87,205	37,891	42,640	6,674	87,040	3,237,704
75 to 79 years	2,152,393	137,295	85,449	28,099	52,729	4,621	51,846	2,015,098
80 to 84 years	1,125,358	97,420	69,780	16,678	50,115	2,987	27,640	1,027,938
85 years and over	576,901	70,165	54,314	9,955	42,307	2,052	15,851	506,736
PERCENT DISTRIBUTION								
35 to 44 years	100.0	3.1	1.0	0.5	(1)	0.4	2.1	96.9
45 to 54 years	100.0	3.6	1.2	0.7	0.1	0.3	2.4	96.4
55 to 64 years	100.0	4.2	1.5	0.9	0.3	0.3	2.7	95.8
65 years and over	100.0	5.7	3.1	1.2	1.8	0.2	2.6	94.3
65 to 69 years	100.0	4.5	1.8	1.0	0.6	0.2	2.7	95.5
70 to 74 years	100.0	5.1	2.6	1.1	1.2	0.2	2.6	94.9
75 to 79 years	100.0	6.4	4.0	1.3	2.4	0.2	2.4	93.6
80 to 84 years	100.0	8.7	6.2	1.5	4.5	0.3	2.5	91.3
85 years and over	100.0	12.2	9.4	1.7	7.3	0.4	2.7	87.8

[1] Less than 0.1 percent.

Source: Table E-1; *1950 Census of Population*, Vol. IV, *Special Reports*, Part 2, Chapter C, Institutional Population, tables 3, 5, and 7.

TABLE **E-3.**—LIVING ARRANGEMENTS OF THE POPULATION 25 YEARS OLD AND OVER,
BY PRESENCE OR ABSENCE OF RELATIVES AND AGE: 1950

Living arrangements and presence or absence of relatives	25 to 34 years	35 to 44 years	45 to 54 years	55 to 64 years	65 years old and over		
					Total	65 to 74 years	75 years and over
Total...................	23,619,780	21,246,570	17,184,900	13,182,060	12,244,380	8,391,450	3,852,930
Relatives present.....	21,966,720	19,730,880	15,411,730	11,234,310	9,361,080	6,578,640	2,782,440
No relatives present..	1,653,060	1,515,690	1,773,170	1,947,750	2,883,300	1,812,810	1,070,490
Head or wife in own household...............	17,768,380	17,992,340	14,749,540	10,938,570	8,437,520	6,268,830	2,168,690
As married couple.......	16,892,680	16,607,630	12,907,250	8,866,980	5,377,460	4,288,530	1,088,930
As other male head......	331,920	454,020	584,980	661,710	993,030	628,950	364,080
Relatives present.....	147,150	215,490	268,330	274,890	400,830	247,800	153,030
No relatives present..	184,770	238,530	316,650	386,820	592,200	381,150	211,050
As female head..........	543,780	930,690	1,257,310	1,409,880	2,067,030	1,351,350	715,680
Relatives present.....	345,390	620,550	755,920	737,040	890,820	586,740	304,080
No relatives present..	198,390	310,140	501,390	672,840	1,176,210	764,610	411,600
As relative of head of household...............	4,181,190	2,009,700	1,276,380	1,216,080	2,582,970	1,378,170	1,204,800
Child...................	2,974,560	1,202,580	443,790	110,670	14,940	14,940	...
Parent..................	...	39,660	225,930	606,090	1,899,900	945,390	954,510
Other...................	1,206,630	767,460	606,660	499,320	668,130	417,840	250,290
Other living arrangements.	1,670,210	1,244,530	1,158,980	1,027,410	1,223,890	744,450	479,440
Relatives present.....	400,310	277,510	203,850	139,320	109,000	77,400	31,600
No relatives present..	1,269,900	967,020	955,130	888,090	1,114,890	667,050	447,840
In households but not related to head........	775,640	573,520	530,550	470,490	523,540	349,020	174,520
Relatives present.....	227,150	138,100	93,150	58,380	48,190	33,540	14,650
No relatives present..	548,490	435,420	437,400	412,110	475,350	315,480	159,870
In institutions.........	220,050	214,440	205,530	201,060	378,120	172,770	205,350
In other quasi households.............	674,520	456,570	422,900	355,860	322,230	222,660	99,570
Relatives present.....	173,160	139,410	110,700	80,940	60,810	43,860	16,950
No relatives present..	501,360	317,160	312,200	274,920	261,420	178,800	82,620
PERCENT DISTRIBUTION							
Total...................	100.0	100.0	100.0	100.0	100.0	100.0	100.0
Relatives present.....	93.0	92.9	89.7	85.2	76.5	78.4	72.2
No relatives present..	7.0	7.1	10.3	14.8	23.5	21.6	27.8
Head or wife in own household...............	75.2	84.7	85.8	83.0	68.9	74.7	56.3
As married couple.......	71.5	78.2	75.1	67.3	43.9	51.1	28.3
As other male head......	1.4	2.1	3.4	5.0	8.1	7.5	9.4
Relatives present.....	0.6	1.0	1.6	2.1	3.3	3.0	4.0
No relatives present..	0.8	1.1	1.8	2.9	4.8	4.5	5.5
As female head..........	2.3	4.4	7.3	10.7	16.9	16.1	18.6
Relatives present.....	1.5	2.9	4.4	5.6	7.3	7.0	7.9
No relatives present..	0.8	1.5	2.9	5.1	9.6	9.1	10.7
As relative of head of household...............	17.7	9.5	7.4	9.2	21.1	16.4	31.3
Child...................	12.6	5.7	2.6	0.8	0.1	0.2	...
Parent..................	...	0.2	1.3	4.6	15.5	11.3	24.8
Other...................	5.1	3.6	3.5	3.8	5.5	5.0	6.5
Other living arrangements.	7.1	5.9	6.7	7.8	10.0	8.9	12.4
Relatives present.....	1.7	1.3	1.2	1.1	0.9	0.9	0.8
No relatives present..	5.4	4.6	5.6	6.7	9.1	7.9	11.6
In households but not related to head........	3.3	2.7	3.1	3.6	4.3	4.2	4.5
Relatives present.....	1.0	0.6	0.5	0.4	0.4	0.4	0.4
No relatives present..	2.3	2.0	2.5	3.1	3.9	3.8	4.1
In institutions.........	0.9	1.0	1.2	1.5	3.1	2.1	5.3
In other quasi households.............	2.9	2.1	2.5	2.7	2.6	2.7	2.6
Relatives present.....	0.7	0.7	0.6	0.6	0.5	0.5	0.4
No relatives present..	2.1	1.5	1.8	2.1	2.1	2.1	2.6

Source: *1950 Census of Population*, Vol. IV, *Special Reports*, Part 2, Chapter D, Marital Status, table 1.

APPENDIX E

TABLE **E-4.**—WIDOWS BY LIVING ARRANGEMENTS AND PRESENCE OR ABSENCE OF RELATIVES, FOR SELECTED AGE GROUPS: 1950

Living arrangements and presence or absence of relatives	35 to 44 years	45 to 54 years	55 to 64 years	65 years old and over		
				Total	65 to 74 years	75 years and over
All widows.....................	407,790	964,170	1,644,000	3,541,500	2,032,740	1,508,760
Relatives present...........	313,410	660,720	1,034,910	2,212,350	1,227,090	985,260
No relatives present.........	94,380	303,450	609,090	1,329,150	805,650	523,500
As head..........................	283,530	673,730	1,028,250	1,751,340	1,124,580	626,760
Relatives present............	222,840	455,300	568,710	773,520	500,790	272,730
No relatives present.........	60,690	218,430	459,540	977,820	623,790	354,030
As relative of head..............	82,320	193,230	452,430	1,418,100	714,450	703,650
Child........................	42,360	36,660	20,460	4,050	4,050	...
Parent.......................	11,610	101,430	344,100	1,199,700	591,480	608,220
Other relative...............	28,350	55,140	87,870	214,350	118,920	95,430
Other living arrangements........	41,940	97,210	163,320	372,060	193,710	178,350
Relatives present............	8,250	12,190	13,770	20,730	11,850	8,880
No relatives present.........	33,690	85,020	149,550	351,330	181,860	169,470
PERCENT DISTRIBUTION						
All widows.....................	100.0	100.0	100.0	100.0	100.0	100.0
Relatives present...........	76.9	68.5	63.0	62.5	60.4	65.3
No relatives present.........	23.1	31.5	37.0	37.5	39.6	34.7
As head..........................	69.5	69.9	62.5	49.5	55.3	41.5
Relatives present............	54.6	47.2	34.6	21.8	24.6	18.1
No relatives present.........	14.9	22.7	28.0	27.6	30.7	23.5
As relative of head..............	20.2	20.0	27.5	40.0	35.1	46.6
Child........................	10.4	3.8	1.2	0.1	0.2	...
Parent.......................	2.8	10.5	20.9	33.9	29.1	40.3
Other relative...............	7.0	5.7	5.3	6.1	5.9	6.3
Other living arrangements........	10.3	10.1	9.9	10.5	9.5	11.8
Relatives present............	2.0	1.3	0.8	0.6	0.6	0.6
No relatives present.........	8.3	8.8	9.1	9.9	8.9	11.2

Source: Same as table E-2.

A P P E N D I X   F

HOUSING

Section 1: Data on housing of older persons available from the 1950 Census of Housing

Housing data from the 1950 Census of Housing for dwelling units classified by the age of the head of the household occupying dwelling units are presented in Vol. II, *Nonfarm Housing Characteristics*. These are the data which provide some indication as to the character of the housing of older persons. With the exception of data on tenure and number of rooms which appeared in Vol. III, *Farm Housing Characteristics*, the information by age of head is limited to the nonfarm population. The data presented in the following tables are derived from Part 1, U. S. Summary, Vol. II. The definitions of the concepts used in the classifications appear in the introductory statement to Vol. II. The basic data on which the analysis in Chapter 7 is based are presented in tables F–1 to F–9.

TABLE **F–1.**—TENURE OF NONFARM DWELLING UNITS, BY AGE AND SEX OF HEAD OF HOUSE-HOLD: 1950

Tenure and type of household	Total, 14 years and over	Under 45 years	45 to 64 years	65 years and over
All household heads...................	35,933,525	17,503,580	12,974,640	5,455,305
Owner..............................	19,014,765	7,645,775	7,840,610	3,528,380
Percent..........................	52.9	43.7	60.4	64.7
Renter.............................	16,918,760	9,857,805	5,134,030	1,926,925
Male head, wife present................	26,230,660	14,682,070	9,011,435	2,537,155
Owner..............................	14,363,985	6,753,470	5,822,495	1,788,020
Percent..........................	54.8	46.0	64.6	70.5
Renter.............................	11,866,675	7,928,600	3,188,940	749,135
Other male head.......................	3,739,865	1,256,200	1,496,845	986,820
Owner..............................	1,863,455	485,205	785,880	592,370
Percent..........................	49.8	38.6	52.5	60.0
Renter.............................	1,876,410	770,995	710,965	394,450
Female head...........................	5,963,000	1,565,310	2,466,360	1,931,330
Owner..............................	2,787,325	407,100	1,232,235	1,147,990
Percent..........................	46.7	26.0	50.0	59.4
Renter.............................	3,175,675	1,158,210	1,234,125	783,340

Source: *1950 Census of Housing*, Vol. II, *Nonfarm Housing Characteristics*, Part 1, United States and Divisions, table 8.

205

TABLE **F-2.**—TYPE OF STRUCTURE OF NONFARM DWELLING UNITS, BY AGE AND SEX OF HEAD OF HOUSEHOLD AND TENURE: 1950

Tenure and type of household	Total, 14 years and over				Under 45 years			
	Total	1 dwelling unit, detached		All other	Total	1 dwelling unit, detached		All other
		Number	Per-cent			Number	Per-cent	
All household heads...	35,933,525	20,754,535	57.8	15,178,990	17,503,580	9,640,200	55.1	7,863,380
Owner..............	19,014,765	15,456,955	81.3	3,557,810	7,645,775	6,490,795	84.9	1,154,980
Renter.............	16,918,760	5,297,580	31.3	11,621,180	9,857,805	3,149,405	31.9	6,708,400
Male head, wife present.	26,230,660	15,896,260	60.6	10,334,400	14,682,070	8,445,420	57.5	6,236,650
Owner..............	14,363,985	11,953,700	83.2	2,410,285	6,753,470	5,792,500	85.8	960,970
Renter.............	11,866,675	3,942,560	33.2	7,924,115	7,928,600	2,652,920	33.5	5,275,680
Other male head........	3,739,865	2,060,340	55.1	1,679,525	1,256,200	618,655	49.2	637,545
Owner..............	1,863,455	1,451,005	77.9	412,450	485,205	382,900	78.9	102,305
Renter.............	1,876,410	609,335	32.5	1,267,075	770,995	235,755	30.6	535,240
Female head...........	5,963,000	2,797,935	46.9	3,165,065	1,565,310	576,125	36.8	989,185
Owner..............	2,787,325	2,052,250	73.6	735,075	407,100	315,395	77.5	91,705
Renter.............	3,175,675	745,685	23.5	2,429,990	1,158,210	260,730	22.5	897,480

Tenure and type of household	45 to 64 years				65 years and over			
	Total	1 dwelling unit, detached		All other	Total	1 dwelling unit, detached		All other
		Number	Per-cent			Number	Per-cent	
All household heads...	12,974,640	7,750,160	59.7	5,224,480	5,455,305	3,364,175	61.7	2,091,130
Owner..............	7,840,610	6,245,380	79.7	1,595,230	3,528,380	2,720,780	77.1	807,600
Renter.............	5,134,030	1,504,780	29.3	3,629,250	1,926,925	643,395	33.4	1,283,530
Male head, wife present.	9,011,435	5,753,895	63.9	3,257,540	2,537,155	1,696,945	66.9	840,210
Owner..............	5,822,495	4,736,710	81.4	1,085,785	1,788,020	1,424,490	79.7	363,530
Renter.............	3,188,940	1,017,185	31.9	2,171,755	749,135	272,455	36.4	476,680
Other male head........	1,496,845	827,265	55.3	669,580	986,820	614,420	62.3	372,400
Owner..............	785,880	609,215	77.5	176,665	592,370	458,890	77.5	133,480
Renter.............	710,965	218,050	30.7	492,915	394,450	155,530	39.4	238,920
Female head...........	2,466,360	1,169,000	47.4	1,297,360	1,931,330	1,052,810	54.5	878,520
Owner..............	1,232,235	899,455	73.0	332,780	1,147,990	837,400	72.9	310,590
Renter.............	1,234,125	269,545	21.8	964,580	783,340	215,410	27.5	567,930

Source: Same as table F-1.

TABLE **F-3.**—NUMBER OF ROOMS IN NONFARM DWELLING UNITS, BY AGE AND SEX OF HEAD OF HOUSEHOLD AND TENURE: 1950

Tenure, age, and type of household	Total	Not re-ported	Reporting on number of rooms					
			Total	1 room	2 rooms	3 and 4 rooms	5 rooms or more	
							Number	Per-cent
TOTAL, 14 YEARS AND OVER								
All household heads..	35,933,525	549,515	35,384,010	1,013,010	2,701,605	13,276,255	18,393,140	52.0
Owner..............	19,014,765	283,915	18,730,850	198,545	458,915	4,755,610	13,317,780	71.1
Renter.............	16,918,760	265,600	16,653,160	814,465	2,242,690	8,520,645	5,075,360	30.5
Male head, wife present..............	26,230,660	322,100	25,908,560	352,115	1,539,060	9,996,580	14,020,805	54.1
Owner..............	14,363,985	173,015	14,190,970	97,655	280,160	3,651,315	10,161,840	71.6
Renter.............	11,866,675	149,085	11,717,590	254,460	1,258,900	6,345,265	3,858,965	32.9
Other male head........	3,739,865	122,725	3,617,140	372,650	431,625	1,043,550	1,769,315	48.9
Owner..............	1,863,455	62,385	1,801,070	69,405	86,870	373,980	1,270,815	70.6
Renter.............	1,876,410	60,340	1,816,070	303,245	344,755	669,570	498,500	27.4
Female head..........	5,963,000	104,690	5,858,310	288,245	730,920	2,236,125	2,603,020	44.4
Owner..............	2,787,325	48,515	2,738,810	31,485	91,885	730,315	1,885,125	68.8
Renter.............	3,175,675	56,175	3,119,500	256,760	639,035	1,505,810	717,895	23.0
UNDER 45 YEARS								
All household heads..	17,503,580	261,620	17,241,960	484,240	1,561,915	7,649,740	7,546,065	43.8
Owner..............	7,645,775	122,780	7,522,995	82,915	208,615	2,310,910	4,920,555	65.4
Renter.............	9,857,805	138,840	9,718,965	401,325	1,353,300	5,338,830	2,625,510	27.0
Male head, wife present..............	14,682,070	177,805	14,504,265	244,470	1,118,290	6,560,725	6,580,780	45.4
Owner..............	6,753,470	86,400	6,667,070	60,755	174,445	2,079,890	4,351,980	65.3
Renter.............	7,928,600	91,405	7,837,195	183,715	943,845	4,480,835	2,228,800	28.4
Other male head........	1,256,200	51,690	1,204,510	123,220	158,525	399,655	523,110	43.4
Owner..............	485,205	25,405	459,800	14,655	15,900	103,130	326,115	70.9
Renter.............	770,995	26,285	744,710	108,565	142,625	296,525	196,995	26.5
Female head..........	1,565,310	32,125	1,533,185	116,550	285,100	689,360	442,175	28.8
Owner..............	407,100	10,975	396,125	7,505	18,270	127,890	242,460	61.2
Renter.............	1,158,210	21,150	1,137,060	109,045	266,830	561,470	199,715	17.6
45 TO 64 YEARS								
All household heads..	12,974,640	201,080	12,773,560	318,705	724,250	3,958,930	7,771,675	60.8
Owner..............	7,840,610	111,090	7,729,520	68,290	147,060	1,617,315	5,896,855	76.3
Renter.............	5,134,030	89,990	5,044,040	250,415	577,190	2,341,615	1,874,820	37.2
Male head, wife present..............	9,011,435	111,900	8,899,535	83,580	315,570	2,659,190	5,841,195	65.6
Owner..............	5,822,495	66,515	5,755,980	28,120	75,520	1,156,775	4,495,565	78.1
Renter.............	3,188,940	45,385	3,143,555	55,460	240,050	1,502,415	1,345,630	42.8
Other male head........	1,496,845	47,690	1,449,155	141,190	161,200	393,505	753,260	52.0
Owner..............	785,880	24,420	761,460	27,815	36,550	147,430	549,665	72.2
Renter.............	710,965	23,270	687,695	113,375	124,650	246,075	203,595	29.6
Female head..........	2,466,360	41,490	2,424,870	93,935	247,480	906,235	1,177,220	48.5
Owner..............	1,232,235	20,155	1,212,080	12,355	34,990	313,110	851,625	70.3
Renter.............	1,234,125	21,335	1,212,790	81,580	212,490	593,125	325,595	26.8
65 YEARS AND OVER								
All household heads..	5,455,305	86,815	5,368,490	210,065	415,440	1,667,585	3,075,400	57.3
Owner..............	3,528,380	50,045	3,478,335	47,340	103,240	827,385	2,500,370	71.9
Renter.............	1,926,925	36,770	1,890,155	162,725	312,200	840,200	575,030	30.4
Male head, wife present..............	2,537,155	32,395	2,504,760	24,065	105,200	776,665	1,598,830	63.8
Owner..............	1,788,020	20,100	1,767,920	8,780	30,195	414,650	1,314,295	74.3
Renter.............	749,135	12,295	736,840	15,285	75,005	362,015	284,535	38.6
Other male head........	986,820	23,345	963,475	108,240	111,900	250,390	492,945	51.2
Owner..............	592,370	12,560	579,810	26,935	34,420	123,420	395,035	68.1
Renter.............	394,450	10,785	383,665	81,305	77,480	126,970	97,910	25.5
Female head..........	1,931,330	31,075	1,900,255	77,760	198,340	640,530	983,625	51.8
Owner..............	1,147,990	17,385	1,130,605	11,625	38,625	289,315	791,040	70.0
Renter.............	783,340	13,690	769,650	66,135	159,715	351,215	192,585	25.0

Source: Same as table F-1.

TABLE F-4.—Nonfarm Occupied Dwelling Units, by Tenure, Number of Persons per Unit, and Age and Sex of Head of Household: 1950

Tenure, age, and type of household	Total	1 person	2 persons	3 and 4 persons	5 persons or more	Percent in--	
						1-person household	5-person-or-more household
TOTAL, 14 YEARS AND OVER							
All household heads..	35,933,525	3,562,810	10,517,440	14,942,005	6,911,270	9.9	19.2
Owner................	19,014,765	1,411,415	5,342,750	8,129,440	4,131,160	7.4	21.7
Renter...............	16,918,760	2,151,395	5,174,690	6,812,565	2,780,110	12.7	16.4
Male head, wife present..............	26,230,660	...	8,174,820	12,418,565	5,637,275	...	21.5
Owner................	14,363,985	...	4,233,405	6,741,785	3,388,795	...	23.6
Renter...............	11,066,675	...	3,941,415	5,676,780	2,248,480	...	18.9
Other male head.......	3,739,865	1,279,445	714,750	1,066,080	679,590	34.2	18.2
Owner................	1,863,455	472,985	338,875	624,785	426,810	25.4	22.9
Renter...............	1,876,410	806,460	375,875	441,295	252,780	43.0	13.5
Female head..........	5,963,000	2,283,365	1,627,870	1,457,360	594,405	38.3	10.0
Owner................	2,787,325	938,430	770,470	762,870	315,555	33.7	11.3
Renter...............	3,175,675	1,344,935	857,400	694,490	278,850	42.4	8.8
UNDER 45 YEARS							
All household heads..	17,503,580	774,470	3,796,230	8,802,140	4,130,740	4.4	23.6
Owner................	7,645,775	144,025	1,182,980	4,060,855	2,257,915	1.9	29.5
Renter...............	9,857,805	630,445	2,613,250	4,741,285	1,872,825	6.4	19.0
Male head, wife present..............	14,682,070	...	3,132,710	7,963,315	3,586,045	...	24.4
Owner................	6,753,470	...	1,007,515	3,748,575	1,997,380	...	29.6
Renter...............	7,928,600	...	2,125,195	4,214,740	1,588,665	...	20.0
Other male head.......	1,256,200	337,830	241,515	354,855	322,000	26.9	25.6
Owner................	485,205	78,310	75,400	152,390	179,105	16.1	36.9
Renter...............	770,995	259,520	166,115	202,465	142,895	33.7	18.5
Female head..........	1,565,310	436,640	422,005	483,970	222,695	27.9	14.2
Owner................	407,100	65,715	100,065	159,890	81,430	16.1	20.0
Renter...............	1,158,210	370,925	321,940	324,080	141,265	32.0	12.2
45 TO 64 YEARS							
All household heads..	12,974,640	1,407,875	4,391,415	4,834,130	2,341,220	10.9	18.0
Owner................	7,840,610	566,780	2,594,885	3,129,890	1,549,055	7.2	19.8
Renter...............	5,134,030	841,095	1,796,530	1,704,240	792,165	16.4	15.4
Male head, wife present..............	9,011,435	...	3,442,625	3,757,190	1,811,620	...	20.1
Owner................	5,822,495	...	2,116,435	2,490,810	1,215,250	...	20.9
Renter...............	3,188,940	...	1,326,190	1,266,380	596,370	...	18.7
Other male head.......	1,496,845	505,595	271,665	455,925	263,660	33.8	17.6
Owner................	785,880	188,280	135,250	285,325	177,025	24.0	22.5
Renter...............	710,965	317,315	136,415	170,600	86,635	44.6	12.2
Female head..........	2,466,360	902,280	677,125	621,015	265,940	36.6	10.8
Owner................	1,232,235	378,500	343,200	353,755	156,780	30.7	12.7
Renter...............	1,234,125	523,780	333,925	267,260	109,160	42.4	8.8
65 YEARS AND OVER							
All household heads..	5,455,305	1,380,465	2,329,795	1,305,735	439,310	25.3	8.1
Owner................	3,528,380	700,610	1,564,885	938,695	324,190	19.9	9.2
Renter...............	1,926,925	679,855	764,910	367,040	115,120	35.3	6.0
Male head, wife present..............	2,537,155	...	1,599,485	698,060	239,610	...	9.4
Owner................	1,788,020	...	1,109,455	502,400	176,165	...	9.9
Renter...............	749,135	...	490,030	195,660	63,445	...	8.5
Other male head.......	986,820	436,020	201,570	255,300	93,930	44.2	9.5
Owner................	592,370	206,395	128,225	187,070	70,680	34.8	11.9
Renter...............	394,450	229,625	73,345	68,230	23,250	58.2	5.9
Female head..........	1,931,330	944,445	528,740	352,375	105,770	48.9	5.5
Owner................	1,147,990	494,215	327,205	249,225	77,345	43.1	6.7
Renter...............	783,340	450,230	201,535	103,150	28,425	57.5	3.6

Source: Same as table F-1.

TABLE **F–5.**—CONDITION AND PLUMBING FACILITIES OF NONFARM OCCUPIED DWELLING UNITS, BY AGE AND SEX OF HEAD OF HOUSEHOLD AND TENURE: 1950

Tenure, age, and type of household	Total[1]	Standard		Dilapidated		All other[1]
		Number	Per-cent	Number	Per-cent	
TOTAL, 14 YEARS AND OVER						
All household heads......	34,983,540	24,721,805	70.7	2,766,040	7.9	7,495,695
Owner......................	18,593,730	14,225,480	76.5	912,035	4.9	3,456,215
Renter.....................	16,389,810	10,496,325	64.0	1,854,005	11.3	4,039,480
Male head, wife present....	25,634,900	18,859,880	73.6	1,654,280	6.5	5,120,740
Owner......................	14,088,815	11,095,100	78.8	552,560	3.9	2,441,155
Renter.....................	11,546,085	7,764,780	67.3	1,101,720	9.5	2,679,585
Other male head...........	3,563,300	2,164,495	60.7	490,190	13.8	908,615
Owner......................	1,785,920	1,246,075	69.8	162,505	9.1	377,340
Renter.....................	1,777,380	918,420	51.7	327,685	18.4	531,275
Female head................	5,785,340	3,697,430	63.9	621,570	10.7	1,466,340
Owner......................	2,718,995	1,884,305	69.3	196,970	7.2	637,720
Renter.....................	3,066,345	1,813,125	59.1	424,600	13.8	828,620
UNDER 45 YEARS						
All household heads......	17,030,625	11,905,830	69.9	1,339,435	7.9	3,785,360
Owner......................	7,461,590	5,735,470	76.9	328,285	4.4	1,397,835
Renter.....................	9,569,035	6,170,360	64.5	1,011,150	10.6	2,387,525
Male head, wife present....	14,336,345	10,252,185	71.5	988,630	6.9	3,095,530
Owner......................	6,612,815	5,135,235	77.7	260,900	3.9	1,216,680
Renter.....................	7,723,530	5,116,950	66.3	727,730	9.4	1,878,850
Other male head...........	1,185,050	753,050	63.5	138,835	11.7	293,165
Owner......................	456,575	338,960	74.2	30,675	6.7	86,940
Renter.....................	728,475	414,090	56.8	108,160	14.8	206,225
Female head................	1,509,230	900,595	59.7	211,970	14.0	396,665
Owner......................	392,200	261,275	66.6	36,710	9.4	94,215
Renter.....................	1,117,030	639,320	57.2	175,260	15.7	302,450
45 TO 64 YEARS						
All household heads......	12,641,865	9,387,800	74.3	909,620	7.2	2,344,445
Owner......................	7,677,225	6,082,470	79.2	344,740	4.5	1,250,015
Renter.....................	4,964,640	3,305,330	66.6	564,880	11.4	1,094,430
Male head, wife present....	8,816,875	6,866,380	77.9	491,070	5.6	1,459,425
Owner......................	5,719,025	4,671,055	81.7	202,180	3.5	845,790
Renter.....................	3,097,850	2,195,325	70.9	288,890	9.3	613,635
Other male head...........	1,429,045	892,685	62.5	190,115	13.3	346,245
Owner......................	755,265	540,695	71.6	64,810	8.6	149,760
Renter.....................	673,780	351,990	52.2	125,305	18.6	196,485
Female head................	2,395,945	1,628,735	68.0	228,435	9.5	538,775
Owner......................	1,202,935	870,720	72.4	77,750	6.5	254,465
Renter.....................	1,193,010	758,015	63.5	150,685	12.6	284,310
65 YEARS AND OVER						
All household heads......	5,311,050	3,428,175	64.5	516,985	9.7	1,365,890
Owner......................	3,454,915	2,407,540	69.7	239,010	6.9	808,365
Renter.....................	1,856,135	1,020,635	55.0	277,975	15.0	557,525
Male head, wife present....	2,481,680	1,741,315	70.2	174,580	7.0	565,785
Owner......................	1,756,975	1,288,810	73.4	89,480	5.1	378,685
Renter.....................	724,705	452,505	62.4	85,100	11.7	187,100
Other male head...........	949,205	518,760	54.7	161,240	17.0	269,205
Owner......................	574,080	366,420	63.8	67,020	11.7	140,640
Renter.....................	375,125	152,340	40.6	94,220	25.1	128,565
Female head................	1,880,165	1,168,100	62.1	181,165	9.6	530,900
Owner......................	1,123,860	752,310	66.9	82,510	7.3	289,040
Renter.....................	756,305	415,790	55.0	98,655	13.0	241,860

[1] Excludes "not reported."

Source: Same as table F-1.

TABLE **F-6.**—VALUE OF NONFARM OWNER-OCCUPIED DWELLING UNITS, BY AGE AND SEX OF HEAD OF HOUSEHOLD: 1950

[Restricted to 1-dwelling-unit structures in 1-dwelling-unit properties]

Value and type of household	Total, 14 years and over	Under 45 years	45 to 64 years	65 years and over
ALL HOUSEHOLD HEADS				
All dwelling units..............	15,298,250	6,409,630	6,198,895	2,689,725
Value not reported...................	818,760	315,345	330,505	172,910
Number reporting on value.............	14,479,490	6,094,285	5,868,390	2,516,815
Under $2,000......................	1,136,310	441,445	406,505	288,360
$2,000 to $2,999..................	839,085	344,520	303,980	190,585
$3,000 to $3,999..................	1,056,675	433,895	392,840	229,940
$4,000 to $4,999..................	1,065,845	445,135	404,835	215,875
$5,000 to $5,999..................	1,236,875	504,760	491,005	241,110
$6,000 to $7,499..................	2,058,075	880,115	807,710	370,250
$7,500 to $9,999..................	2,532,395	1,172,055	989,830	370,510
$10,000 to $14,999................	2,901,735	1,269,985	1,236,980	394,770
$15,000 to $19,999................	958,215	375,440	467,615	115,160
$20,000 and over..................	694,280	226,935	367,090	100,255
Median value............dollars..	7,338	7,445	7,772	6,325
MALE HEAD, WIFE PRESENT				
All dwelling units..............	11,827,060	5,719,885	4,703,725	1,403,450
Value not reported...................	571,620	259,565	230,910	81,145
Number reporting on value.............	11,255,440	5,460,320	4,472,815	1,322,305
Under $2,000......................	742,665	364,430	254,115	124,120
$2,000 to $2,999..................	607,010	298,925	211,655	96,430
$3,000 to $3,999..................	789,045	378,445	285,280	125,320
$4,000 to $4,999..................	810,390	394,720	300,345	115,325
$5,000 to $5,999..................	945,775	446,260	369,590	129,925
$6,000 to $7,499..................	1,619,285	790,755	622,990	205,540
$7,500 to $9,999..................	2,052,890	1,076,480	770,615	205,795
$10,000 to $14,999................	2,384,375	1,169,710	995,135	219,530
$15,000 to $19,999................	785,760	348,150	381,800	55,810
$20,000 and over..................	518,245	192,445	281,290	44,510
Median value............dollars..	7,588	7,582	8,074	6,461
OTHER MALE HEAD				
All dwelling units..............	1,424,525	377,340	597,150	450,035
Value not reported...................	119,460	34,060	49,585	35,815
Number reporting on value.............	1,305,065	343,280	547,565	414,220
Under $2,000......................	164,815	33,640	63,655	67,520
$2,000 to $2,999..................	87,445	22,575	33,295	31,575
$3,000 to $3,999..................	104,645	30,130	40,415	34,100
$4,000 to $4,999..................	95,085	26,375	37,075	31,635
$5,000 to $5,999..................	113,460	32,845	44,315	36,300
$6,000 to $7,499..................	169,080	50,850	67,995	50,235
$7,500 to $9,999..................	185,665	53,160	79,285	53,220
$10,000 to $14,999................	213,295	57,855	95,015	60,425
$15,000 to $19,999................	73,355	13,425	37,370	22,560
$20,000 and over..................	98,220	22,425	49,145	26,650
Median value............dollars..	6,723	6,719	7,164	6,129
FEMALE HEAD				
All dwelling units..............	2,046,665	312,405	898,020	836,240
Value not reported...................	127,680	21,720	50,010	55,950
Number reporting on value.............	1,918,985	290,685	848,010	780,290
Under $2,000......................	228,830	43,375	88,735	96,720
$2,000 to $2,999..................	144,630	23,020	59,030	62,580
$3,000 to $3,999..................	162,985	25,320	67,145	70,520
$4,000 to $4,999..................	160,370	24,040	67,415	68,915
$5,000 to $5,999..................	177,640	25,655	77,100	74,885
$6,000 to $7,499..................	269,710	38,510	116,725	114,475
$7,500 to $9,999..................	293,840	42,415	139,930	111,495
$10,000 to $14,999................	304,065	42,420	146,830	114,815
$15,000 to $19,999................	99,100	13,865	48,445	36,790
$20,000 and over..................	77,815	12,065	36,655	29,095
Median value............dollars..	6,423	6,103	6,780	6,167

Source: Same as table F-1.

TABLE **F–7.**—GROSS MONTHLY RENT OF NONFARM RENTER-OCCUPIED DWELLING UNITS, BY AGE AND SEX OF HEAD OF HOUSEHOLD: 1950

Rent and type of household	Total, 14 years and over	Under 45 years	45 to 64 years	65 years and over
ALL HOUSEHOLD HEADS				
Total.........................	16,918,760	9,857,805	5,134,030	1,926,925
Rent free or not reported.............	2,070,240	1,075,680	619,780	374,780
Number reporting on rent...............	14,848,520	8,782,125	4,514,250	1,552,145
Under $10.....................	219,625	104,530	65,500	49,595
$10 to $14....................	433,725	212,935	127,745	93,045
$15 to $19....................	686,165	356,500	200,885	128,780
$20 to $24....................	975,855	543,505	280,330	152,020
$25 to $29....................	1,167,805	689,285	328,935	149,585
$30 to $34....................	1,456,460	895,510	408,425	152,525
$35 to $39....................	1,583,335	995,580	442,885	144,870
$40 to $49....................	3,095,855	1,913,500	924,130	258,225
$50 to $59....................	2,218,800	1,324,295	717,230	177,275
$60 to $74....................	1,686,480	999,255	553,895	133,330
$75 to $99....................	905,290	535,070	300,845	69,375
$100 and over.................	419,125	212,160	163,445	43,520
Median rent............dollars..	42.41	42.60	43.85	36.24
MALE HEAD, WIFE PRESENT				
Total.........................	11,866,675	7,928,600	3,188,940	749,135
Rent free or not reported.............	1,335,855	841,365	359,435	135,055
Number reporting on rent...............	10,530,820	7,087,235	2,829,505	614,080
Under $10.....................	107,575	71,460	26,470	9,645
$10 to $14....................	218,015	144,100	53,370	20,545
$15 to $19....................	380,670	255,080	93,010	32,580
$20 to $24....................	583,655	401,060	138,000	44,595
$25 to $29....................	759,850	531,460	175,735	52,655
$30 to $34....................	1,006,720	707,885	236,760	62,075
$35 to $39....................	1,156,670	817,170	275,395	64,105
$40 to $49....................	2,319,070	1,589,430	607,890	121,750
$50 to $59....................	1,703,180	1,117,380	496,615	89,185
$60 to $74....................	1,301,790	843,750	393,210	64,830
$75 to $99....................	694,420	444,390	217,025	33,005
$100 and over.................	299,205	164,070	116,025	19,110
Median rent............dollars..	44.04	43.37	46.34	41.21
OTHER MALE HEAD				
Total.........................	1,876,410	770,995	710,965	394,450
Rent free or not reported.............	346,320	123,305	126,840	96,175
Number reporting on rent...............	1,530,090	647,690	584,125	298,275
Under $10.....................	57,965	14,620	20,965	22,380
$10 to $14....................	99,570	27,575	36,440	35,555
$15 to $19....................	120,560	37,075	47,175	36,310
$20 to $24....................	144,555	53,635	57,065	33,855
$25 to $29....................	137,635	55,970	53,600	28,065
$30 to $34....................	144,650	65,130	54,745	24,775
$35 to $39....................	131,955	61,030	50,220	20,705
$40 to $49....................	244,520	116,135	93,735	34,650
$50 to $59....................	170,715	80,375	66,015	24,325
$60 to $74....................	137,500	66,030	51,935	19,535
$75 to $99....................	85,260	43,990	30,680	10,590
$100 and over.................	55,205	26,125	21,550	7,530
Median rent............dollars..	36.78	40.26	36.70	28.25
FEMALE HEAD				
Total.........................	3,175,675	1,158,210	1,234,125	783,340
Rent free or not reported.............	388,065	111,010	133,505	143,550
Number reporting on rent...............	2,787,610	1,047,200	1,100,620	639,790
Under $10.....................	54,085	18,450	18,065	17,570
$10 to $14....................	116,140	41,260	37,935	36,945
$15 to $19....................	184,935	64,345	60,700	59,890
$20 to $24....................	247,645	88,810	85,265	73,570
$25 to $29....................	270,320	101,855	99,600	68,865
$30 to $34....................	305,090	122,495	116,920	65,675
$35 to $39....................	294,710	117,380	117,270	60,060
$40 to $49....................	532,265	207,935	222,505	101,825
$50 to $59....................	344,905	126,540	154,600	63,765
$60 to $74....................	247,190	89,475	108,750	48,965
$75 to $99....................	125,610	46,690	53,140	25,780
$100 and over.................	64,715	21,965	25,870	16,880
Median rent............dollars..	38.16	38.18	40.15	34.30

Source: Same as table F-1.

TABLE F-8.—VALUE-INCOME RATIO FOR NONFARM OWNER-OCCUPIED DWELLING UNITS, BY AGE AND SEX OF HEAD OF HOUSEHOLD: 1950

[Restricted to 1-dwelling-unit structures in 1-dwelling-unit properties]

Age and type of household	Total	Not reported[1]	Reporting on rent and income						
			Total	Less than 1.0	1.0 to 1.4	1.5 to 1.9	2.0 to 2.9	3.0 or more Number	3.0 or more Percent
All household heads	15,298,250	2,917,585	12,380,665	1,708,205	2,124,965	2,087,170	3,066,105	3,394,220	27.4
Under 45 years	6,409,630	924,065	5,485,565	841,345	1,032,225	1,057,020	1,532,305	1,022,170	18.6
45 to 64 years	6,198,895	1,278,080	4,920,815	694,280	884,770	829,290	1,186,355	1,325,820	26.9
65 years and over	2,689,725	715,440	1,974,285	172,580	207,970	200,860	346,545	1,046,230	53.0
Male head, wife present	11,827,060	1,945,050	9,882,010	1,422,315	1,826,185	1,801,130	2,592,445	2,239,935	22.7
Under 45 years	5,719,885	753,735	4,966,150	767,310	956,890	982,325	1,411,500	848,125	17.1
45 to 64 years	4,703,725	885,295	3,818,430	556,545	740,415	694,130	962,315	865,025	22.7
65 years and over	1,403,450	306,020	1,097,430	98,460	128,880	124,675	218,530	526,785	48.0
Other male head	1,424,525	374,925	1,049,600	156,575	156,840	146,690	227,020	362,475	34.5
Under 45 years	377,340	94,830	282,510	45,550	48,965	47,525	72,040	68,430	24.2
45 to 64 years	597,150	153,975	443,175	75,270	71,920	66,400	99,725	129,860	29.3
65 years and over	450,035	126,120	323,915	35,755	35,955	32,765	55,255	164,185	50.7
Female head	2,046,665	597,610	1,449,055	129,315	141,940	139,350	246,640	791,810	54.6
Under 45 years	312,405	75,500	236,905	28,485	26,370	27,170	49,265	105,615	44.6
45 to 64 years	898,020	238,810	659,210	62,465	72,435	68,760	124,615	330,935	50.2
65 years and over	836,240	283,300	552,940	38,365	43,135	43,420	72,760	355,260	64.2

[1] Ratio not computed when value or income is not reported, value is less than $100 or $99,900 or more, or income is less than $100 or $10,000 or more.

Source: Same as table F-1.

TABLE F-9.—Gross Rent as Percent of Income for Nonfarm Renter-Occupied Dwelling Units, by Age and Sex of Head of Household: 1950

Age and type of household	Total	Not reported[1]	Reporting on gross rent and income						
			Total	Less than 10	10 to 14	15 to 19	20 to 29	30 or more	
								Number	Percent
All household heads............	16,918,760	3,744,275	13,174,485	1,892,345	3,083,680	2,751,510	2,788,275	2,658,675	20.2
Under 45 years............	9,857,805	1,805,930	8,051,875	1,170,240	2,019,925	1,831,805	1,762,845	1,267,060	15.7
45 to 64 years............	5,134,030	1,233,865	3,900,165	632,520	924,760	770,610	782,455	789,820	20.3
65 years and over.........	1,926,925	704,480	1,222,445	89,585	138,995	149,095	242,975	601,795	49.2
Male head, wife present........	11,866,675	2,220,525	9,646,150	1,544,605	2,568,755	2,204,945	2,012,325	1,315,520	13.6
Under 45 years............	7,928,600	1,316,210	6,612,390	1,028,800	1,800,070	1,583,180	1,413,975	786,365	11.9
45 to 64 years............	3,188,940	676,070	2,512,870	468,410	689,970	540,645	482,120	331,725	13.2
65 years and over.........	749,135	228,245	520,890	47,395	78,715	81,120	116,230	197,430	37.9
Other male head...............	1,876,410	579,890	1,296,520	211,650	253,570	222,430	258,195	350,675	27.0
Under 45 years............	770,995	205,875	565,120	92,895	117,325	106,825	118,745	129,330	22.9
45 to 64 years............	710,965	217,000	493,965	95,125	108,700	86,170	91,250	112,720	22.8
65 years and over.........	394,450	157,015	237,435	23,630	27,545	29,435	48,200	108,625	45.7
Female head..................	3,175,675	943,860	2,231,815	136,090	261,355	324,135	517,755	992,480	44.5
Under 45 years............	1,158,210	283,845	874,365	48,545	102,530	141,800	230,125	351,365	40.2
45 to 64 years............	1,234,125	340,795	893,330	68,985	126,090	143,795	209,085	345,375	38.7
65 years and over.........	783,340	319,220	464,120	18,560	32,735	38,540	78,545	295,740	63.7

[1] Percentage not computed when unit is rent free, rent or income is not reported, rent is $999 or more, or income is less than $100 or $10,000 or more.

Source: Same as table F-1.

Section 2: Percentage of the older population covered by the 1950 housing statistics

As indicated in the text of Chapter 7, although the data on the housing characteristics of persons 65 and over relate only to those dwelling units in which the head is 65 and over, appreciable numbers of other persons 65 and over live in such households. It has also been indicated that the housing data are limited to the nonfarm population. It is, therefore, of some interest to develop a figure on the proportion of the total population 65 and over covered by the housing statistics.

In the family tabulations from the Current Population Survey of April 1955 data on the number of family members by age were classified by age of head, type of family, and relationship. These figures suggest that there were approximately 5.4 million families in which the head was 65 and over, and about 8.2 million persons 65 and over living in these families (table F–10). Data from 3⅓-percent marital status tabulations of the 1950 Census indicate that there were approximately 4.6 million families in which the head was 65 and over. The application of ratios derived from the Current Population Survey, by type of family, yields a figure of approximately 6.9 million persons 65 and over in these families. In addition to this number there were in 1950 approximately 1.8 million primary individuals (that is, household heads living in the absence of relatives and thus household but not family heads). It appears then, that there were roughly 8.7 million persons 65 and over living in households headed by persons 65 and over, or approximately 71 percent of the total population 65 and over. The corresponding figures for nonfarm households were 7.4 million and 60 percent, respectively.

Since the 1955 ratios are derived from data covering both primary and secondary families and estimates for 1950 are based on primary families only, the estimated population for 1950 is perhaps slightly understated (that is, generally speaking, ratios for primary families would be slightly larger than those for all families). A further small understatement is involved in the use of primary individuals to obtain a figure for households. It is quite probable that there are a small number of secondary individuals 65 and over living in the households of primary individuals 65 and over. Since in both cases, however, the numbers involved are extremely small, the understatement is not appreciable.

TABLE **F-10.**—ESTIMATED NUMBER OF PERSONS 65 YEARS OLD AND OVER IN HOUSEHOLDS
HEADED BY PERSONS 65 YEARS OLD AND OVER, FARM AND NONFARM: 1950

| Subject | All persons | In families | | | | Primary individuals[1] |
		Total	Husband and wife families	Other families with male head	Families with female head	
1950 ESTIMATE						
Primary family heads...........	6,414,000	4,646,000	3,354,000	401,000	891,000	1,768,000
Nonfarm[2].....................	5,489,000	3,854,000	2,733,000	319,000	802,000	1,635,000
Farm[3]........................	925,000	792,000	621,000	82,000	89,000	133,000
Estimated persons..............	8,724,000	6,956,000	5,338,000	506,000	1,112,000	1,768,000
Nonfarm[2].....................	7,388,000	5,753,000	4,350,000	402,000	1,001,000	1,635,000
Farm[3]........................	1,336,000	1,203,000	988,000	104,000	111,000	133,000
1955 CURRENT POPULATION SURVEY						
Family heads...................	...	5,402,000	4,099,000	381,000	922,000	...
Persons........................	...	8,156,000	6,524,000	481,000	1,151,000	...
Persons per family head........	...	...	1.5916	1.2625	1.2484	...

[1] Household heads with no relatives living in their households.
[2] Urban and rural nonfarm.
[3] Rural farm.

Source: U. S. Bureau of the Census, *Current Population Reports*, Series P-20, No. 67, table 7; *1950 Census of Population*, Vol. IV, *Special Reports*, Part 2, Chapter D, Marital Status, tables 1 and 3.

A P P E N D I X G

AGE AND INCOME

Section 1: Sources of data on income

The 1950 data on individual income (tables G–1 and G–2) are based on tabulations of the 20-percent sample, and summary statistics by age appear in tables 139 and 140 of the U. S. Summary, Vol. II, of the population reports. The introduction to this report outlines the concept of income as it was applied in the 1950 Census and indicates the relation of census data on income to other income series. The information on family income and individual income of family heads, by age of head, is based on a 1⅛-percent sample and appears in tables 22 and 23 of the special report on the characteristics of families. The information on the age and income of persons falling into various household relationship categories (table G–3) is based on a 3⅓-percent sample and appears in table 6 of the special report on marital status.

TABLE **G-1.**—PERSONS WITH AND WITHOUT INCOME IN 1949, BY AGE AND SEX

Age and sex	Total population	Income not reported	Income reported						
				With income				Without income	
			Total	Total	Me-dian	Income under $2,000		Number	Per-cent of total rptd.
						Number	Per-cent of total with income		
Male, 14 yrs. old and over..	54,601,105	3,861,790	50,739,315	44,389,170	$2,434	17,678,450	39.8	6,350,145	12.5
14 to 19 years...	6,413,490	627,700	5,785,790	2,582,790	435	2,418,420	93.6	3,203,000	55.4
20 to 24 years...	5,559,265	389,230	5,170,035	4,614,270	1,669	2,742,125	59.4	555,765	10.7
25 to 34 years...	11,467,290	701,300	10,765,990	10,344,890	2,737	3,042,930	29.4	421,100	3.9
35 to 44 years...	10,402,195	679,700	9,722,495	9,390,155	3,073	2,322,315	24.7	332,340	3.4
45 to 54 years...	8,484,515	609,005	7,875,510	7,503,240	2,979	2,123,155	28.3	372,270	4.7
55 to 64 years...	6,540,100	453,000	6,087,100	5,623,060	2,551	2,083,130	37.0	464,040	7.6
65 and over......	5,734,250	401,855	5,332,395	4,330,765	1,128	2,946,375	68.0	1,001,630	18.8
Female, 14 yrs. old and over..	57,102,295	3,623,145	53,479,150	22,945,550	$1,029	17,136,785	74.7	30,533,600	57.1
14 to 19 years...	6,369,125	615,260	5,753,865	1,817,640	419	1,732,870	95.3	3,936,225	68.4
20 to 24 years...	5,878,040	317,630	5,560,410	3,078,010	1,276	2,331,680	75.8	2,482,400	44.6
25 to 34 years...	12,174,105	660,685	11,513,420	4,749,475	1,309	3,282,930	69.1	6,763,945	58.7
35 to 44 years...	10,837,650	618,910	10,218,740	4,366,450	1,358	2,936,015	67.2	5,852,290	57.3
45 to 54 years...	8,687,605	521,795	8,165,810	3,522,555	1,316	2,379,125	67.5	4,643,255	56.9
55 to 64 years...	6,633,170	410,065	6,223,105	2,473,635	1,006	1,855,335	75.0	3,749,470	60.3
65 and over......	6,522,600	478,800	6,043,800	2,937,785	602	2,618,830	89.1	3,106,015	51.4

Source: *1950 Census of Population,* Vol. II, *Characteristics of the Population,* Part 1, U. S. Summary, table 139.

TABLE **G-2.**—PERSONS WITH INCOME IN 1949, BY INCOME LEVEL, AGE, AND SEX

Income and sex	Total, 14 years and over	14 to 24 years	25 to 34 years	35 to 44 years	45 to 54 years	55 to 64 years	65 years and over
Male............	44,389,170	7,197,060	10,344,890	9,390,155	7,503,240	5,623,060	4,330,765
Under $2,000........	17,678,450	5,160,545	3,042,930	2,322,315	2,123,155	2,083,130	2,946,375
$2,000 to $3,999....	18,497,525	1,875,080	5,532,050	4,492,375	3,310,650	2,321,575	965,795
$4,000 to $6,999....	6,395,825	142,035	1,551,255	2,031,500	1,519,485	875,315	276,235
$7,000 to $9,999....	888,690	10,670	132,670	285,750	252,300	149,680	57,620
$10,000 and over....	928,680	8,730	85,985	258,215	297,650	193,360	84,740
Female.........	22,945,550	4,895,650	4,749,475	4,366,450	3,522,555	2,473,635	2,937,785
Under $2,000........	17,136,785	4,064,550	3,282,930	2,936,015	2,379,125	1,855,335	2,618,830
$2,000 to $3,999....	5,098,425	802,670	1,374,275	1,262,250	954,705	484,435	220,090
$4,000 to $6,999....	534,030	20,620	73,820	133,860	146,230	98,290	61,210
$7,000 to $9,999....	79,310	4,090	9,440	16,505	19,130	15,205	14,940
$10,000 and over....	97,000	3,720	9,010	17,820	23,365	20,370	22,715
PERCENT DISTRIBUTION							
Male............	100.0	100.0	100.0	100.0	100.0	100.0	100.0
Under $2,000........	39.8	71.7	29.4	24.7	28.3	37.0	68.0
$2,000 to $3,999....	41.7	26.1	53.5	47.8	44.1	41.3	22.3
$4,000 to $6,999....	14.4	2.0	15.0	21.6	20.3	15.6	6.4
$7,000 to $9,999....	2.0	0.1	1.3	3.0	3.4	2.7	1.3
$10,000 and over....	2.1	0.1	0.8	2.7	4.0	3.4	2.0
Female.........	100.0	100.0	100.0	100.0	100.0	100.0	100.0
Under $2,000........	74.7	83.0	69.1	67.2	67.5	75.0	89.1
$2,000 to $3,999....	22.2	16.4	28.9	28.9	27.1	19.6	7.5
$4,000 to $6,999....	2.3	0.4	1.6	3.1	4.2	4.0	2.1
$7,000 to $9,999....	0.3	0.1	0.2	0.4	0.5	0.6	0.5
$10,000 and over....	0.4	0.1	0.2	0.4	0.7	0.8	0.8

Source: Same as table G-1.

TABLE **G-3.**—INCOME IN 1949 OF PERSONS 65 YEARS OLD AND OVER, IN SELECTED TYPES OF LIVING ARRANGEMENTS

Age and type of living arrangement	Total	No income	Under $1,000	$1,000 to $1,999	$2,000 and over	Percent			Median in-come [1]
						No income	Under $850	Under $1,000	
RELATIVE OF HOUSEHOLD HEAD									
Total..................	2,404,870	1,282,680	861,730	141,060	119,400	53.3	83.8	89.2	...
Male relative..............	715,520	279,490	292,270	71,880	71,880	39.1	73.8	79.9	$268
65 to 74 years..........	361,970	116,110	141,280	48,600	55,980	32.1	65.3	71.1	459
75 years and over.......	353,550	163,380	150,990	23,280	15,900	46.2	82.5	88.9	89
Parent....................	515,310	214,320	205,620	47,970	47,400	41.6	75.5	81.5	211
65 to 74 years..........	232,650	78,660	88,350	30,060	35,580	33.8	66.1	71.8	426
75 years and over.......	282,660	135,660	117,270	17,910	11,820	48.0	83.3	89.5	48
Other relative.............	200,210	65,170	86,650	23,910	24,480	32.6	69.3	75.8	403
65 to 74 years..........	129,320	37,450	52,930	18,540	20,400	29.0	63.7	69.9	514
75 years and over.......	70,890	27,720	33,720	5,370	4,080	39.1	79.5	86.7	229
Female relative other than wife.....................	1,689,350	1,003,190	569,460	69,180	47,520	59.4	88.0	93.1	...
65 to 74 years..........	914,420	526,130	307,650	48,690	31,950	57.5	86.1	91.2	...
75 years and over.......	774,930	477,060	261,810	20,490	15,570	61.6	90.3	95.3	...
Parent....................	1,273,220	796,460	414,480	37,590	24,690	62.6	90.2	95.1	...
65 to 74 years..........	657,440	403,880	214,800	24,360	14,400	61.4	89.2	94.1	...
75 years and over.......	615,780	392,580	199,680	13,230	10,290	63.8	91.3	96.2	...
Other relative.............	416,130	206,730	154,980	31,590	22,830	49.7	81.3	86.9	9
65 to 74 years..........	256,980	122,250	92,850	24,330	17,550	47.6	78.3	83.7	67
75 years and over.......	159,150	84,480	62,130	7,260	5,280	53.1	86.3	92.1	...
NO RELATIVE PRESENT IN HOUSEHOLD									
Total..................	2,336,580	518,130	1,194,090	336,660	287,700	22.2	65.6	73.3	$544
As male head of household...	558,690	85,620	298,680	85,500	88,890	15.3	60.8	68.8	649
65 to 74 years..........	360,000	47,880	181,380	62,310	68,430	13.3	56.1	63.7	728
75 years and over.......	198,690	37,740	117,300	23,190	20,460	19.0	69.2	78.0	525
As female head of household.	1,111,920	257,700	595,860	144,810	113,550	23.2	68.7	76.8	501
65 to 74 years..........	724,440	156,300	377,910	106,920	83,310	21.6	65.9	73.7	545
75 years and over.......	387,480	101,400	217,950	37,890	30,240	26.2	74.0	82.4	424
As male household or quasi-household member..........	347,430	71,130	155,580	60,150	60,570	20.5	58.5	65.3	659
65 to 74 years..........	240,030	41,640	99,630	46,410	52,350	17.3	52.6	58.9	787
75 years and over.......	107,400	29,490	55,950	13,740	8,220	27.5	71.7	79.6	433
As female household or quasi-household member.....	318,540	103,680	143,970	46,200	24,690	32.5	71.0	77.7	386
65 to 74 years..........	208,110	60,690	91,200	36,810	19,410	29.2	66.4	73.0	475
75 years and over.......	110,430	42,990	52,770	9,390	5,280	38.9	79.5	86.7	232

[1] For all persons including those reporting no income.

Source: *1950 Census of Population*, Vol. IV, *Special Reports*, Part 2, Chapter D, Marital Status, table 6.

INDEX

Ability to work and disability, 45, 46

Abrahams, Albert J., 51

Age discrimination and retirement, 51, 66

Age of household head, and home ownership, 104, 105

and number of rooms, 106

and occupancy of single family dwelling unit, 105, 106

and persons per household, 106, 107

and substandard housing, 107–109

and value and rental of dwelling unit, 109, 110

see also Housing

Age-income cycle, 112, 113

Age at marriage and sex differences in marital status, 93

Age statistics from 1950 Census, 136–137

Age structure, of counties, special factors in, 39

and future growth of older population, 20

and immigration, 15, 16

of major occupation groups, 71

and mortality, 16, 17

of States, and fertility, 29

and migration 25–30

and mortality, 29

of suburbs, 32–37

and age of suburb, 33, 36

and migration, 35, 36

and trends in births, 15

trends 1900–1950, 10–14

variation within each major occupation group, 71–74

see also Older population

Aging, ancillary contributing factors, 6, 7

changes in household and family organization, 5, 6

evolution of the phenomenon, 5–7

and Federal activities in the field of, 1–4

growth of interest in, 1–4

and increasing numbers of older persons, 5

and industrial revolution, 5

and interest of professional societies, 2

of older population and labor force rates, 59

and State and local activities in the field of, 2, 3

Alabama, 27

Albuquerque SMA, 39

Architects, 75

Arizona, growth 1860–1950, 25

in-migration and age structure, 28

Arkansas, 32

Assets of older persons, 122

Atlanta, Ga., 120

Beverly Hills, Cal., 35

Birth rate, crude, 1820–1950, 19, 20, 143

Birth trends, and age structure, 15

and future growth of older population, 21

and growth of older population, 15, 125

and increase in number of older persons, 15, 18, 143, 144

and increase in the proportion of older persons, 13–20

see also Fertility

Births, estimates of 1810–1910, 15, 137, 143

Blacksmiths, decrease in and age trends, 74

self-employed, 79, 80

"Blue collar" workers, 70

Budgets for older persons, 117

California, county variation in percent 65 and over, 39

in-migration and age structure, 28, 126

migration to, 24

Career line and occupational age structure, 75, 76

Charwomen, janitors and porters, 78

Chicago, Ill., 33

Chicago Urbanized Area, 34

Cities of 100,000 or more, range in proportion of older persons, 39

Clergymen, career line and age structure, 75

occupational survival rates, 76

219

DATE DUE

DEC 0 9 1997			
DEC 1 1 1997			